Chalice Introduction
to the
New Testament

D1366776

Chalice Introduction to the
New Testament

Dennis E. Smith, editor

CHALICE
P R E S S

ST. LOUIS, MISSOURI

© Copyright 2004 by Dennis E. Smith

All rights reserved. For permission to reuse content, please contact Copyright Clearance Center, 222 Rosewood Drive, Danvers, MA 01923, (978) 750-8400, www.copyright.com.

Bible quotations, unless otherwise noted, are from the *New Revised Standard Version Bible,* copyright 1989, Division of Christian Education of the National Council of the Churches of Christ in the United States of America. Used by permission. All rights reserved.

Scripture quotations marked (NIV) are taken from the HOLY BIBLE, NEW INTERNATIONAL VERSION®. NIV®. Copyright © 1973, 1978, 1984 by International Bible Society. Used by permission of Zondervan Publishing House. All rights reserved.

Those quotations marked RSV are from the *Revised Standard Version of the Bible,* copyright 1952, [2nd edition, 1971] by the Division of Christian Education of the National Council of the Churches of Christ in the United States of America. Used by permission. All rights reserved.

Scripture quotations marked (TLB) are taken from *The Living Bible,* copyright © 1971. Used by permission of Tyndale House Publishers, Inc., Wheaton, Illinois 60189. All rights reserved.

Translations of ancient Greek and Latin sources are taken from the Loeb Classical Libary from Harvard University Press.

Cover image: ©Broderbund, Click Art: Christian Graphics
Cover design: Mike Foley
Interior design: Elizabeth Wright
Art direction: Michael Domínguez

ChalicePress.com

Library of Congress Cataloging-in-Publication Data

The Chalice introduction to the New Testament / Dennis E. Smith, editor.
p. cm.
Includes index.
ISBN-13: 978-0-827204-85-0
ISBN-10: 0-827204-85-X (pbk. : alk. paper)
1. Bible. N.T.–Introductions. I. Smith, Dennis Edwin, 1944-
  BS2330.3.C48 2004
  225.6'1–dc22

Printed in the United States of America   2004008672

Contents

Contributors

RONALD J. ALLEN, who holds a Ph.D. from Drew University and a M.Div. from Union Theological Seminary in New York, is Nettie Sweeney and Hugh Th. Miller Professor of Preaching and New Testament at Christian Theological Seminary. He is the author of almost thirty books, including *Preaching Luke-Acts, Interpreting the Gospel, Patterns of Preaching: A Sermon Sampler, Wholly Scripture: Preaching Biblical Themes* (all by Chalice Press), and *Preaching Is Believing: The Sermon as Theological Reflection* (Westminster John Knox Press). In his research, he continues to probe the relationship between the Bible and preaching and the theological and philosophical dimensions of preaching.

M. EUGENE BORING, who holds a Ph.D. from Vanderbilt University, is I. Wylie and Elizabeth M. Briscoe Professor of New Testament (Emeritus) at Brite Divinity School. His writings include "The Gospel of Matthew" in *The New Interpreter's Bible* (Abingdon Press), "1 Peter" in *The Abingdon New Testament Commentary* (Abingdon Press), *Revelation* (Westminster John Knox Press), *Disciples and the Bible* (Chalice Press), and (with Fred B. Craddock) *The People's New Testament Commentary* (Chalice Press). His research interests focus on theological interpretation of the Bible in the life of the church, especially the gospels, christology, and early Christian prophecy and apocalypticism.

STEPHANIE BUCKHANON CROWDER holds a Ph.D. in religion (New Testament) from Vanderbilt University and has most recently served as adjunct professor at Shaw University Divinity School and Fisk University. Her published dissertation is *Simon of Cyrene: A Case of Roman Conscription* (Lang Publishing), and she is currently writing the chapter on the Gospel of Luke for the upcoming *African American New Testament Commentary* (Fortress Press). Her interests include cultural studies and ideological criticism.

LARRY PAUL JONES, who received a Ph.D. in New Testament from Vanderbilt University, serves as pastor and head of staff with the First Presbyterian Church in Birmingham, Michigan. He is the author of *The Symbol of Water in the Gospel of John* (Sheffield Academic Press) and *Preaching Apocalyptic Texts* (Chalice Press), in addition to other articles and curriculum resources.

RODNEY L. PARROTT is dean and professor of Disciples Studies and New Testament at the Disciples Seminary Foundation in Claremont,

California. He received a Ph.D. from the Claremont Graduate School (now Claremont Graduate University), and has taught courses in Paul at the Claremont School of Theology and San Francisco Theological Seminary/Southern California. He has written a number of scholarly articles and reviews and is a contributing author in *The Five Gospels* (Polebridge Press). His research interests are in the social formation of the Jesus movement and early Christianity as evidenced in narrative and rhetorical traditions.

NANCY CLAIRE PITTMAN is pastor of First Christian Church in Tahlequah, Oklahoma, and adjunct professor of New Testament and preaching at Phillips Theological Seminary. She earned a Ph.D. in New Testament Studies at Southern Methodist University before serving as a missionary on the faculty of Tainan Theological College and Seminary, a school related to the Presbyterian Church of Taiwan, from 1994–2001. Currently, she is working on a book on christology in the book of Revelation.

DENNIS E. SMITH, who holds a Th.D. degree from The Divinity School of Harvard University, is professor of New Testament at Phillips Theological Seminary. He is coeditor of *The Storytellers Companion to the Bible* series (Abingdon Press), coauthor of *Many Tables: The Eucharist in the New Testament and Liturgy Today* (Wipf and Stock Publishers), and, most recently, author of *From Symposium to Eucharist: The Banquet in the Early Christian World* (Fortress Press). His research interests range from the social history of early Christianity to the interface between ancient and modern storytelling as a resource for biblical interpretation and proclamation.

RICHARD E. STURM is associate professor of Christianity and the Arts at New Brunswick Theological Seminary, New Jersey, and director of the Seminary's New York Program, having received a Ph.D. degree in Comparative Literature from Washington University in St. Louis, and a Ph.D. in New Testament from Union Theological Seminary in New York City. His published work includes essays in *Apocalyptic and the New Testament* (Sheffield Academic Press) and *Towards Tragedy: Reclaiming Hope* (Ashgate Press), as well as in journals on homiletics and biblical studies. In his teaching and research, he explores questions of biblical hermeneutics, the authority of scripture, and the interrelationship of theology and the arts.

BONNIE B. THURSTON earned her Ph.D. from the University of Virginia and has done postdoctoral work at Harvard Divinity School, Eberhard Karls University, and the Ecole Biblique. Now writing and doing retreat work, she taught for twenty-seven years at the university level and was most recently William F. Orr Professor of New Testament at Pittsburgh

Theological Seminary. She is the author of eleven books including most recently: *Women in the New Testament* (Crossroad Press), *Preaching Mark* (Fortress Press), and *Philippians* (Liturgical Press, forthcoming). Her research interests include the gospels of Mark and John and the deutero-Pauline canon. She is also a widely published poet.

JUDITH HOCH WRAY, who holds a Ph.D. in New Testament Studies from Union Theological Seminary in New York City, is an independent scholar, writer, editor, and preaching consultant. She is author of *Rest as a Theological Metaphor* (Scholars Press), a contributor to *Kitchen Talk* (Chalice Press), and former assistant editor and writer for *The Living Pulpit*. Her current research ranges from exploring biblical texts as resources for preaching styles and ethics to providing local congregations with language options that will invite rather than exclude those previously marginalized.

Preface

Today it often seems as if as many different views exist about what the Bible really says as do interpreters. In such a situation, the serious student of the Bible needs help to be able to make intelligent and informed decisions about biblical interpretation. *Chalice Introduction to the New Testament* is written to help address that need. It is designed for seminary students, pastors, and biblically literate laypeople.

Many introductions to the New Testament that are available today will often stop short of drawing theological conclusions. This introduction is different; here we will be explicitly addressing the meaning of the text for the church of the twenty-first century.

This introduction is also different from most in that it is written not by one author but by many. This offers a significant advantage for the reader. It is often difficult for a single author to be equally adept at interpreting the gospels as well as Paul, not to mention Acts, the Pastorals, Hebrews, and Revelation, all of which can represent subspecialties in New Testament scholarship. Here, however, each New Testament book is introduced by an author who specializes in and has a passion for the text being interpreted. The authors are all connected with the Christian Church (Disciples of Christ), and many are ordained. However, they all write from a broad ecumenical perspective and draw on the latest in New Testament scholarship.

Though the chapters are not all organized the same, they all address the same basic issues of interpretation, including date and authorship, methodology, social and religious context, literary features, a summary of the argument or plot of the text, its primary theological teachings, its importance for the church today, and a recommended bibliography.

The chapters have been arranged in three groups corresponding to a rough chronological order. Paul and his letters are discussed first, since they are the earliest documents we have and derive from the pre-60s period of Christianity. The gospels are discussed next, since they derive from the 70s and later. The third group of remaining documents represents a varied mix of genres and dates.

The New Testament and Its World

DENNIS E. SMITH

The New Testament is made up of twenty-seven separate documents, all of which arise out of specific historical settings of the first and second centuries. These documents were written by many different authors, some of whom are known to us and others unknown. None of them were written to be part of "The New Testament," since such an entity did not exist when they were written. Later generations put them together in one collection that we now call "The New Testament."

Christianity began without a master plan—in a sense, it just happened. Literature developed only as the need arose, and it was written to meet the needs of the moment. The earliest documents we have are the letters of Paul, written in the 50s C.E., about twenty years after the death of Jesus. Paul's letters were originally written with individual churches in mind. They were not written to be saved for future generations, much less to be placed in a collection of Christian scriptures.

The earliest gospel we have is the gospel of Mark, written about the year 70 according to conclusions reached by a large number of scholars. We know that sayings of Jesus and stories about Jesus had been circulating in oral form from the very beginning of the Jesus movement. In the 40s and 50s we think some of the Jesus material began to be written down. But it was as much as a full generation after the death of Jesus when the first narration of the story of Jesus was composed and written down, namely the gospel of Mark.

These early writings became part of a growing collection of early Christian writings that mushroomed all over the Mediterranean world. They represented a variety of communities with a variety of theological perspectives, as seen in the rich theological diversity to be found in the noncanonical as well as canonical material. As yet there was not an official list of authoritative writings. Rather, these writings all had different levels of "authority" depending on the value placed in them by specific early Christian communities. It took many generations for the concept of an "orthodox" list of writings to develop, and many more generations for such a list to take definitive and authoritative shape. Over time controversies arose about which of the various writings were orthodox and which were not. Such controversies led to the development of a list of writings verified by the church to be "apostolic" and authoritative. The list was called by the Latin word for list, *canon.*

Canon

Canonization was a process that took place over a period of over three hundred years. During that time the church developed a list of writings deemed "canonical" and elevated them to a status of "scripture" alongside the Jewish scripture they had inherited. So the decision to collect these writings together and designate them the "New Testament" (as opposed to the Christian designation for the Hebrew Bible, the "Old Testament") was a decision not of the writers themselves, but of the church of later generations that preserved and revered their writings. The entire idea that there would be a set of Christian scriptures to supplement the Jewish scriptures took several generations to take shape and several more generations to come to final fruition.

The concept of canon took place in an atmosphere in which battle lines were being drawn between "orthodoxy" and "heresy." Each side in the debate had its own literature and apostolic patron saints. In the latter stages of the debate, ca. 323, Eusebius wrote an analysis of the state of the question as he saw it. His discussion provides us with a glimpse into the issues as they had developed.

Eusebius defined four categories of early Christian literature. At the highest level were the writings he deemed "acknowledged." Under this category he listed most of the writings that eventually made the final list: the four gospels, Acts, epistles of Paul (by which he probably meant the traditional thirteen), 1 John, 1 Peter, and the Apocalypse (or Revelation) of John, though he admitted that the latter was still debated by some. In the next category were those writings he deemed "disputed," by which he meant that some accepted them as scripture and some did not. Here he listed James, Jude, 2 Peter, 2 John, and 3 John. Of course, all of these writings made the final list, but in the time of Eusebius they had not. His third category was called "spurious," by which he meant writings that had no valid claim to scripture though they still might have value. Here he listed *Acts of Paul, Shepherd of Hermas, Apocalypse of Peter, Barnabas, Didache,* and *Gospel of the Hebrews.* Also in the spurious category "according to some," as

Eusebius put it, was the Revelation of John. Eusebius's final category was the "heretical" writings, which he defined as "altogether monstrous and impious," thus having no value for faith at all. In this category he listed *Gospel of Peter, Gospel of Thomas, Gospel of Matthias,* the *Acts of Andrew* and *Acts of John.*

Eusebius, of course, represented one side in the debate, the side that eventually was able to claim orthodoxy for its point of view. But clearly there were a variety of voices and points of view in Christianity in his time, and among those points of view there would be those who would champion a different list of authoritative writings than his. Eusebius had to specify writings by name in order to clarify to his public which ones were acceptable and which were not.

In the course of his discussion he also summarized the categories by which writings were to be judged:

> None [of the "heretical" writings] has been deemed worthy of any kind of mention in a treatise by a single member of successive generations of churchmen; and the character of the style also is far removed from the apostolic manner, and the thought and purport of their contents is so absolutely out of harmony with true orthodoxy, as to establish the fact that they are certainly the forgeries of heretics. (*Ecclesiastical History,* 3:25.6–7)

Both "acknowledged" and "heretical" writings were claimed to have been written by apostles. For example, alongside the Bible's gospel of Matthew some communities could champion *Gospel of Peter* and alongside the biblical Acts of the Apostles, some would champion *Acts of Paul.* Eusebius, therefore, could not argue on the basis of apostolic authorship, because everyone made such claims for their preferred writings. Rather, he argued on the basis of "orthodox" church tradition. In effect, he claimed that the writings on his list were the true apostolic ones because the "apostolic" church, namely the church tradition Eusebius represented, had acknowledged them as such over the years. Eusebius won the debate because the church position he represented won the political battle for dominance. By the year 367 the debate seems to have ended. In that year, Bishop Athanasias, in a festal letter to his churches, provides a list of canonical writings identical to what we have today. There is no record of any continuing debate over canon after that point.

Text and Translation

All of the New Testament documents are written in Greek. Some of the writers were undoubtedly Jewish, yet they wrote in Greek. Jesus was Jewish also, and is thought to have taught in Aramaic, yet the gospels record his sayings in Greek, with only a few Aramaic terms left untranslated.

A New Testament text in its raw form would look something like this:

ΕΝΑΡΧΗΗΝΟΛΟΓΟΣΚΑΙΟΛΟΓΟΣΗΝΠΡΟΣΤΟΝΘΕΟΝΚΑΙΘΕΟΣΗΝΟΛΟΓΟΣ

To read this text, one would need a sufficient competence in the ancient Greek language and a basic understanding of the world from which it came. Fortunately, a lot of this work has been done for us, so that today we can read the Bible in modern English. The text quoted above in its original Greek form would read like this in English: "In the beginning was the Word, and the Word was with God, and the Word was God."

The process of bringing that original text into English form is more complex than one might realize. First, decisions had to be made about which version of the text to use. We have no originals of any New Testament text. We have only copies, and the earliest copies we have, in only fragmentary form, date from the second to third centuries C.E. These copies take a shape commonly found in ancient documents; that is, they manifest numerous textual variants from copy to copy, so that it is impossible to know exactly what the original form of the text was. We can only apply our best research and analysis to make educated guesses about what might have been the most likely original text. The name given to this kind of research is Textual Criticism.

To be sure, most textual variants in the manuscripts can be easily dealt with. They represent errors in the transmission of hand copying of manuscripts that we can fairly easily identify and correct. Nevertheless, there are a number of textual variants that pose more significant problems. In these cases, scholars try to choose the reading that is most likely the earliest, but will often place other options in the footnotes in order to indicate that the differences in the manuscripts cannot be finally decided. In the *New Revised Standard Version Bible* (NRSV), other textual options are identified in the footnotes by the phrase "other ancient authorities." Such notes indicate that the decision about the earliest text cannot completely rule out the possibility that the text in the footnote may be the earlier.

An example of a text criticism problem is found at the end of the gospel of Mark. Some Greek manuscripts end the gospel at 16:8 with the phrase, "and they said nothing to anyone, for they were afraid." Other manuscripts follow this phrase with a short summary of the commission of the disciples by the risen Lord. Other manuscripts add after 16:8 a more lengthy resurrection appearance story. The evidence strongly supports the view that the earliest version of Mark ended at 16:8. That is because it is the version found in a significant group of our earliest and generally more reliable manuscripts and also because it is "the more difficult reading." The more difficult reading is generally preferred to be the earlier, because one can then explain how the other variant readings arose as attempts to correct a difficulty in the text.

Once a text is decided upon, a process of translation must take place before it can be read and interpreted by people today. The process of translating these texts from their original ancient Greek to today's modern languages is a complex process as well. No translation from one language to another can be an exact copy; all translations must be only approximations of the original. For example, it is virtually impossible to translate a pun from one language to another. A famous pun in the New Testament occurs in the gospel of John in the conversation between Jesus and Nicodemus (3:1–15). When Jesus says one must be "born *anothen*" he is using a pun (3:3, 7). The Greek word *anothen* means both "again" and "from above." The conversation takes an ironic twist when Nicodemus fails to understand the pun and puzzles over how one can be born again from his mother's womb (3:4). The story uses this pun to illustrate the difference between one who has the insight of faith and one who is still tied to this world. But the translator cannot fully catch this nuance of the Greek with any comparable English term. The best one can do is resort to a footnote, as most translations do. Such footnotes in the NRSV version indicate translation options with the term "Greek" followed by the literal meaning of the term, or with the term "or" followed by another translation option. In the case of John 3, the NRSV translates "born from above" in the text and "born anew" in the footnote.

In other cases, translation problems are presented by differences in customs between their time and ours. For example, ancient people reclined when they dined, and so Jesus is always described as reclining at meals. Yet the NRSV prefers to translate such references with the phrase "sit at table" (see, e.g., Mark 2:15) because in today's world, we sit when we eat. Ancient people who spoke Greek often used male references generically to refer to both male and female people. Today our language has developed differently and a generic use of a male reference no longer communicates clearly. For this reason, the NRSV often translates "brothers" with "brothers and sisters" in an attempt to render in current English usage a more precise equivalent to the original meaning of the Greek (see, e.g., 1 Cor. 1:10, 2:1, 3:1, etc.).

These examples serve to illustrate the point that no translation is final; all translations have their good and bad points. The best translations are generally those that derive from a committee made up of scholars who are representative of a wide variety of points of view. The NRSV is a good example; it is a translation prepared specifically by a representative, ecumenical committee of scholars. It is also a translation that defines itself as needing renewal every generation, because the English language itself changes over the years. Thus the NRSV takes the place of the *Revised Standard Version Bible* (RSV) which itself was a revision of a revision that goes back several centuries, eventually to the *King James Version*. The purpose is to continue the heritage of the *King James Version,* that is, to provide a "standard" translation useable in the worship of the church but to update the translation on a regular basis.

Why not simply use the *King James Version,* since it is still so widely revered today? The problem with the *King James Version* (KJV) is that it is based on scholarship of the seventeenth century, and we have learned a lot in the nearly 400 years since. Furthermore, our language has changed significantly since the days of Shakespearean English. So while the KJV was a fine translation for its day, it no longer suffices for today. Of course, it is still the version that is the most well-known to the general public. But the serious student of the Bible must read for understanding, and for ease of understanding the KJV is actually a hindrance rather than an aid. In this book we will use the NRSV as our standard translation, and recommend that the reader always consult this or another modern translation in order to get at the meaning of the text most readily.

The World of the New Testament

Alexander and Hellenistic Civilization

The New Testament documents were all written in the Greek language, though most were not written in Greece itself nor were they written by "Greeks" per se. But Greek was the common language of the entire eastern half of the Mediterranean world. To understand why this was so, we have to go back to the time of Alexander the Great and assess his importance for setting the stage for the world of the New Testament.

In the mid-fourth century B.C.E., the dominant empire in the eastern Mediterranean region was that of the Persians, and it stretched from Asia Minor through the Mesopotamian region and Palestine all the way to Egypt and, from time to time, threatened Greece as well. In response, the Greek city-states ceased their wars among themselves and organized under the leadership and rule of King Philip of Macedon in order better to address the Persian threat.

With the death of Philip, the Macedonian kingdom was passed on to his son, Alexander. Alexander then began an ambitious military campaign against the Persians. His strategy was brilliant, his forces were clearly superior, his ambition was boundless, and in a few short years his armies had succeeded in conquering the entire Persian empire, including the rich prize of Egypt, and had extended as far east as India. Alexander had succeeded in uniting the entirety of the eastern Mediterranean world under one rule and one culture, and had in the process changed the course of world history.

Alexander had been schooled by the famous philosopher Aristotle, and so, applying those lessons, he set about to spread Greek civilization throughout the lands he conquered. He died while still engaging in military campaigns, and was not able to fulfill this mission himself. But the heirs to his kingdom, his generals, were successful in installing a single language and culture for the lands that had been conquered. Greek became the official language throughout the region, and Greek values and traditions became the resources for what we now call Hellenistic civilization.

Although there was a single language and a single culture, there was no longer a single kingdom after Alexander's death. He had left no will, and so his generals divided up the spoils and set up ruling dynasties in their respective kingdoms. Ptolemy set up a kingdom in Egypt, Seleucus a kingdom in Syria, and Antigonus a kingdom in Macedonia. Then they and their heirs began to engage in continual skirmishes and wars with one another for the next several centuries.

Judaism and the Hellenistic Kingdoms

Judea, located midway between the kingdoms of the Ptolemies and the Seleucids, was fought over by the two empires. At first it was part of the Ptolemaic Empire, which ruled from Egypt, and Judea prospered under their rule. It was during this time that Judaism began to adopt the Greek language and aspects of Hellenistic civilization.

By the second century B.C.E., Judaism had become so thoroughly Hellenistic that the Jewish scriptures had to be translated into the Greek language so that Jews could read their own scriptures. We call that Greek translation the Septuagint (abbreviated LXX), a Latin term that means "seventy." It refers to the official legend that the translation was originally done by seventy (or, according to some versions of the story, seventy-two) scribes who all worked independently, yet whose translations miraculously all agreed in every detail (a wonderful public relations tool to sell the new translation; for the official story of the miraculous translation, see the *Letter of Aristeas*). The Septuagint was also the Bible of the early Christians, as seen by the fact that all of the New Testament writers, when they quote the Jewish scriptures, are quoting from the Greek version (with few if any exceptions).

Though the Jews had come to terms with Greek civilization, they had not quite come to terms with foreign rulers. During the Hellenistic period, Judaism had begun to divide into two groups, diaspora Jews, namely those that lived away from Judea, and Palestinian or Judean Jews. Diaspora Judaism prospered especially in intellectual centers like Alexandria in Egypt, where the Septuagint translation was presumably made and where the great Jewish intellectual and philosopher, Philo, lived and worked in the first half of the first century C.E. Diaspora Jews were still loyal to the temple in Jerusalem, paying a temple tax to support it, but they also had their local synagogues and their own form of piety.

Palestinian Judaism saw itself as the keeper of the traditions. Aramaic, a derivative of Hebrew, was the spoken language in much of the region, though Greek language and civilization was still present and influential. The piety of Palestinian Judaism especially centered on the temple and the land. The land of Judea was the "promised land" given to them by God, and there was a continuing longing for the return of sovereignty over the land, often expressed as a longing for the reestablishment of the kingdom of David.

The Maccabean Revolt and the Hasmonean Kingdom

Judea under the rule of the Ptolemies in Egypt enjoyed a period of peace and prosperity. But this came to an end in the early part of the second century B.C.E. when it was taken over by the Seleucid Kingdom in Asia Minor, now ruled by the Antiochid dynasty. Their style of rule was much more oppressive, and soon tensions came to a head, eventually resulting in open rebellion by the Jews.

It was Antiochus IV Epiphanes who provoked the rebellion, as chronicled in the official Jewish history of the conflict contained in the four books of the Maccabees. In a misguided attempt to unify his kingdom under a common allegiance to the state, he commanded that pagan offerings be offered in every Judean city, beginning with Jerusalem. In the year 167 B.C.E., an altar to Zeus was set up in the Jewish temple and a sacrifice to Zeus was made. This event is defined as the "abomination that makes desolate" in Daniel 11:31, signifying that it was considered a profaning of the temple. The policies of Antiochus fueled a "holy war" rebellion led by Judas Maccabaeus and his brothers. Largely because Antiochus was occupied with battles elsewhere, the Maccabees succeeded in driving out the foreign rulers and establishing a new kingdom of Israel. One of the first acts of the Maccabees was to purify the temple, an event that is still commemorated in Judaism today in the festival of Hanukkah.

The new kingdom of the Jews, the first since the exile, came to be known as the Hasmonean kingdom, named after its ruling family. The Hasmonean dynasty ruled from 140 to 63 B.C.E., at which time the rule over Judea passed into the hands of the Romans. The period of the Hasmonean kingdom was remembered in subsequent Judaism as a time when the land given by God had been restored to its proper rulers.

The Roman Empire

In the third to first centuries B.C.E., Rome began to emerge as a new power, first dominating in the western region of the Mediterranean, and then gradually extending its rule over hte eastern region as well. By the time Augustus took charge as the first emperor of Rome (prior to that, Rome had been a republic), the entire Mediterranean world was under Rome's control. The rule of Augustus (31 B.C.E. to 14 C.E.) inaugurated an extended period of "Roman peace" *(pax Romana)*. No longer were there petty wars between rival kings; now the iron hand of Rome kept the peace. Rome built roads connecting the various parts of its empire, and travel and trade increased exponentially. While Latin was the official language of Rome itself and the Western half of the empire, Greek remained the common language of the Eastern Mediterranean region (the former Hellenistic kingdoms) under Roman rule. This was the context within which Christianity began and grew.

Roman rule of Judea began when the Roman legions led by Pompey took Jerusalem in 63 B.C.E. From the beginning, however, Judea was a difficult area for Rome to control. Herod, from the royal family of the Idumeans, was given kingship over Judea by the Roman Senate, and ruled as client king from 37 B.C.E. until his death in 4 B.C.E. The Jews hated Herod from the start, seeing him as a tyrant who tried to pretend he himself was Jewish. For his part, Herod tried to ingratiate himself with the Jews by various public building programs, including a lavish refurbishing of the temple. "Herod's temple," as it came to be called, was described by the first century C.E. Jewish historian Josephus as a marvel of the ancient world. But it did not lessen Jewish hatred of Herod. Herod's temple was the temple of Jesus and of Paul.

According to the gospels, Jesus was born under the rule of Herod (Mt. 2:1, Lk. 1:5), leading scholars to date his birth at about 6 B.C.E. Although written years afterward, the gospel of Luke may capture some of the political feeling of the day when he has Mary proclaim that the birth of Jesus would bring about a new political order, when God would bring "down the powerful from their thrones" (Lk. 1:52). After the death of Herod in 4 B.C.E., his kingdom was parceled out among his sons. Judea, however, eventually came to be governed by prefects, who were officials directly appointed by Rome. Thus during the ministry of Jesus, Galilee was ruled by Herod Antipas, whereas Judea was governed by a prefect, Pontius Pilate.

The Jews of Judea continued to chafe under Roman rule. There were many attempts at popular uprisings. In fact, Jesus' own death probably occurred because he was identified as a political rabble-rouser. Finally, a full-fledged uprising of the Jews against Rome took place in 66 C.E. It was fated to be a failure. Rome first sent Vespasian to lead the legions. Then, when he was called back to Rome to become emperor, he turned the generalship over to his son Titus, who would one day become emperor himself. Titus placed Jerusalem under siege, and eventually succeeded in destroying Jerusalem and the temple in 70 C.E. The war came to its official close after a long siege of the last rebel stronghold at Masada in 73 C.E. Josephus tells the story of that siege, and how the rebels, when their cause appeared lost, agreed to a suicide pact. When the Romans finally breached the walls, they found that all were already dead.

Titus' victory over the Jews was commemorated in a victory arch that is still standing in Rome today near the Coliseum. One of the interior reliefs of the arch pictures the plundering of the temple and shows the soldiers carrying away a menorah and other sacred items. The destruction of the temple was a watershed in Jewish history. Never again would there be a temple of the Jews. Judaism was changed forevermore.

Paul had been dead ten years when the temple was destroyed; forty years had passed since the crucifixion of Jesus. But the course of Christianity was changed by this event. The gospels, which are written after the destruction of the temple, refer to the trauma of the event in grisly terms. It became a point of reference for the eventual separation of Christianity from Judaism.

Second Temple Judaism

The Judaism of Jesus and Paul is known as second temple Judaism. This refers to the phase of Judaism from the time of the rebuilding of the temple after the Babylonian exile (ca. 520 B.C.E.) to the destruction of the temple in 70 C.E. It was during this period that the synagogue arose and the various sects of Judaism took shape.

We do not know for sure exactly when the institution of the synagogue arose in Judaism, but we do know that it existed in the Hellenistic period. The term actually refers to the gathering itself, and only secondarily came to be applied to the meeting place. A synagogue gathering was an occasion for study of the Torah and prayer. It was not a substitute for the temple, but a supplement to it, since sacrifice, the central ritual in Jewish religious practice, could not take place at a synagogue but only at the temple. Whereas there was only one temple in Judaism, the temple in Jerusalem, there could be a synagogue anywhere Jews were found. The synagogue structures that have been excavated from this period are designed with benches around the walls so that people could gather and study and discuss the Torah. The focus of the synagogue assembly room was the Torah shrine, often a niche in one of the walls, where the copy of the Torah was kept.

The primary parties that had developed in Judaism by the time of Jesus were the Sadducees, the Pharisees, and the Essenes. The Sadducees were the priestly party and controlled the temple priesthood. This gave them a significant power base within Judaism. They also subscribed to a rather narrow view of Jewish scripture, acknowledging only the Pentateuch as authoritative. Thus, since the Pentateuch did not teach the doctrine of resurrection, the Sadducees did not believe in resurrection.

The Pharisees were students of the law, and prided themselves on keeping the law to a greater degree than other Jews. They were highly respected as scholars in the law, and at various times during the second temple period seemed to have had some influence over Jewish society at large. They utilized as their authority not only the Pentateuch but also other Jewish scriptures as well as the "oral torah," or what later became known as the rabbinic tradition. Because they accepted a wider collection of Jewish writings than just the Pentateuch, they also included apocalyptic beliefs in their theology, and therefore believed in the doctrine of resurrection. Paul identified himself as a Pharisee (Phil. 3:5), though his form of diaspora Pharisaism was probably somewhat different from the more strict form of Pharisaism found in Judea.

The Essenes were a sect of rival claimants to the temple priesthood. Since the Sadducees controlled the priesthood, however, the Essenes, in protest, withdrew to the desert and lived apart from the rest of Judaism. They built a colony at Qumran on the Dead Sea where they practiced a strict form of purity and a ritualized communal life. Their community was destroyed by the Romans during the Jewish War in 68 C.E. and they disappeared from history, but their literature has been preserved in the Dead Sea Scrolls.

Jesus lived his life totally within a Jewish world, only encountering non-Jews occasionally. As for Paul, even though he saw himself as "apostle to the Gentiles" (Gal. 1:16) and argued against "judaizers" (namely, those who "compel the Gentiles to live like Jews," Gal. 2:14), he was not yet at the point of declaring Christianity a separate religion. He saw his mission as an extension of Jewish religious traditions, and Gentile Christianity as a "graft" onto the root that was Israel (Rom. 11:17–18).

When the temple was destroyed in 70 C.E., Judaism entered a period of severe crisis. Since the Jews no longer had a place where sacrifices could be offered, they, in effect, could no longer practice their religion, or at least a major component of it. Without a temple, the Sadducees disappeared. But two parties survived to fight over the Jewish heritage, namely the Pharisees and the Christians. What remained of Jewish piety was the synagogue, and both Pharisees and Christians made claims on it. The Pharisees were actually well positioned to pick up the pieces that remained of Judaism, because they had already developed a strict view of piety that, in effect, substituted for temple piety. But the Jewish sect of Christians also made claims upon the Jewish heritage. Allusions to conflicts between Jewish Christians and other Jews can be found in the gospels and in Acts and often reflect conditions in the period after the destruction of the temple.

Christians under Roman Rule

Jews in the diaspora largely escaped the persecution suffered by their countrymen in Judea during the revolt against Rome. Indeed, the animosity against the Romans that was felt so strongly in Judea was apparently not shared by most diaspora Jews. Paul, for example, while engaging in his ministry in the 40s and 50s, clearly benefited from the Roman peace and prosperity which allowed him to travel all over the Empire spreading his message. When he wrote the letter to the Romans in the late 50s, he advised this congregation of Christians in the capital city of the ancient world to "be subject to the governing authorities; for there is no authority except from God, and those authorities that exist have been instituted by God" (Rom. 13:1). For Paul, Rome ruled by God's own authority, a far cry from the feelings about Rome among the Jews in Judea. Paul lived prior to the rebellion against Rome, of course, and most likely eventually died at the hand of Rome. (According to legend, he died in Rome under Nero in the early 60s C.E.) But his sentiments expressed here in Romans are not very different from those of his contemporary, Josephus, the Jewish historian. Josephus had joined the Romans during the Jewish revolt, and later wrote a history in which he emphasized the folly of the rebellion.

Yet the early Christians did not always have an easy time against Rome. Sporadic persecution broke out against Christians, but was usually localized rather than empire-wide. A classic record of a trial of Christians before the Roman authorities is contained in a letter of Pliny, governor of Bithynia, to the Emperor Trajan in about 112 C.E.:

> Having never been present at any trials of the Christians, I am unacquainted with the method and limits to be observed either in examining or punishing them...In the meanwhile, the method I have observed towards those who have been denounced to me as Christians is this: I interrogated them whether they were Christians; if they confessed it I repeated the question twice again, adding the threat of capital punishment; if they still persevered, I ordered them to be executed...Those who denied they were, or had ever been, Christians, who repeated after me an invocation to the Gods, and offered adoration, with wine and frankincense to your [the Emperor's] image, which I had ordered to be brought for that purpose, together with those of the Gods, and who finally cursed Christ—none of which acts, it is said, those who are really Christians can be forced into performing—these I thought it proper to discharge. (*Letters* 10.96)

What Pliny pictures here is the clash between emperor worship, considered a patriotic duty, much like saluting the flag is today, and Christian worship of Christ. Christians, like Jews and unlike everyone else in their polytheistic world, considered it sacrilegious to worship any other deity except the one God and the Lord Christ. Pliny also records that trials such as this had evidently happened under Roman rule before. Indeed, a similar clash with Rome must lie behind the language in the Revelation of John. Here the faithful must choose either to worship "the image of the beast," clearly a reference to emperor worship, or die (13:15). Revelation defines the primary sin of the Roman Empire to be the shedding of the blood of the martyrs (17:6). Unlike Paul, who saw the Roman Empire as having been instituted by God, Revelation, written a full generation later under different circumstances, saw the Roman Empire as having been instituted by Satan (12:9; 13:1–8).

Yet if Christianity was to survive, it had to learn to accommodate itself to the Roman Empire. Luke-Acts seems to make a case for that accommodation when it presents a story of the origins of the church in which no Roman official, beginning with the trial of Jesus by Pilate and Herod (Lk. 23:4, 14–15, 22) and ending with the trial of Paul (Acts 23:29; 25:25; 26:31–32), ever found anything illegal in Christianity. Luke's story seems to have an apologetic function, and to make the case that Christianity could survive and prosper under a benign Roman rule.

Social and Religious Life in the Greco-Roman World

When Paul wrote the Corinthian Christians about divisions in their community, he provided a window into significant aspects of their social and religious life. This primarily Gentile community of new Christians had been quickly formed and, while it saw itself as distinctive from other similar communities around it, it was also in many respects very much like them. Paul refers to this reality when he warns them, "You cannot drink the cup of the Lord and the cup of demons; you cannot partake of the table of the Lord and the table of demons" (1 Cor. 10:21). Clearly it was possible to do both; clearly religious meals were being practiced by a variety of groups in Corinth, not just by the Christians. On the surface, there must have seemed to be little difference; that is why Paul had to present this warning. This text opens for us a window into the religious world of the New Testament period.

Sacrifice

One issue at Corinth was meat "sacrificed to idols" (1 Cor. 8:1–12; 10:14–22). This issue arose because the prevailing form of worship in the ancient world was animal sacrifice, and a constituent part of that animal sacrifice was the accompanying meal in which a portion of the sacrificed animal was eaten by the worshipers. This was the universal practice in ancient religion, whether among the Greeks and Romans or among the Jews, as Paul notes when he refers to both groups in his discussion (1 Cor. 10:18–20).

When Paul walked through Corinth he would have passed numerous temples to the various deities of the Greco-Roman world. There was an archaic temple, perhaps to Apollo, that was already several hundred years old when Paul visited Corinth. Temples dominated the public marketplace or forum, temples to Hermes, Dionysus, wives of the emperors, and a variety of others. Nearby in the outskirts of Corinth, there were elaborate and highly popular temples dedicated to the worship of Asclepius, Demeter and Persephone, and Aphrodite. To Paul's Jewish mind, these were all "idol temples" containing images of false gods or "demons." When he visited the holy sanctuary of his own religion in Jerusalem, he worshiped at the temple that, according to Jewish belief, served as the only temple to the one true God.

For all their differences, nevertheless the Jewish temple and the Greco-Roman temples had one thing in common. The center of worship was always the altar where the sacrifices took place. It is difficult for us today to fully comprehend the differences between the ancient views of piety and our views. For the ancients, whether Greek, Roman, or Jewish, the height of religious worship was to be found in animal sacrifice.

There was a similarity in the practice of animal sacrifice throughout the ancient world. An animal, preferably an unblemished one, would be brought to the altar by the worshiper. The animal would then be taken by the priest and slaughtered by cutting the throat and letting the blood flow over the altar. The act of slaughter itself was a high point of the ceremony. The animal would then be butchered and a portion (or the entire animal in the case of the whole-burnt offering practiced by Jews) would be burned on the altar as the portion given to the deity. The rest of the meat would be divided among the priest and the worshipers, who would often consume it in a meal immediately following the sacrifice.

The meal that followed the sacrifice could evidently be conducted in a variety of ways. Sometimes there would be specifications that the meat had to be eaten on the site. At other times it could be taken home and eaten later (though not much later, since it would quickly spoil unless preserved with salt). It might even show up at the meat market, as Paul suggests in 1 Corinthians 10:25. Temples often provided elaborate facilities for dining and must have functioned somewhat like an ancient version of a restaurant, that is, as a facility where anyone might gather a group of friends and have a meal together. This is the situation Paul has to address in 1 Corinthians 8. Here a problem had developed between two groups in the Christian community, the "weak" and the "strong." The "strong" were those who thought that meat "sacrificed to idols" was okay to eat, since the idols, in their view, had no power (8:4–6). The "weak" were those who "still think of the food they eat as food offered to an idol; and their conscience, being weak, is defiled" (8:7). Paul seems to side with the "strong" on theology, but not in regard to practice. "If others see you, who possess knowledge, eating in the temple of an idol, might they not, since their conscience is weak, be encouraged to the point of eating food sacrificed to idols?" (8:10). What is especially remarkable about this verse is the extent to which it takes for granted the phenomenon of the "temple restaurant" and the apparent common practice by many in the Christian community to take meals there. Indeed, one wonders to what extent Paul himself may have had personal experience of such a practice.

Meals

The communal meal was a social institution in the ancient world that provided a means for community formation among a variety of groups. Whether the group came together around shared religious beliefs or philosophy, or whether they were organized around a shared ethnicity or occupation, or whether they were simply formed as a funerary society to insure that their members would be guaranteed a really nice funeral celebration—whatever the circumstances, whether they were Greek, Roman, or Jewish, groups tended to meet together around a common table. The communal meal gave structure and focus to their meetings.

When early groups of Christians began to organize into communities, our evidence suggests that more often than not they met around a common table. From at least the 40s in Antioch, to the 50s in Corinth and Rome, and probably in all of Paul's churches, communal meals were the norm for the early Christian gatherings. Paul called the Christian meal a "Lord's supper" (1 Cor. 11:20) and indicated that the normal practice included a remembrance of Jesus' last meal and interpretation of his death in the form of a benediction over the cup and the wine. This ceremony, also echoed in the gospels and thus probably also found in their communities, was held as part of a larger communal meal, as is clear from Paul's reference to the entire event as a "supper" or "banquet" (*deipnon*, 1 Cor. 11:25).

The ancient form for a formal communal meal was that of the banquet or *deipnon*. This was an evening meal at which diners reclined on couches arranged in a traditional format, such as the *pi*-shaped arrangement in the typical *triclinium*, so that they faced one another for conversation. They were also arranged in such a way that they tended to share from tables together. The meals of Jesus in the gospels are pictured in this form. The posture is always reclining and sharing of common dishes is assumed (see e.g. the references to reclining at Mark 6:39–40; 8:6; 14:3; 18; and the reference to shared dishes at 14:20).

There were normally two courses in the ancient banquet, the *deipnon* proper, or eating course, and the *symposion*, or symposium, which was the drinking course. The two courses were divided by a formal ceremony in which the tables from the first course were taken out and the wine was mixed for the drinking course. A reference to the two-course meal is contained in Paul's version of Jesus' Last Supper, in which the cup benediction is pronounced by Jesus "after supper" (or after the *deipnon*, 1 Cor. 11:25).

The banquet was an occasion for social formation. Paul referred to this power of the meal when he argued, "Because there is one bread, we who are many are one body, for we all partake of the one bread" (1 Cor. 10:17). Here he echoed the common interpretation of the banquet as expressed also by the Greek writer Plutarch in the second century C.E. when he argued for "the friend-making character of the table" which is symbolized especially by the "wine that must be common to all" (*Table Talk* 612D, 614E).

The banquet was a time for the marking of social boundaries. Normally one's social status was indicated by the position one was assigned at the table. In Luke, Jesus used this convention to teach a lesson about humility and the reversal of social roles in the new age (14:7–11). The marking of social status could also be indicated in a variety of other ways at the meal, including providing a different quality or quantity of food at the meal based on social class, or not sharing the same portions of the meal with everyone. Some sort of social distinction must have been the cause of the problems at the community meal in Corinth. In that situation, Paul deplored the fact that "when the time comes to eat, each of you goes ahead with your own supper, and one goes hungry and another becomes drunk" (1 Cor. 11:21). His final advice was, in effect, that if their meal was truly to be the "Lord's supper" (11:20) then they should "wait for one another" (11:33) and eat together as a community. The social status marked by the meal was also used as a means to symbolize the breaking down of barriers. In the Jesus tradition, Jesus was stigmatized as a "friend of tax collectors and sinners" (Mt. 11:19; Lk. 7:34), a catchall term for social outcasts, because he ate with them (Mk. 2:16; Mt. 9:11; Lk. 5:30). He interpreted his actions in this way: "I have come to call (*kaleo*, "invite") not the righteous but sinners" (Mk. 2:17; Mt. 9:13; Lk. 5:32) thus indicating, in effect, how the borders of the table were to serve as a symbol for the borders of the kingdom of God.

Other Forms of Piety

Besides the sacrificial ritual, there were other forms of piety in the ancient world. Many of the sanctuaries also offered healing rituals of various kinds. The cult of Asclepius, for example, was renowned for the healing it offered. The large sanctuary of Asclepius at Corinth was typical of such sanctuaries. Besides the standard temple housing the image of the deity and the altar where the sacrifices were held, the sanctuary also included an accessory room and a set of dining rooms. The accessory room was probably the *abaton*, an area set aside in a healing sanctuary where the supplicant could sleep overnight and receive the healing he or she sought. The Asclepius sanctuary at Corinth, like other such sanctuaries all over the Greek world, was found by its excavators to contain dozens of votive offerings in the form of images and inscriptions that detailed the successful healings that had been accomplished there. The phenomenon of healing by various deities and divinely empowered individuals throughout the ancient world reminds us that Jesus as a healer would have been but one among many such healers in the world of his day.

Other rituals in ancient religious practice served a different set of religious needs. The practices grouped under the category of mystery religions were widespread in a variety of cults and dated back for centuries in Greek religion to the early forms of the Demeter and Dionysus cults. They are called "mystery" religions because their central ritual was a "secret" rite in which the individual was enabled to experience some kind of personal encounter with the deity. These rituals were routinely kept secret, so we know little about how they were actually practiced. But they apparently served a longing among the people for a greater religious experience than was available in the normal sacrificial cult. Paul may have borrowed and adapted some of the mystery religion terminology when he refers to the Christian ritual of baptism as one in which there is the experience of a spiritual "death and burial" followed by a "newness of life" (Rom. 6:4).

In the Hellenistic and Roman period, there also arose a longing for more assurance about the afterlife. In traditional Greek and Roman religious thought, and early Jewish tradition, the afterlife was only a vague idea, a place where the "soul" might go but where little actual consciousness was found. Greeks and Romans, in effect, went on a quest to find more sufficient data about the afterlife than their traditional resources provided. Many found it in the new cults that grew up in the Hellenistic period that were based on Egyptian tradition. It was well known that the ancient Egyptian religion, with its *Book of the Dead* and its elaborate, and very impressive, embalming practices, provided expert knowledge about the afterlife. The Hellenistic version of Egyptian religion, the Egyptian cult of Isis and Sarapis, became one of the most popular mystery religions in the ancient world, largely because of its connection with Egyptian lore on the afterlife. In fact, the cult of Isis was one of the primary competitors with Christianity for much of the second century C.E.

The other ancient religion that had developed an elaborate theology about the afterlife was Judaism. Its afterlife doctrine was part of its apocalyptic theology. Jewish apocalyptic ideology became the foundation for early Christian theology and undoubtedly provided part of its appeal to the ancient world. Paul had to address issues about the afterlife over and over again in his letters. Early Christian groups, with their regular meetings at table and their highly developed theology about the afterlife, must have resembled funerary societies to outside observers.

In the ancient world, there was not a distinction between the sacred and the secular as there is today. One's religion and religious practices tended to be imbedded in one's identity. Most people followed the religion of their ethnic group, and their religious practices were fully integrated into their family, social, and civic life and responsibilities. One of the challenges of the early Christian missionaries was to convince people to break with this pattern and form religious alliances across the traditional ethnic and social boundaries.

Theology

Apocalyptic thought was the matrix out of which early Christian theology developed. Apocalyptic theology had been adopted by Jews during the time they lived under Persian rule and was modeled on Persian dualism. It was based on a concept of temporal dualism, a view that time had a beginning and would have an end. This was unlike the circular view of time more widely found elsewhere in the Greco-Roman world. According to apocalyptic thought, the current age would end and be supplanted by a new age. This represented the divine purpose for the world, for the world had been created free of defect, but corruption had since crept in. So God's plan was to destroy this world and replace it with a "new heaven and new earth" that would reestablish the perfection it had at creation in the beginning of time. The current age was characterized as a time in which "the ruler of this age" was in control and was corrupting the world and persecuting the faithful. This time was rapidly coming to a close, to be brought on by a great cosmic battle between the powers of evil and the powers of good, or between the "angels of Satan" and the "angels of God." The angels of God would prevail, the righteous would take their proper place as rulers, while the current rulers would be punished, and a new world order would be created.

Apocalyptic thought generated not only a theology but also a distinct form of literature, the apocalypse. There were numerous such writings that emerged in second temple Judaism, and many more emerged in popular Christian literature. Only one such Christian writing made the final canon, the Apocalypse (or Revelation) of John. But in its day it was but one among many of this type of writing. Apocalyptic literature was a form of visionary literature in which a seer recounted a vision about current events and a glimpse into the future of the new age. Such literature arose primarily in times of turmoil, and provided a theological interpretation for current events so that the righteous, who were always the oppressed, could be encouraged by the knowledge that in the new age, which was always at hand, conditions would be reversed, the current rulers overthrown, and the righteous given power in a new heaven and new earth. Such visions defined current events in symbolic language and spoke of "signs of the end" that could be identified in various significant events of the time in which the seer was living.

The apocalyptic doctrine about the new age provided a basis for a highly developed doctrine of the afterlife, expressed in the form of resurrection terminology. Jewish belief did not distinguish between body and soul as the Greeks did, so existence in an afterlife was based on a belief in bodily resurrection. For the Greeks, body and soul were distinct; the body was doomed to decay, but the soul was considered immortal. Consequently, bodily resurrection made no sense to Greeks. Nevertheless, Paul fought for the centrality of bodily resurrection to Christian theology in 1 Corinthians 15, although he adapted somewhat to Greek thought by speaking of a resurrection of a "spiritual body" (1 Cor. 15:44). Ironically, as Christian theology developed in centuries following Paul, it would be the Greek view of the immortality of the soul that would prevail.

Apocalyptic thought also provided the foundation for Paul's doctrine of salvation or "justification." This doctrine was based on the belief in the resurrection of Christ, which was interpreted not as an event of personal vindication, but rather as an event of cosmic significance. Resurrection, in the code language of apocalyptic thought, meant that the new age was now erupting among us. The new age was a time of radical social transformation, a time when all people would gather equally before God. Thus Paul saw the mission to the Gentiles as demanded by the fact that Christ had been resurrected. The chasm between Gentiles and Jews was now bridged, because now Gentiles could be recreated by the power of the resurrection to become heirs of the promise of Abraham just as Jews were (Gal. 3:6–14). This was not something that Gentiles could simply claim as their birthright.

Rather it was a condition granted to them by the grace of God. Paul's language in regard to newness of life, justification, reconciliation, redemption, and so on, was all based on this basic apocalyptic foundation. It gave him the ability to proclaim a truly revolutionary doctrine of a universal faith for all humankind.

Another dualistic system of thought that prevailed in the ancient world was Platonism. This system, which derived from the teachings of Plato, provided the structure by which virtually all people of the ancient world, including hellenized Jews, understood reality. The basic idea was illustrated by Plato's famous myth of the cave (*Republic* 7.1–2). This parabolic story imagined human existence to be comparable to people being chained inside a cave in such a way that they could not see out to the outside world but could only see the shadows of the outside world passing before them on the interior wall of the cave. In this circumstance they would naturally assume that the shadows they saw were real. If one then imagined someone escaping and visiting the outside world, then coming back to explain what he saw, people might have difficulty accepting it. But that was exactly the task of the philosopher, to explain to people that the world of their experience was not the "real" world, but was like a shadow. The real world, the world of the "forms," existed in another realm. To be sure, the shadow world presented a reasonable image of the real. But the real was the ideal, eternal form, and should not be confused with the shadow form. Accompanying this doctrine was the idea of the separation of the body and soul. The body belonged to this mortal world. The soul, however, belonged to the eternal world of the forms. Physical activity was ephemeral. But reason, as an activity of the mind and soul, was what connected the human with the Divine.

As a person fully at home in the Hellenistic world, Paul was certainly familiar with Platonic thought. He seems to reflect that point of view in 2 Corinthians 5:1–4 when he speaks of the physical body as an "earthly tent" which we long to escape so that we may be "clothed with our heavenly dwelling." The book of Hebrews, an anonymous work that is often grouped with the Pauline letters, utilizes Platonic thought throughout, as it contrasts Jewish tradition, unfavorably, with the newly developed Christian theology. In Hebrew 8:1–5, for example, the author refers to Jesus as our high priest, one who presides at the "sanctuary and the true tent that the Lord, and not any mortal, has set up" as opposed to the earthly sanctuary, the temple, "that is a sketch and shadow of the heavenly one."

Platonic dualism was taken to a more radical extreme by gnosticism. Gnostic thought began to develop in the second half of the first century C.E. Some of the ideas were around in Paul's day, but the fully developed gnostic theology had not yet taken shape. By the latter part of the first century and throughout the second century C.E., gnosticism mushroomed as a major new form of theological speculation. Variations of gnostic thought appeared in Greek philosophy, in Jewish theology, and in Christian theology.

The basic gnostic religious point of view took Platonic dualism one step further toward a radical form of dualism. In this view, physical life on this earth was totally corrupt and entrapping to the soul. Some, however, contained within themselves a divine spark that would allow them to escape this corrupt world. Unfortunately, they were unaware of this condition because the all-pervading corruption of this world kept that knowledge from them. By some external means, however, such as by a divine mediator (e.g. the Christ according to Christian Gnostics), the true "knowledge," or *gnosis,* of their divine origin would be revealed. Armed with this knowledge that the soul had a divine origin and was only trapped on this corrupt earth, the supplicant could then escape the bonds of this earth through some form of spiritual transformation in order eventually to dwell with the Divine. Meanwhile, the Gnostic would follow a lifestyle on this earth that represented a denial or devaluing of physical existence. This could be expressed in the form of asceticism, especially sexual asceticism. Or it could be expressed in the opposite way, in the form of libertinism, especially sexual libertinism, based on the view that what one did in the physical body did not matter anyway. The problem that Paul addressed in 1 Corinthians 5:1–2, in which a particular form of sexual immorality is being practiced out of arrogance, is often interpreted as an early form of gnostic-style libertinism.

According to gnostic theology, the true God dwelled far away from this world and had no connection with it. In fact, this world was created not by the true God but by a false god. In the process of that creation, by some kind of cosmic accident, a spark or emanation of the true God became trapped here. This theology produced a distinct form of christology known as docetism. According to this viewpoint, the Christ who came to earth as an emissary from the true God could not have actually taken on fleshly form, because the flesh is corrupting and because the immortal cannot take on mortality. Thus the earthly figure of Christ only "appeared" (Greek: *dokeo*) to be in human form and only "appeared" to die on the cross. This version of christology made a lot of sense philosophically and was a matter of much debate in the formative years of Christian theology. It is thought that the gospel of John, while seeming to present a figure compatible with a docetic view, since the Jesus of John is so pervasively divine, nevertheless attempted to avoid that perspective by proclaiming "the Word became flesh" (1:14). Despite this, John became a favorite gospel for Gnostic Christians. In response, 1 John was written to "save" the Johannine tradition for "orthodoxy." It proclaimed "orthodox" christology in these terms: "every spirit that confesses that Jesus Christ has come *in the flesh* is from God, and every spirit that does not confess Jesus is not from God; and this is the spirit of the antichrist" (4:2–3, emphasis mine). Another New Testament writing that fought against gnostic thought, was 1 Timothy. Here the writer enjoins, "Avoid the profane chatter and contradictions of what is falsely called knowledge [Greek: *gnosis*]" (6:20). Throughout the second century C.E. and into the third, the early church would continue to be roiled by debates between Gnostic Christians and "Orthodox" Christians.

Social Class and Social Formation

From which social level of ancient society did early Christians come? The earliest clear evidence we have for the social class of an early Christian community comes from Paul. Paul defines the members of the Corinthian Christian community in this way: "not many of you were wise by human standards, not many were powerful, not many were of noble birth" (1 Cor. 1:26). What Paul tells us then is that *most* of them were not classed as upper class, yet *some* of them were from an upper class level. Consequently there was a great deal of social stratification in this community.

At the lower end of the social order in the Christian community would be the slaves, whom Paul mentions in 1 Corinthians 7:21–24. At the upper end would apparently be the homeowners who hosted the church at various times in their houses or who otherwise are identified as being heads of households. Such individuals included the woman household head, Chloe (1:11), who might have been a widow, and the couple Aquila and Prisca (16:19), who were no longer in Corinth but who seemed to host the church wherever they were.

Social class in the ancient world was not the same as it is today. For one thing, there was no middle class. Furthermore, social class was not defined by money alone. As Paul indicated in 1 Corinthians 1:26, quoted above, it was defined by family and ethnic connections and political status. People got along by means of social networks, that is, by means of their family and ethnic connections. Power was brokered through a patronage system. Those in power served as "patrons" of the less powerful who were their "clients" and gave them honor in return. Status and honor were more important than wealth, and it provided the motivation for the patronage system. An example of the patronage system at work was the house church in early Christianity. The early Christian communities did not have church buildings to meet in. Instead they met in homes. Those who provided the homes then became "patrons" of the group. As hosts, they would receive status and would have a certain degree of power in the group. Paul often mentions such individuals with gratitude in his various letters (see, for example, Rom. 16). Another example of a patron is Theophilus, to whom the writer of Luke-Acts dedicated his work (Luke 1:3; Acts 1:1). Paul also uses patronage language when he refers to the fact that he is "owed" a debt by those to whom he brought to the faith (see, for example, Philemon 19).

The patronage system was a standard way in which social interaction took place, and so it was natural for the early church to utilize it. But earliest

Christianity also developed a bold new form of social experimentation. Christians saw themselves as a society of equals, where normal barriers of rank and status did not hold. The gospels date this idea of radical egalitarianism to the teachings of Jesus. They spotlight the revolutionary nature of Jesus' message as seen in such acts as eating with tax collectors and sinners (Mk. 2:15–17; Mt. 9:10–13; Lk. 5:29–32). Paul inherited a similar perspective, but for him it was based on a different tradition than the teachings of Jesus. For Paul, the idea was expressed in a primitive baptismal liturgy in which baptism would transfer the individual into a new community "in Christ" in which "there is no longer Jew or Greek, there is no longer slave or free, there is no longer male and female; for all of you are one in Christ Jesus" (Gal. 3:27–28).

Paul's initial discussion of this principle was in support of his theology of the equality of Gentiles and Jews before God. He did not apply it so clearly to male and female relations nor to slave and free. To be sure, women were often designated by Paul as co-workers (Rom. 16:3–4, 6, 12), even as "deacons" (see Phoebe in Rom. 16:1–2), and, in the case of Junia, as an "apostle" (Rom. 16:7). Yet Paul was still troubled by gender questions, and, in one of his least inspiring moments, tried to argue for the necessity of women being veiled when they preached (or "prophesied") in the churches, in effect merely arguing for a personal sense of what constituted "propriety" (1 Cor. 11:2–16). Similarly, Paul does not seem to have thought much about the "neither slave nor free" concept. At one point, in 1 Corinthians 7:21–24, he seems to argue that the problem of slave and free in the same community could simply be solved by everyone treating everyone else as an equal. But in the letter to Philemon, after he had come face to face with a Christian slave, Paul seems to have moved to a position in which one who is a equal brother "in the Lord" should also be an equal brother "in the flesh" thus implying that the escaped slave, Onesimus, who had now become a Christian, should therefore be freed by his Christian master, Philemon (Philem. 15–16).

This bold new venture into radical egalitarianism struck a chord with ancient people, because it was reminiscent, for Greeks, of the Hellenistic ideal of a utopian state, and, for Jews, of the new world order of the apocalyptic new age. But it could also be worrisome to society at large, because it could suggest that Christians were not law-abiding people who kept to the proprieties of society. So it was that later generations of Christians began to back away from this primitive Christian vision, and seek for greater respectability in their society. A further motivation at this point was solidifying the leadership of the church in order to fight against "heretics" from within. Thus the church began to adopt a standard view of the orderly society, one in which order was based on a strong sense of boundaries between social, sexual, and political structures. The "household rules" illustrate this development. They represent the use by later Christian leaders of conventional rules of morality in which each level of society had a responsibility to act in accord with their social class, so that the lot of "children," "wives," and "slaves" was to obey and the lot of "fathers," "husbands," and "masters" was to rule wisely (see Eph. 5:22–6:9; Col. 3:18–4:1; 1 Tim. 2:8–15; 6:1–2; Titus 2:1–10; 1 Pet. 2:13–3:7).

From Judaism to Christianity

Many New Testament documents represent the struggle of the early Jewish Christian communities as they faced opposition in the larger Jewish world. The gospel of Matthew, for example, reflects the struggle between Jewish Christians and other Jewish groups when it emphasizes the disease and conflicts Jesus faced in "their synagogues" (4:23; 9:35; 10:17; 12:9; 13:54; 23:34) and spotlights Jesus' call for Christians to have a righteousness, in essence, like that of the scribes and Pharisees, only better (5:17–20). Clearly, Matthew's community saw itself as a claimant to the tradition of the Torah and the synagogue. Similarly the community represented by the gospel of John was also in a struggle over the synagogue. They too had come to a crisis point, so that their story paralleled that of the blind man and his parents in John 9. If they confessed Jesus, they too would be kicked out of the synagogue, which would obviously represent an estrangement from the only religious community they had known (9:18–23). Yet that was exactly what they were being challenged to do, just as was the blind man (9:34–41).

What is represented in these texts is the phase in the development of post-temple Judaism when the synagogue became the locus for the survival of Judaism and when the Pharisees emerged as leaders and keepers of correct interpretation of the Torah. Christianity had begun as a Jewish sect and only began to spread to Gentiles in fits and spurts, most notably as a result of the mission work of Paul. Clearly Paul saw "Christianity" as a form of Judaism. But over time Gentile Christianity came to dominate the Christian movement and Jewish Christianity declined. Most of the New Testament writings derive either from Gentile Christian groups per se or from groups that were in the process of including Gentiles in their midst.

As the Christian movement evolved from a primarily Jewish movement to a mixed movement to, finally, a purely Gentile movement, its developing theology began to address these changes. A major theological conundrum was the question, how could it be that the Messiah could be rejected by his own people? Paul answered the question by asserting that "through their stumbling salvation has come to the Gentiles" (Rom. 11:11) and that, in any case, "all Israel will be saved" by the "unsearchable...judgments" and "inscrutable...ways" of God (Rom. 11:26, 33). Later generations were more caustic. The Jewish Christian gospel of Matthew asserted that the Jerusalem mob cried out, "His [Jesus'] blood be on us and on our children!" (27:25), which contributed to the later development of the unfortunate doctrine that Jews were "Christ-killers." The gospel of John referred to the enemies of Jesus throughout as "the Jews" though the community of John itself was clearly Jewish as well. Consequently, when John is read by a non-Jewish readership, it appears to suggest that "the Jews" alone were responsible for the death of Jesus.

These traditions of anti-Judaism in early Christian theology clearly developed in the period in which early Christian groups were seeking to establish their own identity over against their Jewish forebears. In the passions of the debate, harsh statements were made, statements that are understandable in their historical context. But when taken out of context and interpreted not as historically contingent but as foundational Christian theology, these statements began to fuel a theology of anti-Semitism. Driven by this mistaken form of piety, Christians over the centuries have committed many heinous crimes against Jews. In our post-Holocaust age, we must step back and reexamine these dark aspects of our history. Out of the multivarious voices and seemingly conflicting perspectives that make up the New Testament, we must learn how to seek out its core theology, a theology that proclaims God's grace for all people, a grace that is founded on God's judgment, not ours. As Paul stated centuries ago, Gentile Christians are but "grafts" on the "rich root" that is Judaism. Therefore, he urged that we not "boast over the branches. If you do boast, remember that it is not you that support the root, but the root that supports you" (Rom. 11:17–18).

Contextual Interpretation of the New Testament

As any astute student of the Bible knows, the Bible can be interpreted in a myriad of ways to support completely opposing ideas. In such a situation, it is difficult to affirm the authority of the Bible while simultaneously acknowledging that there is no consensus on what it actually says. What is called for is a method of biblical interpretation that has both intellectual and spiritual integrity.

It is when the Bible is read out of context that it is subject to the greatest variety of conflicting interpretations. Reading the Bible in its context is a way of letting the Bible speak for itself on its own terms and not according to what we want it to be and say. Of course, no method can be perfect and there will always be disagreement on what the Bible actually says and means. But it must also be acknowledged that every reading of the Bible that finds "meaning" in what it says is therefore an interpretation, and it behooves any interpreter to be clear and forthcoming about how he or she arrived at any particular interpretation.

A contextual interpretation takes into account the historical circumstances out of which the Bible came, or the *historical context.* The New Testament was not written with us in mind; rather its individual writings were written for specific needs of specific churches in another time and place. In order to interpret it for today, we have to take into account those historical differences. For example, when Paul talks about meat "sacrificed to idols" as an issue in Corinth (1 Cor. 8), we can clearly recognize that he is addressing an issue that he faced in his day but that we do not face today. However, we do face what we might consider to be similar issues that divide our churches. On the other hand, some issues mentioned in the New Testament seem to address us directly, such as scriptures that enjoin wives to obey their husbands. Nevertheless, such texts are also historically conditioned, as seen by the fact that, in the same context, slaves are enjoined to obey their masters (see, e.g., Eph. 5:22; 6:5). Such instruction clearly applies to specific historical and cultural circumstances of that day and should not be read as laying down a law for every generation. Consequently, even texts that seem to be directly relevant need to be understood first in their own context before being applied to today.

A contextual interpretation should also give attention to *literary context.* The writings of the New Testament all represent forms of literature of their day. Literary standards in the ancient world were not the same as they are today. It was common, for example, for people to write in the names of famous people, rather than in their own names, and a great deal of the religious literature of the day was clearly written in that form. It is not unlikely, therefore, that some of the documents that made it into our New Testament canon could also have been written under those same literary rules. This issue will be discussed in more detail in the chapters that follow.

Writings also differ in terms of the *genre* of literature to which they are related. For example, Paul writes letters and uses the letter form of the day to do so. Understanding ancient letter form provides us with insights in interpreting Paul's letters. On the other hand, the gospels are all forms of narrative literature, perhaps related to the ancient form of the biography. As narratives, they partake of the motifs and formulas common to storytelling. For example, the author of a narrative must take responsibility to make the story make sense, in so far as the author has an opinion about what it means. Thus we can observe the gospel writers interpreting the Jesus story according to their own views about its meaning by the way in which they tell the story. This is especially clear when we notice that it is the narrator who gives us interpretive information. For example, in the gospel of Mark, it is the narrator who makes the connection between John the Baptist and Isaiah 40:3 (Mk. 1:2–4). Other aspects of narrative analysis will be noted in the chapters on the gospels.

Literary context also refers to the context of a verse within its own writing. The most common error of biblical interpreters throughout the generations is to interpret a text from the Bible out of context. When one takes a text out of its context, you can make it mean just about anything you want it to mean. The most consistent way to let the Bible speak for itself is to let it speak in its own context.

Interpretation of the Bible should also give attention to *theological context.* By that I mean interpreting a text in the context of the theology of its document or writer. For example, in the gospel of John the death of Jesus is interpreted by means of the words of Jesus in John 10:18: "No one takes [my life] from me, but I lay it down of my own accord. I have power to lay it down, and I have power to take it up again." Consistent with this view, when John portrays the death of Jesus, Jesus is shown to be in charge, from directing his own arrest (18:4–9), to being in charge of his own trial before Pilate (19:10–11), to carrying his cross with no help from anyone (19:17), to choosing the moment of his death and then "giving up his spirit" (19:30).

Similarly, texts from Paul must be interpreted in the context of Paul's overall theology. Thus when Paul addresses factions at the Lord's supper in Corinth (1 Cor. 11:17–34), he urges that everyone should "examine himself" lest they partake in an "unworthy manner," for all who "eat and drink without discerning the body, eat and drink judgment against themselves" (11:27–29). To interpret Paul's meaning here, we should note that in Paul's theology, the term "body of Christ" refers not only to the bread that is shared (11:24), but also to the community that shares it (12:12–13), a community that is unified into one body precisely by the ritual of sharing bread together (10:17). In the context of 11:17–34, Paul's advice is meant to address divisions at the meal and cause the community, when they come together to eat, to "wait for one another" and eat together (11:33). Consequently, Paul's advice to "discern the body" means, in effect, to "discern the community" and eat together in unity rather than in factions.

The New Testament reminds us over and over of the historical circumstances out of which it came, circumstances that are as messy as real life always is. Nowhere is this more apparent than in the story Paul tells of his confrontation with Peter in Antioch (Gal. 2:11–14). Here we see Paul and Peter virtually coming to blows because they disagreed about how the gospel was to be applied to the life of the church. Could you have two groups meeting under separate theological perspectives and still maintain the unity of the gospel, as Peter seemed to believe? Or, as Paul proposed, do you undermine the very integrity of the gospel by implying that there are distinctions before God rather than affirming by the life of the church that "there is no longer Jew or Greek... slave or free... male and female" before God (Gal. 3:28)? What is remarkable about this story is that these two giants of the faith could disagree on such a basic point. This story reminds us that the church and its Bible are products of history, just as we are products of history. And if we are to know God's presence among us today, we must seek the witness of God in our day just as they did in their day through the medium of imperfect "clay jars," namely the human witnesses who testify to the faith in the Bible and down through the centuries.

Contextual interpretation must also pay attention to the social and cultural context of the interpreter. Today biblical interpreters have become aware of a variety of different possible readings of the Bible based on the context of the interpreter. Examples include perspectives derived from feminist theology, womanist theology, African American theology, and liberation theology. Indeed, as our global awareness has increased, so has our appreciation for the fact that biblical interpretation can vary depending on the cultural context of the interpreter. These perspectives represent alternative points of view, often underrepresented in traditional Western scholarship, which an interpreter can bring to the text and which can provide new insights into its meaning.

Contextual interpretation has also guided the organization of this book. The chapters are arranged not by the order of books in the New Testament, but rather by reference to their chronological order. To be sure, we can only guess as to the date of any of the New Testament writings, since none of them actually tell us when they were written. Sometimes a writing may give a lot of clues as to date; at other times, there are very few clues. These issues are discussed in more detail in the chapters that follow.

We begin our analysis with the earliest writings in our collection, namely the letters of Paul. By beginning here, the student is able to assess the state of early Christian thought in the 50s, prior to the destruction of the temple. All of the other writings in the New Testament date to a period after the destruction of the temple, and represent developments in the second and third generations of early Christianity. It is here where the gospels are located, so they come next in the order of analysis. After an introduction to the study of the gospels and the historical Jesus, we then take up the gospels in rough chronological order, starting with the earliest, Mark. The remaining writings of the New Testament are also discussed in a rough chronological order, so that at the end of the period represented by the New Testament writings we have arrived at the beginning of the second century. In those one hundred plus years since the birth of Jesus the Jesus movement went through radical changes, changes that are reflected in the New Testament writings themselves. Consequently, it is wise to keep chronology in mind as we read the books of the New Testament. In that way we can avoid assuming that they all came from the same time period and point of view. Rather, we can properly place each writing in its own historical context.

Suggested Resources for the Pastor's Library

Brown, Raymond E. *Introduction to the New Testament.* New York: Doubleday, 1997.

Koester, Helmut. *Introduction to the New Testament.* Volume 1. Second edition. New York: Walter de Gruyter, 1995.

_____. *History and Literature of Early Christianity: Introduction to the New Testament.* Volume 2. New York: Walter de Gruyter, 2000.

Powell, Mark Allan. *The New Testament Today.* Louisville: Westminster John Knox Press, 1999.

Smith, Dennis E. *From Symposium to Eucharist: The Banquet in the Early Christian World.* Minneapolis: Fortress Press, 2003.

A Chronology of the New Testament and Its World

Date	Christian History	Christian Literature	Political Events
31 B.C.E.—14 C.E.			Reign of Emperor Augustus
37 B.C.E.—4 B.C.E.			Rule of Herod the Great, King of the Jews
Ca. 6 B.C.E.	Birth of Jesus		
4 B.C.E.—6 C.E.			Herod Archelaus, Ethnarch of Judea, Samaria, Idumea
4 B.C.E.—39 C.E.			Herod Antipas, Tetrarch of Galilee
Ca. 5—10 C.E.	Birth of Paul		
14—37			Reign of Emperor Tiberius
26—36			Pontius Pilate, Prefect of Judea
Ca. 31 C.E.	Death of Jesus		
30s—40s	Jesus Movements rise up in Judea and surrounding regions	Oral traditions about Jesus circulating; written collections of sayings of Jesus appear (example: "Q")	
35	Paul's "conversion" (Gal. 1:15–17)		
37—41			Reign of Emperor Caligula
38	Paul's first visit to Jerusalem (Gal. 1:18)		

Date	Christian History	Christian Literature	Political Events
39—41, 41—44			Herod Agrippa I, Tetrarch of Galilee (39–41), Ruler of Palestine (41–44)
41—54			Reign of Emperor Claudius
46—48	Paul in Antioch and "first journey" to south Asia Minor (Acts 13:1—14:28)		
48	Jerusalem Conference (Gal. 2:1–10; Acts 15:1–29)		
49—52	Paul's "second journey" to Galatia, Macedonia, Corinth	Paul's First Letter to the Thessalonians	
53—58	Paul's "third journey" to Ephesus, Macedonia, Corinth (Acts.)	Galatians, 1 Corinthians, 2 Corinthians, Philippians, Philemon, Romans	Felix, Procurator of Judea
54—68			Reign of Emperor Nero
58—61	Paul's arrest in Jerusalem, imprisonment in Caesarea, journey to Rome (Acts)		Festus, Procurator of Judea
Ca. 61—64	Paul's house arrest in Rome and execution under Nero		
Ca. 65—75		Gospel of Mark	
66—73			Jewish Revolt vs. Rome in Judea
69—79			Reign of Emperor Vespasian
70			Jewish Temple Destroyed

Date	Christian History	Christian Literature	Political Events
79—81			Reign of Emperor Titus
80s		Colossians, James, Jude	
80s—90s		Gospel of Matthew, Luke-Acts, 1 Peter	
81—96			Reign of Emperor Domitian
90s		Gospel of John, 2 Thessalonians, Ephesians, 2 Peter, Hebrews, Revelation	
96—98			Reign of Emperor Nerva
98—117			Reign of Emperor Trajan
Early 100s		Pastoral epistles (1 Timothy, 2 Timothy, Titus), 1, 2, 3 John	
117—138			Reign of Emperor Hadrian

2

The Early Paul
Galatians, 1 & 2 Thessalonians

Richard E. Sturm

Paul's Life and Work

Besides Christ Jesus himself, there is no one more central to the New Testament than the figure we know as "the apostle Paul." Paul's importance lies not only in his impact–for better and for worse–on the history of Christian faith and thought through his influence on such major theologians as Marcion, Augustine, Martin Luther, and Karl Barth. Even more dramatically, Paul's influence is evident within the New Testament itself. He is the author–or traditionally purported to be the author–of thirteen of the twenty-seven New Testament documents. Moreover, through the centuries, many have associated him also with the letter to the Hebrews, and fully half of Luke's Acts of the Apostles focuses on his ministry. Indeed, in the canon of the New Testament the Pauline literature follows Acts, as if he were *the* apostle. Both in the New Testament and in church history, whether heralded as a libertarian wholly committed to our freedom and unity in the gospel–or as a conservative advocating respectful submission to our superiors in society, family, and the church–Paul is a figure with whom we must reckon. But with so many different understandings of Paul and his thought, how can we discern Paul himself, as distinguished from the images of him that evolved–often in distorted ways–after his death?

Our primary sources must be Paul's own letters. Even though these letters were not meant to chronicle his life and work (as was in part the intent of the book of Acts), and although Paul often recounted his personal experiences in the heated context of polemic, his own letters must be our definitive resource regarding his biography and theology. While Acts is acknowledged to contain valid historical data, it is not always considered reliable. That said, we need not discount everything we hear in Acts. True, Luke has his own theological perspective and sometimes questionable traditions of biographical information on Paul's mission(s) to the Gentiles, which differ at significant points from the apostle's own recounting; nevertheless, Luke's work is a valuable repository of memories of Paul. John Knox, the noted mid–twentieth–century American interpreter of Paul, has best stated our criteria of evaluation: "We may, with proper caution, use Acts to supplement the autobiographical data of the letters, but never to correct them" (Knox, 32).

In addition to the portrait of Paul we see in Acts, we see his image in letters that, though traditionally ascribed to him, are now viewed as products of one or more of his later followers. In these "deutero-Pauline" epistles, several features of vocabulary and pastoral concern characterize a shift of circumstance and theology that argue not for a merely older or "wiser" Paul but for another author, time, and situation. Because the ancient world valued such "pseudonymous" writing (as in biblical works like Daniel, portions of Isaiah, and the ascription of all the Pentateuch to Moses), we need to distinguish Paul's authentic letters from those that come later to discern the apostle's own thought and experience.

Over the last several generations biblical research has identified seven of the Pauline letters as "undisputed" with regard to authorship: 1 Thessalonians, Galatians, Philippians, 1 and 2 Corinthians, Philemon, and Romans. Interpreters are divided regarding 2 Thessalonians, Colossians, and Ephesians (moving in that order toward pseudonymity). A scholarly majority sees 1 and 2 Timothy and Titus as pseudonymous. Hebrews has long been recognized as coming from an entirely different hand.

Considering these multiple sources, we may attempt responsibly to reconstruct a "life of Paul," cherishing the apostle's crucial role for the thought of the early church and the contents of its canon of scripture. Based mainly on the book of Acts, we can calculate that Paul was probably born around 5–10 C.E., during the reign of Caesar Augustus, in Tarsus, the impressive capital of Cilicia, on the northeast shore of the Mediterranean Sea in what is now Turkey. Moreover, since we know (from Rom. 11:1; 2 Cor. 11:22; and Phil. 3:5) that he was Jewish, referring to himself as circumcised on the eighth day, a member of the people of Israel, a Hebrew, a Pharisee, and a Benjaminite, we have every reason to believe that he was originally named Saul (as he is first called in Acts, after Israel's first king, from the tribe of Benjamin). His intellectual brilliance is evident in the thought and composition of his letters (all believed to be written in Koine Greek), so we can assume he was well educated, with expert knowledge of Jewish scripture (i.e., the Torah, Prophets, and Writings, encompassing what we now refer to as the Old Testament, but for Paul also including deutero-canonical literature such as Wisdom of Solomon, Sirach, Baruch, and 1 and 2 Maccabees) both in Hebrew and in Greek (primarily the Septuagint, the Greek translation of the Hebrew scriptures that was already centuries old by the time of Paul). His training to become a Pharisee suggests that a major part of Paul's education would have occurred in Jerusalem, and Acts 22:3 would have it that Paul was brought up in Jerusalem, studying under the esteemed Pharisee Gamaliel I the Elder. Paul himself says, "I advanced in Judaism beyond many among my people of the same age, for I was far more zealous for the traditions of my ancestors" (Gal. 1:14). Most of these details are consistent with—if not substantiated by—Paul's own letters.

But Paul would not have begun his "autobiography" with details such as these. On the contrary, Paul himself gives us something quite different: His account of his own identity and vocation begins with an "apocalypse," that is, an *apocalyptic revelation* of Jesus Christ (Gal. 1:12), "when God, who had set me apart before I was born and called me through his grace, was pleased *to reveal* his Son to me, so that I might proclaim him among the Gentiles" (Gal. 1:15–16, emphasis mine). Using the Greek verb/noun, *apokalypto/apokalypsis*, Paul describes the crucial event of his life.

This is the event Acts dramatizes three times (9:3–7; 22:6–9; 26:13–18) in what has become known as Paul's "conversion." Today, in spite of important connections between Paul's own words and the accounts of Acts (e.g., Paul's having "seen the Lord" [1 Cor. 9:1 and 15:8; cf. Acts 9:27] and the link with Damascus [Gal. 1:13–17; cf. Acts 9:1–9]), we need to recognize the sharp distinction between "apocalypse" and "conversion," at least as generally conceived. The term "conversion" usually implies both a moral turnabout, so that one ceases doing evil and starts leading a "good" or upright life, and/or a change of religions, say, from Judaism or no religion to Christianity. On both counts "conversion" is inadequate to describe what Paul says happened for him. Before he encountered Christ, Paul was, "as to righteousness under the law, blameless" (Phil. 3:6), so it would be wrong to say that he became morally upright only after becoming a follower of Christ. And although it is common to think that, on the road to Damascus, Paul stopped being Jewish and became a Christian, as if he were changing religious affiliations, Paul never stopped thinking of himself as "Jewish." For him, becoming an apostle of Christ Jesus in no way meant changing religions.

Where "conversion" suggests a significant change within a linear progression of events, like the *peripeteia* or "turning point" in a Greek drama, "apocalypse" connotes a radical disjuncture in time and space, like the discovery of an entirely different plot. *Apocalypse* is the word Paul chooses to describe the sudden encounter with the risen Christ that transformed him into Christ's "slave" and "apostle," commissioning him to proclaim the gospel of Christ Jesus to the Gentiles. And as we shall see in the Galatians commentary below, this revelation is *apocalyptic* for Paul, in that it manifests God's ultimate and intrusive action of power into "the present evil age" (Gal. 1:4).

In Paul's "earlier life in Judaism, [he] was violently persecuting the church of God and was trying to destroy it" (Gal. 1:13), which Acts (7:58; 8:1; 9:1) associates with the martyrdom of Stephen and which Paul describes as motivated by religious zeal (Phil. 3:6). After his apocalyptic revelation, Paul characterizes himself as an "apostle," that is, a person *sent out* or *commissioned*, and he declares his commission to be directly from God and Christ (Gal. 1:1), with no ambiguity about his being called by God to proclaim Jesus Christ among the Gentiles (Gal. 1:16). After three years, which he spent in Arabia (i.e., Nabatea, in the Transjordan, rather than present-day Saudi Arabia) and Damascus, which he may have had to escape, when the Nabatean king Aretas tried to seize him (Gal. 1:17–18; 2 Cor. 11:32–33; cf. Acts 9:23–25), Paul made his first trip to Jerusalem. There Paul spent a brief time with Peter and James, the brother of Jesus–but none of the other apostles; and Paul says he did not return to Jerusalem until eleven (or fourteen) years (in Gal. 2:1 Paul is probably counting from his apocalyptic revelation, rather than from his prior visit to Jerusalem) had passed. For these next eleven (or fourteen) years, we have no direct account of Paul's activity, but Acts (9:30) places him back in Tarsus and then in Antioch of Syria, a city exceeded in population throughout the Roman Empire only by Rome and Alexandria. Acts (13:3–14:28) has Paul begin from here an extensive mission to Cyprus and several cities in Asia Minor, including Perga, Pisidian Antioch, Iconium, Lystra, and Derbe, before returning. This is generally referred to as Paul's "first missionary journey," although the numbering and nomenclature are certainly not Paul's–nor even Luke's.

After several years of proclaiming the gospel among the Gentiles, Paul came a second time to Jerusalem, where, at the "mother church," which is what the Jerusalem church seemed to have become, an important meeting was held regarding Paul and his work. This event is now referred to as "the Jerusalem Council," differing accounts of which are found in Galatians 2:1–10 and Acts 15:1–29. According to Paul, "false brothers" challenged the legitimacy of his ministry because his gospel did not require Gentiles to get circumcised as part of becoming followers of Christ. But James (the brother of Jesus), Cephas (Peter), and John, "who were acknowledged pillars" of the church (Gal. 2:9), were not at all persuaded by Paul's accusers. Instead, they recognized God's grace at work in Paul and extended to him and his co-worker Barnabas "the right hand of fellowship, agreeing that we should go to the Gentiles and they to the circumcised" (2:9). It is hard today to appreciate the magnitude of this conclusion, since for most of us the organic link between Christian faith and Judaism is long lost, but Paul saw it as a confirmation of "the freedom we have in Christ Jesus" (2:4). The one thing that was asked of Paul was something he fully intended, namely, to "remember the poor" (2:10).

Paul's triumph at the meeting with church leaders in Jerusalem was in some ways short-lived and shallow. After returning to Antioch, Paul and

Barnabas were joined by Peter, and at first apparently everyone in the congregation (of both Jewish and Gentile background) ate in common table fellowship. But once "certain people came from James" (Gal. 2:12), Peter began to eat only with them, separating himself from Gentile Christians—which Paul could interpret only as exposing his "fear of the circumcision faction" (2:12). For Paul, Peter's change of behavior at meals was hypocritical, contradicting the resolution achieved at Jerusalem. Instead of basing actions on "the truth of the gospel" (Gal. 2:14), that is, "the freedom we have in Christ Jesus" (2:4), Peter was acting as if human religious practices mattered more than what *God* had done to save humanity in the cross of Christ. Paul's argument was unambiguous: Whether it be circumcision or table fellowship, if for their salvation human beings rely on practices of religion rather than faith in the gospel, they act as if "Christ died for nothing" (2:21). However compelling this argument may sound today, apparently Paul lost the day at Antioch, for "even Barnabas was led astray" (2:13), so that Jewish and Gentile members of the Antioch church separated themselves at meals, losing the unity Paul knew Christ had won for them.

Our window directly onto the apostle Paul, through the letters he wrote primarily to churches he founded and for whom he had deep pastoral concern, is a period of less than a decade, perhaps only eight years. During this time, Paul probably first returned to the cities he had visited in southeast Asia Minor before travelling to new territory: north to Galatia (the area around present-day Ankara, in Turkey), west to Phyrgia, and then over to the European mainland. Here, in what we now call Greece, Paul stayed in Philippi, Thessalonica, Beroea, Athens, and Corinth. Paul's sojourn in Corinth probably lasted a year and a half, and it was probably from Corinth (see Acts 18:1) that he wrote the church he had recently established in Thessalonica. Galatians was probably composed in this early period, too.

The book of Acts records a return trip to Jerusalem at this point, followed by what has generally been called Paul's "third" missionary journey: back through Galatia and on to Ephesus, the major city in the Roman imperial province of Asia. Paul apparently spent three years in Ephesus (part of that time very likely in prison) and here probably wrote Philippians, 1 Corinthians, and Philemon. The present 2 Corinthians was almost certainly written as multiple letters, probably on Paul's way from Ephesus through Macedonia back to Corinth. Although his stay in Corinth this time was only three months of winter, there Paul wrote the church at Rome and finished collecting donations for the Jerusalem church.

Sailing back along the coast, Paul made his way for the last time to Jerusalem, where Acts recounts a riot occurring as a result of his presence in the temple. When the Sanhedrin could not resolve the matter, Paul was taken to Caesarea Maritima to be judged by the Roman governor Felix. After two years of inaction, during which Paul was imprisoned, Festus became the new procurator and Paul's case was taken up again. This time Paul's appeal to Caesar postponed final judgment until he could be taken, as a prisoner, to Rome. After a perilous journey by sea, including shipwreck and a winter on Malta, Paul arrived in Rome–where he spent probably two years under house arrest, before being executed by beheading as part of a persecution of Christians by the emperor Nero.

There is little scholarly support today for additional episodes in the life of Paul, but the Pastorals and a purported journey west to Spain show that as early as the first three decades after his death, Paul had become *the apostle*, par excellence. His thought and long-suffering witness for the gospel–particularly to the Gentile world–became inspiring and influential in ways far beyond the limited success he experienced in his own lifetime.

It is difficult to determine dates for the events in Paul's life, but a point in Acts helps fix his chronology. Acts 18:12 records a tribunal hearing charges

---

A Chronology

(?)5–10 c.e.	Date of birth
35	The apocalypse/revelation of Jesus Christ
38	First visit to Jerusalem, meeting with Peter and James
46–48	Antioch stay and mission ("First Journey") to south Asia Minor
48	Meeting with Jerusalem church leaders ("Jerusalem Conference")
49–52	Mission ("Second Journey") to Galatia, Macedonia, Corinth
53–58	Mission ("Third Journey") to Ephesus, Macedonia, Corinth
58–61	Arrest in Jerusalem, imprisonment in Caesarea, on to Rome
61–64	House arrest in Rome, execution under Nero

---

against Paul during the Achaean proconsulship of Gallio, whose governance an inscription in Corinth dates to 52 c.e., a date that would need to coincide with Paul's stay in Corinth. The following timetable reflects my assessment of the current biblical research on the topic:

It is less difficult to reconstruct the likely sequence of the apostle's letters. In Galatians 2:10, Paul mentions a concern for the poor, to which he was eager to respond. Although "the poor" is sometimes synonymous with a pious movement in Jewish Christianity, the term here probably refers to the church in Jerusalem, suffering years of famine. Paul responded by taking a collection from his (primarily Gentile Christian) churches, a task that fulfills part of the great commandment, in love to one's neighbor, and expresses the unity the faithful–Jew and Gentile–have in Christ. Noting other references to this collection (in 1 Cor. 16:1–4 and Rom. 15:25–27), we can assume that 1 Thessalonians, Galatians, and Philippians were written (probably in that order) before Paul's official undertaking of this task–followed by the letters now extant in 1 and 2 Corinthians and ending with Romans. First Thessalonians is usually dated around 50 or 51 c.e., and Romans in 57 or 58. Of the undisputed letters, this omits Philemon, written to an individual, and its place in the sequence of Paul's correspondence is almost impossible to determine. The sequence is important not so much to trace a supposed "progression" of Pauline thought, as if the apostle were composing his letters like a systematic theologian writing a book, but rather to reflect on the changing counsel of a pastor exploring the truth of the gospel while addressing needs and concerns unique to congregations he knew and loved.

Paul's Letter Type, Context, and Format–and Methods of Interpretation

In the Greco-Roman world letter writing–in a wide variety of forms and types–was a major form of communication. Early in the twentieth century, the German biblical scholar A. Deissmann distinguished "letters" from "epistles," characterizing "letters" as personal correspondence and "epistles" as literary essays presenting a lesson or argument meant to persuade general audiences. The two terms are often used synonymously, but it is good to consider the difference for interpretation between an intimate request (like that found in Philemon) and careful deliberation (like that in Romans). For Paul, letters were generally dictated, rather than personally drafted, and they would need to be delivered by trusted persons travelling slowly (usually by boat and/or foot) to the place and persons addressed. In addition, Paul's letters were generally intended to be read aloud–in a congregation meeting for worship (see, e.g., 1 Thess. 5:27).

Students of Hellenistic rhetoric have long discerned a format for the letters now in our New Testament: (1) Opening Formula. Recipients of a letter in the Greco-Roman world never had to turn to the last page to read the name of the person sending it; the first word (*superscriptio*) is the name of the writer. Following the sender's name is the name of the person(s) addressed (*adscriptio*). Next would come a word or phrase of greeting (*salutatio*) and a statement of remembrance or wish for good health. This last element opening a Hellenistic letter is usually omitted in New Testament examples; instead, Paul has here a theological expression of grace and peace. (2) Thanksgiving. The second element, offering thanks (to God) for reasons specified, can vary greatly in length–or be omitted altogether (as in Galatians). (3) Body. This section covers the message of the letter, the issues or concerns that prompted correspondence. (4) Concluding Formula. Paul never uses two of the conventional conclusions of Hellenistic letter-writing: a(nother) wish for good health or a word of farewell. Instead he prefers a doxology and/or benediction, and several times he includes here a statement that he says is written in his own hand, probably indicating his approval of the previous content drafted by another.

Methods for responsible interpretation of Paul's letters include historical, literary, sociological, canonical, and liberation criticisms. Historical criticism has become, in the last two centuries, the single most important method of biblical interpretation; indeed, sometimes the term is used synonymously with biblical criticism in general. Although often under attack, particularly by church conservatives who believe its critical approach opposes biblical truths and authority, its only shortcoming is that it must be complemented by other methods of interpretation; no single method is sufficient. The goal of historical criticism is to place a text within its original setting, so that vocabulary, literary forms, and socio-political and theological currents of the author's time and place are respected. By so honoring a text's first hearing, listening as much as possible with the ears of its original audience, we may discern aspects of the argument that go unnoticed in the context of a different time or place—including our own. This discipline has proven invaluable, for example, in appreciating ways in which the apostle Paul's concerns are different in Galatians than in Romans or 1 Corinthians, as well as ways in which the theological issues and controversies of the undisputed letters differ from those of the disputed and/or pseudonymous letters.

Literary criticism is helpful for distinguishing the role of conventions of Greco-Roman rhetoric and epistolary format that Paul employs, alters, or rejects. Sociological criticism concentrates on the social, political, and economic aspects of the original setting of a text to consider, for example, the diversity in Paul's congregations as well as in the larger Greco-Roman world. Canonical criticism reflects on the biblical traditions behind a text (e.g., Paul's citation of the Old Testament), as well as on the relationship between a biblical text and the community of faith, as in the historical and theological process toward canonization and the church's ongoing interpretation of a biblical text. This approach respects the authority of a text, while acknowledging that scripture may well include different—or even conflicting—voices on a particular issue, and requiring the interpreter's sensitivity to a community's changing condition and needs for faithful hearing. Canonical criticism is especially valuable, for example, in valuing the different apocalyptic scenarios in 1 and 2 Thessalonians without regard to authorship. Under the rubric liberation criticism I would include the perspectives of biblical interpretation from voices that have traditionally been neglected or excluded in the exegesis of scripture, and the themes of Christian unity and freedom in Galatians have inspired needed insight from, for example, feminist, African American, gay and lesbian, and two-thirds world hermeneutics.

1 Thessalonians
Basic Data: Authorship, Date, Addressees, Prompting, Structure

There is scholarly consensus that 1 Thessalonians was written by the apostle Paul; its authorship is undisputed. Written from Corinth in 50 or 51 C.E., it is generally believed to be the first of Paul's letters. It is therefore the oldest preserved document of Christian literature. Paul wrote the letter to the church he had founded during a several month stay in Thessalonica, capital of the Roman province of Macedonia, not long after he arrived in Corinth. (There is considerable evidence in 1 Thessalonians that Paul's time with them was much longer than the three weeks indicated in Acts 17:2.) Paul had come to Thessalonica, accompanied by Silvanus and Timothy, after having been "shamefully mistreated" (1 Thess. 2:2; Acts 16:23 records an imprisonment) in Philippi. Paul was no stranger to controversy, and indeed, his preaching of the gospel to the Thessalonians also met with "great opposition" (1 Thess. 2:2). The book of Acts makes such controversy understandable, stating that it was Paul's "custom" to enter a local synagogue, encountering not only Jews but also Greek "God-fearers" involved in Jewish worship and respectful of Jewish thought. Paul then "argued with them from the scriptures, explaining and proving" (Acts 17:2–3) that his gospel of the crucified Christ was biblical and true–persuading some of the Jews, a great many of the Greeks, and "not a few of the leading women" (Acts 17:4), but antagonizing everyone else.

Paul's departure from Thessalonica was abrupt, leaving the apostle anxious about his new congregation's welfare. When he "could bear it no longer" (1 Thess. 3:1), Paul sent Timothy back to them in order to learn about their current situation and report back. What prompts Paul's writing of 1 Thessalonians is the fact that "Timothy has just now come to us from you, and has brought us the good news of your faith and love" (1 Thess. 3:6)–and their longing to see Paul again. Paul's own desire to return to them produces in 1 Thessalonians a tone of love and encouragement, even when giving pastoral advice and theological instruction, equaled only by his loving letter to the church in Philippi.

The structure and unity of 1 Thessalonians are matters of little dispute, although the severity of statements against "the Jews" in 2:14–16 have made these verses problematic. Since the harsh criticism here is both unparalleled in Paul's other letters and contradicts arguments presented elsewhere (particularly Romans 9–11), some interpreters have proposed that these three verses are a later interpolation [note: an interpolation is a section of an ancient document that appears to have been added by a later editor]. The structure of 1 Thessalonians is somewhat unusual. After the opening formula of 1:1, a thanksgiving comprises over half the letter (from 1:2–3:13; cf. Galatians, where no thanksgiving occurs at all). The body of the letter (4:1–5:22) covers some issues for instruction and/or exhortation, followed by a concluding formula (5:23–28) in the form of a beautiful prayer and benediction.

Commentary

The opening formula is simple, in that Paul adds nothing to his name–not even *apostolos*, as he does in Galatians, 1 and 2 Corinthians, and Romans; apparently his apostolic authority is not in question among the

Thessalonians. Most striking in this letter outline is the thanksgiving; in none of Paul's other correspondence does his gratitude attain such length. Such cordial affection expresses the love and concern Paul has for this congregation, his children in the faith from whom he must now be absent. Paul's thanks is to God, but his reason is the faith, love, and hope (1:3; cf. 1 Cor. 13:13) of the Thessalonians. Paul knows that God has "chosen" them, because they received his gospel "not in word only, but also in power and in the Holy Spirit and with full conviction" (1:5). Despite persecution, these early Christians embraced the gospel "with joy inspired by the Holy Spirit," becoming an example for the church both in neighboring provinces but also everywhere else (1:6–7). Note that when Paul describes their becoming part of the church, he combines language characteristic of Hellenistic Judaism (e.g., Jewish/Gentile differentiation) with the imagery of apocalyptic expectation: "you turned to God from [Gentile] idols, to serve a living and true God, and to wait for his Son from heaven, whom he raised from the dead–Jesus, who rescues us from the wrath that is coming" (1:9–10). As we shall see, the "coming of the Lord" and its implications for the church constitute the single most important issue in the body (4:13–5:11) of this letter.

In 2:1–12, Paul describes his proclaiming of the gospel among the Thessalonians in ways foreshadowing Galatians, but here contrasting his methods with those of Greco-Roman philosophers seeking their own gain. Paul "worked night and day" (2:9; cf. 1 Cor. 9:6–18; 2 Thess. 3:7–10), probably in labor related to tent making, so that he would not burden the church. His imagery of care here is quite touching, employing both masculine and feminine examples: "like a nurse tenderly caring for her own children" (2:7), "like a father with his children" (2:11). He thanks God that they received the Gospel "not as a human word but as what it really is, God's word" (2:13). In 2:17–3:13, Paul speaks personally about his relationship with the Thessalonians: his longing to be with them, his sending Timothy to them, and Timothy's return with the good news of their faith and love even in the face of persecution.

The body of 1 Thessalonians begins and ends with exhortation on "how you ought to live, and to please God" (4:1). In 4:1–12, Paul reminds his readers of previous instruction he gave them in person, covering such basics as sex and marriage, love for one another, and guidelines for everyday life and labor. Likewise, in 5:12–22, he gives counsel on respect for leaders within the church community, as well as on constructive attitudes toward idlers, the faint-hearted, and the weak, not repaying evil for evil but refraining from evil altogether–testing everything and holding fast to the good, always rejoicing, praying, and giving thanks to God. Such counsel provides ethical standards that are not uniquely Christian, but characteristic also of Hellenistic Judaism or Stoic philosophy. The positive words on work, wherein Paul uses his own labor while among them as an example opposing idleness, may reflect a problem some within the congregation had with the apocalyptic aspect of Paul's gospel, but it could also simply reflect a tendency toward Epicurean withdrawal from the world. In any case, in these moral imperatives, Paul is reminding the Thessalonians not to act "like the Gentiles who do not know God" (4:5).

Paul's central topic in this letter is "the coming of the Lord" (for this phrase alone, see 1:10; 2:19; 3:13; 4:15; 5:23). In 4:13–18, Paul instructs the Thessalonians on their grieving for those who have died ("fallen asleep" in the Greek)–in distinction from the grief of those "who have no hope" (4:13). Paul declares "by the word of the Lord" that the dead will not be forgotten when "the Lord himself, with a cry of command, with the archangel's call and with the sound of God's trumpet, will descend from heaven" (4:16). Paul reassures them that then both the living and the dead "will be caught up in the clouds together with them to meet the Lord in the air; and so we will be with the Lord forever" (4:17). In 5:1–11, Paul continues his instruction, "concerning the times and the seasons" of the day of the Lord (5:1–2), with words of encouragement for their obtaining salvation rather than wrath, since they are children of light and of the day: "since we belong to the day, let us be sober, and put on the breastplate of faith and love, and for a helmet the hope of salvation" (5:8; for the battle imagery cf. 2 Cor. 6:7; 10:4; Phil. 1:27–30; Rom. 13:12; Eph. 6:13–17).

It is impossible to know what Paul is saying here without some understanding and appreciation of his apocalyptic eschatology. This theological perspective on time and history, in which the past is reinterpreted in light of history's ultimate goal and its imminent end, is derived from certain Old Testament traditions. Although in the Old Testament only the book of Daniel from the genre of apocalyptic literature achieved canonical authority for Judaism and the church, the prophetic works of Ezekiel, Joel, Zechariah, and Isaiah included apocalyptic imagery and content. In this regard, especially noteworthy are the visions of Ezekiel (1–3; 27–28; 37; 40–48; cf. Zech. 4:1–6:8; 9–14; and Isa. 24–27) and the revelation of God's perspective on human history, often to a prophet transported to the courts of heaven, as seen in 1 Kings 22:19–23; Amos 3:7; and Isaiah 6. In Hellenistic Judaism, 1 Enoch (from the third century B.C.E.), Daniel (165 B.C.E.; see especially chapters 7 and 9), and the literature of the Dead Sea Scrolls (from the mid-second century B.C.E. into the first century C.E.) are steeped in apocalyptic thought and imagery (as are 4 Ezra and 2 Baruch, from the late first or early second century C.E.).

What issues are most significant for our hearing 1 Thessalonians today? We find here our oldest window into the life and thought of the apostle Paul and the early church. We learn the depth of pastoral concern Paul has for the Thessalonians, as well as their love of him and his guidance for their ethical and theological instruction. But two matters present problems for contemporary interpretation. First, regarding Paul's apocalyptic eschatology, it has been tempting for many to get stuck in a literal reading of "the rapture" and/or chronological predictions of the end-time–and neglect or miss entirely the theological wisdom of Paul's apocalyptic gospel. Such literalism can so overemphasize the supernatural elements of a passage like 4:16–17 that faith is reduced to belief in the miraculous–rather than trust in God's sovereignty over time and history, and our hope in God's love and righteousness. As with the creation narratives of Genesis, apocalyptic figures, times, and events need to be interpreted figuratively, not literally.

A second problematic issue for us today is our interpretation of 2:14–16, regarding the relationship between Judaism and the church. Assuming that these verses are original, reflecting actual thoughts of the apostle Paul himself, we must remember that he makes other statements (as in Romans 9–11) that give a different and more loving assessment of the role of the Jews in God's history and of their relationship to the church. We need also to confess the use of this passage (and others like it in the New Testament) by Christians through the centuries in an attempt to "sanctify" anti-Jewish prejudice. To be sure, there is hostility against the Jews expressed in some passages in Paul, Matthew, and the Fourth Gospel, in particular (note that the authors here are, or are believed to be, of Jewish heritage). That hostility is understandable in an historical context of oppression, when the early church was powerless and under persecution from the synagogue. That persecution intensified after the sacking of Jerusalem and destruction of the temple in 70 C.E., when Judaism was struggling to define and preserve its own identity under Roman oppression. But hostility is inexcusable, particularly once the power shifts to the church and the synagogue begins to suffer under the church's oppression. Surely we are called to heed Paul's own exhortation: "See that none of you repays evil for evil, but always seek to do good to one another and to all" (5:15).

2 Thessalonians
Basic Data, Structure, and Commentary

2 Thessalonians bears a striking resemblance to 1 Thessalonians. It is a little over half as long, and about one-third of 2 Thessalonians seems directly influenced by 1 Thessalonians–so much so that a number of scholars believe 2 Thessalonians was written shortly afterward (hence around 51 C.E.), almost as a revision of 1 Thessalonians. The opening formula (1:1–2) repeats the salutation of 1 Thessalonians almost exactly, with only a slightly expanded sentence of grace. The thanksgiving (1:3–12), concluding with a prayer, again recalls 1 Thessalonians (note also the second statement of thanks in 2:13; cf. 1 Thess. 2:13). The body of 2 Thessalonians (2:1–3:15) provides instruction and exhortation on the day of the Lord, a topic anticipated in 1:5–10; as we saw, this topic was central to 1 Thessalonians; and 2 Thessalonians 3:8 copies almost exactly the related statement (in 1

Thess. 2:9) about Paul's working night and day. The concluding formula (3:16–18) gives a final prayer and a benediction virtually verbatim to the one in 1 Thessalonians 5:28–as well as an affirmation (in 3:17) that Paul is signing the letter, writing in his own hand. This hand-written note near the end of a letter is a feature in several undisputed letters (Gal. 6:11; 1 Cor. 16:21; Philem. 19; cf. Col. 4:18); but the emphasis here seems curious: "I, Paul, write this greeting with my own hand. This is the mark in every letter of mine; it is the way I write." Indeed, the extensive verbal repetition of 1 Thessalonians, allusion to false teaching in forged correspondence ("by letter as though from us," in 2:2), and this insistence in 3:17 that *every* one of his letters bears his own handwriting, when only *one* other letter (1 Thessalonians) is likely to have been known to the church in Thessalonica early on–all this seems to "protest too much" that 2 Thessalonians is authentic.

Other content elements in 2 Thessalonians point to problems the church was facing *after* the life and ministry of the apostle Paul. For example, the threat of false teachers leading vulnerable congregations astray (2:2–3, 10–11) sounds very much like the situation Pauline churches faced in 1 Tim. 1:5–7; 4:1–2; and Titus 1:9. But most importantly, the central issue of concern–proper understanding and behavior with regard to the day of the Lord–is described in ways characteristic of the book of Revelation, usually dated in the last decade of the first century C.E., rather than what we saw in 1 Thessalonians or what we find in the other undisputed letters of Paul. First Thessalonians asserts that since we cannot know when Christ's second coming will be, we need to live each day as if it were the last, not worrying about the future, but concentrating on the present, showing our readiness for the last judgment through lives of faithfulness. In contrast, 2 Thessalonians asserts today is not the last day, since certain signs must be fulfilled before that day of the Lord will arrive. Therefore, concern about the future is appropriate, and if the last judgment is not imminent, we do well to look for and interpret signs of the end. The scenario (2 Thess. 2:3–12) sounds more like the intricate apocalyptic time line of Revelation 13 than the few events of 1 Thessalonians 4 or 1 Corinthians 15. Indeed, the false teaching–that is, that the day of the Lord had already come–resembles that fought in 2 Tim. 2:16–18. Moreover, if the "man of lawlessness" ("son of perdition" KJV; 2 Thess. 2:3) is an allusion to the emperor Domitian, referred to elsewhere as *Nero redivivus* (his predecessor even more cruelly reborn), then 2 Thessalonians would need to be dated after Nero's death in 68 C.E..–and hence also after the death of the apostle Paul. All these elements in 2 Thessalonians therefore argue for a composition date nearer the time of the Pastorals, around the end of the first century C.E.

To conclude that this letter is one of the pseudonymous works of the New Testament does not negate its authority for the church of the twenty-first century. As noted above, pseudonymity is a venerable element of biblical tradition. A more historical-critical reading of this letter may alter our identification of its author, but does not erase the centuries of church history in which it has had authority as part of the New Testament canon. And even if apostolic authorship was a major argument toward canonization in the first four centuries of the church, it was never the only argument. Indeed, by no means was every letter or gospel that claimed apostolic authorship included in the New Testament. The essential value of a biblical text is its ability to speak from faith to faith, and the theological content of 2 Thessalonians continues to speak authoritatively to the church today.

Significant details distinguish the apocalyptic eschatology of 2 Thessalonians from that of the apostle Paul, but that apocalypticism does reflect the particular expectation of the leaders of the church in Asia Minor near the beginning of the second century c.e., as they confronted misunderstandings of the gospel. And there are Christians today, so many centuries later, who need to hear the exhortation against idleness spoken so forcefully in 2 Thessalonians. Whether it derives from philosophical withdrawal from the world or from simplistic apocalypticism that devalues all human enterprise and effort, a life of idleness is not only opposite from the life of the apostle Paul–it is also turning a deaf ear to the truth and power of the gospel.

Galatians

Basic Data: Authorship, Date, Addressees, Prompting, Structure, and Synopsis

Paul's authorship of the letter to the Galatians is undisputed. Indeed, through the centuries it is this New Testament letter, more than any other, that has inspired some of the most thoughtful to believe that they had come to know Paul and the gospel: For example, Luther referred to this letter as his beloved Katie von Bora; John Wesley found in it peace of heart and spirit. Many present-day interpreters date Galatians in the mid-fifties, but, as J. Louis Martyn argues (in his commentary that is the major influence on the present chapter), it may well have been written perhaps as early as 50 c.e., shortly after 1 Thessalonians and before Philippians. The place of composition is unknown, but Thessalonica or Philippi are likely possibilities; and the Galatians' sudden "turning to a different gospel" (1:6) suggests sometime soon after Paul left Galatia for his first visit into Macedonia and Achaia, on his way to Corinth.

The "churches of Galatia" (1:2) are named as recipients of the letter, and much discussion has been given to the question of whether these congregations might be in the southern area of the Roman province called "Galatia" (which would include the cities of Pisidian, Antioch, Iconium, Lystra, and Derbe)–or in its original, northern area (around Ancyra, now Ankara), the name of which was given to the expanded Roman province, including also the southern region, less than a century before, in 25 b.c.e.

Paul's address in 3:1 to "Galatians" could be ethnic, referring to his addressees as Gauls, or Celts, the (Gentile) Indo-Europeans who migrated not only into what is now France (the Roman province of "Gaul") and Britain, but also into central Asia Minor. This reference argues in favor of the north, where Paul would initially have encountered no synagogue and few if any links with Judaism, including its rites regarding calendar events, dietary practices, and circumcision. What prompts the letter to these churches from their recently departed founder is the success of certain men—rival missionaries J. L. Martyn calls "the Teachers"—from Jerusalem, claiming the authority of the church there, in convincing the Galatians that Paul had failed to give them adequate instruction on what it means to become followers of Christ. By ignoring religious practices essential to Christian life and worship, they asserted, Paul had left them and their salvation incomplete. No wonder Paul's tone is one of urgency and outrage, like that with which he had rebuked Peter in Antioch: the Galatians' salvation *is* at stake, as is the very truth of the gospel.

The compositional structure of Galatians is straightforward—with one notable exception. An opening formula (1:1–5) identifies Paul not only as the sender of the letter, but also as an "apostle;" in the Galatian churches, his authority is under attack. Instead of a thanksgiving, in which the theme of a letter is expressed, and which is missing in none of his other letters, Paul launches immediately into the heated argument of the body (1:6–6:10). First in the body comes a rebuke (1:6–9) stating the theme and cursing anyone proclaiming a perversion of the gospel. After a transition (1:10), in which he rejects the methods of human rhetoric in favor of only pleasing God by being the slave of Christ, Paul begins a series of theses and supporting arguments. The first of these (1:11–2:21) declares Paul's gospel to be apocalyptically revealed to him by God, not something taught or handed down to him by other human beings; God has acted for human salvation not, finally, in the law, but in "the faith of Jesus Christ" (2:16). A second rebuke (3:1–5) differentiates the hearing of the gospel that evokes faith, which the Galatians experienced in their encounter with Paul, from religious observation of the law's commandments, as advocated by newly arrived rival missionaries.

Two exegetical arguments confirm Paul's assertion that faith and religion are quite different. First (in 3:6–4:7), reflecting on various passages of scripture (including Gen. 15:6; Hab. 2:4b; and Gen. 17:8), Paul demonstrates that inheriting the blessing of the patriarch Abraham is not a matter of ritual observance of the Jewish law but trusting in God's promise, as manifested by the Spirit of Christ in our hearts. Another transition (4:8–20) expresses, first, Paul's fear that the Galatians might return to their former state, before they had experience of faith or knowledge of God, and second, Paul's appeal to them not to do so on the basis of their initial cordial relationship with him. The second exegetical argument (4:21–5:1), reflecting especially on Genesis 16 and 21, and Isaiah 54, demonstrates that scripture itself testifies that only faith in Christ brings freedom. A third transition (5:2–12) reiterates Paul's concern for the Galatians, his warning against circumcision, and an attack on those who are unsettling them. The body ends (in 5:13–6:10) with pastoral instruction and exhortation, contrasting life guided by the Spirit with slavery to evil (embodied in the impulsive desires of the flesh, as conceived within the context of apocalyptic eschatology). The concluding formula (6:11–18), which Paul says is written in his own hand, summarizes the whole letter by restating its theme, lobbing a final attack on the circumcisers, witnessing to God's new creation in the church, and recalling his own body's scars as evidence of his slavery to Christ—as well as giving a benediction.

Remembering that, as with 1 Thessalonians (and Paul's other letters), the Galatians would be hearing Paul's letter read aloud in the context of worship, let us now explore these sections somewhat more thoroughly.

Commentary

Immediately after stating his name, with the second word of Galatians Paul begins his polemic against rival missionaries in the Galatian churches: he claims for himself the title of "apostle," one *sent*, or *commissioned*, not by human beings or on the basis of human authorities, but one commissioned by Christ Jesus and God. The implication is clear: Paul considers the rivals as "authorized" not by God or Christ but by human beings, albeit such "pillars" of the Jerusalem church as James and Cephas (Peter) and John. Paul sees these rivals not really as *his* rivals—but as *God's* adversaries, since in being seduced to their teachings, the Galatians are "deserting the one [i.e., God] who called" them, and turning to a perversion of the gospel (1:6). Whatever their pious intentions, the new missionaries who are "confusing" (or better, "troubling") the Galatians deserve to be cursed, according to Paul—not because they are opposing *Paul* and/or his authority, but because they are seeking to pervert the gospel of Christ and *causing* the Galatians to desert *God*. This (1:6–9) is the theme of Galatians, but as the salutation already underscored, it is conceived by Paul within the context of an apocalyptic understanding of the death and resurrection of "the Lord Jesus Christ, who gave himself for our sins to set us free from the present evil age" (1:3–4; for descriptions of God's triumphant justice expected in "the age to come" according to Jewish apocalyptic, see, e.g., Isa. 60; 65:17–25; 2 Esd. 7:50, 113; and *1 En*. 91:15–17). There is but one gospel, to which Paul holds himself—as well as everyone else—accountable. Paul knows that the origin of the gospel is in God—not in human beings, their teachings, or their traditions. (*Lambano*, the first verb in 1:12, is a technical term for handing down tradition.) And Paul received the gospel directly from God and Christ, in the form of an apocalypse. (For Paul, the Greek *apokalypsis*, usually translated "revelation," conveys something more apocalyptic or cosmically intrusive than the mere "unveiling" of some truth or vision.)

If the rival Teachers criticize Paul for his lack of close ties to the Jerusalem church, Paul is proud of his independent calling grounded solely in God's apocalypse. Therefore, Paul can emphasize his distinction from Jerusalem (in 1:15–24 and 2:1–10), noting that instead of adding anything to his gospel, the authorities there "recognized the grace that had been given to [him]" and confirmed that God had "entrusted" him with the "gospel for the uncircumcised" (2:6–9). Here Paul is challenging the rivals' claim of having the backing of the Jerusalem church leaders–while defending his gospel to the Gentiles from needing anything added to it, in case those leaders had changed their minds since meeting with him. Indeed, even when a pillar like Cephas can miss the implications of the gospel in regard to table fellowship, in which it should *unite* the faithful of both Jewish and Gentile background, Paul does not–and has the courage and commitment to that gospel to oppose him to his face (2:11–14).

Paul's criterion for such clear discernment is the gospel, namely, that humanity's salvation is not a matter of observance of the law, however religious or meaningful these rites may seem to be, but only "by the faith of Christ" (2:16). The Greek possessive here is generally translated "faith *in* Christ," which is a possible translation and would underscore the inclusion of the Galatians among the justified, those reckoned as righteous by God, solely on the basis of faith; but the "faith *of* Christ" is the stronger meaning, underscoring *Jesus'* faithfulness to God in giving up his life "for our sins to set us free" (1:4). Paul sees no ambiguity here: salvation depends in no way on what *we* do, even as religious human beings; we are justified only by what *God* has done for us in Christ, that is, in his death on the cross. And our being reckoned as righteous by God is not God's response to our faith, as if faith were our religious work; instead, the initiative is God's, and faith is defined for Paul not by what we do or believe but by Christ's faithful death on our behalf. If justification were based on what we do with regard to religion, Paul asserts, then Christ was crucified and died for no purpose at all (2:21).

"You foolish Galatians!" (3:1): this harsh rebuke is a fitting climax to Paul's argument so far. Paul is astonished that the same persons who had come to faith hearing preaching in which Christ crucified was made so dramatic for them they recognized God's spirit among them working miracles–that having so started in the spirit, they would now determine their perfection depended on flesh (3:2–5; note especially *epiteleo*, "to end, complete," in v. 3). Here Paul is using language the Galatians would know from both Greco-Roman philosophy and Jewish apocalyptic. "Flesh" (*sarx*) carries considerable weight in the argument of Galatians (see also *epithymia sarkos*, the impulsive "desires of the flesh," in 5:16). On the simplest level of meaning, Paul is referring to the foreskin that the Teachers are requiring to be circumcised. But on a deeper level, Flesh is a terrible power, identified in Epicurean thought as the seat of desire, which is inevitably insatiable and destructive, and identified in the Qumran sect (among others) in Judaism as synonymous with the *yetser ha ra*, or Evil Impulse. Hellenistic Judaism perceived humanity as possessing both an Evil and a Good Impulse (the *yetzer ha tov*); and the law (*Torah*) was viewed as the antidote God has given humanity to enable the Good Impulse to overcome the Evil Impulse. Moreover, the patriarch Abraham was seen as having achieved a kind of perfection, or victory over the impulsive desire of the flesh, in his covenant with God sealed in the rite of circumcision. Apparently the Teachers have the pious desire to bring the Galatians within the household of God through a few simple acts (chief among which is circumcision, but probably also including holy days and dietary rules–see 2:12 and 4:10) that will demonstrate their rejection of instinctive desires of the Flesh. Since the (Gentile) Galatians are without any knowledge of the law, they are all the more vulnerable to the Evil Impulse. These missionaries surely perceive their gospel as "Christian," since it includes belief in Jesus as the Messiah; but it goes beyond Paul by requiring a few religious acts. They would see Paul's focus solely on faith in/of Christ as inadequate and incomplete, a theological risk the Galatians do not need to take.

Paul counterattacks the Teachers' "fuller gospel" with biblical exegesis on Abraham. Both view Abraham as a central figure of salvation history, the one of special significance for Gentiles. But instead of portraying the patriarch as the paradigm of *religion*, demonstrated in his act of covenantal circumcision, in 3:6–4:7 Paul presents Abraham as the paradigm of *faith*. The Teachers have missed this distinction, Paul argues, because they fail to discern the apocalyptic antinomy (i.e., following Martyn, opposing pairs of cosmic forces) between law and faith. They do not understand that Habakkuk 2:4 (cited in Gal. 3:11) and Leviticus 18:5 (Gal. 3:12) constitute a contradiction between faith and the law. It is not that faith *and* observance of the law both lead to life; for Paul it is an either/or proposition, as he will demonstrate. This argument is clinched by Paul's reading of Deuteronomy 21:23 (in Gal 3:13): "Cursed is everyone who hangs on a tree." Having already evoked the cross of Christ (in 2:19–21 and 3:1), Paul shows that in being crucified, Christ took upon himself "the curse of the law" (3:13) in order to redeem everyone else from it. In this way Christ's death gives Gentiles–and all humanity–access to the blessing of Abraham, that is, "the promise of the Spirit through faith" (3:14). One more exegetical argument at this point confirms Paul's point. Using a rabbinic method of interpretation, in which he argues for significance in the use of a singular form of the collective noun "seed," Paul claims (in 3:16–17, NIV) that the promises were actually made by God only to Abraham and his one seed, Christ Jesus. The law, which came four hundred thirty years after Abraham, neither added to nor annulled God's original covenant of promise made to him.

Another argument–even more startling to the Teachers than these previous exegetical ones–answers the question of the origin and purpose of the law (3:19–25). Here Paul makes use of tradition (based primarily on

Deut. 33:2 and Lev. 26:46) that the law was instituted by *angels* through a *mediator* (Moses, whose name is powerfully absent). Paul articulates (in 3:21) the horrifying conclusion toward which he seems headed: "Is the law then opposed to the promises of God?" His immediate answer, "Certainly not!" is followed not with claims that the law, even for a time, could be the means of righteousness or life, but with the image of the law as humanity's confining custodian (*paidagogos*, 3:24, 25), disciplining everyone until Christ came to justify us by faith. One sentence is particularly weighty, asserting that "scripture imprisoned all things under the power of sin, so that what was promised might be given through the faith of Jesus Christ to those who have faith" (3:22, translation mine). What Paul has done here is show, first, a positive side of law (that is, the sense of *Torah/Nomos* as scripture; cf. 4:21b), and second, to introduce sin as another apocalyptic force. Galatians 3–5 uses the Greek phrase for "to be under the power of" ten times (3:10; 3:22; 3:23; 3:24–25; 4:2; 4:3; 4:4; 4:5; 4:21a; 5:18), and in seven of these occurrences the enslaver is the law! In stark contrast to the Teachers, Paul realizes that the law can be—and has been—aligned with sin, and since the law is valued as salvific by the Teachers, Paul makes this counterpoint emphatic.

Now Paul's polemic reaches a lyrical conclusion. Apparently utilizing a baptismal liturgy (3:27), traditionally associated with imagery of clothing, Paul proclaims unequivocally to the Galatians that the blessing of Abraham has come to include them fully:

> For in Christ Jesus you are all children of God through faith. As many of you as were baptized into Christ have clothed yourselves with Christ. There is no longer Jew or Greek, there is no longer slave or free, there is no longer male and female; for all of you are one in Christ Jesus. And if you belong to Christ, then you are Abraham's offspring, heirs according to the promise. (3:26–29)

Of the three comprehensive categories of 3:28, Paul's argument concentrates on the first, since distinction based on religion is so contested in Galatia. The full significance of such religious, social, and gender inclusiveness is not yet realized in the church. Yet in the very worship and fellowship of his struggling congregations, where all these barriers were broken down, Paul had seen more than a glimpse of God's promises fulfilled. Unity in Christ underscores the apocalyptic dimension of Paul's gospel. It requires the use of new creation imagery, affirming that even the division of male and female—as ancient as Genesis 1:27—is no more.

In 4:1–7 Paul continues with the theme of inheritance, here with the analogy of coming of age, when heirs become free of guardians and trustees—as well as custodians, we may add. Surprisingly, Paul describes Jews as sharing with Gentiles enslavement to "the elemental spirits of the world" (*stoicheia tou kosmou*, 4:3), until they might become adopted as children.

These powers were conceived in Greco-Roman philosophy and Hellenistic Judaism (see Sirach 33:15) as the building blocks of the universe (including heat/cold, wetness/dryness), and for Paul they would include Jew/Gentile, law/lawless, as well as religious/secular calendars (4:10). These "beggarly elemental spirits" (4:9) define the divided and fallen nature of things that is inherently limiting and oppressive. But Paul sees proof that he and the Galatians have been liberated from these powers by the fact that "God has sent the Spirit of his Son into our hearts, crying 'Abba! Father!'" (4:6).

After pleading with the Galatians to remember their former relationship—in which Paul was treated like a messenger (or angel) from God, and in which he is "again in the pain of childbirth until Christ is formed" in them, calling them his "little children" (4:19)—Paul begins another exegetical argument. This time he gives an extended reading of Genesis 16 and 21, the story of Hagar and Sarah, and quotes Isaiah 54:1, on the promise of children to the barren woman. He characterizes his exegesis as "an allegory" (4:24), although today we might better use the term, *typological.* In any case, Paul reverses the traditional identification of Abraham's two sons (Isaac as Israel, and Ishmael as the Gentiles) and identifies Hagar and her children of slavery as "the present Jerusalem" and Sarah as "the Jerusalem above; she is free, and she is our mother" (4:25–26). Paul finds confirmation of his reading in the fact that "just as at that time the child who was born according to the flesh persecuted the child who was born according to the Spirit, so it is now also" (4:29). After quoting Genesis 21:10, ordering that the slave-woman and her child be driven out, clearly Paul's advice regarding what the Galatians should do with the Teachers, he concludes his exegesis with one of the boldest verses in scripture: "For freedom Christ has set us free. Stand firm, therefore, and do not submit again to a yoke of slavery" (5:1).

In a transitional passage (5:2–12), Paul adds that if a man lets himself be circumcised, he is obliged to obey the entire law—and to want to be justified by the law is to cut oneself off from Christ, to fall away from grace. "For in Christ Jesus neither circumcision nor uncircumcision counts for anything; the only thing that counts is faith working through love" (5:6). Faith working through love will become the focus of the rest of Galatians, but before Paul turns to his pastoral counsel, he gives another warning to the Galatians, anguished that they would be persuaded to stop running well, as they were when he was with them, and a warning to the Teachers, wishing that they would not merely circumcise but castrate themselves. It is hard to miss the depth of Paul's indignation.

Paul's counsel is expressed much more in the indicative than in the imperative. He is careful to distinguish the Galatians' freedom to love from mere opportunity to be self-indulgent. Instead of being consumed in mistreatment of one another, they need to become slaves of one another—for to love your neighbor as yourself (Lev. 19:18) sums up the whole of the Law "in a single *sentence*" (5:14, following Martyn's translation–note that Paul deliberately avoids the term "commandment" here). In 5:16–26 Paul contrasts living in the Spirit with yielding to the desires of the flesh. Again, Paul is speaking apocalyptically, differentiating two cosmic forces opposing one another in human affairs. The list of the works of the flesh is long, and the sense of moral judgment reflected here is probably close to that of the Teachers. Jewish Christian sensibilities are reflected in what Paul believes persons should not do, but such sentiments would be shared by some Gentile thinkers as well, particularly the Stoics. What is surprising is Paul's list naming "the fruit of the Spirit": "love, joy, peace, patience, kindness, generosity, faithfulness, gentleness, and self-control" (5:22–23). This is a shorter list, and Paul's reference to "fruit" is singular, as if such things embodied a congregation's unity in Christ. There can be no question now that Paul sees these all as fruit of the spirit *of Christ*, and there is nothing in the law prohibiting them. Indeed, bearing one another's burdens is to fulfill what Paul describes as "the law *of Christ*" (6:2, emphasis mine). Here Paul proclaims that it is Christ who seizes the law from sin and hands it back to God.

After giving the imperative to "work for the good of all, and especially for those of the family of faith" (6:10), Paul writes his conclusion. Here he gives a few final jabs at the Teachers' boasting over matters of the flesh–in contrast to Paul himself, who would boast only in the cross of Christ: "by which the world has been crucified to me, and I to the world. For neither circumcision nor uncircumcision is anything, but a new creation is everything!" (6:14b–15). This last summary statement repeats 5:6, but now with explicit apocalyptic reference to the new creation begun on the cross. A final benediction is given, but not until Paul has prayed for the church as the new creation's "Israel of God" (6:16) and identified his own scars of persecution with the stigmata of Jesus. This last reference suggests branding, which evokes a favorite self-designation of Paul as Christ's *slave*.

What significance do we find in Galatians for the twenty-first–century church? To begin, as interpreters we see the value of scripture's particularity. To be sure, a biblical text can speak forcefully to a time and place inconceivable to its own author and audience, but we need first to honor a text's original setting and significance. Failure to do so results in attempts to harmonize the content of Galatians with that of, say, 1 Corinthians or Romans–when the apostle Paul may be saying quite different things in each letter. For example, if the church in Corinth needs exhortation regarding disciplined life in the Spirit, Paul would not emphasize a critique of the law, as in Galatians. Llikewise, if time has brought Paul awareness of the danger of negative statements about the Jews, his letter to the church in Rome would need to present a different argument regarding the relationship of church and synagogue than that implied in Galatians or expressed in 1 Thessalonians. Listening for a diversity of views, even from a single author, is a way of respecting Paul and any one of his letters.

Galatians also has special significance for the church today in its expression of Paul's apocalyptic theology. Perhaps the single most important "discovery" of New Testament research in the twentieth century, beginning with Johannes Weiss and Albert Schweitzer, is the role of apocalyptic thought on Judaism and the early church, particularly in the first century of our present era. If an apocalyptic perspective on cosmos, time, and history is not simply a footnote or epilogue on–but rather the whole outline and structure of–the thought of Jesus or Paul, then we need to study its every expression. But again, as interpreters we need to be mindful that the literary genre of apocalyptic, rooted in Old Testament prophetic and wisdom traditions, is symbolic and figurative, like the creation narratives of Genesis. It is valuable to consider metaphoric allusions to an author's own time and place, but it is myopic and irresponsible to assume that the author coded these images for our present generation.

An appreciation of Paul's apocalyptic framework of thought can help us understand his discernment of the crucifixion and resurrection of Christ as the turning of the ages, exposing once and for all the depths of cosmic conflict between God (and the children of God) and the forces of evil, sin, and death. Reflecting on the substance of apocalyptic, rather than its surface, can help us grasp Paul's argument. When he refers, for example, to the impulsive desires of the flesh, we can be sure Paul means much more than bodily lust. Likewise, when he affirms Christian unity, freedom, faith, and love, Paul is not imagining human achievements but the grace of God, the gift and the power of the spirit of Christ.

Finally, the church of the twenty-first century, as in every other century, needs to hear in Galatians the apostle Paul's critique of the law, distinguishing religion from faith, or what we do in our religious acts, rather than our trust in what God has done for us in Jesus' death on the cross. In a superficial reading of Galatians, many are tempted to think that here Paul is contrasting Judaism with Christianity–so that in a competition of religions, the church replaces the synagogue as the new and perfected household of God. Such Marcionite dualism would seek to insulate the church from the judgment and righteousness of God, denying that the Christian religion has often fallen under the power of sin and committed crimes of arrogance and cruelty unequalled by the synagogue. Without self-critical humility, the church can place–and has placed–scripture in the hands of sin, so that its letter kills. But scripture in the hands of Christ, read through his Spirit, his heart, and mind, brings freedom and life. In every age, Paul's letter to the Galatians condemns religious idolatry and challenges the church instead to nurture the manifold fruit of the Spirit that is summed up in love.

Suggested Resources for the Pastor's Library

Betz, Hans Dieter. *Galatians*. Philadelphia: Fortress Press, 1979.

Doty, William G. *Letters in Primitive Christianity*. Philadelphia: Scholars Press, 1973.

Gaventa, Beverly R. *1 and 2 Thessalonians*. Interpretation. Louisville: Westminster John Knox Press, 1998.

Keck, Leander E. *Paul and His Letters*. Revised edition. Minneapolis: Fortress Press, 1988.

Knox, John. *Chapters in a Life of Paul*. Revised edition. Macon, Ga.: Mercer University Press, 1987.

Krentz, Edgar, et al. *Galatians, Philippians, Philemon, 1 Thessalonians*. Minneapolis: Augsburg, 1985.

Martyn, J. Louis. *Galatians*. Anchor Bible 33A. New York: Doubleday, 1997.

_____. *Theological Issues in the Letters of Paul*. Nashville: Abingdon Press, 1997.

Meeks, Wayne A., *The First Urban Christians: The Social World of the Apostle Paul*. New Haven, Conn.: Yale University Press, 1983.

3

Paul as Missionary/Pastor

Corinthian Correspondence, Philippians, Philemon

Rodney L. Parrott

Are they ministers of Christ? I am talking like a madman–I am a better one: with far greater labors, far more imprisonments, with countless floggings, and often near death. Five times I have received from the Jews the forty lashes minus one. Three times I was beaten with rods. Once I received a stoning. Three times I was shipwrecked; for a night and a day I was adrift at sea; on frequent journeys, in danger from rivers, danger from bandits, danger from my own people, danger from Gentiles, danger in the city, danger in the wilderness, danger at sea, danger from false brothers and sisters; in toil and hardship, through many a sleepless night, hungry and thirsty, often without food, cold and naked. And, besides other things...(2 Cor. 11:23–28a)

This single passage from 2 Corinthians, a catalog of apostolic hardships found nowhere else in Paul's writings (but see also 1 Cor. 4:9–13; 2 Cor. 4:8–9; 6:4–10; and Phil. 4:11–12), is a sober reminder of the paucity and fragmentary character of our information about the ministry of the apostle. Presented with obvious rhetorical purpose (the defense of his status as an apostle) and flourish (note the extended *repetitio*, "danger...," in v. 26), it lacks any annotations or further descriptions that would provide concrete locations in Paul's ministry. As a result, the student of Paul is tantalized-and frustrated: Where and when were the imprisonments, floggings, near-death experiences, lashings, beatings, stoning, shipwrecks, or journeys? These questions have no ready answers.

Indeed, reconstructing the contours of Paul's ministry requires detective work of the first rank: reading with sensitivity and astuteness the material we do have, connecting bits and pieces of information from various places, and venturing an imaginative reconstruction of church life in Corinth, Macedonia, Ephesus, Galatia, and even Jerusalem. Only so can the reader probe the structure of relationships between Paul, the congregations he founded, and the other figures who enter upon the scene.

Social Context of Paul's Ministry

By contrast, the general context of Paul's ministry is relatively well-known. The Roman presence in Greece and the eastern Mediterranean that had begun two centuries before received a new impetus when Octavian (Augustus) defeated the forces of Cleopatra and Antony at Actium (31 B.C.E.). The resulting consolidation of Octavian's power inaugurated a period of peace and prosperity–and building–as Roman presence settled deeper into provincial soil. Diverse, mobile populations traversed the routes of commerce, carrying goods and culture to Roman colonies established to ensure stability and control across the eastern Mediterranean. With them moved a variety of ethnic and religious traditions. The hellenization that had begun with Alexander the Great continued under the imperial aegis and in Latin dress.

Paul's well-known missionary work was focused in a few prominent cities: Philippi, Thessalonica, Corinth, and Ephesus. Colossae is the probable location of his contact with Philemon; precisely where in Galatia he labored is not certain. The first three cities were key Roman colonies, two of them provincial capitals and the other on the *Via Egnatia*. They were hubs of Roman influence, centers of urban life among smaller villages and towns. Biblical and classical scholars have assembled a considerable amount of information about life in each of them. It is impossible, however, to place Paul's ministry in a concrete social setting in any one of them or to link the subject matter or theological perspective of a given letter to the character of a particular colony.

For example, scholars once made much of the legendary sexual promiscuity of Corinth, suggesting it was why Paul dedicated so much attention to sexual immorality (*porneia*) in his correspondence with the congregation there. But the city to which the notorious reputation belonged was destroyed in 146 B.C.E., and a new Roman city–with a new population–was built on the ruins in 44 B.C.E. So, deprived of its former reputation, some scholars have portrayed this latter city, the provincial capital of Achaia, as a status-conscious center of commercial and political competition, thereby explaining the interest in position and power that is evident in the Corinthian correspondence! The perceptive reader should note two things: (1) Paul also devotes attention to sexual immorality in 1 Thessalonians (4:1–8)–and in much the same tone as 1 Corinthians; and (2) Thessalonica was also a Roman provincial capital.

Attempts to situate Paul's ministry in a particular economic stratum have met varied results. Some believe the gospel moved primarily among the lower classes; others, across a wide range of the population; and still others, primarily within the middle class. An important passage in this discussion is Paul's description of the Corinthians in 1 Cor. 1:26: "not many of you were wise by human standards, not many were powerful, not many were of noble birth." On the basis of this reference, along with Paul's address to slaves in 1 Cor. 7:21–23, some have concluded that the Corinthian church was primarily a church of the lower classes. But the obverse also must be seen: *some* were wise, *some* were powerful, *some* were of noble birth; and *some* sought liberation from slavery.

Other relevant passages include Paul's reference to his manual labor (1 Thess. 2:9; 1 Cor. 4:12; 2 Cor. 11:7–9) and the indications that some members of his congregations were individuals of economic means. Aquila and Prisca, for example, were mobile enough to host the church in two locations (1 Cor. 16:19; Rom. 16:3) and Erastus held the office of city treasurer in Corinth (Rom. 16:23). While we have no absolute indicators of economic status, the predominance of the evidence suggests that Paul's ministry embraced persons from a wide spectrum: Paul effusively celebrates the support of the Macedonian churches (2 Cor. 11:9; Phil. 1:5; 2:25; 4:10–18), but on several occasions also acknowledges times of hunger, thirst, nakedness, and cold (cf. 1 Cor. 4:11; 2 Cor. 11:27; Phil. 4:12); Phil. 4:11–12 suggests that Paul's standard of living had its contrasts, if not extremes; the description of the Corinthian practice of the Lord's supper (1 Cor. 11:21–22) indicates that some in the congregation did not have enough, while others had (and ate) plenty; and a major agenda of Paul's ministry is the collection of an offering for the poor in Jerusalem (cf. 2 Cor. 8:2–3).

The religious context of Paul's ministry is basically twofold. As a Jewish Christian missionary pastor seeking to hold together a regional ministry to Gentiles (Galatia, Asia, Macedonia, Achaia), and to link it to the mother church in Jerusalem, Paul worked among Jews and Gentiles. As Gerd Lüdemann has shown in *Paul, Apostle to the Gentiles*, however, the scene was not that simple. Paul worked not only among a variety of Greek, Roman, or eastern religions, but among a variety of Jewish and Christian options as well. Although Acts consistently portrays Paul entering first and primarily into conversation with Jews (and Gentile God-fearers) in and around synagogues and turning to the Gentiles only when frustrated in that attempt, Paul's letters lack such a programmatic presentation. Indeed, Paul indicates that from the beginning he was called to ministry among the Gentiles (Gal. 1:16). There are indications, however, that he addressed both Jews and Gentiles, and interpreted the gospel against the backdrop of Jewish life and faith. Indeed, Paul claims his Jewish heritage at several key points (Phil. 3:3–6; 2 Cor. 11:22).

Paul's letters for the most part address unidentified conversation partners or, in some cases, outright opponents. Whether they are members of his congregation is not always clear; it appears Paul faces challenges both from within and without. The intruders from outside seem to oppose his law-free, spirit-generated gospel; the insiders, to believe he has not gone far enough in that direction. Older studies named the former *Judaizers* (law-observant Jews; see Gal. 2:14) and the latter *Gnostics* or enthusiasts (as in 1 Cor. 12). Today there is something approaching a scholarly consensus that these opponents were other workers in the pluriform Hellenistic Jewish Christian mission, ranging from spirit enthusiasts rooted in Jewish wisdom (*sophia*) traditions to strict advocates of Torah-observance.

The evidence is of three kinds. First, the theological "slogans" Paul deals with (and assumes his readers share) in 1 Corinthians—*all things are lawful* (6:12; 10:23), *nothing beyond what is written* (4:6), *all of us possess knowledge* (8:1), *no idol in the world really exists* (8:4), *there is no God but one* (8:4), *food will not bring us close to God* (8:8)—are striking for their lack of specifically *Christian* character. All of them make sense as part of a Hellenistic Jewish dialogue with God-fearers or others in a pagan environment. Second, there is the striking correspondence between Paul's concerns about sexual immorality (*porneia*) and idol-meat (*eidolothuton*) in 1 Corinthians (see chaps. 5, 7, 8, and 10) and the stipulations placed on the Gentile church by the "mother" church in Jerusalem (according to Acts 15:29 but contrary to Gal. 2:10). Third, there are the various suggestions that many of the frictions around Paul's ministry clustered around the role of the Spirit (see Gal. 3:3–5; 2 Cor. 10:1–12:13).

Paul's work among non-Jews is attested to in his description of church members in Thessalonica (1 Thess. 1:9), Galatia (Gal. 4:8–9), and Corinth (1 Cor. 12:2). Richard Horsley recently has suggested that beginning with Augustus and the institution of the cult of the emperor, there developed a pervasive civil religion throughout the Empire (*Paul and Empire,* 10–24). Much of ordinary social activity was thereby overlaid with religious ritual and meaning, effectively eliminating the separation of sacred from secular. The extent to which Paul and other early Christians were affected is evident from the fact that virtually all of the meat available in the meat markets of the cities derived from temple altars, as suggested by 1 Corinthians 10:25. With the internal Christian conflict between Jewish Christian spirit enthusiasts on his left and legalists on his right, Paul also had to deal with how his congregations could coexist within the socio-religious practices of the dominant culture.

Theology and Ethics

Paul's letters indicate that the apostle tried to address these issues by providing concrete advice and instruction. As a rule he writes in order to reply to an identified crisis or a verbal or written inquiry, and to outline a recommended course of behavior. Only in Romans does his theological focus widen beyond particular matters at hand, and then only slightly. Put another way, Paul as we know him from the letters is a *practical theologian.*

His letters are *working ecclesiology*, employing doctrinal bits and pieces (on God, Christ, the Spirit, or even salvation) to instruct his readers on churchly behavior. As Romans indicates (and 1 Cor. 2 assures!), Paul is capable of profound theologizing. But in most of the letters he employs only as much theology as needed to provide guidance to his newborn congregations. In fact, at times he even eschews theological discourse in favor of political rhetoric. Consequently those who seek the broader outlines of his theology must carefully extrapolate them from his reflection on particular occasions or situations.

Having said that, how may we describe Paul's theological position? To begin with, Paul was a Hellenistic Jew who maintained a belief in the oneness of God and in the reliability of God's covenants (see Gal. 4 and Rom. 9–11). But Paul also believed God had acted decisively through Jesus of Nazareth. By raising him up as an exalted heavenly "Lord" (Phil. 2:9–11) who was present in the community as an empowering Spirit (Gal. 3:1–5), God had not only effected the redemption of the believer but inaugurated a new age and a new kind of human community appropriate to that age (see Rom. 1:16–4:25; Gal. 2:15–21; 3:26–29; Phil. 3:7–11; 1 Cor. 12:12–13; 2 Cor. 5:16–21). Hence theology, christology, and eschatology eventuate in ecclesiology (and subsequently, ministry). For that reason, the two concerns that claim a major share of Paul's attention–the unity of the church and the defense of his own ministry (see 1 Thess. 2:1–16; Gal. 1:6–9; 1:10–2:10; 2:11–21; 1 Cor. 1:10–4:7; 4:8–21; 9:1–27; 11:2–14:40; 2 Cor. 1:15–6:13; 7:2–16; 10:1–13:10; Phil. 1:15–26; 3:1b–4:1; Rom. 14–15)–are not digressions, but are central to Paul's theological activity. God's action in Christ has refigured the social/symbolic world, and a whole range of practices and relationships must be rethought: definitions of power, freedom, and responsibility; traditional social institutions; sexual mores; and so on. In all of this, apostolic ministry is geared toward *oikodome* ("upbuilding"), promoting the health and welfare of the church (see esp. 2 Cor. 10:8; 13:10).

Scholars often explain the connection between Paul's theology and its practical, ecclesiological application by using the terminology of "indicative" and "imperative." The "indicative" refers to the present, already-accomplished status of the believer–what he or she has come to by virtue of baptism and incorporation into the body of Christ. The "imperative" refers to what remains to be done, to the life of discipleship as it is to be lived out. For Paul, the former ("indicative") grounds or gives rise to the latter ("imperative"). The shape of discipleship is in large measure determined by one's new Christian status. This heuristic model is by no means unambiguous. As Paul's letters attest, there were substantive disagreements among early Christians about the nature of the indicative, with subsequent divergence on the character of discipleship. With many different answers to "What has God done?" (depending on one's perspective and social location) there were many ideas about "What shall we do?"

Baptism and the Lord's Supper in Paul

Because Paul was constructing a new community, baptism and the Lord's supper occupied important places in his churches. Recent studies have even suggested that his churches were unique in that regard. Anthropological and sociological studies have helped to describe how baptism was a primary entrance rite into Paul's churches, establishing the boundaries between who was *in* and who was *out.* The Lord's supper confirmed and reinforced these boundaries and identity, refreshing in the minds of church members the commitments made when they embraced the risen Lord and received the Spirit. Hence what was said about Paul's theology as ecclesiology also applies to the place of baptism and the Lord's supper in Paul: the rites are construed in their relationship to particular facets of the church's life.

The primary Pauline texts on baptism are Galatians 3:27–28 and Romans 6:1–11. In Galatians 3:27–28, where Paul is concerned with the unity of different persons in the church (Jew, Greek, slave, free, male, female), he equates baptism with being "clothed." According to this metaphor (which may, in fact, have been enacted in the liturgy itself by taking off one's garments to be baptized and putting on new garments afterwards), baptism, as an initiatory rite, is seen as an incorporation *into* Christ, or a *putting on* of Christ. Here also there is a spatial or locative aspect to baptism. It puts one in a new place, in a new community, where social roles have been radically redefined. In Romans 6:1–11, Paul invokes baptism in order to discourage sinful behavior. Again he uses the image of baptism *into* Christ, but this time is much more specific about his meaning: Baptism is a ritual participation in the crucifixion (6:6), death (6:3), burial (6:4) and resurrection (6:5–11) of Jesus. Paul here takes ritual very seriously: a real "death to sin" has occurred, both for Christ and for the believer incorporated into Christ by baptism. Yet the Christian continues to live in an evil age, so the initiatory ritual must carry over into everyday life: The Christian must *consider* himself/herself dead to sin (6:11). Such a perceptual or volitional move is possible because the believer is empowered by the Spirit (Rom. 8:1–2). This is often referred to as the doctrine of *realized eschatology* in Paul, whereby one is empowered by God to live *as if* the new age had already come. It is a variation of the *indicative* out of which the Christian practices the *imperative* of Christian living.

This passage also contains one of the finer points to be noted in Paul's theology, namely, what scholars call his "eschatological reservation." The careful reader of Rom 6:4–8 will observe that in these verses Paul alternates tenses and moods in his choice of verbs. Christ's crucifixion, death, and resurrection are expressed in past tense (as is the believer's baptism into them). The resurrection of the believer, however, is lodged in future tense and subjunctive mood, as something yet to be realized. While others in Paul's churches may have disagreed (e.g. some at Corinth, who may have argued that the resurrection had passed already, 1 Cor. 15:12), Paul identified the *full* riches of resurrection with the end-time, not his own present.

Paul also provides us with our earliest data about the Lord's supper in early Christianity. In 1 Corinthians 10:14–22, he interprets the meal in contrast with other religious meals of the day, namely meals at pagan temples. At all such religious meals of the day there was a sense that worshipers somehow engaged in a "communion" with the deity being honored at the meal. Thus Paul argues that instead of partaking of "the table of demons" (10:21) and thereby becoming "partners with demons" (10:20), Christians were to participate only in the "table of the Lord" (10:21). For it was at the Lord's table that they "shared" in the "blood… [and] body of Christ" (10:16), a phrase that indicated that the efficacy of the death of Christ in creating a new community was somehow communicated in the sharing of the community in "the cup of blessing" and in the bread. Furthermore, the sharing in a common bread also created a unified community (10:17).

The concept of unity at the table recurs in 1 Corinthians 11:17–34. Here he addresses an issue of divisions that had begun to take place at their community meal (11:17–22), which he refers to as the Lord's supper (11:20). To address this issue, Paul quotes the earliest known tradition of Jesus' words at the Last Supper, a tradition that Paul acknowledges had been passed on to him (11:23–25). The divisions in question evidently involved some form of eating separately or individually rather than as a community, with the result that some were not getting enough to eat while others were getting too much (11:21). Paul considers this a serious issue, one that challenges the whole concept of "Lord's supper" (11:20). He quotes the words of Jesus defining the bread as "my body" (11:24), then pronounces a curse on anyone who would defile the body of Christ (11:29), which, by implication, they are in the act of doing by their divisions. Indeed, the "body of Christ" is the community itself, entered into by baptism (12:12–13) and participated in by the sharing of bread together (10:17). Thus Paul concludes the whole affair with the recommendation, "when you come together to eat, wait for one another" (11:33), or, to put it succinctly, "eat together." For Paul, the very essence of the meal is that it creates and sustains community, a community that defines itself over against the outside world (thus no eating at the table of demons) and a community that is unified and that lives out that unity by showing care and responsibility for the other, a theme found throughout 1 Corinthians.

Paul and the Twenty-first Century

A new reading of Paul (and his churches) may be useful for the church in the missionary situation of contemporary North America at the beginning of a new millennium. Certainly there are factions (or, by its more polite name, *diversity*) in the contemporary church like those Paul faced in his.

The fragmentation and polarization of the American Church continues to surface some of the very issues referenced in Paul's writings: the promise and limits of a spirit-based gospel, the inclusive character of the church, sexual morality, and the relation between the church and social status. Paul's emphasis on community is a lesson sorely needed in a world awash in individualism.

Paul's letters might also usefully be approached as one would a contemporary case study in ministry. Like every minister, the apostle struggles to apply theological insight to real problems. To be sure, his concerns focused on the founding and construction of congregations, but some of his struggles may inform the work of pastors who seek to reinvent the church in a new generation. In particular, Paul could help at two points: (1) understanding the church in relation to diverse cultures; and (2) fleshing out a ministry of *weakness* in a social context that values power and numerical size. In both cases, Paul's focus on Christ (his *suffering* and his *body*) can shed light on the way forward. For it is in the working out of that *indicative* that the church can better define its *imperative* for the world today.

Corinthians, Philippians, Philemon

Rhetorical criticism is a particularly helpful tool to use in reading Paul. However, even without formal training in rhetoric the reader will find substantial benefit in reading widely in Paul's letters themselves. Corinthians, Philippians, and Philemon (and, for that matter, Galatians, Thessalonians, and Romans) should be read together, because Paul's ministries, though geographically spread, were not compartmentalized and discrete. As the Corinthian correspondence shows (see especially 2 Cor. 8–9), Paul himself linked them, boasting of the activities in one church in order to instruct or encourage the members of another.

When examined side by side, the letters to Corinth and Philippi are a study in contrasts. With the exception of 3:2 and 3:18–19, the tone of Philippians is congenial and mild. The letter is full of gratitude and joy. Paul clearly cherishes his relationship to the congregation. By contrast, the Corinthian correspondence bristles with surprise, dismay, disappointment, and frustration. Paul carefully–almost torturously–measures his words and struggles mightily with a combative Corinthian congregation. Philippi is a positive valence on the screen, while Corinth is, at the minimum, more ambiguous.

What happens, then, when these two congregations become part of the same rhetorical situation? That is what the reader must imagine. Especially in 2 Corinthians, Paul plays off Macedonia (i.e. Philippi and Thessalonica) against Corinth (Achaia), accepting support for his ministry from Macedonia while refusing it from Corinth, holding up the example of Macedonia in presenting the offering for Jerusalem, and admonishing the Corinthians to follow their pattern (8:1–7; 9:1–5). Even his travel plans seem to favor Macedonia, for he confesses at the end of 1 Corinthians that he planned to journey to Corinth on his way to and from Macedonia (16:5), but in 2 Corinthians reports that he has traveled to Macedonia without stopping in Corinth, in order that he might spare the Corinthians "a painful visit" (1:16; 2:1). Reading Corinthians and Philippians together helps the reader imagine the effect (and effectiveness) of what Paul wrote.

1 Corinthians

1 Corinthians comprises a portion of the correspondence written by Paul in the early 50s to members of the Christian community he founded in Corinth. It probably is the second letter written by Paul to the congregation. The first, now probably lost, is mentioned in 1 Cor. 5:9. Some suggest that it may be found in 2 Cor. 6:14–7:1, but that passage is focused on those Paul eliminates as the subject of the letter: the immoral *outsider* (1 Cor. 5:10). The present letter was likely written from Ephesus (1 Cor. 16:8). Admittedly Paul does not say, "I will stay *here* in Ephesus...," but the inclusion of greetings from "the churches of Asia" (1 Cor. 16:19) confirms that provenance. When it was written is unclear. In view of its focus on two of the items proscribed for Gentile Christians at the Jerusalem conference as described in Acts 15, namely *porneia* (sexual immorality) and *eilothuton* (idol-meat), one is tempted to place it after that conference. On the other hand, Paul's own description of the conference (Gal. 2:1–10) does not mention either of the proscriptions. It is possible that the proscriptions in Acts are dependent on Paul's letter, or that Paul's concerns in the letter were widely shared by diverse Hellenistic Jewish Christian missionaries before being formalized at the conference.

Several things appear to have occasioned the letter. Sometime earlier, Paul had received a report about factiousness from "Chloe's people," (1 Cor. 1:11), a report from an unnamed source about a specific instance of sexual immorality in the congregation (5:1), and a letter requesting advice about several matters (7:1). First Corinthians responds to a number of these issues and includes Paul's travel plans.

Paul structures his responses in the familiar letter form (see description in the previous chapter), and utilizes a broad range of rhetorical devices and strategies. Since Paul seeks to persuade his readers to follow particular courses of action, he tends to use here the deliberative form of ancient rhetoric. The major sections of the letter may be outlined as follows:

1:1–9	Letter opening (address, greetings)
1:10–4:21	Discourse on dissension and factions
5:1–7:40	Clarification of instructions about sexual immorality (*porneia*), including a digression on court lawsuits (6:1–8)
8:1–11:1	Discourse about idol-meat (*eidoluthon*), with a digression on apostolic freedom (9:1–27)

11:2–34	Instructions about community life (women prophets; Lord's supper)
12:1–14:40	Discourse on prophecy and tongues
15:1–58	Discourse on the resurrection
16:1–24	Letter closing (misc. remarks and instructions)

We use the term "discourse" for several sections because of their speech-like organization. That should not detract from the fact that all of the letter was intended to be read aloud in the congregation. The overarching subject of the letter is the unity of the church and each part of the letter focuses on some aspect of that.

1:1–9. The letter opening is typical of Pauline letters. Formally listed as authors are Paul and Sosthenes (1:1). As chapter 16 indicates, also with Paul in Ephesus are Apollos (16:12), Stephanas, Fortunatus, Achaicus (16:17), and Aquila and Prisca (16:19). Timothy is apparently away from Ephesus (16:10–11), having been dispatched to Corinth separately from the letter (4:17). Members of the church in Corinth are addressed only in general (1:2), although some individual members are named in the body of the letter (Crispus and Gaius, 1:14, and perhaps Chloe's people, 1:11). The focus on sanctification (1:2) reflects Paul's interest in preserving the community's integrity and honor.

1:10–4:21. The first major section of the letter focuses on the problem of factions in the church. The sources of the division are not named but it is clear from Paul's response that some possess an "eloquent wisdom" (1 Cor 1:17). References to Apollos (1:12; 3:4, 5, 22; 4:6) suggest that this early Christian missionary and contemporary of Paul (see Acts 18:24–19:1) has figured somehow in the situation, but the letter does not directly accuse him of any misconduct. Paul's reference at the end of the letter (16:12) to his unsuccessful effort to persuade Apollos to return to Corinth with his (Paul's) associates may signal some distance between the two leaders, but is hardly enough to cast aspersions on Apollos.

Antoinette Wire, in *The Corinthian Women Prophets*, is probably correct in placing Paul in dialogue with women prophets whose reception of the gospel has liberated and empowered them. Perhaps they have embraced a *sophia*-theology (a stream in Jewish and early Christian thought that imagined a feminine incarnation of wisdom and celebrated her presence in prophetic insight and revelation) and have precipitated the choosing up of sides (1:12), which Paul finds abhorrent. In any case, Paul emphasizes three things: (1) the fundamental grounding he has provided *in the crucified Christ.* (1:21–24, 30–31); (2) the inclusive, cooperative character of ministry (3:5–9); and (3) absence of any place for arrogance (3:21; 4:1–21). In addition, he sends Timothy (4:17) to work with the situation in person, and promises to come soon (4:19).

5:1–7:40. The second section of the letter focuses on the subject of sexual immorality (*porneia*; cf. 5:1, 9, 11; 6:9, 13, 18; 7:2), particularly as it impinges on Christian community. As noted above, Acts 15 makes *porneia* part of the agenda at the Jerusalem Council, perhaps reflecting similar concerns in the wider Hellenistic Jewish community. Paul has written about the subject in general (5:9), and perhaps his letter has prompted the report to which he now responds. It is possible that the boastful attitude of the persons involved (5:2; cf. 4:18–21) has led Paul to turn to the subject here, but its location does not necessarily indicate that the *porneia* is an outgrowth of the theology of a particular faction. Rather, Paul's note about the Corinthians' pre-Christian state (6:11, see below) suggests that their theology has not eradicated the unwelcome practice.

The section begins with Paul's announcement of his judgment on a man in the church who is living with his father's wife (5:1–8). Claiming to be present in the spirit, *with power,* Paul announces his judgment, and calls for the man's expulsion from the community. His language here exposes the world of raw (some might say *brutal*) religious power within which Paul worked. In that dangerous world, Paul moves immediately (5:9–6:20) to focus on the integrity of the community, explaining his earlier letter and specifying the boundaries of the community's membership. A digression about believer-vs.-believer lawsuits (6:1–8) interrupts the focus on *porneia*, but is congruent with the expectation that the community will police itself. Paul returns to the topic by reminding the Corinthians of their past. Listing ten different categories of evil persons, Paul adds, "and this is what some of you used to be" (6:11a). Baptism (6:11b) has provided a transition from the past to the present. But baptism and its concomitant gift of the Spirit can be misunderstood (6:12–13a), and Paul must rein in the liberties of the Corinthians by reminding them to whom they belong (6:13b–20).

It is clear from 1 Corinthians 7:1–40 that sexual behavior–or perhaps more precisely, sexual roles–were problematic for Paul's churches. The gospel meant liberation, especially for women, and resulted in the interruption of established social patterns. Consequently, Paul found it necessary to clarify the meaning of the gospel for those social roles, and apparently provided rules for all his churches (7:17). The rules in 1 Corinthians 7 are comprised of different degrees, from a command of the Lord (7:10) to Paul's rule (7:17), to Paul's opinion (7:25), to his concession (7:6). They treat appropriate sexual behavior for different groups within the community: married couples (7:1–7, 10–16), unmarried and widows (7:8–9), virgins and unmarried (7:25–35), engaged (7:36–38), and widows (7:39–40). Unlike the earlier prescriptions, these seem less concerned with discouraging sexual immorality, although it is mentioned (7:2), than with encouraging a self-control that prevents distraction and disorder (7:15, 32, 34, 35), that is, that enhances the general social stability of the churches. Like other Hellenistic Jewish missionaries, Paul wants nothing (including the disruptive power of sexual passion, see 7:5, 9, 36–37) to put the infant communities at risk, so he invokes a generally conservative rule that religious conversion not be associated with changing social roles (7:17–24).

What this rule means when he applies it to the issue of slavery (7:21–24), however, has been the subject of much discussion. At 7:21, when Paul addresses slaves with "Were you a slave when called?" the Greek phrase that follows can be translated in two opposite ways: either "if you can gain your freedom, do so," or "if you can gain your freedom, remain a slave instead." Some scholars prefer the latter reading because it clearly correlates with Paul's theological principle, "let each of you remain in the condition in which you were called" (7:20, 24). But when one recognizes that some slaves' "condition" included the possibility of gaining their freedom without social threat or upheaval, the first reading also becomes possible without violating this principle. Paul's basis for not changing one's social role is an ad hoc one, namely the distinctively Christian expectation of the imminent end of the world (7:26, 29–31), but he does not want life to come to a total standstill. Furthermore, he will have occasion to revisit the issue of slavery, and perhaps revise his position on it somewhat, when he writes to Philemon concerning the slave Onesimus.

If there is any doubt about the extent to which Paul is focused on the safety and security of the congregation, the four words with which he ends his instruction regarding the remarriage of widows (*only in the Lord*, 7:39) should be sufficient to dispel it. Likewise, his friendly jab in the next verse at some of his critics–"And I think that I *too* have the Spirit of God" (7:40, emphasis mine)–displays not only the liveliness of the engagement, but some of what is at issue.

8:1–11:1. When Paul turns to the matter of eating food offered to idols (*eidololuthon*), it becomes clear that his thinking about it (along with *porneia*) is rooted in the Old Testament story of the Hebrews' wilderness disobedience. This may signal that again we are in touch with material from the Hellenistic Jewish community, modified slightly for use in Christian circles (8:6b, 11–12; 10:4, 9, 16–22, 32; 11:1). The flow of his argument is obscured by a digression on the subject of apostolic rights and freedoms (9:1–27), but can be recovered by reading around the digression. Paul first engages in the critical analysis of a series of slogan-like statements that originate in the Hellenistic Jewish community, but are also shared by Corinthian Gentiles (cf. 8:1, 4, 8). The phrase "all of us possess knowledge" appears to have been a slogan among the Corinthians that developed in a context of spirit enthusiasm. To their slogan, Paul proposes a counter statement, "knowledge puffs up, but love builds up" (8:1). Here, in contrast to what he perceives as the individualism of "knowledge" (thus the term "puffs up"), he introduces the term "love" and the concept of "building up the community" that he will develop further in chapters 13–14. Then he identifies the principle of selective abstinence by which he himself lives (8:13), making clear that his adherence to the principle is justified by adherence to the principle of "building up" the community. When he resumes the argument following the digression, he appeals to the lessons of the Hebrew wanderings (10:1–22; see Ex. 32:4, 6; Num. 25:1–9; Num.

16:13–14, 41–49) as a negative precedent for the churches. Distinctively Christian interpretations are interwoven with his readings, so that the exodus is likened to baptism (10:1–5) and the Lord's supper is invoked as a buffer against eating idol-meat (10:16–22). The discourse comes to a close with another critical analysis of a slogan (10:23–30; cf. 6:12). To their slogan "all things are lawful," Paul once more opposes a principal of community concern, "not all things are beneficial...not all things build up [the community]." He then clarifies the meaning of "beneficial" and "build up" with his own slogan based on a traditional Jewish teaching (which we know as the "golden rule"): "Do not seek your own advantage, but that of the other." Finally, he closes with an appeal (10:31–11:1) that repeats in slightly different language the principle Paul enunciated at the end of the first section. A Hellenistic Jewish "rule" about cultural sensitivity appears to have been modified with the church's welfare in mind: "Give no offense to Jews or to Greeks *or to the church of God*" (10:32, emphasis mine). In effect, Paul has adapted the emphasis on giving no offense to an ethic of community concern, designated especially by the term "build up."

11:2–34. Paul follows up on the sharing of this more general instruction with two critiques of specific behavior in the Corinthian congregation. Against their presumably different practice, he advocates the veiling of women during prayer or prophecy (11:2–16), as is the practice in all the other congregations (11:16). Notable in this discussion is the clear implication that women are participating as worship leaders in the church at Corinth, namely as "prophets," which can be understood as a form of inspired preaching (as defined in 14:24–25). Paul has no problem with the practice, only with what they are wearing when they do it. It is an argument based in an arcane cultural tradition, the practice of veiling, and Paul's attempts to justify this cultural tradition are often lame (as in his argument that long hair on men is "degrading," 11:14). This is not Paul at his best. But since he leaves untouched the fact that women were taking a leadership role in worship, many scholars see a direct contradiction between 11:2–16 and 14:33b–36, where women are told to be silent in church. For this reason, many argue either that 14:33b–36 was not by Paul and was added later to the letter (it is also a bad fit in its context), or that 14:33b–36 arose in response to a very specific issue no longer accessible to us, so that it was originally intended to be a reprimand to a particular group of women in this community, not a teaching directed to all women in all churches.

As already discussed above, in 11:17–34, when Paul addresses the Corinthians' corrupted and fractious practice of the Lord's supper, he recalls the tradition he shared with them (11:23–25) and, drawing on that tradition, develops still another variation on the theme of community concern, this time as exemplified in a meal centered on unity.

12:1–14:40. This section on spiritual gifts (*to pneumatikoi*) is a well-crafted discourse, which, replete with trinitarian formulas (12:4–6), analogies (12:12–26), contrasts (13:8), and other rhetorical devices (12:3, 7–11, 28, 29, 30), lays bare a spiritual endowment of the church that both empowers it (12:7–11) and threatens its order (14:33, 40). Lest anyone suggest that the gifts are simply hypothetical, Paul claims (14:18) to be proficient in the very one which is so problematic: tongues (*glossai*). Noteworthy in this section is the list of gifts (12:27–28), the hymn to love (13:1–13) with its trinity of graces (13:13), and the description of a typical (and ideal) Corinthian gathering (14:26–31). Underlying the entire discussion is Paul's core theology and ethics. He notes that the purpose of the Spirit is to serve "the common good" (12:7) and that "the spirits of prophets are subject to the prophets" (14:32). Thus Paul proposes a responsible use of spiritual gifts. They were not to be used for the purpose of self-glorification, in the sense of "building up" the self; this was the problem with "speaking in tongues," or *glossolalia* (14:4). Rather they had as their purpose to "build up" the church, as exemplified especially by prophecy (14:4–5). In essence, Paul has moved the discussion of spiritual gifts to a higher level, placing the emphasis on theological and ethical *function* on behalf of the community rather than on personal meaning. Indeed, the highest spiritual gift of all, greater than any form of spectacular manifestation, is altruistic love itself, a form of love that seeks the good of the other (thus 13:1–3).

15:1–58. The final section of the letter, dealing with the resurrection of the dead, appears to have been written to respond to a reported situation at Corinth (15:12). As in earlier sections, Paul continues to use the rhetorical strategy of invoking traditions the Corinthians had received, reciting a creedal narrative of the facts of the gospel (15:1, 3b–5) before appending a more extended history of appearances (15:5b–7) and modifying it to include himself (15:8–11). This focus on his continuity with the other apostolic witnesses, something Paul plays down in Galatians (see Gal. 1:18–19), establishes a backdrop against which he can express astonishment at the Corinthians' denial of the resurrection. That he can hardly believe the report he has received is evident from the structure of the rhetoric itself: Paul displays a chain of logical inconsistencies (15:13–19) before attempting to turn the matter in a positive direction (15:20–28), only to find himself returning to additional inconsistencies (15:29–33). How can some Corinthians think this! When he has adequately vented his amazement, he utilizes two diatribe-like questions at 15:35 (that is, questions he raises himself as if they have been raised by a member of his audience) to introduce an extended explanation of the *how* of resurrection (15:36–49). Then he privileges his readers with an abbreviated apocalyptic *mystery* (15:51–52) before rounding out the discourse with an exhortation to steadfastness (15:58).

16:1–24. The closing of the letter includes instructions about the collection (16:1–4), travel plans (16:5–9; cf. 4:17–21), and miscellaneous admonitions and greetings (16:10–20). To all of this, Paul apparently affixed his own handwritten greeting–and curse! (16:21–24).

2 Corinthians

When Paul's letters were collected for distribution to the church at large, they went through a process of editing. In some cases, we can see evidences of that editing. 2 Corinthians is a letter that many scholars feel exhibits such signs of editing. It appears to be not one letter, but a composite of several discrete letters that Paul sent to this church over time. Even though there is no extant manuscript evidence for multiple letters, there are portions of the text of 2 Corinthians that do not fit together well as a single letter. Aside from the letter opening (1:1–2) and closing (13:11–13) with its trinitarian benediction (13:13), at least four sections can be identified. They are listed below in the order in which they might have been written as separate letters:

1) 6:14–7:1–a letter fragment about interfaith marriages, written before any tensions had developed between Paul and the Corinthians.
2) 10:1–13:10–a combative letter of reprimand and apostolic self-defense. This letter fragment may be the same as the "tearful letter" referred to in 2 Corinthians 2:3–4 and may be in response to the "painful visit" mentioned at 2 Corinthians 2:1.
3) 1:3–6:13; 7:2–16–a letter of consolation and reconciliation. The connection of these verses as one fragment is seen in the flow of thought from 6:13 to 7:2. It presupposes a "painful visit" (2:1) and a "tearful letter" (2:3–4) that have already taken place before this reconciliation.
4) 8:1–9:15–instructions about the offering for Jerusalem. This section could perhaps be made up of two letter fragments rather than one, both written about the offering, but apparently written at different times.

These letter fragments will be examined below in the order in which they occur in our current version of 2 Corinthians.

1:1–2. The opening of the current letter carries an address from Paul and Timothy (1:1) to the church in Corinth *as well as in Achaia* (1:1). One may surmise that Phoebe, mentioned in Rom. 16:1 as a deaconess at Cenchreae, is among those addressed. Silvanus is listed as one who has preached in Corinth (1:19), but not as a co-sender; Titus appears prominently as part of the missionary team (2:13; 7:6, 14; 8:6, 16; 12:18). Also mentioned in the body of the present letter is "the brother who is famous" for his preaching (8:18), "our brother whom we have often tested" (8:22), and "the brother" (12:18). But no names are given.

1:3–6:13; 7:2–16. Paul's rhetorical technique in this section is interesting. He shapes an opening blessing (1:3–4) around the theme of *consolation*, and returns to the theme with the closing description of Titus' recent experience at Corinth (7:13b–15). In a similar fashion, a two-part narrative of apostolic work specifically related to Corinth (1:15–2:13; 7:5–16) forms an *inclusio* around a discourse on the true practice of apostolic ministry (2:14–6:13; 7:2–4) which remains relatively general until it arrives at the appeal (6:11–13; 7:2–4). In this central section, only Paul's defensiveness about self-commendation (3:1–3; 4:2; 5:12; 6:4) and a brief reference to the fading glory of Moses (3:7–18) give a hint of the troubled relationship between the apostle and his estranged congregation (cf. 1:15–2:5). The rest of the material can be seen as the kind of *apologia* any Christian missionary pastor might have given in the midst of the diverse and competing religious (and philosophical) voices of the first century.

It is worth noting that Paul suggests in 1:6 that the Corinthians suffer as he does. Paul says this also of the Thessalonians (1 Thess. 1:6; 2:14–16) and Philippians (1:29) but one hears little elsewhere of Corinthian suffering. Rather it is *Paul's* suffering that is in view. As in 1 Corinthians, Paul makes it clear that his ministry is grounded in the Spirit (3:3, 6, 8, 17–18; 5:5). But it is the death and resurrection of Jesus that provides the paradigm for ministry, so that Paul connects his afflictions with Jesus' suffering (1:5; 4:10–11) and can rejoice in the hope (and comfort) of resurrection (1:9; 4:10–5:10). With the noteworthy catalogs of hardships (4:8–9; 6:4–10) he claims the heroic high ground. The report of ministry plans, decisions, and activities (1:8–11;1:15–2:13; 7:5–16) provides some details about Paul's work with the congregation–especially the "painful visit" (2:1) and the "letter of tears" (2:4)–as well as at least one indication of what some Corinthians say about Paul (1:17).

6:14–7:1. This passage interrupts its immediate context (6:11–3; 7:2ff.), both in subject matter and in tenor. The focus is strongly on drawing boundaries between the Christian community (see 6:15) and those around it, especially idolators (6:16). Whether it is Pauline is debated; it could be an interpolation added by a later editor. This is because the basic admonition (6:14) is supported by scripture proofs (16c–18) quite different from anything we have seen elsewhere in Corinthians (cf. 1 Cor. 3:16–17; 6:13b–19).

8:1–9:15. In two successive chapters that may have originally been separate letters, Paul takes up again the matter of the collection for Jerusalem. In 1 Corinthians 16 he referred to instructions given to the churches in Galatia; here he cites the progress of the offering in Macedonia (Thessalonica, Philippi). Common to the two chapters is some apostolic boasting. In 8:1–5 he boasts of the Macedonians to the Corinthians; in 9:1–5 he seeks to make good his boast to the Macedonians about the Corinthians. Both chapters focus on the completion of the offering (8:10–11; 9:5), but there also are differences. Chapter 8 underscores the eagerness of the Corinthians with respect to the offering, and indicates that they had begun it the previous year (8:10). Chapter 9 mentions the Corinthian desire, and reports Paul's boast that Corinth *has been ready* for a year (9:2). Chapter 8 also mentions the return of Titus to Corinth, with two of the brothers

(8:18, 22); chapter 9 mentions the brothers (9:3, 5) but omits Titus. If the present chapters were in fact different letters, they seem to have been preserved in correct chronological order.

Motivation for the offering is grounded in various ways: (1) comparison with Macedonia (8:1–5); (2) consistency of character (excelling in everything; 8:7); (3) Christ-like generosity (8:9); (4) following through (8:10–11); (5) the balance of abundance and need (8:13–15); (6) the rule of sowing and reaping (9:6); (7) the promise of God's abundance (9:8–11a); and (8) public recognition (which produces thanksgiving to God; 9:11b–12).

10:1–13:10. The remainder of the present letter illustrates what first-century missionary work (pastoral ministry?) is all about: oaths (11:11, 31; 12:19) and threats (10:11), foolishness (11:1—12:10), caricatures and name-calling ("super-apostles," 11:5; 12:11; "false apostles," 11:13), boasting (11:10, 17–18, 21b–29; 12:1–10), and sarcasm (11:19–21). This may be Paul's "letter of tears" (see above, 1:23–2:11; 7:6–12); the identification is still debatable. What is certain is that there is an in-your-face character to the section (cf. 10:7). Paul's description provides even more indication that some of the troubles of the Corinthian church stem from the arrival of people who challenge Paul's leadership style (10:2, 10; 11:6, 7–10), who speak about him in his absence (10:10–11), and who even impugn his honesty and integrity (12:16). He says they commend themselves (10:12) and boast in their work in comparison to him (11:12–13) even as they take offence at his boasting (10:8–11). In several places Paul reveals again the *raw* religious power with which he works (10:3–6; 11:13–15; 12:1–10, 12; 13:1–4).

Here Paul again articulates the principle by which he operates his missionary enterprise, and which undergirds his boast: boasting within limits, of work in one's own sphere of action (10:12–18). Perhaps the decree of the apostolic council has opened the floodgates of the Gentile mission, and brought new missionaries into the regions where Paul has worked. In Corinth, as with the Galatian churches, Paul is concerned lest "another Jesus," "a different spirit," or "a different gospel" become lodged in his congregations (11:4; cf. Gal. 1:6–9).

The extended section that Paul labels "foolishness" (11:1–12:13) is fascinating. Even though he claims a special relationship to his readers (11:1–4), Paul treats them as a fickle and uncritical (if not also hostile) audience. He launches into a carefully constructed "defense speech" that amounts to a verbal jousting match—an intense, wide-ranging comparison of his ministry with that of the "super-apostles" the Corinthians apparently favor. The thesis is stated in 11:5, stated negatively in 11:6a, and presented as the conclusion in 12:11b–12. In between, Paul describes his behavior that has so offended the Corinthians (11:7–12), hurls a counter accusation (11:13–14), questions his readers sensibilities (11:16b–21), and engages in an extended boast (11:21b–12:10). Underlying all of the argumentation is a steady insistence on a theology of suffering and weakness, consistent with the theology of "Christ crucified" (1 Cor. 1:23). Thus, even though Paul is forced to defend himself in order to preserve the integrity of his message, he recognizes the irony of a powerful defense of a gospel that is based on weakness. Therefore he engages in self-described "speaking as a fool" (2 Cor. 11:21), in which he "boast[s] of the things that show my weakness" (11:30).

The announcement of his impending third visit to Corinth (12:14–13:10) provides additional details about Paul's interaction with the congregation. We learn that Paul had sent Titus (and "the brother") to Corinth earlier (12:18), and that Titus had completed his ministry with the same integrity Paul himself displayed. We learn that Paul had warned a number of folk on his second visit (13:2). But perhaps more importantly, Paul completes in this section the point he began in 10:8, a point that defines the purposes of his ministry: Whether in weakness, foolishness, or power, Paul seeks to build up (*oikodomein*) the church (13:10).

Philippians

The letter is addressed by Paul and Timothy to the members of the church Paul founded at Philippi, a Roman army colony in northern Greece (Macedonia). Epaphroditus, a member of the church, probably carried the letter when he returned from conveying to Paul a gift of support from the church (see 2:25; 4:18). Except for Epaphroditus, Euodia and Syntyche (4:2), Clement (4:3), and, perhaps Syzygus (see 4:3), other members of the church are anonymous. Alone among Paul's letters, Philippians is addressed to "bishops and deacons"–a puzzling reference since otherwise such church leaders are not commonly mentioned by Paul (but see Rom. 16:1).

The letter was written during one of the imprisonments Paul suffered (1:13–14, 17; cf. 2 Cor. 11:23), perhaps at Ephesus. Its occasion may have been a number of things: (1) Paul's imprisonment (1:12–20); (2) the arrival of opponents in Philippi (1:15–17, 28; 3:2; 3:18–19); (3) Epaphroditus' illness (2:25–30); (4) trouble between Euodia and Syntyche (4:2–3); or (5) the receipt of a gift (4:18).

The letter as it currently appears follows the form of other Pauline letters. Its literary integrity, however, is not without question; like 2 Corinthians it may be an edited version of more than one letter. What appears to be the beginning of a conclusion at 3:1a is broken off, followed by an extended section of warnings and exhortations (3:1b–4:3), and then resumed at 4:4 or perhaps 4:10. As a result, what otherwise is a friendly letter updating Paul's (and Epaphroditus') condition takes on a more menacing and controversial tone. Perhaps the intervening section was a separate letter sent to the Philippians at another time, and was combined with the primary letter when Paul's letters were collected.

1:1–11	Letter opening
1:12–3:1a	Body A: letter of encouragement
3:1b–4:3	Body B: warnings and admonitions
4:4–23	Letter closing

1:1–11. After the basic elements of the letter opening (sender, recipient, greeting) Paul sets its tone by focusing the thanksgiving on his partnership with the Philippians (1:3–5) and by appending an extended compliment (called a *captatio benevolentia* in ancient rhetoric) to them (1:6–11). He emphasizes the mutuality of their ministries and acknowledges the emotional bond between them (1:7–8) before revealing the content of his prayer on their behalf (1:9–11). His reference to the coming *day of Christ* (1:10; see also 2:16) provides an insight into how Paul maps time.

1:12–3:1a. The first part of the body of the letter includes four sections. Paul begins by describing his current imprisonment, and the effects it has had on his ministry and the ministry of others (1:12–18a). Then he turns his view to the immediate future. He expects deliverance and vindication (1:19b–20a), but reflects on other options (1:20b–26). As in 2 Corinthians (see above), the death and resurrection of Jesus shapes his ministry strategy.

Having explained his own plans, Paul then composes a third section (1:27–2:18) encouraging the Philippians in their discipleship. Acknowledging that they face opposition (1:28) and are undergoing suffering (1:29), he urges them to remain faithful. A variety of rhetorical forms (*inclusio*, 1:27–30; *repetitio*, 2:1; paired exhortations, 2:3, 4) are part of his appeal, but the most prominent is the *Christ-hymn* in 2:6–11, the theological high point of the letter to the Philippians.

Paul probably inherited this hymn, since it is a type of poetry, and Paul elsewhere uses and modifies segments of poetry or liturgy (cf. Gal. 3:28; Rom. 10:9; 1 Cor. 8:6; 15:3–5). Similar hymnic material can also be found in Ephesians 2:11–22, Colossians 1:15–18, and the pastoral epistles (1 Tim. 2:5–6; 3:16; 2 Tim. 2:11–13. Its poetic recital of the self-emptying of Christ and his subsequent exaltation testifies to the existence of early christological reflection. At some point before Paul, early Christians looked back on and gave words to the whole course of what they believed God had done in Christ. At least two decades before the birth narratives of Matthew and Luke, they affirmed a belief in the pre-existence of Christ "in the form of God," and marveled at the subsequent course of his birth, death, and exaltation. Although the hymn itself does not report Christ's salvific work for believers, as, for example, does the brief credo in Rom. 4:25, it shares with such credos a two-part movement correlated with death and resurrection. This simple but clear movement, along with its antiquity and (probably) its familiarity in the church, give it considerable rhetorical force. Much as the admonition to faithfulness in Hebrews 12:1–2, this hymn celebrates Christ as an exemplar, as a pattern for emulation by disciples

(2:5). In that respect it is crucial that one be clear about Paul's use of it. He does *not* use it to say "salvation through suffering." Reading the passage as an invitation to martyrdom is a misreading of it. The issue in the immediate context of the hymn is humility, and a mutuality of concern and care within the church at Philippi. While Christ's suffering included his death, and the Philippians' discipleship may also, Paul's focus here is simply on the self-emptying *(kenosis)* of Christ. That the hymn speaks so powerfully, and reverberates with Paul's theology of the cross as well as the shape of his ministry (see below on 3:1b–4:3), may not be unlike the preacher whose sermon illustration is more powerful than the point it is to support. Yet it also illustrates the strong connection between *indicative* (theology) and *imperative* (ethics) in Paul.

The concluding section (2:19–3:1a) is a report of travel plans for Timothy (2:19–23a), Epaphroditus (2:25–30), and Paul himself (2:23b–24). The appearance of such plans at or near the end of Paul's other letters supports the conclusion that this letter may have ended shortly after 3:1a.

3:1b–4:3. This portion of the body of the letter differs dramatically in tone and (some) content from what precedes. Heretofore Paul has expressed confidence in the Philippians, simply urging them to continue doing what they are currently doing (2:12–13). Now he writes in a way that resembles sections of Galatians or 2 Corinthians 10–13: calling names (3:2, 15, 18); boasting (3:4b–6); appealing to emotion (3:18); and using caricature (3:19). The transition to this section (3:1b) suggests that this portion of the letter mirrors what he has written elsewhere, a suggestion supported by several pieces of material. The "pedigree" in 3:4b–6 is similar to the first part of the catalog of hardships in 2 Cor. 11 (see also Gal. 1:13–14), and the distinction between two kinds of righteousness (3:9) resonates with the extended discussions in Galatians 2:11ff. and Romans 1:16ff.

At the same time, this portion of the letter parallels the earlier section. On his way to a basic appeal that the Philippians stand firm in their faith (3:16; 4:1), Paul incorporates an extended narrative of his own self-emptying (3:4–14) and invites his readers to imitate him (3:15–17). There is little doubt that this portion stands in close relation to the *Christ-hymn* (2:6–11). It is difficult to know to how profoundly the *Christ-hymn* has influenced the development of the *imitatio*-motif that is a basic component of Paul's ministry (see especially 3:7, 10–11, 17).

Of interest also in this section are the two descriptions of opponents at Philippi. The *repetitio* at 3:2 seems to describe Torah-observant Jews or Jewish Christians, since Paul immediately seeks to strip the opponents of any claim to the identity of "circumcision" (3:3). The description at 3:18–19 is less clear, and may refer to opponents in the wider culture around the church. Such an identity would explain the (contrasting) description of the Christian "commonwealth" *(politeuma)* which follows (3:20–21). Elsewhere in the letter (2:15), Paul places the Philippians in the midst of a "crooked and perverse generation."

4:4–23. As we suggested earlier, the original letter closing begins anew in 4:4. Here, as in 3:3a, Paul repeats the word rejoice (*chairete*) that gives the entire letter the rhetorical character of celebration (*epideixis*) as well as deliberation. Then, with a variety of exhortations (4:4, 5, 6, 8–9), declarations (4:5b), promises (4:7, 19); thanksgivings (4:10–18), and ascriptions (4:20), Paul leads the reader to the culminating greetings and blessing of 4:21–23. In four words, the Philippians are reminded of the eschatological horizon (4:5b; see 1:10; 2:16; 3:20–21); with a memorable *repetitio* (4:8), of the community's virtues. An extended section (4:10–19) acknowledges the arrival of their support (brought by Epaphroditus), and gives Paul another chance to highlight his model of apostolic ministry (4:11–13). Greetings from anonymous members in "the emperor's household" (4:22) perhaps echo an earlier reference to "the imperial guard" (literally "whole praetorium," 1:13), and serve as final punctuation to the positive movement of the gospel.

Philemon

The letter to Philemon exhibits all of the customary marks of a letter: letter opening (address, v. 1; addressees, 1b–2; salutation, v. 3), body (vv. 4–22), and letter closing (greetings, v. 23; blessing, v. 25). In the body of the letter, an initial thanksgiving (vv. 4–7) and a closing travel-related request (v. 22) bracket the main section (vv. 8–21).

Paul probably wrote the letter from Ephesus during an imprisonment (cf. vv. 1, 9–10, 23) there. Philemon may have resided in Colossae, since his runaway slave Onesimus (vv. 10–21) is identified elsewhere with the city (cf. Col. 4:9) as are Archippus (Col. 4:17) and Epaphras (Col. 4:12). The identity of Apphia, "the sister," is unclear; she may be a member of Philemon's household as well as the church that meets there (v. 2). Timothy is listed as a coauthor (v. 1), and others with Paul as he writes are Onesimus (v. 10), Epaphras (v. 23), Mark, Aristarchus, Demas, and Luke (v. 24). These seven also are mentioned in Colossians (1:1; 4:9–16).

By means of a narrative analysis, Norman Peterson has reconstructed the story line (plot) which lies behind the letter. Paul had converted Philemon at some earlier point and thereby had put Philemon in his debt (v. 19). He now appeals to Philemon on behalf of Philemon's slave, Onesimus, who apparently has fled to Paul and has also become a Christian (v. 10). Paul's rhetoric seeks to persuade Philemon to receive Onesimus on different terms from those under which he left (vv. 16–17), and provide an example of the application of Paul's theology of baptism (cf. Gal. 3:28; 1 Cor. 12:13).

Two important issues emerge with the letter. Both have to do with the relation of the gospel and social structures. Does Paul's return of Onesimus represent, in the final analysis, an acknowledgment of the primacy of existing social institutions (in this case, slavery) over the gospel? Or does it illustrate how the gospel changes them? In that regard, 1 Cor. 7:21–24 is a key passage, with its similarity of language (esp. 7:22) to Philemon 16. That Paul asks Philemon to receive Onesimus as his brother *in the flesh* as well as *in the Lord* (v. 16) is tantamount to asking him to acknowledge Onesimus' liberation by freeing him. That he offers to reimburse Philemon for anything Onesimus owes (vv. 18–19) may in effect be the fiscal side of that liberation, that is, a redemption, even though Paul does not call it that.

Philemon also illustrates the way in which Paul deals with a particular person of some financial means. The Colossian leader not only owns slaves, but has a church meeting in his house (v. 2), and can provide Paul with a guest room (v. 22). It is hardly coincidental that after flattering Philemon (v. 4–7), Paul declines to command him (v. 8), but chooses to plead and cajole (vv. 9–21), invoking Philemon's partnership with him (v. 17). As the gospel moves forward in the Greco-Roman world, carrying within it the power of irreversible liberation, Paul seems intent to assure more-privileged members of society that it is no threat to their status. At the same time, he leaves very little room for Philemon to ignore his plea, since he notes that he will be coming soon (v. 22) and is confident that Philemon will do the right thing (vv. 17–21).

Here we may, in fact, see Paul's theological "indicative" catching up with his pastoral "imperative." Embedded in the baptismal theology of the Pauline communities was a statement of radical egalitarianism: "As many of you as were baptized into Christ have clothed yourselves with Christ. There is no longer Jew or Greek, there is no longer slave or free, there is no longer male and female; for all of you are one in Christ Jesus" (Gal. 3:27–28). But how was it to be lived out? Paul's own understanding seemed to grow as he faced new situations. Whereas he could argue in 1 Corinthians 7:21–22 that slave and free should coexist in the church as if they are equal, he can no longer be so naïve about social reality after meeting Onesimus. Now he is convinced that to be equal "in the Lord" must imply equality "in the flesh" as well. It is not enough to say that all are equal in God's eyes. One must go further and seek to apply that equality in the social setting as well.

Suggested Resources for the Pastor's Library

Beardslee, William A. *First Corinthians: A Commentary for Today*. St. Louis: Chalice Press, 1994.

Conzelmann, Hans. *1 Corinthians*. Hermeneia. Philadelphia: Fortress Press, 1975.

Craddock, Fred B. *Philippians*. Interpretation. Atlanta: John Knox Press, 1985.

Dunn, James D. G. *The Epistles to the Colossians and Philemon.* The New International Greek Testament Commentary. Grand Rapids: Eerdmans, 1996.

Fee, Gordon D. *The First Epistle to the Corinthians.* The New International Commentary on the New Testament. Grand Rapids: Eerdmans, 1987.

_____. *Paul's Letter to the Philippians.* The New International Commentary on the New Testament. Grand Rapids: Eerdmans, 1995.

Furnish, Victor. *II Corinthians.* Anchor Bible 32A. Garden City, N.Y.: Doubleday, 1984.

Hays, Richard B. *First Corinthians.* Interpretation. Louisville: Westminster John Knox Press, 1997.

Horsley, Richard A. *Paul and Empire.* Harrisburg, Pa.: Trinity Press International, 1997.

_____. *1 Corinthians.* ANTC. Nashville: Abingdon Press, 1998.

Lüdemann, Gerd. *Paul, Apostle to the Gentiles: Studies in Chronology.* Philadelphia: Fortress Press, 1984.

Meeks, Wayne. *The First Urban Christians: The Social World of the Apostle Paul.* Philadelphia: Westminster, 1986.

Neyrey, Jerome. *Paul, In Other Words.* Louisville: Westminster/John Knox Press, 1990.

Peterson, Norman R. *Rediscovering Paul: Philemon and the Sociology of Paul's Narrative World.* Philadelphia: Fortress Press, 1985.

Sampley, J. Paul. *Walking Between the Times: Paul's Moral Reasoning.* Minneapolis: Fortress Press, 1991.

Talbert, Charles H. *Reading Corinthians: A Literary and Theological Commentary on 1 and 2 Corinthians.* New York: Crossroad, 1987.

Theissen, Gerd. *The Social Setting of Pauline Christianity.* Philadelphia: Fortress Press, 1982.

Wire, Antoinette. *The Corinthian Women Prophets.* Minneapolis: Fortress Press, 1990.

4

Paul as Theologian
Romans

DENNIS E. SMITH

Paul is, without doubt, one of the most important theological thinkers of earliest Christian history. It is Paul who gave us the foundational Christian doctrine of justification by faith and the most highly developed doctrine of grace in the New Testament. Of all of his writings, Romans stands out as the most comprehensive presentation of his theology. It was recognized early on as a classic of early Christian literature and given first place in the collection of Paul's letters in the canon. It has remained influential throughout Christian history down to the present day.

The history of the interpretation of Paul's thought has had its ups and downs, however. In his own lifetime, Paul had to fight against those who misinterpreted him. His detractors would raise this question: "Should we continue in sin in order that grace may abound?" Paul's answer was, "By no means!" (Rom. 6:1–2). But the charge of being soft on obedience stuck with him and throughout Christian history continued to surface among Christian interpreters. In fact, within only a generation or two after Paul's death, the writer of 2 Peter felt it necessary to warn his readers that although "our beloved brother Paul wrote to you according to the wisdom given to him" nevertheless "there are some things in [his letters] hard to understand, which the ignorant and unstable twist to their own destruction" (3:15–16). Although it is unclear what problems 2 Peter had in mind, two issues have tended to dominate all debates about Paul, namely the issue of faith versus works and the issue of Paul's relation to Judaism.

One of Paul's earliest champions was Marcion, a second-century church leader. Although he eventually came to be condemned as a heretic, he started out as an influential Christian teacher in Rome. Marcion based his interpretation of the Christian message on the writings of Paul and the gospel of Luke. To be sure, he felt that these writings had been corrupted, so he published his own "corrected" or edited version of Paul and Luke. Marcion took Paul so seriously and read him in such stark terms that he took a step that Paul himself did not take, though Marcion was sure that he had. According to Marcion's interpretation, Paul had thoroughly discredited and rejected the Jewish scriptures. These scriptures, Marcion said, derived from a false God, the Jewish God. Jesus, on the other hand, came to witness to a different God, a loving God, who was not to be confused with the Jewish God. Marcion's stark dualism was condemned as heresy, but his radical reading of Paul nevertheless brought to the surface the question, to what extent did Paul reject the Jewish law and Judaism itself?

The issue of "faith vs. works" surfaced again in Christian history in the early fifth century C.E. A Christian teacher named Pelagius began to argue that the initial move toward God was taken by the individual prior to grace, thus taking a position positive to "works." In opposition, Augustine of Hippo in North Africa argued for the doctrine of original sin and for the necessity of grace before one was capable of any response to God. Both Pelagius and Augustine had based their teachings on the writings of Paul. Augustine, in fact, had discovered what he saw as the essence of Christian faith by reading Romans. In a famous passage in his *Confessions* (8.12.29) he spoke of his experience when, in a state of despair at his own sin, he heard a child say, "Pick up and read." Taking this to be a divine message, he returned to the text of Romans that lay before him and found in Romans 13:13–14 what seemed to him to be a direct response to his despair over the desires of the flesh. Augustine won the debate with Pelagius, and the Augustinian version of the doctrine of salvation by faith and not by works became official church doctrine. Pelagius was condemned as a heretic. But, unofficially, Pelagianism continued to coexist in Christian thought. Today theologians will often point out that, while church leaders speak of salvation by faith through the grace of God, popular theology is still imbued with a form of "semi-Pelagianism," the idea that salvation depends first of all on what one does.

In the sixteenth century, many years after Augustine, Martin Luther began another major debate about "faith vs. works." He, too, had discovered the essence of Christian theology in Romans, most especially in the doctrine of justification by faith. His debate with the church of his day concentrated on such issues as the granting of indulgences, which he interpreted as salvation by works rather than by faith. His radical new vision of Christian theology was derived primarily from Paul, and it led to his eventual split with the church of his day and the beginning of the Protestant Reformation. To a great extent, then, the Protestant Reformation was founded on a rediscovery of Paul.

Although Luther represented a corrective of Christian theology on the issue of faith vs. works, the other problem of Pauline theology, its relationship to Judaism, remained unresolved. Luther, who was one of the most gifted interpreters of Paul in Christian history, was also anti-Jewish in his theology. And so it is that the issue of anti-Judaism has continued to plague the interpretation of Paul down to the present day.

In the twentieth century, the champions of Paul included Karl Barth, one of the greatest Christian theologians of that era who, like Augustine and Luther before him, rediscovered the essence of Christianity by a close study of Romans. The movement he led, known as "neoorthodoxy," is considered to have begun with the 1918 publication of his classic commentary on Romans. But it was the twentieth century that also brought to light once and for all the dark side of Pauline theology. The slaughter of six million Jews by the Nazis during World War II brought Christians everywhere face to face with the dangers and implications of the anti-Semitism that had become embedded in Christian theology. It was especially expressed in the doctrine of supercessionism, the idea that God had rejected the Jews and replaced them with the Christians, and Paul was seen as its champion.

After World War II, reflections on the Nazi atrocities against the Jews caused a radical reassessment of anti-Semitism in Christian theology, as well it should. Leading this reassessment among Pauline theologians in the '50s and early '60s was Krister Stendahl, who argued that Paul had been misinterpreted because we had overlooked the original context in which he wrote. Stendahl pointed out that Paul was a Jew and that he argued strongly in Romans 9–11 that God would never forsake God's own people, the Jews. God had made a covenant with the Jewish people, Paul argued, and it was inconceivable that God would go back on his promises. Consequently, Stendahl concluded, rather than concentrating on a mission to Jews, Paul saw his call and his mission as directed to Gentiles, and all of his arguments were directed toward defining the gospel for the Gentiles.

A large majority of Pauline scholars today have followed Stendahl's lead and sought to come to grips with the anti-Semitic heritage of Pauline theology. But they differ on how this is to be done. A major reason that the debate continues today is the often unstated presupposition among many theologians that supercessionism cannot be separated from Paul's basic doctrine of justification by faith. But this presupposition is problematic both theologically and historically. Theologically, the argument that in order to affirm the universal nature of the Christ event one must argue that God rejected the Jews catches one in the trap first identified by Paul, namely that one then accuses God of breaking promises. Historically, to argue that Paul turned his back on his Jewish heritage to become a Christian does not do justice to the specific historic context within which Paul lived and in which he wrote Romans, a context in which "Christianity" as such did not exist as a separate religion but only as a sect within Judaism.

This introduction to Romans will attempt to tackle these issues directly in order to alert the student both to the treasures and to the pitfalls to be found in this Christian classic. Our starting point will be to define as precisely as possible the context in which Paul wrote. Then we will move to a brief commentary on Romans that will attempt to deal with the issues under debate in scholarship today.

Historical Context

Paul wrote Romans to a church community he had never visited. His stated purpose for writing is revealed in chapter 15. Here he states that he has now finished his mission to the Gentiles in the eastern Mediterranean area, or, as he puts it "from Jerusalem and as far around as Illyricum" (15:19). Indeed, it has been because of his devotion to that mission that he had "so often been hindered from coming to you" (15:22). But now that he is on his way to a new mission in Spain (15:24), he plans to stop off in Rome both to enjoy their company and to be "sent on" by them, which probably means he was seeking their financial support.

Our best evidence suggests that Paul never made it to Spain. He tells the Romans that, before he comes to visit them, he will travel to Jerusalem with the contributions he has gathered from Gentile Christian communities for "the poor among the saints at Jerusalem" (15:26). According to Acts, this visit to Jerusalem results in his arrest and resulting trip to Rome as a prisoner (Acts 21–28). It is from the apocryphal *Acts of Paul* that we get the information that Paul was executed while still a prisoner in Rome (*Acts of Paul* 11).

Based on this information, Romans is identified as the last extant letter Paul wrote, which would date it ca. 57 or 58 C.E. We do not know who founded the Christian community in Rome, nor do we know much about its early history and makeup. Even more intriguing, we do not know how much Paul knew about them. But as Paul addressed the Romans in this letter, he seemed to exhibit some familiarity with them. On the one hand, he identified the recipients of the letter as Gentiles (see, for example, 1:5–6, 13; 11:13). On the other hand, in chapters 14–15, he alluded to a situation that would arise in a mixed community of Gentile Christians and Jewish Christians, namely the problem of table fellowship within a community in which "some believe in eating anything, while [others] eat only vegetables" (14:2). This situation would most likely have occurred in a mixed community that included Jewish Christians practicing some form of dietary laws regarding "unclean" meat and Gentile Christians who did not follow any food restrictions (14:20–21). The question is whether Paul is referring to an actual situation in the Roman church, and if so, how he knew about it, or whether he is referring hypothetically to a situation like many he had faced in his missionary career.

Our data about the probable origins of the Roman church suggests that it began as an offshoot of Judaism. According to Acts 18:1–3, Paul met up with the Jewish couple Aquila and Priscilla in Corinth. They "had recently come from Italy," according to Acts, "because Claudius had ordered all Jews to leave Rome." This expulsion of Jews from Rome in about 49 C.E. during the reign of Claudius is also mentioned by the Roman historian Suetonius, who attributed it to unrest connected with a certain "Chrestus" (*Life of Claudius* 25.3). It is thought that "Chrestus" might be a misspelling of "Christos," or Christ, and that therefore the expulsion was related to disturbances in the Jewish Christian community. Some have argued that the expulsion of Jews may have resulted in the Roman Christian community becoming more Gentile in its makeup. In any case, while Paul addressed the Romans as if they were primarily a Gentile community, he nevertheless included greetings in chapter 16 to a number of Jewish Christians, including Aquila and Priscilla who by then were evidently back in Rome (16:3–5). Chapter 16 therefore suggests that not only did Paul know several members of the Roman church, and so might have had some idea of the issues present there, but also that the church was in some sense a mixed community of Jewish and Gentile Christians.

Rhetorical Context

The rhetoric of Romans has always presented problems for interpreters. John Gager has pointed out how easily Paul can be seen to contradict himself. On the one hand, there is the anti-law/anti-Israel Paul, who said, "For 'no human being will be justified in his sight' by deeds prescribed by the law" (3:20), and who said, "Israel, who did strive for the righteousness that is based on the law, did not succeed in fulfilling that law" (9:31). On the other hand, there is the pro-law/pro-Israel Paul, who said "Do we then overthrow the law by this faith? By no means! On the contrary, we uphold the law" (3:31). And "so the law is holy, and the commandment is holy and just and good" (7:12). And "I ask, then, has God rejected his people? By no means!" (11:1). Gager notes that these contradictions have usually been resolved by assuming that the anti-law/anti-Israel Paul was the real Paul. The reason this conclusion was drawn so easily is that Romans was interpreted not according to its original context but according to the later context of the church. In the later context of the church, which extended from the generation right after Paul to the present day, Christianity became a religious movement separate from and in competition with Judaism. In that context, the anti-Israel Paul made sense. But was that the original context of Romans? Gager says no, and he bases his argument on new research into the rhetorical style of Romans.

That Romans follows ancient rhetorical style should come as no surprise. Ancient schooling emphasized instruction in rhetoric or how to construct an argument for public discourse. Paul was clearly a person who had been educated in the proper use of the Greek language and utilized a wide range of rhetorical devices in Romans. Especially important for the argument in Romans is his use of the form of the diatribe. Diatribe was a form of written and oral discourse that was popular especially among the Cynic and Stoic philosophers of Paul's day. In this rhetorical style the speaker/author carries on a debate with an "imaginary" questioner. Thus the speaker/author raises the questions of the supposed questioner himself and then answers them. This can be seen in such texts as Romans as 6:1–2: "What then are we to say? Should we continue in sin in order that grace may abound? By no means!" Or 7:7: "What then should we say? That the law is sin? By no means!"

Stanley Stowers has pushed this research even further. Like Stendahl, he argues that Paul was addressing a primarily Gentile audience in Romans. He then identifies in great detail how the ancient method of *prosopopoiia* or "speech in character" can be traced in Paul. "Speech in character" is the method whereby a speaker/writer would present the argument of a detractor in the language of the detractor and then refute it. Stowers argues that the use of this style explains the seeming contradictions in Paul. That is to say, Paul seems to contradict himself because we do not notice, as his original ancient audience would have, how he is speaking at certain points not in his own voice but in the voice of a detractor. Thus Paul, instead of contradicting himself, is rather contradicting the detractor with whom he carries on his imaginary rhetorical debate. It is this "rereading of Romans" (to borrow a phrase from Stanley Stowers) in scholarship today that will especially inform the interpretation presented here.

The Argument and Theology of Romans
1:1–17. The Salutation and Introduction to the Argument of the Letter.

In the salutation to this letter, Paul sets forth his self-understanding as a called apostle. It means first of all that he has been "set apart for the gospel of God, which he promised beforehand through his prophets in the holy scriptures" (1:1–2). The "gospel" is thus founded on Jewish scripture; it can be no other way. Secondly, since the term "apostle" denotes one who is commissioned for a task, Paul reminds his readers what his specific commission from God was. He was commissioned "to bring about the obedience of faith among all the Gentiles for the sake of his name, including yourselves who are called to belong to Jesus Christ" (1:5–6). Throughout this letter, Paul will be arguing for the legitimacy of Gentiles as now part of God's people because of the event of Jesus Christ. And he will be building his argument on scripture, namely the Jewish Bible.

Paul sets forth a summary of his argument with his opening thesis statement: "For I am not ashamed of the gospel; it is the power of God for salvation to everyone who has faith, to the Jew first and also to the Greek" (1:16). It is as if someone might say to Paul, "shame on you," for his is truly a revolutionary message. The "shamefulness" of the message is seen in this opening statement of the scope of God's good news or gospel, namely that now both Jews *and* Gentiles are brought together under a single religious vision.

1:18–3:20. The Problem of Sin.

In this first section, Paul makes a broad case for the argument that all human beings ("Jews and Gentiles" encompasses all humanity) "are under the power of sin" (3:9). He thus begins with anthropology, with the state of humanity, and traditional interpretation of Paul has often emphasized this point. According to this traditional interpretation, Paul would be starting with a universal human experience of being estranged from God, an experience that is then understood to be elaborated further in Romans 7. The problem with this view is that it assumes that Jews as well as Gentiles were estranged from God. But such a view would undermine the covenant God made with Israel and the law God gave to Moses; how could God's covenant people be described as estranged from God? To properly interpret this section, therefore, one must pay close attention to the rhetorical style of Romans.

1:18–2:16. PAUL ADDRESSES A GENTILE DETRACTOR.

How does one indict Gentiles, when, after all, they were never given the law? Paul argues that God's divine nature is revealed in creation, and thus "what can be known about God is plain to them" (1:19). What he is after is an indictment of idolatry, which he views as worshiping "the creature rather than the creator" (1:25). Paul is here using a commonplace argument found in Jewish preaching of the day as seen, for example, in Wisdom of Solomon 13:10–14:31 (this is a Hellenistic Jewish oration dated to the early first century C.E.). To the Jewish mind, the basic Gentile sin was idolatry, and the result of that idolatry was Gentile immorality: "For the idea of making idols was the beginning of fornication" (Wis. 14:12). Here in Romans Paul provides a virtual laundry list of Gentile sins as seen from a Jewish view, with an emphasis on homosexual acts, which were seen by Jews as inherently related to the worship of idols.

The basic sin here is that they did "not honor [God] as God" (Rom. 1:21, 25, 28), which to the Jewish mind was the essence of idolatry. As a consequence of this, "God gave them up...to impurity," that is, to living outside the Jewish laws of purity (1:24; see also 1:26, 28). The emphasis on homosexual acts as the example of life outside the realm of purity (1:26–27) comes directly out of the Old Testament laws of purity which distinguish Jews from other nations, as seen in Leviticus 18:22 and 20:13, and as echoed in *Wisdom of Solomon* 14:26, which lists "sexual perversion" as one of the results of idolatry. In effect, Paul is defining what it is like to live outside the sphere of God's grace, that is, outside the law as seen from the viewpoint of a first-century Jew.

Paul's views on homosexual acts should be understood in their cultural and theological context. Paul was working with a conventional first-century Jewish view of homosexual acts as a sign of pagan idolatry. He had no concept of homosexuality as a natural form of sexual orientation, which is a common view today. Furthermore, since today most Christians no longer live according to Jewish purity laws, and since today the institution of idolatry as it existed in Paul's day no longer exists, Paul's argument against homosexuality loses its primary force. What is of value in his argument is the overall principle he was setting forth, namely the importance of acknowledging God as God as a basic religious stance, a stance he will later identify as "faithfulness." If we wish to apply Paul's teaching to today, therefore, we will re-examine what it means to "acknowledge God as God," or what it means to be faithful to God, in our own time. Furthermore, since Paul throughout Romans is arguing against legalism in religion, we miss his point if we indict homosexuality today on the basis of law. If we follow Paul's lead, our discourse on sexuality will be founded on a theology of grace.

Paul closes this section by addressing an imaginary interlocutor in the style of the diatribe, that is, in the second person (2:1–16). While traditional interpreters have often proposed that it is the pretentious Jew Paul has in mind, Stowers argues that it is rather the pretentious Gentile that Paul is addressing. This pretentious Gentile who "judge[s] others" but is guilty of "doing the very same things" (2:1) can be likened to the boastful Gentile that Paul addresses at 11:17–21.

2:16–3:20. PAUL ARGUES WITH A JEWISH CHRISTIAN TEACHER.

In this section, the question for interpreters is this: If "all Jews" are also "under the power of sin" (3:9) then is not Paul indicting Judaism as a religion? This is a traditional reading of Paul, but it is inconsistent with his overall argument, as suggested above. Here again we need to give closer attention to Paul's rhetoric.

In this section, Stowers argues that the interlocutor with whom Paul is debating represents not Judaism as a whole, but rather represents the viewpoint of a certain type of Jewish teacher who would argue that Gentiles may become righteous by merely keeping the law. For Paul, that does not work because, as he has already argued, Gentiles, lacking a covenant with God, have been consigned to sin by God. Thus, he indicts the Jewish teacher of Gentiles in 2:17–24 in this way: "But if you call yourself a Jew and rely on the law and boast of your relation to God…[and] teach others, will you not teach yourself?…You that boast in the law, do you dishonor God by breaking the law?" That is to say, since sin is still to be found where there is law, introducing the law to Gentiles is not the answer. Rather the answer is to be found in the religious principle that lies behind the law. Thus the "true Jew" in Paul's argument here is not the one whose righteousness is expressed solely by "outward" means, namely by circumcision, but "rather a person is a Jew who is one inwardly, and real circumcision is a matter of the heart—it is spiritual and not literal" (2:28–29). This was a traditional argument in Judaism, Stowers points out, and was not a critique of circumcision per se but rather a reminder of the religious principle that lies behind the law, namely faithfulness (as in Deut. 10:16; 30:6).

Rather than indicting Judaism, Paul proclaims the advantage of the Jew and the value of circumcision (3:1–2), both of which are dependent upon the reliability of God's promises (3:3–4). At the same time, he argues that the "uncircumcised" can keep the just requirements of the law and thus be considered as if circumcised (2:26). So when Paul argues that "all are under the power of sin" (3:9), his point is that all are dependent on God's mercy (3:3). As God's response to sin, Jews have been given "the adoption, the glory, the covenants, the giving of the law, the worship, and the promises" as Paul argues in 9:4. What Gentiles now have available, based on the same mercy of God, Paul will explain in the next section.

3:21–8:39. The Solution: The Righteousness of God.
3:21–31. THE CHRIST EVENT.

The turning point in Paul's argument from problem to solution is indicated at 3:21: "But now, apart from law, the righteousness of God has been disclosed, and is attested by the law and the prophets." The term "now" is an eschatological term. It refers to the new state of affairs since the Christ event, as seen in the course of Paul's argument in 3:21–26. But for whom is this new state of affairs intended? Here once again the traditional view is a supercessionist one in which Paul is interpreted to mean that now all Jews along with Gentiles must become Christians. That interpretation no longer suffices, however. Rather we should notice, for example, the point that Paul makes as he concludes his argument at 3:29–31: "Or is God the God of Jews only? Is he not the God of Gentiles also? Yes, of Gentiles also, since God is one; and he will justify the circumcised on the ground of faith and the uncircumcised through that same faith. Do we then overthrow the law by this faith? By no means! On the contrary, we uphold the law." Paul is therefore arguing that Gentiles are now able to take their place within God's grace along with Jews because of the Christ event.

For Paul, the key term "righteousness of God" derives from the very nature of God. It is "attested by the law and the prophets," and thus is characteristic of God from the beginning of God's interaction with humanity, and it is "now" attested in the Christ event. The Christ event is specifically described in 3:21–26 as an action of God and as "[proving that] at the present time [God] is righteous." The background for Paul's view of grace, therefore, comes right out of Jewish scripture. It is based on the Jewish concept of God's election of Israel as an act of grace.

Paul describes the Christ event with four weighty metaphors, translated in the NRSV as "justification" (3:24), "redemption" (3:24), "sacrifice of atonement" (3:25), and "reconciliation" (5:10–11). These are all mediated through "faith in Jesus Christ" (3:22, 25, 26; 5:1). However, the Greek phrases that these terms translate are subject to differing interpretations based on differing perceptions about the central focus of Paul's theology.

In order to highlight some of the issues in this debate, we will compare two recent translations of Romans 3:22–25a, the first from the NRSV and the second from Stanley Stowers.

> The righteousness of God [has been disclosed] through faith in Jesus Christ for all who believe. For there is no distinction, since all have sinned and fall short of the glory of God; they are now justified by his grace as a gift, through the redemption that is in Christ Jesus, whom God put forward as a sacrifice of atonement by his blood, effective through faith. (NRSV)

> God's plan to make things right has come by means of Jesus' faithfulness, intended to elicit an appropriate faithfulness (like Jesus') among all peoples (and not the Jews only), since Jews and gentiles have been equalized and shown lacking [when God consigned all to sin]. All the ungodly, then, are made right as a gift through God's graciousness by means of the deliverance in Jesus Christ whom God intended (accepted) as a solution to the problem of his anger [against the gentiles] by means of the faithfulness manifested in Jesus' death. [Stowers, 195]

The phrase translated by the NRSV as "faith in Jesus Christ" has two possible meanings in Greek. The word translated "faith" is followed by a Greek genitive which literally means "of Jesus Christ." Greek uses the genitive with two possible meanings. It may be used as an objective genitive, in which case the "faith" in question has as its object "Jesus Christ." This is the interpretation represented by the NRSV translation, which is then understood to refer the response of faith that is essential to salvation. However, a Greek genitive may also be used as a subjective genitive. In this case, it would mean that the phrase "Jesus Christ" functions not as the object of faith but as its subject. The phrase would then be translated "faithfulness of Jesus Christ" with the emphasis being placed on the means whereby the gift of God's grace is transmitted, that is, by means of the faithfulness of Jesus Christ rather than by the believer's faith. This is the interpretation represented by Stowers' translation.

The term "justified," which metaphorically evokes courtroom imagery and has the sense of an "acquittal" in a court of law, is here rendered by Stowers as "made right." The term "redemption," which metaphorically evokes the world of slavery and has the sense of having one's freedom bought and paid for, is here rendered by Stowers as "deliverance." The third term is especially problematic. The Greek word is *hilasterion*, a term that seems to evoke the world of sacrificial worship. The traditional translation has tended to combine this term with the phrase "his blood" and interpret the phrase as a reference to Jesus' death as a sacrifice for sins; such an interpretation can be read into the NRSV translation "sacrifice of atonement by his blood." The interpretation of the death of Jesus as a sacrifice for sins, while it became dominant in later Christian discourse, is unlikely for the time of Paul, a time when Jews as well as Gentiles still practiced animal sacrifice [note that the Jewish temple in Jerusalem was still standing in Paul's day]. Many scholars now argue that the term *hilasterion* in Paul is intended rather to evoke the imagery of martyrdom. Paul and his contemporaries would have utilized the suffering servant imagery in Isaiah 53:4–9 as well as the martyrdom stories of the Maccabees (as in, e.g., 4 Macc. 6:28–29) as their proof texts for this point of view. The theology of martyrdom speaks of an innocent one dying for a cause and thereby as a "*hilasterion*" on behalf of the people (4 Macc. 17:22). Utilizing martyrdom imagery, Stowers therefore interprets the phrase in Romans 3 in this way: "accepted as a solution to the problem of his anger [which Paul introduced as a problem in 1:18] by means of the faithfulness manifested in Jesus' death [i.e. his blood]." In this translation, Stowers is interpreting the reference to "blood" to be a reference to death rather than a reference to the ritual use of blood in temple sacrifice.

In this part of Paul's argument, the opposition of "faith vs. works" is given explicit expression. Paul argues that "deeds prescribed by the law" cannot lead to justification (3:20); rather his position is "that a person is justified by faith apart from works prescribed by the law" (3:28). The law being referenced here is, of course, the Torah, or the law of Moses. Lest he be misunderstood, Paul very quickly affirms that he is not attacking the law per se. "On the contrary," he says, "we uphold the law" (3:31). Rather the issue here is how the concept of "works of law" applies to his primary audience for the letter, Gentiles. Thus the question is whether, for Gentiles, simply following the law alone is enough. Paul argues that it is not, since, as his argument clearly assumes, the law cannot function as it is intended to function outside of a relationship with God. For Jews, that relationship is defined by their covenant with God. For Gentiles, Paul argues, that relationship, described with such metaphorical terms as justification and reconciliation, has now been established by God through the death of Christ. "Works of law" would then represent an attempt to apply the law outside of a relationship with God, or, one might say, outside of a spiritual context, and thereby one would be setting out on a path of futility (described eloquently in Rom 7:7–24). Rather, for Gentiles there must first be "justification by faith," or a relationship with God founded on and mimicking the faithfulness of Jesus Christ.

4:1–25. How Abraham Is the Father of All.

Paul continues his scriptural argument in 4:1–25, where he repeats in a somewhat revised form an interpretation of the Abraham story that he first presented in Galatians 3. Here Paul expounds further on the theme of "faithfulness." His basic text is Genesis 15:6, which states that Abraham "believed," or "was faithful," and that this was counted as "righteousness." Using interpretive methods that any rabbi might use, he then argues that since, at this point in the Abraham story, he had not yet been circumcised, and of course the law had not yet been given, then "righteousness" was based not on "works" but on "faith," or "faithfulness." Through this basic principle, Abraham becomes the "father" of "many nations" (4:16–17, quoting Gen. 17:5), namely the "faithful" who are circumcised as well as those who are uncircumcised (4:11–12). "Faithfulness," then, means responding to God, or trusting in God, in the context of a relationship initiated by God.

5:1–21. RECONCILIATION.

In addition to the terms we noted in chapter 3, namely *justification, redemption,* and *hilasterion,* Paul here in chapter 5 uses a fourth metaphorical term, "reconciliation" (5:6–11). This is a term that suggests a response to a condition of estrangement. Paul himself elaborates on the imagery by referring to "the ungodly" or "sinners" being in the condition of "enemies" when God acted through the death of Christ to heal that chasm and bring about "reconciliation." The language fits the state of Gentiles who are outside the covenant and thus subject to the "wrath of God" (1:18) and "given over" to a life without God (1:18–32). Reconciliation means that God through Christ has now created a relationship with Gentiles "while [they] still were sinners" just like the covenant with Abraham created a relationship with Jews.

Just as Paul compared Christ to Abraham earlier, in 5:12–21 he compares Christ to Adam. This has become a famous passage in Christian theology, but its interpretation has tended to far outstrip what Paul actually says. Joseph Fitzmyer, for example, reminds us that Paul does not here talk of original sin or inherited sin or a fall from grace. Such doctrines come into play in later Christian history. Rather Paul is making the case that sin entered human history with Adam and, as a result, rather than saying humans were born in sin he simply says, "all have sinned" (5:12). Stowers points out that in Paul's argument the circumstances changed with Moses ("death exercised dominion from Adam to Moses," 5:14), because the law was given to Moses and the law was God's answer to sin for the Jewish people. Just as Paul argued in the Abraham story, so also here, the point is to define the condition of Gentiles as being comparable to that of the Jews before the giving of the law.

6:1–23. BAPTISM.

In chapter six, Paul presents his theology of baptism. Using imagery reminiscent of mystery religion terminology of his day ("buried with him by baptism into death," 6:4), he argues that baptism effectively ritualizes the move from one state of existence into another. The old state of existence is that of the Gentile "ungodly" (5:6; see also "Gentile sinners" in Gal. 2:15) who exist outside of a covenant relationship with God. But because the new age has come, signified by the resurrection of Christ (6:4), it is now possible to create a new person, one who is "dead to sin" (6:11) and now can walk "in newness of life" (6:4). The same sense for the power of baptism is also found in Galatians 3:27–29, where it signifies entering a new fictive family where all now live in unity and harmony. For Paul, then, baptism effects the creation of a new community inclusive of all and characterized by faithfulness or "righteousness" (Rom. 6:18) to be lived out in community with others. Paul will address the issues of living in community in chapters 12–15.

7:1–25. THE ANGUISH OF A LIFE LIVED OUTSIDE OF THE GRACE OF GOD.

Chapter seven characterizes living outside the grace of God as a "wretched" existence (7:24). Traditional interpretations have often taken the "I" of chapter seven to represent Paul speaking of his own experience as a Jew. However, although chapter seven speaks of a stricken conscience, Paul says elsewhere that, as a Jew, he lived with a good conscience before God, "as to righteousness under the law, blameless" (Phil. 3:6). Consequently, it is better to interpret Paul here as speaking with the voice of an everyman Gentile. The "wretched" condition he describes is this: "I can will what is right, but I cannot do it" (7:18). The law is implicated in this situation, for it makes known what sin is (7:7). But "the law is holy, and the commandment is holy and just and good" (7:12). So the problem is not the law, but rather is sin (7:13) which holds the individual in slavery (7:14) and dwells within the flesh (7:17–18). Chapter seven ends with the plaintive cry of verse 24: "Who will rescue me from this body of death?" The answer is, of course, "Thanks be to God through Jesus Christ our Lord" (7:25). This forms the transition to the next section.

8:1–39. THE FREEDOM AND PEACE OF A LIFE LIVED WITHIN THE GRACE OF GOD.

Chapter eight begins with a summary statement of "newness of life" in Christ: "There is therefore now no condemnation for those who are in Christ Jesus" (8:1). Here Paul elaborates on the "realized eschatology" that lies at the heart of his theology. Realized eschatology refers to the idea that the end has already begun but has not been fully consummated. Consequently, one can already experience a taste of the blessings that will be fully known at the end. As Paul expresses it, we "have the first fruits of the Spirit" and "groan inwardly while we wait for adoption, the redemption of our bodies" (8:23). In this in-between state, "the law of the Spirit of life in Christ Jesus has set you free from the law of sin and of death" (8:2). This perspective provides the power behind Paul's revolutionary theology. It makes it possible for him to imagine that people can actually change, for it is by the power of God that they do so. Just as Jews maintain their identity as God's people by means of their ethnic identity, Gentiles can now have a fictive ethnic identity through "adoption" as children of God (8:15). Already they can call on God as "Abba! Father!" (8:15), yet their full adoption still awaits in the future (8:23). Meanwhile, they have the Spirit of God to empower them to live "not according to the flesh but according to the Spirit" (8:4). Living within the sphere of God's grace, they live in a zone of "no condemnation" (8:1). That in itself is liberating, freeing the Christian to live for others, a lifestyle that Paul describes so eloquently in 1 Corinthians 10:24 and 13:1–13 and that he characterizes here in Romans as "suffer[ing] with [Christ]" (8:17). In this eloquent paean to apocalyptic theology in chapter 8, Paul makes his case for the importance of the Christ event. For Paul it is only by God's grace that one's basic identity (as "Gentile sinners") can be changed, and that grace is available for Gentiles through the Christ event understood as an eschatological event.

9:1–11:36. Jews and Gentiles Considered Together Theologically.

Paul has made a passionate argument to this point in Romans for the inclusion of Gentiles as children of God through the faithfulness of Jesus Christ. Yet there is still a problem to be dealt with. If Jesus is the Messiah, why is it that the Jewish people as a whole have not acknowledged him as such? Paul proposes that somehow this was all part of God's plan. It is because all of Judaism did not accept Jesus as the Messiah, Paul says, that Gentiles have now been given an opportunity to respond (11:11, 25). But Paul categorically rejects the idea that God has now rejected the Jews in favor of Gentile Christians: "Has God rejected his people? By no means!" (11:1). To make such a claim would be to imply that "the word of God had failed" (9:6) or "there [is] injustice on God's part" (9:14) rather than recognizing that "the gifts and the calling of God are irrevocable" (11:29).

But what are we to make of 10:4: "For Christ is the end of the law so that there may be righteousness for everyone who believes"? This text has often been interpreted to mean that Judaism ended with Christ. In its context, however, it refers back to the principle that Paul had been defining, whereby "Israel…did not succeed in fulfilling the law…because they did not strive for it on the basis of faith, but as if it were based on works" (9:31–32). This is a repetition of his argument in 4:1–25, in which Abraham was "justified by faithfulness" not by "works," and his argument at 2:28–29, that a "real Jew" is defined not by the "outward" sign of circumcision but "a person is a Jew who is one inwardly, and real circumcision is a matter of the heart." That is to say, Paul is not indicting Judaism as a religion but rather is calling Jews to account when they miss, in his view, the essence of their own religion. That essence, he is arguing, is expressed once again in

Christ, so that "Christ is the goal [Greek: *telos*, which means "end" or "goal"] of the law." It is the same point he makes in chapter 4, when he argues for the parallelism between the faithfulness of Abraham and the faithfulness of Christ.

In the end, Paul acknowledges that he does not know the answer to the mystery he poses, for the "judgments" of God are "unsearchable" and the "ways" of God are "inscrutable" (11:33). But he expresses confidence in the "depth of the riches and wisdom and knowledge of God" (11:33). Consequently, because "as regards election they [Jews] are beloved" then he must proclaim that "all Israel will be saved" (11:26–28).

Meanwhile, he speaks directly to Gentiles about how they are to perceive their place in God's plan (11:13–24). He uses the metaphor of an olive tree to make his point. Judaism is like the olive tree, and Gentiles are like a "wild olive shoot" that has been grafted onto the olive tree (11:17). Gentiles, then, like a new graft, draw their sustenance from "the root that supports you" (11:18). The problem is when Gentiles think they *are* the tree and then "boast over the branches" (11:18). It is the sin of supercessionism that Paul specifically and prophetically condemns here. Yet Paul's teaching on this point has been consistently overlooked in much of Christian history, and this omission has contributed to centuries of Christian anti-Semitism.

12:1–15:13. Jews and Gentiles Together in Community.

Based on what has been said so far, how is the Christian then to live, or what does it mean to live a life of faithfulness? Living in a condition of "realized eschatology," the Christian is not to live "conformed to this world," but rather is to be "transformed by the renewing of your minds" (12:2). He defines what he means further by summarizing an argument he first made to the Corinthians (1 Cor. 12:1–30), when he says "we, who are many, are one body in Christ" even though we have "gifts that differ according to the grace given to us" (Rom. 12:5–6). Here in Romans he signals that the "transformed life" is to be lived in community, just as he emphasized to the Galatians and Corinthians. Next comes a list of virtues that should characterize life in community, starting with "love one another with mutual affection" (Rom. 12:10; see also 1 Cor. 12:31–13:13). After applying the principle of the harmonious life to their relationship to the Roman government (13:1–7), an important concession to the tenuous existence of this community under the thumb of an all-powerful Roman rule, Paul returns to the theme of love (13:8–10) and life together in the Christian community.

The issue in Romans 14–15 is similar to one Paul addressed earlier in one of his letters to the Corinthians. According to 1 Corinthians 8:1–13, the problem in Corinth had developed around meat "sacrificed to idols." Here in Romans, the issue is similar, but expressed a bit differently. The problem seems to center on divisions that have developed at their community meals. It is manifested by their division into those who "eat anything" on the one hand and those who "eat only vegetables" (who are also "those who abstain") on the other (14:2–3). Consequently, the vegetarians here are best understood as Jewish Christians who, because they are following some version of the Jewish dietary laws, all of which refer to meat products, have qualms about eating meat that has not come from "kosher" sources. Paul later refers more specifically to issues of "clean" and "unclean" in regard to table customs, thus affirming that Jewish dietary laws are under discussion (14:14–21). We do not know for sure exactly what version of the dietary laws is in question here, but the general principal applies nevertheless. Eating vegetables has for centuries been a way in which a devout Jew can eat at a Gentile table. So also here, in a mixed community of Jewish and Gentile Christians, certain Jewish Christians have decided to abstain from the meat at the community meal, and as a result, a conflict has developed.

What makes the conflict especially important is that it evidently takes place at the community meals. Paul's argument here is based on principles similar to those he applied to issues at the table at Antioch, and repeated to the Galatians (2:11–14), and at Corinth (1 Cor. 11:17–34). The principle is that the unity of the community is symbolized by unity at the community table. Indeed, the table is such a powerful symbol for the community functioning as community that Paul connects table ethics with some of his most profound statements on the implications of his gospel for Christian living. In Galatians 2:11–14, he answers the issue of eating at separate tables with a discourse on the very core meaning of the gospel (Gal. 2:15–21) and how a community should live out the ethic of neither "Jew nor Greek" (Gal. 3:28). In 1 Corinthians 11:17–34, factions at the table (1 Cor. 11:18–21) represented the profaning of the "body of Christ" (1 Cor. 11:29), a rich term that referred at the same time to the bread as body of Christ (1 Cor. 11:24) and to the community as body of Christ (1 Cor. 12:12–13) that was constituted as such by the sharing of the bread (1 Cor. 10:17). In that same vein, Paul here in Romans focuses on the issue of tension at the table as a way to draw conclusions about Christian living.

In such a diverse community of God, Paul argues, they are to "welcome one another, therefore, just as Christ has welcomed you" (15:7). Here he is drawing on the entirety of his weighty theological argument presented throughout Romans, namely how it is that "Christ welcomed you" when, for example, all of you were "ungodly" and "enemies [of God]" (5:6–10). The ethical outcome of "newness of life" (6:4) and "life in the Spirit" (8:4–6), then, is to apply that same gracious welcome to the other as God had applied it to them and to live out that principle in every part of their life in community.

The irony is that this core theological principle, which Paul saw as the essence of the revolutionary nature of his gospel, almost immediately was overlooked by his ardent admirers. In Galatians, he seemed to be arguing for the inclusion of Gentiles in a Jewish Christian world in which Gentiles were considered second-class citizens. Here in Romans, in what had by then become a primarily Gentile community, he argues for Gentile Christian acceptance of Jewish Christians in their midst. In both cases, his vision was that of the eschatological community of God in which all of God's people, Jews and Gentiles alike, lived together in harmony. Almost immediately, however, his teachings were used to create divisions rather than harmony. When in later history Gentile Christianity eventually triumphed, it turned on the Jews with a vehemence that lasted for centuries. If Paul were alive today, one can imagine that his message would be the same, but directed more specifically to our situation today. One could imagine Paul, once more, urging humility upon Gentile Christians, who owe all they have to their Jewish heritage. One could imagine him arguing for rapprochement and peace between Jews and Christians today. One could imagine him arguing that "welcome one another as Christ has welcomed you" has to mean that the church today, which is so fond of deciding who is worthy of membership, should instead open its doors equally to all people and, following Paul's theme of radical hospitality, should proclaim a message of social justice in a world of injustice.

15:14–16:27. Closing Comments: Plans and Greetings.

In 15:14–33, Paul details his plans to visit them after he has traveled to Jerusalem with the collection he has gathered from the Gentile churches for "the poor among the saints at Jerusalem" (15:26). This collection (see also 1 Cor. 16:1–4) is apparently in response to the agreement reached in Jerusalem years before in which Paul was urged in his mission work among the "uncircumcised" to "remember the poor" (Gal. 2:10). As Paul defined it, it was not only an act of charity but also an act of diplomacy in which Gentile Christians acknowledged their debt to the Jewish Christian community that preceded them (15:27).

Chapter 16 tells us a great deal about how early Christian churches were organized. First we must note how many of the early church leaders Paul mentions here were women. Phoebe (16:1–2), who may, in fact, have been the messenger who delivered the letter, is "commended" to the Romans by Paul. She is a "deacon," which at this time in history designated some form of ministry to the church, as well as a "benefactor" or patron of the church and its leaders. At 16:7, Junia, along with Andronicus (perhaps her husband), is identified as an "apostle," indicating that she held a significant leadership role in this early Christian community. Other women co-workers of Paul include Mary (16:6), Tryphaena, Tryphosa, Persis (16:12), the mother of Rufus (16:13), Julia, the sister of Nereus, and Olympas (16:15).

Paul's special friends, Prisca and Aquila (16:3–5), who are most probably husband and wife, are praised as prominent co-workers who not only "risked their necks for my life" but also hosted the church in their house. They had been co-workers with Paul earlier in Corinth (1 Cor. 16:19). Acts 18:2 includes information from an unknown source that they met Paul in Corinth after having been among the Jews exiled from Rome by Claudius. If that information is correct, they have now returned to Rome where, once more, they have become leaders in the Christian community. Since Paul mentions Prisca first here in Romans (rather than Aquila and Prisca as in 1 Cor. 16:19), it suggests that she had now emerged as the more prominent of the two.

Prisca and Aquila hosted an *ekklesia* (assembly or church) in their house both in Corinth and in Rome. This reminds us that Christian groups met primarily in homes in the first two hundred plus years of Christianity. Indeed, there may be an indication here in Romans 16 of at least five different household churches in Rome: besides the Prisca and Aquila assembly there were also household churches of Aristobulus (16:10), Narcissus (16:11), "the brothers and sisters" mentioned together in 16:14, and the "saints" mentioned together in 16:15. In large cities like Rome and Corinth we should imagine not one large congregation but several "cells" that met in individual homes.

Paul for the Twenty-first Century

Paul's gospel still speaks with power today. His concluding charge to the Romans offers a good summary of his message for today's church: "Welcome one another, therefore, just as Christ has welcomed you" (15:7).

Paul has provided the most powerful vision in the New Testament of a universal gospel, a gospel for all humanity, as encapsulated in the phrase, "as Christ has welcomed you." This vision was based on the biblical themes of the oneness of God and the mercy of God. It was based on the concept of justification by faith through the grace of God, which for Paul was the functional equivalent of Old Testament covenant theology. In effect, Paul understood the Christ event as the means whereby God was now extending his mercy outward from the Jews to embrace all people. When Paul's universalism is properly understood, it negates all forms of theological arrogance, especially supercessionism, which Paul specifically rejected in Romans.

Paul's is a vision that embraces all humanity while acknowledging diversity. It is a vision that is to be lived out in community, encapsulated in the phrase, "welcome one another." Paul imagined the community of God as one without boundaries, where there "is no longer Jew or Greek, there is no longer slave or free, there is no longer male and female" (Gal. 3:28). Life in community is to be lived out in faithfulness to the same ethic as exhibited by the faithfulness of Christ (see also Phil. 2:1–13). The charge to offer open hospitality to all could hardly be defined more radically, for the Christian is to model the same hospitality that is present in the open-ended welcome extended by Christ.

Suggested Resources for the Pastor's Library

Achtemeier, Paul. *Romans*. Atlanta: John Knox Press, 1985.

Beker, J. Christiaan. *Paul the Apostle: The Triumph of God in Life and Thought*. Philadelphia: Fortress Press, 1980.

Boyarin, Daniel. *A Radical Jew: Paul and the Politics of Identity*. Berkeley: University of California Press, 1994.

Cousar, Charles B. *A Theology of the Cross: The Death of Jesus in the Pauline Letters*. Overtures to Biblical Theology. Minneapolis: Fortress Press, 1990.

Cranfield, C. E. B. *Romans*. International Critical Commentary. Two volumes. Edinburgh: T. & T. Clark, 1975, 1979.

Dunn, James D. G. *Romans*. Word Biblical Commentary. Two volumes. Dallas: Word Books, 1988.

_____. *The Theology of Paul the Apostle*. Grand Rapids: William B. Eerdmans, 1998.

Elliott, Neil. *Liberating Paul: The Justice of God and the Politics of the Apostle*. Maryknoll, N.Y.: Orbis Books, 1994.

Fitzmyer, Joseph A. *Romans*. Anchor Bible 33. New York: Doubleday, 1993.

Gager, John G. *Reinventing Paul*. New York: Oxford University Press, 2000.

Gaston, Lloyd. *Paul and the Torah*. Vancouver: University of British Columbia Press, 1987.

Hay, David M., and E. Elizabeth Johnson, eds. *Romans*. Vol. 3 of *Pauline Theology*. Minneapolis: Fortress Press, 1995.

Horsley, Richard A., ed. *Paul and Empire*. Harrisburg, Pa.: Trinity Press International, 1997.

Keck, Leander E. *Paul and His Letters*. Second edition, revised and enlarged. Proclamation Commentaries. Philadelphia: Fortress Press, 1988.

Lampe, Peter. *From Paul to Valentinus: Christians at Rome in the First Two Centuries*. Minneapolis: Fortress Press, 2003.

Nanos, Mark D. *The Mystery of Romans: The Jewish Context of Paul's Letter*. Minneapolis: Fortress Press, 2003.

Sanders, E. P. *Paul, the Law, and the Jewish People*. Philadelphia: Fortress Press, 1983.

Stendahl, Krister. *Paul Among Jews and Gentiles*. Philadelphia: Fortress Press, 1976.

Stowers, Stanley. *A Rereading of Romans: Justice, Jews, and Gentiles*. New Haven, Conn.: Yale University Press, 1994.

White, John L. *The Apostle of God: Paul and the Promise of Abraham*. Peabody, Mass.: Hendrickson, 1999.

5

The Pauline Tradition
Colossians and Ephesians

BONNIE B. THURSTON

The study of Colossians and Ephesians is particularly interesting. Along with Philippians and Philemon, both belong to the group of letters known as the prison epistles, in which the author makes reference to his imprisonment. But did Paul write these two letters or are they products of Paul's disciples? I am reasonably sure Colossians and Ephesians are written toward the end of the first century. As such they are primarily documents showing how Christianity evolved as it moved from its Jewish and Semitic roots into the Hellenistic communities of the early Pauline mission, and, finally, into being the church in the Roman Empire. Their theology is formative for the church even if their study may raise more questions than it answers.

Colossians

Basic Data

Colossians engenders lively debate about authorship. As such it provides an opportunity to examine how scholars go about deciding the question of authorship. Discussions of the authenticity of an epistle revolve around two poles: language and style, and the absence or presence of Pauline concepts.

Careful examination of the language of Colossians reveals that it contains twenty-five words not found elsewhere in Paul's uncontested letters and thirty-four not found elsewhere in the New Testament. At minimum, it has a distinctive vocabulary. Stylistically, Colossians has long sentences with strings of synonyms heaped together and complex strings of participial phrases. The style of Colossians is more liturgical and hymnlike than the

96

briefer, crisper rhetoric (probably borrowed from Cynic-Stoic diatribe) of other Pauline letters. It can be argued that this distinctive vocabulary is due to the fact that the letter quotes traditional materials (hymns, confessions, vice and virtue lists, household codes), and that the longer, more complex sentences are due to the fact that the imprisoned author can be more reflective in his writing. Since language and style alone are not conclusive, scholars look for the absence or presence of Pauline concepts.

Paul's great theological themes—righteousness, justification by faith, salvation, and revelation—are largely absent from Colossians. And at least two theological issues are treated differently in Colossians than elsewhere in Paul. In Colossians, Christ does not reflect the likeness of God, but is God's true representative, making visible what was before invisible (cf. Rom. 8:29, 2 Cor. 4:4, and Col. 1:15.) In Colossians, Christ is the goal of creation (1:16), the subject of the authoritative tradition the believer receives and in which she or he lives (2:6–7). In Colossians the church as body of Christ is a cosmic reality (1:18), not a metaphorical way of expressing mutual Christian dependence as in 1 Corinthians 12:12–27 or Romans 12:4–8. Other departures from Pauline thought include the comparison of baptism with the Jewish rite of circumcision (2:11–12) and the use of the word "mystery" rather than the Pauline term "gospel" (1:26; 4:3).

In my view the debate about authorship is inconclusive. Scholars who hold that Paul wrote Colossians suggest either that it was written from Ephesus between 54 and 56 or from Rome at the end of Paul's life, between 59 and 62. Scholars who think Colossians is pseudonymous believe it was written in Asia Minor by a Christian leader, trained by Paul, between 65 and 90.

Pseudonymity, or the practice of writing in another's name, was common in Paul's world. Proverbs, Ecclesiastes, and the Hellenistic works *Wisdom of Solomon* and *Psalms of Solomon,* are all attributed to King Solomon. Plato wrote philosophical dialogues by putting words in the mouth of Socrates. Jewish works of the second and first centuries B.C.E. claim the authorship of such heroes as Daniel, Baruch, and Enoch. Similarly, disciples of Paul took up the task of preserving his teaching; they wrote for their own circumstances in Paul's name. This was not considered either dishonest or plagiarism. It honored Paul's teaching and gave authority to their own message. The issue is not one of "making things up" but of preserving the apostolic witness and applying it to a new day. Paul's students were making his teaching "relevant."

While the question of authorship is cloudy, we know a fair amount about the Colossian church. Although Phrygians are mentioned at Pentecost (Acts 2:10), the church in Colossae was the result of missionary work in the Lycus valley during the time of Paul's Ephesian ministry. The church existed by mid-century, was apparently founded by Epaphras (1:7–8), and did not know Paul personally (2:1). The many allusions to their non-Christian past suggest the church was made up of Gentiles (1:21, 27; 2:13). Colossae may be the least important city to which a Pauline letter was addressed. Although an important city in the Hellenistic period, its prominence had waned by New Testament times both because its neighbor Laodicea was the seat of Roman administration and because of an earthquake in the early 60s. Strabo calls it a "small town." In Paul's time its population included indigenous Phrygians and Greeks and Jews from Mesopotamia and Babylon. Cicero notes that 11,000 Jewish men lived there.

Methods for Interpretation

In my view there is no substitute for the "old-fashioned" historical-critical method, which includes textual study, careful translation of the text, lexical studies, analysis of Greek style, comparison with other New Testament works, and placing the letter and its issues in historical context. That said, three other and more recent New Testament disciplines have added much to our understanding of Colossians and a fourth is yielding new insights.

Excellent studies have been done of the use of traditional materials in Colossians and, relatedly, of the literary forms in the letter. Having noticed that Colossians seems to quote other documents (a Christ hymn, for example) and to use traditional Hellenistic literary forms (vice and virtue lists, a household code), scholars have studied the parallel forms and their uses and noted how the Colossian author has appropriated and/or adopted them. A seminal work in this field is George E. Cannon's book *The Use of Traditional Materials in Colossians.*

Second, rhetorical studies of Colossians, particularly careful analysis of the way the author deals with the false teachers in Colossae, has revealed much about both the Colossian church and the problems faced by first-century Christianity in a religiously plural environment. Third, sociological analysis of the Greco-Roman environment, particularly marriage legislation and analysis of the Greco-Roman household, has enriched our understanding of the parenetic (practical instruction) material in Colossians, particularly the household code (3:18–4:1).

Finally, feminist analysis, which begins with a "hermeneutic of suspicion" and insists that texts which are not liberating are not scripture, has yielded fascinating new readings of Colossians. When one begins with the question "who benefits from this text?" new insights occur. Feminist analysis, especially of the household code, has challenged traditional views.

Social and Religious Context

Because they are closely related, I treat the social and religious contexts of the Colossian letter together. The situation of the writer of Colossians is unclear since we do not know with certainty who wrote it or its provenance, although I suspect it dates from the last quarter of the first century in Asia Minor. The context of the Colossian church is much clearer.

Colossae was a "has been" town. Having been the principal city in the Lycus Valley and on the main trade route from Ephesus to the Euphrates, it had been eclipsed by its neighbors, Ephesus, Laodicea, and Hierapolis. Long known for its wool industry, the city had shrunk in size, but was still cosmopolitan in population, home to Phrygians, Greeks, and Jews from Mesopotamia and Babylon. And it was religiously pluralistic. There is evidence from the coinage of Colossae of the worship of the Ephesian Artemis, Laodicean Zeus, and Artemis. Other Greek deities, as well as Egyptian Isis and Serapis, the cult of Cybele, and Mithraism were in evidence. The text of the letter also suggests that a syncretized form of Judaism was present in Colossae as well as an early form of gnostic thought.

As far as the writer of Colossians is concerned, the primary "social problem" is false teaching. This is frequently referred to as the "Colossian heresy." The letter describes this "heresy" as "philosophy" (2:8) and "self-imposed piety" (2:23). It is understood to be in accordance with "the elemental spirits of the universe" (2:8), to teach worship of angels (2:18), Jewish cultic practices and ascetic rigor (2:16, 20–21), and to stress wisdom and knowledge (2:22–23). The possible sources of this false teaching include sectarian Judaism, some form of syncretistic Judaism, wisdom speculation, Pythagorean philosophy, and incipient gnosticism. Recent scholarship favors some form of Jewish Christianity as the "culprit," although one highly influenced by Hellenistic astrology and the mystery cults.

The writer's refutation of this false teaching centers in his christology. Christ, he argues, is superior to any supernatural beings (1:15–20). The cosmic principalities and powers are captives in Christ's triumphal procession (2:15). The absolute supremacy of Christ is the theological core of the letter.

Literary Data

Colossians follows the usual pattern of a Hellenistic letter. An opening formula (1:1–2) is followed by a prayer for the recipients and a thanksgiving (1:3–12), which moves seamlessly into the body of the letter (1:13–4:6). As is characteristic of Paul's letters, the body is divided into a theoretical/theological section (1:14–2:23) followed by practical exhortation/parenesis (3:1–4:6). The letter closes in standard form with greetings (4:7–17) and a closing formula (4:18). The closing greetings are unusually extensive. This is characteristic of Paul when he writes to churches that do not know him personally; it is his way of establishing relationship.

Beyond the epistolary form, the other literary issue in Colossians is related to the traditional materials embedded in the letter. Clearly discernable in Colossians are a hymn (1:15–20), vice and virtue lists (3:5, 8, 12), and a household code (3:18–4:1).

The bulk of scholarly literature on Colossians deals either with the false teachers or with the "Christ hymn" of 1:15–20. As does Paul in Philippians 2:6–11, the Colossian writer seems to be quoting an already existing Christian hymn. These hymns are of immense importance because they are the earliest articulation of the church's christology and reflect its earliest liturgy. Reading the text in Greek, one notices the shift of pronouns from the surrounding material. Verses 13–14 are first person, vv. 15–20 third, vv. 21–23 second and first. Verses 15–20 exhibit repeated words, an almost metrical rhythm, and the use of relative constructions, all of which characterize liturgical material. Additionally five words found here do not appear elsewhere in Paul. This evidence suggests vv. 15–20 are an insertion.

Within this text there are several nominal sentences beginning with "he" (1:15, 17, 18). In two (1:15a, 18b) "he" is "firstborn," followed by the clauses "for in him" (1:16, 19). These repetitions suggest two ways of viewing the hymn's stanza structure: a two-part division with vv. 15–18a describing Christ and creation and vv. 18b–20 describing Christ and reconciliation, or a three part division of vv. 15–16 discussing creation, vv. 17–18a its preservation, and vv. 18b–20 its redemption. Either way, the hymn is introduced to establish the preeminence and supremacy of Christ. Everything is subject to him; "all" appears eight times in the hymn, "heaven and earth" twice.

The full text of the hymn is as follows (printed in a three stanza format):

He is the image of the invisible God, the firstborn of all creation;
for in him all things in heaven and on earth were created,
things visible and invisible,
whether thrones or dominions or rulers or powers–
all things have been created through him and for him.

He himself is before all things,
and in him all things hold together.
He is the head of the body, the church;

He is the beginning, the firstborn from the dead,
so that he might come to have first place in everything.
For in him all the fullness of God was pleased to dwell,
and through him God was pleased to reconcile to himself all things,
    whether on earth or in heaven,
by making peace through the blood of his cross.

The vice and virtue lists the writer uses in 3: 5, 8, 12 are a standard form of ethical teaching in the period and are found in writings by the Stoics, Hellenistic Jews, and early Christians in *The Didache* (especially 1–6) and *The Epistle of Barnabas* (especially 18–20). The form is hortatory in nature and ethical in content. In them an imperative verb is followed by lists of vices or virtues, usually in identifiable groups. In Colossians, for example, each list contains five vices or virtues related to a central theme; 3:5 lists sexual sins (compare these to the Holiness Code of Leviticus 18), 3:8 detriments to relationship, 3:12 how to deal with other believers. The lists are related to a series of baptismal metaphors ("put to death" 3:5, "stripped off" 3:9, "clothe yourselves" 3: 10, 12, 14).

The household code in 3:18–4:1 has been extensively studied. Again, there are extensive parallels to the form in contemporary literatures. Such codes are found in Stoic sources (Seneca, Epictetus, Diogenes Laertius) and in Hellenistic Judaism (Pseudo-Phocylides, Philo, Josephus). Colossians provides the first Christian example of a form that became widely used in early Christian literature (see Eph. 5:22–6:9; 1 Tim. 2:8–3:13; Titus 2:1–10; 1 Pet. 2:13–3:7; *Didache* 4: 9–11; *Epistle of Barnabas* 19: 5–7 and *1 Clement* 21:6–9). Its philosophic origins are traced to Aristotle's *Politics* (1.1254b), which teaches that the patriarchal domination of women by men enhances the proper functioning of the household and thus the state. The well-run (i.e. male-dominated) household is the foundation of, and associated on a symbolic level with, the well-run state.

The number of words that occur only in 3:18–4:1 suggest it existed prior to the letter. In form, it is characteristic of its literary type. Each exhortation has an addressee and a command to him or her that is followed by the motive for obeying the command; subservient parties are addressed first. In Colossians there are three sets of reciprocal exhortations arranged from closest to least close relationship. As in all the codes, the greatest attention is paid to wives and slaves suggesting that they were a particular problem. (Note that Paul's letter to Philemon, which deals with the issue of slavery, is also thought to have been written to Colossae.)

Organization

As noted above, Colossians follows the usual form of a Hellenistic letter: opening formula (1:1–2), prayer and thanksgiving (1:3–12), body (1:13–4:6), greetings (4:7–17), closing (4:18).

1:1–12. SALUTATION, PRAYER, THANKSGIVING

The opening lines of the letter are conventional. Timothy, frequently listed as Paul's co-author, is known to the churches of Asia Minor and could corroborate Paul's teaching, since the apostle is not known personally to them (1:4). In view of the false teaching, I wonder if "faithful brethren" in v. 2 intends to exclude the unfaithful. The absence of reference to Jesus Christ in the grace wish in verse 2b is an anomaly.

The thanksgiving (1:3–8) is one long Greek sentence and is intended to establish friendly relations with the Colossian church. It begins and ends with love (1:4, 8) and introduces the major concern of the letter by stressing the "word of the truth" (1:5) and its teacher, Epaphras, who brings the Pauline gospel.

Deciding where the petitionary prayer ends is difficult. I suggest that vv. 9–12 are the prayer and that vv. 13–14 begin a description of what God has done that moves smoothly into Christ's work in the hymn (1:15–20).

The prayer lifts up four petitions: (1) that they may be filled with knowledge of God, spiritual wisdom, and understanding (1:9); (2) that they may lead worthy lives and "bear fruit" (1:10); (3) that they may be made strong with God's power (1:11); and (4) that they may be able to endure "everything" with patience (1:11, a hint of persecution in Colossae?).

1:13–23.

This section stresses the all-sufficiency of Christ. The letter's purpose hinges on the author's ability to convince the Colossian church that Christ is the ultimate power and authority in the universe. Verses 13–14 describe in the language of the exodus (and in the vocabulary of the Dead Sea Scrolls) what God has already accomplished in Christ: delivered, transferred, redeemed.

As noted above, 1:15–20 is a hymn, "worked over" and inserted to demonstrate how everything falls into the sphere of Christ's authority. The hymn makes seven christological claims: Christ is the image (*ikon*) of God; he is before all things; he is the firstborn of creation; through his agency all things are created; in him all holds together (a word used by Plato and the Stoics for world unity); he is head of the church; and he is firstborn from the dead. Because of this "fullness," nothing is outside the scope of Christ's redeeming power.

Verses 21–23 form another long Greek sentence made up of an introductory clause ("you who were" 1:21), main clause ("he has now reconciled" 1:22), purpose clause ("to present you" 1:22) and conditional clause ("provided that" 1:23). The sentence applies the terms found in the hymn to the particular situation of the Colossian church. The once-then-now pattern is clearly Pauline (Rom. 6:17–22; 7:5–6, 11:30; Gal. 4:8–9). Verse 23 gives the first hint that all is not well in Colossae; some are drifting from what they first received. The final phrase of the verse about Paul's service of the gospel introduces the section that follows.

1:24–2:5.

Material on Paul's ministry might seem a digression except for the fact that the writer must establish why he has the right to intervene in a situation with which he has had no direct prior connection. Or perhaps the author is worried that Paul's imprisonment called the apostle's ministry into question. The approach is first to address the Colossian situation (1:24–26) and then that of the wider church (1:26–29). The section presents the reasons for Paul's suffering, a comment on the inclusiveness of the gospel, and a call to the Colossian church to be vigilant. Particularly interesting are the six things that the author understands about ministry. It involves suffering (1:24), is by God's commission (1:25), is "for your sake" (1:24), is "to make the word of God fully known" (1:25), is inspired and energized by God (1:29), and understands that physical absence does not mean unconcern (2:1, 5).

Verse 24 is perplexing. I suspect that it does not mean that the writer thought Christ's sacrifice on the cross was incomplete. The remark is best understood in relation to Jewish texts that speak of the suffering and tribulation that must be endured before the Messiah comes (see *Mishnah Sotah* 9:10). The writer may understand that Paul's sufferings shorten the time before Christ's second coming. The verse proposes that Paul had a deep sense of identification with Christ, something of what the mystical union of being "in Christ" meant for the apostle. But it also meant that for him the "word of God" is Jesus Christ who is the central feature in God's plan of history to be made known to the Gentiles (1:26–27).

The vocabulary of 2:2–3 is that of Greek religion ("mystery," "wisdom," "knowledge") and thus well suited to the letter's recipients. False teaching is first raised in 2:4–5. This is rhetorically clever. The author has already made a strong case for Christ's supremacy and has established his authority to speak to the situation.

2:6–23.

What is the problem in Colossae? Determining its exact nature is difficult; we hear only one side of the conversation, and what we hear is polemical. Although I encourage readers of this introduction to consult the substantial literature on the issue, for brevity's sake let me suggest that the problem is that some teachers in Colossae (the "false teachers" or "opponents") are combining faith in Jesus with other religious powers. They suggest Christ is one in a hierarchy of religious powers and seek strictly to regulate "lifestyle" issues (dietary laws, ritual observances, etc.). Their "philosophy" (2:8) teaches that ascetic practices and cultic requirements are a prelude to religious experience that will lead to supernatural knowledge.

The writer objects because Christ as all-sufficient liberates from such legalisms. He describes the false teaching as doctrine (2:8–15) then as practice (2:16–23). The false teaching is "not according to Christ" (2:8), a "shadow" (that is not enduring, 2:17, 22, 23) and useless and ineffective (2:23). In 2:9, 14, 15 the writer lifts up Christ and his accomplishments, the effects of which are described in 2:10–13. Christ the victor has disarmed these so-called "powers" and led them in a triumphal procession (2:15). He has not only disarmed the powers, but delivered the Colossians from their influence. Thus all their "requirements" are "of no value" (2:23).

3:1–4:6.

The practical exhortations in Colossians presuppose the christology of the letter. The writer assumes that if people believe correctly, they will act correctly. These exhortations contain three forms of traditional material: vice and virtue lists, a household code (both discussed above), and *topoi* or brief, pithy admonitions.

The first four verses of chapter 3 provide the theological motivation for what follows. As in 2:12 and 20 the "if" presupposes a "yes" or "it does." The principle is that what one thinks determines who she is and what she does. Since Christians are identified with Christ who is above, they are to live as "above" people. In 3:3 the metaphor of baptism, which dominates 3:5–17, first appears.

The personal behavior of Christians is the subject of 3:5–17. The "things that are on earth" of 3:2 are to be "put to death" (3:5–11) and the things "above" are to be put on (3:12–17). The image of changing clothes alludes to baptism and was a common metaphor in the ancient world for spiritual initiation. The passage contains two lists of five vices (3:5, sexual sins, the characteristic sins of paganism, and 3:8, sins of the tongue, the sins that disrupt Christian fellowship) and one list of five virtues, Christ-like qualities that bear on social relationships (3:12). Chapter 3 verse 11 sounds like an early baptismal formula, but notice that "male and female" is omitted from the list of divisions healed in Christ (cf. Gal. 3:2).

The household code (3:18–4:1) was discussed above. While it reflects the cultural assumptions of the Greco-Roman world and a conservative social stance, the writer uses it to show how domestic relations are to be governed by Christ's lordship (3:18, 20, 23, 24; 4:1). Those preaching and teaching the code today should note that it follows from 3:17.

The final exhortations in the parenesis (4:2–6) are *topoi,* that is, brief, self-contained teachings with only loose connection to their context. *Topoi,* like vice and virtue lists, are probably borrowed from Cynic-Stoic teaching and are often linked together by a theme word. These particular exhortations suggest that the Colossians support the Christian mission through prayer (4:2–4) and through their behavior (4:5–6). They remind that all encounters with nonbelievers are missionary opportunities.

4:7–17.

Paul typically closed his letters with greetings. These greetings are longer in letters to churches the apostle did not found. Here the author, in the name of Paul, commends the messengers carrying the letter (4:7–9), conveys greetings from fellow prisoners and co-workers (4:10–14), and sends his own greetings and messages (4:15–17). The author also respectfully greets Nympha and the house church she leads with no apparent discomfort. (Was it to her home that the letter to Laodicea, no longer extant, was addressed [4:15–16]?) The greetings give "flesh and blood" to the message of the epistle and reveal its "human geography."

4:18.

Colossians closes with a "grace wish," which omits mention of Christ. This is a departure from normal Pauline practice in his other letters.

Colossians also has an autograph. The letter says it is signed by the hand of the imprisoned apostle, by manacled hands, to remind the Colossians of the authority granted by the apostle's suffering.

Theological Themes

The primary theological issues in Colossians are christological and ecclesiological. After Epaphras brought the Pauline gospel to Colossae, teachers arose who attempted to combine faith in Jesus with other religious powers. They taught a hierarchy of such powers and that they could be approached through preparatory aesthetic practices and cultic worship. The writer of the letter counters those claims by rehearsing the extent of Christ's power and authority. Christ is supreme in creation and church (1:15–20) and has through his death reconciled people to God (1:21–23; 2:13–15). Therefore, Christ has supremacy in the lives of individuals (2:9–12) and in Christian households (3:17–4:1). Much of Colossians is praise of the power of Jesus Christ.

In earlier Pauline letters, the church is depicted as the body of Christ with an emphasis on mutual responsibility of all of the members for the welfare of the other (1 Cor. 12:12–27). In contrast, in Colossians the church as the body of Christ has Christ as its head; thus the church is the sphere in which Christ exercises his Lordship. Through baptism, one has not only died and been buried with Christ (as per Romans 6), but is raised with him (2:12; 3:1) and made alive with him (2:13). The writer thinks that the resurrection to new life has already taken place (which contrasts with Paul's language elsewhere, as in Rom. 6:4). What is to be hoped for, then, is not resurrection to new life, which has occurred, but the full manifestation of the life that is "hidden with Christ in God" and "will be revealed with [Christ] in glory" (3:3–4).

Importance for the Church of the Twenty-first Century

Religious pluralism is not a new phenomenon. The writer of Colossians would understand the problematic issues raised by "New Age" religion, with its tendency toward syncretism, toward "picking and choosing" from a great smorgasbord of beliefs and practices. Colossians reminds Christians of every age of the supremacy of Jesus Christ, that, "Jesus Christ is Lord" with all that lordship implies. Christ's Lordship is "sung" in Colossians in the hymn in 1:15–20, a very early example of both the church's liturgy and christology. Christ is understood in terms of the wisdom tradition and exalted as God's image, agent, and co-regent. Whatever the century, this will always be the case.

The letter reminds us not to be taken captive by hollow and deceptive human systems, but to remember who Christ is and what he has done, "to live…in him" (2:6), and to know our lives as "hidden with Christ in God" (3:3) with all the mystery and wonder of that state of life.

Relation of Colossians and Ephesians

Before introducing Ephesians, it is important to note ways it is related to Colossians. Of 155 verses in Ephesians, seventy-three have parallels in Colossians. Roughly twenty-six percent of Ephesians has Colossian parallels. (Compare, for example, Col. 1:1–2/Eph. 1:1–3; Col. 3: 12–15/Eph. 4:2–4; Col. 3:16–17/Eph. 5:19–20.) Furthermore, the two letters exhibit many structural and stylistic similarities.

Several reasons for these similarities are suggested. Some scholars explain that Paul wrote Colossians and Ephesians from prison in a relatively brief time period. Others believe that the author of Ephesians used Paul's letter to the Colossians as an outline, or conversely that Ephesians was written first and Colossians is an abbreviated version of it. Another theory is that both Colossians and Ephesians are dependent upon a third Pauline document no longer extant (the letter to Laodicea?). The issue is not easily resolved. For our purposes it is enough to note the similar structure, themes, and theological vocabulary of the two letters and to posit some literary relationship.

Ephesians

Basic Data

Whether Ephesians was written by Paul or by one of his disciples is debated, and questions have been raised about the recipients of the letter and whether the document is a "letter" (a matter discussed in the "Literary Data" section).

Luke's Acts of the Apostles devotes significant material to the church at Ephesus in Acts 18:24–20:1 and 20:16–21:1. Acts describes Paul's nearly three-year residence at Ephesus in his third missionary journey (ca. 54–57 C.E.). From his Ephesian imprisonment Paul probably wrote 1 Corinthians, parts of 2 Corinthians and perhaps Philippians and Philemon. But this does not square with the text of Ephesians, whose author is under arrest and sends Tychicus to supplement the letter with oral information (3:1–2; 6:20–22) because he and the recipients are unknown to each other (1:15; 3:2). How can this be if Paul spent three years in Ephesus?

Furthermore, those who question Pauline authorship note the difference in Ephesians' vocabulary from the Pauline corpus. It has forty words not found elsewhere in the New Testament and ninety not found elsewhere in Paul's letters. (Many of these appear in noncanonical and early Christian writings, suggesting a later date for Ephesians.) Stylistically Ephesians has long sentences (nine of which are over fifty words long) composed of relative and participial clauses and synonyms amassed in a non-Pauline way. The letter reflects a unity of Jew and Gentile that Paul's communities were working toward but had not yet achieved. There are doctrinal differences as well. In Ephesians the word *church* is used only of the universal church (all believers everywhere) and not as Paul uses it for believers in a particular location. In Ephesians the church is built on the apostles and prophets (2:20), not on Christ as in Paul's undisputed letters. The parousia is absent from the letter. As opposed to Paul's concessionary attitude toward marriage in 1 Cor. 7, here it is treated with the highest honor. Finally, Ephesians does not include the personal details that Paul's letters to churches usually evince.

The best manuscript traditions omit "in Ephesus" in 1:1. Marcion, the second-century collector of Paul's letters, believed Ephesians was the letter to the Laodiceans (Col. 4:16). Other early commentators thought Ephesians was an encyclical sent to various churches. It has also been suggested that Ephesians was originally written as a "cover letter" or summary document to accompany a collection of Pauline letters and later was detached and circulated on its own.

We don't know with certainty who wrote Ephesians or to whom it was written. Three points of view predominate: that Paul wrote Ephesians to the church at Ephesus about 60 C.E.; that Ephesians was written in the last quarter of the first century by a disciple of Paul's as an encyclical to the churches in Asia Minor (of which Ephesus was the most prominent); or that the letter was written *at* Ephesus as a preface to a collection of Paul's letters made there and later it circulated alone.

In my view the author of Ephesians is a Jewish Christian from Asia Minor, a disciple of Paul's who is concerned to promote the apostle's teaching. He knew the Colossian letter well, had mastered Paul's thought, and was applying it to situations that arose after Paul's death. Since Ephesians was known to 1 Clement (95–115 C.E.), it must have been written after Paul's death in the early 60s and before the end of the first century, probably about 90.

Methods for Interpretation

I prefer standard historical-critical methods to approach Ephesians. Tradition-history studies have underlined the Ephesian writer's use of Hebrew scripture and of Jewish thought. Although there are only five direct allusions to the Old Testament in Ephesians, that material was formative in the author's understanding; he reminds Gentile Christians that they are heirs of this heritage from Israel.

Form critical studies compare the structure of Ephesians to that of undisputed Pauline letters and look at the creedal, doctrinal, and catechetical materials in the letter. Perhaps most importantly, they have pointed out the liturgical quality of the letter, especially of chapters 1–3 (which Markus Barth has noted have the character of prayer), and have suggested that the letter contains many hymnic fragments.

This is not to ignore other critical methods. A recent sociological study by C. Arnold, *Ephesians, Power, and Magic,* places Ephesians in the context of religious expression in Asia Minor, noting that Ephesus was a center for magical practice and explaining the effect of that on Ephesian Christianity. Studies of visionary experience in Hellenistic religion have also shed light on Ephesians.

Recent scholarship on the Qumran documents suggests that Ephesians may have its roots not in Hellenistic gnosticism, but in the Judaism of Qumran. Such studies note that the language and style of Ephesians' Greek is replete with Semitic influences, that the vocabulary of Ephesians (especially the term *mysterion*) has Qumran parallels, and that many ideas in Ephesians have parallels in the Qumran documents. Both the dualisms and the parenetic materials in Ephesians are also fundamental to Qumranic thought. (More information on these matters is found in J. Murphy-O'Connor and J. Charlesworth, eds., *Paul and the Dead Sea Scrolls*, New York: Crossroad, 1990.)

Finally, feminist analysis of Ephesians has focused on the household code in 5:21–6:9 and pointed out that no woman is mentioned in the letter, and that its language (see, for example, 4:18) and metaphors (6:11–17) are masculine.

Social Context

In the New Testament period, Ephesus was the first city in the Roman province of Asia, and its capital. A seaport and commercial center, Strabo described it as the "largest emporium in Asia" (Geography, XIV, 1, 24). It ranked with Antioch of Syria and Alexandria as one of the three great cities of the Eastern Mediterranean. Something of its splendor is indicated by the fact that the main street from the harbor to the theater (which seated 24,000) was thirty-five feet wide. Ephesus boasted a stadium rebuilt under Nero (54–68 C.E.) and a library.

For Paul, Ephesus had many of the same attractions as Corinth. It was strategically located and was a major crossroads. What was taught at Ephesus would travel far and wide. It had a strong intellectual tradition (Thales, Anaximander, Anximenes, Herodotus, and Hippocrates were all from near by) and was a meeting place for ideas from the East and West. And the religious traditions of Ephesus were rich and varied.

Ephesus remained a strong Christian center. The Revelation to John was probably written near there. Second-century traditions connect John the Evangelist and Ephesus and an early collection of the four gospels circulated from Ephesus. Jerome Murphy-O'Connor has suggested that half the documents of the New Testament, or two-thirds of its content, originated in Ephesus. According to Christian legend, the Virgin Mary is said to have lived out her days in Ephesus (and modern visitors are taken to see her home there). And Ephesus was the site of the council in 431 C.E. that condemned Pelagian and Nestorian thinking and reaffirmed the Nicene Creed.

Ephesus has been extensively excavated, and a large reconstruction of the city is on display in Vienna. Unfortunately, while the reconstructions at the site of Ephesus are impressive, they are pieced together from various periods and are historically unreliable. The library of Celsus, which dominates the reconstruction, post-dates Paul.

Religious Context

The religious context of Ephesus is crucial to the letter. Before Ionian colonization in the first millennium B.C.E., there existed an Ephesian cult of a goddess similar to the Phrygian Cybele and Phoenecian Astarte, which the Greeks associated with Artemis. A temple of the Ephesian Artemis was built in Ephesus as early as the eighth century B.C.E. and rebuilt in successive stages over the centuries. A larger version was begun about 550 B.C.E. and was dedicated in 430 B.C.E. Tradition says it was burned on the night Alexander the Great was born in 356 B.C.E.

The Hellenistic temple of Ephesian Artemis that Paul knew was one of the seven wonders of the ancient world. Begun before 350 B.C.E., it was 160 feet wide and 340 feet long with one hundred columns each fifty-five feet high. Acts indicates that the worship of Artemis (also known as Diana) included an extensive votive industry (namely, "silver shrines," Acts 19:23–41). Processions on the goddess's birthday were long and elaborate; worshipers entered the city by the Magnesian Gate and left by the Coressian Gate.

A typical statue of Artemis of the Ephesians depicts the goddess with multiple breasts, evidently a fertility symbol. The image wore a necklace made of the twelve signs of the zodiac indicating how popular astrology was in the first century. Furthermore, gods and goddesses were often understood according to astrological formulae.

The terminology of Ephesians (head/body imagery, mystery, fullness, age, etc.) also suggests a gnostic presence in the city. Some scholars have noted that of all the Greco-Roman cities, Ephesus was the most hospitable to magicians and sorcerers. This is attested by many magical papyri from Ephesus and environs and by the fact that magic was an integral part of the worship of Artemis. Judaism in Ephesus would almost certainly have been influenced by these forces as would early Christianity. And both would have had to cope with a lively ruler/Imperial cult in Asia Minor.

It is little wonder that commentators have seen in Ephesians reflections not only of Judaism, but of the mystery religions, of gnosticism, and of the syncretistic magical practices that were part and parcel of first-century religion. Of particular concern were "the powers" (which we encountered in Colossians) and their relationship to the lordship of Jesus Christ.

Literary Data

The most pressing literary matter is whether Ephesians is a letter in the sense of other Pauline letters. The usual opening formula (1:1–2) omits the destination. There is a prayer/thanksgiving, but it is unclear exactly where it ends (1:3–10? 14?). The theoretical section of the letter (1:3–3:13) ends with a prayer (3:14–21) and is highly liturgical. Standard Pauline parenesis follows (4:1–6:20), but as is the case in Colossians, careful readers find much traditional material (vice and virtue lists, a household code) and, unlike Colossians, there are no personal greetings or travel plans of the author at the end of the section. There is a brief reference to Tychicus and his mission (6: 21–22) and a standard closing (6:23–24). The impersonal tone and the absence of individuating information have led many to suggest that Ephesians is best read as a treatise or encyclical rather than a letter.

Ephesians is also remarkably liturgical in tone. Markus Barth's commentary notes that a good deal of the content is public prayer and that the diction of the letter is that of Jewish and pagan prayer=. It contains two long prayers (1:3–20?; 3:14–21), doxologies (1:3; 3:20–21), a benedictory prayer (6:23–24) and several texts that have been called hymns (1:3–14; 1:20–23; 2:4–10, 2:14–18) or hymn fragments (5:14). Furthermore, the language of "sealing" from early baptismal liturgies appears in 1:13–14 and 4:30, and 4:17–24 makes use of baptismal allusions.

As is the case with Colossians, the parenetic section of Ephesians (4–6) contains much traditional material. A virtue list (4:2) and vice list (5:3–5) are followed by exhortations to virtue (5:6–20). The household code (5:21–6:9) is a greatly expanded version of its Colossian counterpart. (For a description of these forms, see the discussion on Colossians above.)

Finally, the writer of Ephesians skillfully unites the scriptural traditions of the Old Testament with the language of Hellenistic religions, especially the mystery religions and gnosticism. It is a way to remind the Gentile Christians of Ephesus of their connection to the God of Israel who, through Jesus Christ, has delivered them from "following the ruler of the power of the air" (2:2) and made them "citizens with the saints and also members of the household of God" (2:19).

Organization

Although without the personalizing elements of a Pauline letter, Ephesians mimics its form: opening formula (1:1–2), prayer and thanksgiving (1:3–23), body (divided into theology in 2:1–3:21 and praxis in 4:1–6:20), and closing (6:21–24). I have refined these divisions somewhat in this brief commentary.

1:1–23. SALUTATION, THANKSGIVING, INTERCESSION

The letter opens by appealing to Paul's authority as an apostle. The author writes in an official capacity (perhaps to Ephesus, see "Basic Data" above) and by the will of God to the "saints" (Christians) "who...are faithful" (or "also faithful," suggesting some were not) "in Christ Jesus" (1:1). The letter opens with the "in Christ" formula that appears thirty-four more times in Ephesians, not so much indicating profound, personal identification with

Christ (as in Paul's undisputed letters) but an instrumental usage, indicating Christ as the channel though which God works. The grace wish in verse 2 is standard Pauline practice.

The prayer begins, in Jewish fashion, with a beatitude ("blessed be the God...who has..."). The thanksgiving (1:3–14) is a long panegyric on what God has done for Christians in Christ: blessed them, chosen them, destined them for adoption, redeemed them, forgiven their trespasses, made known to them the mystery of his will, and provided an inheritance for them. The language of the thanksgiving echoes religious language found in Hellenistic religions (heavenly places, wisdom, mystery, fullness), thus uniting, in literary form, Jewish and Gentile elements whose unity the letter will later proclaim has been accomplished in fact. The thanksgiving stresses the forethought and orderliness of God's initiative and Christ's agency in providing redemption and an inheritance so that Christians might live "for the praise of his glory," a phrase repeated twice (1:12, 14).

If the thanksgiving stresses spiritual blessings, the intercession (1:15–23) stresses "spiritual eyes" with a prayer that the Ephesians will "see" ("with the eyes of your heart enlightened" [1:18]) what God has done for them. Verses 15 and 16 suggest that the author and the letter's recipients are unknown to each other. The prayer proper is that God will, first, give them a spirit of wisdom and revelation (1:17) in order that they may, second, know the hope to which God has called them (1:18) and the greatness of God's power (1:19). Christians are promised the spirit and revelation, the hope of a calling, the riches of an inheritance, and the power of faith.

That power was at work in Christ, about whom six christological assertions are made: God (1) raised him from the dead (1:20); (2) seated him at the right hand in the heavenly places (1:20); (3) put him above any other rule or dominion or power (1:21); (4) put him above every other name in any age (1:21); (5) put all things under his feet (1:22); and (6) made him head over all things for the church, his body (1:22–23). The Ephesian writer is doing exactly what the writer of Colossians did at the outset of that letter: establishing the supremacy of Christ. "In him" is redemption (1:7), an inheritance (1:11), and "the seal of the promised Holy Spirit" (1:13).

2:1–22.

Chapter 2 treats the two things God has done in Christ: saved sinners by grace (2:1–10) and united what was previously estranged (2:11–22). Verses 1 to 10 summarize the Pauline gospel, twice stressing that "by grace you have been saved" (2:5, 8). Verses 1–3 describe the "before" state when Christ was absent from life both externally (2:2) and internally (2:3). The "but" at the beginning of verse 4 rhetorically cancels this "before" state and introduces what God in mercy and love has done (2:4–7; the perfect passive in v. 5 says it has happened and continues to be true): made us alive, raised us up, and seated us with Christ in the heavenly places. This redemption is to show God's grace. Verses 8–10 remind the readers that they are saved by grace through faith, not as a result of works. In fact, any good works that were done were prepared beforehand by God. Grace is God's initiative and faith is the human response. Works are a requisite of faith, not a pre-requisite.

Verses 11–22 move beyond individual salvation to that of the Gentiles as a group and continue the before/after rhetoric with the basic comparisons: far/near (2:13) and aliens/strangers (2:12) to citizens/members of the household (2:19). The main idea is that the estrangement of Gentiles from Israel is now overcome. Both Jewish Christians and Gentile Christians have been built into God's household; the reconciliation is an accomplished fact. Verses 11–12 describe the estrangement. Again the "but" (2:13) introduces what Christ has done (2:13–18) and its positive results (2:19–22). The family language in vv. 19–22 echoes the "inheritance" idea from chapter 1.

This section of the letter introduces the high ecclesiology of Ephesians. This church is different from those reflected in Paul's undisputed letters: the division between Jew and Gentile has been overcome (2:14); the church is built not only on Jesus Christ, but also on the apostles and prophets (2:20). God's shrine is now the people of God. Using the understanding of a temple as the dwelling place of God, the Ephesian writer suggests that together Christians are God's residence. Chapter 2 reminds Gentile Christians of their hopeless condition before Christ, and Jewish Christians that only Christ reconciles to God. The theme of the reconciliation of Jew and Gentile continues in chapter 3.

3:1–21.

Chapter 3 places the reconciliation Christ has effected in the context of the eternal plan of God. Like chapter 2, chapter 3 falls into two sections: verses 1–13, a discussion of "the mystery" (3:3, 4, 5, 9) of God's plan (3:9, 11) (and the most personal part of the letter); and a prayer (3:14–21). The reference to Paul's imprisonment in 3:1 leads to what has been called a "digression" on his ministry. Certainly 3:1 and 3:13 form an inclusio; the bracketed material continues the discussion of reconciliation in chapter 2. The mystery that the Gentiles are now fellow heirs (compare 2:13–20 and 3:6) has been revealed to the apostles and prophets (compare 2:20 and 3:5). Paul is understood to be a servant of this good news, the one appointed to proclaim to the Gentiles "the boundless riches of Christ" (3:8) and the plan of God. The reason for the church's existence is give in v. 10, and what God is doing by means of the church is explained in the language of Hellenistic religions (mystery, wisdom, rulers and authorities in heavenly places).

The wonder of what God has planned and accomplished in Christ sends the writer to his knees (3:14–21) in a prayer of adoration (3:14), petition

(3:15–19), and doxology (3:20–21). Those who think Ephesians is a liturgical document about baptism understand this section of the letter to be a prayer for the newly baptized. That "every family...takes its name" from God (3:15) reminds again of the power of and ownership by God. The writer prays that the letter's recipients may be strengthened in their inner being, that Christ may dwell in their hearts through faith, that they may have power to comprehend the encompassing love of Christ, and thus that they be filled with the fullness of God to whom the writer ascribes glory in vv. 20–21. The "Amen" at v. 21 makes a natural break between the two major sections of the letter.

4:1–6:20.

Following the organization of a Pauline letter, practical instruction on conduct follows theology. In chapters 1 to 3 Christ's work was to unify earth and heaven, Jew and Gentile. The fruit of this work is to be borne by Christians in the church.

For the second time, the author of the letter appeals to the authority gained by his imprisonment (3:1; 4:1) in exhorting the Ephesians to "lead a life worthy of the calling to which you have been called" (4:1). They are "to maintain the unity of the Spirit in the bond of peace" (4:3). This unity is manifested in "one body and one Spirit...one hope of your calling, one Lord, one faith, one baptism, one God and Father of all" (4:4–6). To explain the differences among Christians, and to indicate that unity is not uniformity, the author enumerates various gifts given to the church: "that some would be apostles, some prophets, some evangelists, some pastors and teachers" (4:11). Each gift is given, not for the benefit of the recipient, but for the whole church (4:12–13). Verse 14 (and 5:6–7) suggests that the problem of false teaching may not be peculiar to Colossae. The body metaphor from 3:6 is reintroduced and elaborated on in 4:15–16. The repetition of "love" in 4:1–16 (vv. 2, 15, 16) suggests it is crucial to the unity of the body.

Christians who had been Jews (as the writer of the letter apparently had been) had a moral foundation based on the Torah. Gentiles had no such grounding, and their behavior, especially in sexual matters, was, to say the least, casual. Therefore the writer sounds a clear moral and ethical note in 4:17–5:20 that describes the moral implications of the new life "put on" in baptism, the way of life that will preserve the unity of the church. The old way of life (4:18–19, 22, 25–31; 5:3–5, 18) is to be "put away" or put off (4:22, 25, 31) and the new way put on ("clothe yourselves..." [4:24]). As in earlier sections of the letter, the writer compares before and after. Since one doesn't forbid what isn't being done, we may conclude that the church in Ephesus had difficulty with anger (4:26), thievery (4:28), evil talk (4:29; 5:4), sexual impropriety (5:3, 5) and drunkenness (5:18). The antidote to such behavior is to "be imitators of God" (5:1), to "live in love" (5:2), to "try to find out what is pleasing to the Lord" (5:10) and to be "filled with the Spirit" (5:18). The section 4:17–5:20 exhibits special concern for sins of the tongue and for sexual sins, as both are especially destructive to community. Notice, as well, that for each negative prohibition, the author provides a positive alternative.

The household code in Ephesians (5: 21–6:9; a description of the form occurs in the discussion of Colossians above), depicts the effect Christ's Lordship should have in the domestic sphere. The material is expanded and theologized from its prototype in Colossians. The largest section is devoted to marriage (5:22–33) in part because marriage is related to the central theme of the epistle. Marriage is to reflect Christ's intimate love for the people who exist in union with him. In a culture in which the male head of the household could wield unquestioned authority, Ephesians makes mutual submission (5:21) the principle, but does not question social structure. The general rule for households within the church is mutual subordination in which each person shows more concern for the rights and needs of others than for his/her own.

Note that in Greek "be subject" does not appear in 5:22. In English translations it is carried over from 5:21 or added to bring the verse into conformity with Col. 3:18. The Greek indicates that what the author is interested in here (as in 1 Cor. 7:2) is monogamy. Most of the material in the code is devoted to husbands (5:25–33) and slaves (6:5–8) because, in the first instance, the husband is the party likely to domineer, and in the second, slaves in Christian households were a particular threat to the social order since they were to be treated as siblings in Christ (see Gal. 3:28 and Philemon). Also note that everybody in the list (wives, husbands, children, fathers, slaves, masters) is obedient to somebody and that Christ's Lordship (and likeness to Christ) is the motivation for each group's behavior (5:21, 24, 25, 29; 6:1, 4, 5, 6, 9).

The reader should recall all that was "put off" or "put away" when reading what is "put on" in 6:10–17. Verses 10–18 may well have been addressed to the newly baptized embarking on the Christian life. Their real enemies are spiritual (6:12 recalls the rules and authorities and powers and dominions of 1:21; 2:2; 3:10; 4:9–10, the cosmic focus of the letter) and their strength is derivative (from God, 6:10, 13). The passage is probably influenced by Isaiah 59:17 and the figure of God as warrior who comes to defend. Verses 14–17 catalogue items of equipment. Each piece is needed if vulnerability at some point is to be avoided, and, with one exception ("the sword of the Spirit, which is the word of God" [6:17]), each piece is defensive, not offensive.

The parenetic section of the letter closes with an exhortation to prayer (6:18–20) for the church generally and for the apostle in particular. The theme of the mystery of the gospel is reiterated (6:19) along with the imprisonment of the author (6:20).

6:21–24.

Ephesians 6:21–22 reproduces almost verbatim Colossians 4:7–8. While Tychicus was Paul's messenger and known to the churches of Asia Minor, his introduction at the end of Ephesians, which mentions no other person, seems spurious. The closing formula, 6: 23–24, is long and unusually formal. Grace and peace are typical Pauline words, and certainly any pastor would want peace, love, and faith for his congregations.

Theological Themes

Theologically, the author of Ephesians wants to demonstrate that the unity of Jew and Gentile is the result of a divine plan. Secondarily, the author is reminding a Gentile church of its Jewish origins, of the blessings it receives thereby, and the responsibilities those blessings entail.

The theological center of Ephesians is the unity of all things that is found in Christ. Like Colossians, Ephesians asserts the cosmic dimension of Christ's power and exhibits a "high christology." The unity of Jews and Gentiles has already been effected in Christ (2:11–22); the church is to be the visible symbol of that unity (3:8–11; 4:4–6). Ecclesiology is central to Ephesians. The author uses three images in the letter to depict the church: the body of Christ, the holy temple (2:20–22; 4:12, 16), and the bride. The church's reason for being is to bear witness in the whole universe to God's plan and the unity Christ effects (3:10–12).

But Ephesians is not just abstractly theological. Ethical material figures importantly in the letter. Christians show forth their true identity by the quality of life they live. Through their exemplary lives and good works, Christians in Ephesus show themselves worthy of their high calling (2:10; 4:1).

Importance for the Church of the Twenty-first Century

Ephesians is important for our understanding of the extent and power of Jesus Christ's influence. It describes the cosmic effects of Christ's death and resurrection and the continuity of that "event" with what God had been doing in the history of Israel. Ephesians reminds us that history is not a random series of events, but part of the great plan of God, effected through Jesus Christ, to reconcile all things and all people to God.

Ephesians has a highly developed ecclesiology. It articulates the staggering responsibility that God has laid on the church: to make known God's own wisdom and variety (3:10). With John 17, Ephesians encourages ecumenism and church unity and calls the whole church to maturity, growth, and building itself up in love.

Finally, Ephesians teaches that commitment to Jesus Christ has serious implications for life and action. It is not enough to confess Jesus Christ as personal Lord and Savior unless one is willing to live as the slave of that

Master. Those Christ reconciles, he intends and expects to change, "to lead a life worthy of the calling to which [they] have been called" (4:1), which involves "putting away" behavior that the dominant culture may simply wink at. No aspect of human life is outside Christ's transforming call, certainly not sexual life or family relationships.

Suggested Resources for the Pastor's Library

Arnold, Clinton E. *Ephesians, Power, and Magic.* Cambridge: Cambridge University Press, 1989.

Barth, Markus. *Ephesians.* Anchor Bible 34A and 34B. New York: Doubleday, 1974.

Cannon, George E. *The Use of Traditional Materials in Colossians.* Macon, Ga.: Mercer University Press, 1983.

Dunn, James D. G. *The Epistles to the Colossians and to Philemon.* The New International Greek Testament Commentary. Grand Rapids: Eerdmans, 1996.

Francis, Fred & Wayne A. Meeks, eds. *Conflict at Colossae.* Missoula, Mont.: Scholars Press, 1975.

Lohse, Eduard. *Colossians and Philemon.* Hermeneia. Philadelphia: Fortress Press, 1971.

Mitton, C. Leslie. *Ephesians.* New Century Bible Commentary. Grand Rapids: Eerdmans, 1981.

Pokorny, Petr. *Colossians: A Commentary.* Peabody, Mass.: Hendrickson, 1991.

Schweizer, Eduard. *The Letter to the Colossians.* London: SPCK, 1982.

Thurston, Bonnie. *Reading Colossians, Ephesians, 2 Thessalonians.* New York: Crossroad, 1995.

6

Jesus and the Gospels

DENNIS E. SMITH

Who *was* Jesus? It seems like such an obvious question. And the answer seems obvious as well. The story of Jesus is told in the gospels. And it seems to us to be a straightforward, historical account.

But history is not as easily found in the gospels as it may seem. Even a preliminary investigation will raise questions. First one might note the variations in the gospel accounts. Did the incident in the temple take place at the beginning of Jesus' ministry, as in John, or at the end, as in Matthew, Mark, and Luke? Was the last meal of Jesus with the disciples a passover meal, as in Matthew, Mark, and Luke, or was it on the night before the passover meal, as in John? In that same context, did Jesus therefore die on the afternoon of Passover, as in Matthew, Mark, and Luke, or did he die on the afternoon before Passover when the lambs for the passover meal were being slain, as in John?

Or, one might ask, what do we do with Jesus stories found in noncanonical literature? Given the fact that the canon was fluid for the first few hundred years of Christianity, and that the Jesus stories seem to have floated around in an oral form for some time before being written down, how can we know that only the canonical stories are to be judged reliable? For example, there are a number of fascinating stories about the boy Jesus while still five years old doing amazing and even frightening deeds of power. Once, for example, he was jostled by another child in the village and, upset at this, the boy Jesus struck the child dead on the spot (*Infancy Gospel of Thomas,* 4). Though stories like this may grate on our ears, they were obviously quite popular, and fervently believed, by some groups of early Christians.

What about the widespread use of prophetic literature as the basis for Jesus stories? When the gospel writers tell a story in such a way that it follows exactly the pattern in an Old Testament text, as is often found in the passion narrative, for example, have they constructed their telling to fit the Old Testament text, or did it happen that way and they later found the same pattern in the Old Testament?

Such questions as these are merely the tip of the iceberg. The more one studies the gospels in detail, the more the historical questions grow and the more complex they become.

But this is nothing new in gospel studies. In fact, it has been noticed almost from the beginning of the history of the gospels. Not long after the four gospels began to emerge as the church's definitive versions of the Jesus story, that is, whenever they began to take on canonical force in early Christianity, their differences were being confronted and dealt with. An early attempt to harmonize the gospels is the *Diatessaron* of Tatian. In this late second century work, the variants in the four gospels are harmonized into one story. But Tatian's work was not successful in solving the dilemma. Had it been successful, it might have eventually supplanted the four gospels. But the four gospels remained as they are, four versions of the Jesus story.

Today we often approach the Jesus stories as Tatian did, by harmonizing them. For example, the generic Christmas story is a harmonized one, in which wise men *and* shepherds visit the child Jesus in a stable. In the canonical accounts, however, the visit of the wise men takes place only in Matthew's version, and took place at a house (2:11). It is only in Luke where the child is visited in a stable, and in that case only by shepherds (2:7, 12, 16). Each of these versions of the birth narrative has its own emphasis and theology. To harmonize them creates a new story. And that is, in fact, the problem created by all harmonizations. While a harmony of the gospels seems to fit our need for clarity in storytelling, all harmonies suffer from the fact that they create a new story, with a new emphasis and theology, and thereby they undermine the canon itself. The motivation to produce a harmony is usually innocent and pious. But the end result can be a butchering of the canon, even though that was not the intent.

Thus the first point in gospel analysis has to be this, that since we have four gospels in our canon, each of the four needs to be heard on its own. If we had been in charge of setting up the canon, we might have insisted that there be only one gospel, so as to avoid confusion. But that is not the case. Indeed, there can be an advantage to the multiplicity of gospel stories, for thereby the story of Jesus emerges as much more complex and rich.

When we take these multiple versions of the Jesus story, however, and ask about the singular historical Jesus, then in a sense we are following in the footsteps of Tatian. And we too can be subject to the critique that in attempting to create a single story out of the disparate accounts we are, in fact, proposing a new story to take the place of the canonical "stories." This is a valid critique of historical Jesus studies. Yet, as modern people, we cannot avoid asking historical questions. So we engage in this task with our eyes open, hoping to find insights into the reality of the historical Jesus, but not proposing thereby to overthrow the canon. What we seek instead is to understand the process whereby the Jesus of history became the Christ of faith.

The History of Historical Jesus Research

As late as the 1970s in New Testament studies, the issue of the historical Jesus was virtually off the map. One could do New Testament research at the highest level, or construct a theology of the New Testament as Rudolf Bultmann had done for earlier generations, and relegate the historical Jesus to the briefest of notations. As Bultmann put it, "the message of Jesus is a presupposition for the theology of the New Testament rather than a part of that theology itself" (*Theology of the New Testament,* New York: Scribner, 1951, 3).

For most scholars then as well as now, the issues were nicely defined by the century-old proposition of Martin Kähler, that one had to distinguish between "the historical Jesus" and "the Christ of faith." We can illustrate this point with an analysis of a standard statement of faith like the following: "Jesus died on the cross as a sacrifice for the sins of the world." If we ask ourselves which part of this statement is historical and which is not, we have to conclude the following: the phrase "Jesus died on the cross" describes the historical event; the phrase "as a sacrifice for the sins of the world" represents a christological interpretation of the significance of that event. Clearly Jesus did not die on an altar, which is what a sacrifice would require. The concept that the death on the cross is to be interpreted as "a sacrifice for the sins of the world" is therefore best understood as an after-the-fact interpretation by the early church. The first statement belongs to the category of "the historical Jesus" and the second to the category of "the Christ of faith."

Early scholarly studies of the historical Jesus were analyzed at the beginning of the twentieth century by Albert Schweitzer in his famous work, *Quest of the Historical Jesus* (originally published in 1906). Schweitzer argued that all previous attempts to define the historical Jesus had failed, primarily because, in trying to make Jesus relevant, they had merely succeeded in imposing on the figure of Jesus their own values. Schweitzer's own reconstruction of the historical Jesus presented him as an eschatological prophet who proclaimed, wrongly, that the end of the world was near. Schweitzer's study was so effective in demolishing earlier attempts and so convincing in presenting Jesus as a misguided eschatological prophet that it effectively spelled the end of historical Jesus research for the next fifty years. Scholars became cynical about whether the historical Jesus could ever be successfully reconstructed and, even if it were possible, whether it would matter for New Testament theology. This view is still found among many scholars today.

However, new perspectives began to develop in the '50s and '60s, notably marked by an essay by Ernst Käsemann on "The Problem of the Historical Jesus" in which he argued that the historical Jesus was more than a presupposition but rather was an essential part of New Testament theology.

James M. Robinson marked this new phase with the title of his 1959 book *A New Quest of the Historical Jesus* (Naperville, Ill.: A.R. Allenson). The "new quest" was fueled by the view that not only was it possible to construct a valid profile of the historical Jesus, it was important to do so for properly understanding Christian origins and the foundations of christology. An important study by Norman Perrin followed in the mid-'60s, *Rediscovering the Teaching of Jesus* (New York: Harper & Row, 1967). in which he summarized in readily accessible form the criteria that had developed for determining the historicity of the sayings of Jesus.

Yet a breakthrough in scholarship had not yet taken place. One important "life of Jesus" that did emerge in this period was by Günther Bornkamm (*Jesus of Nazareth*, 1956; English translation (New York: Harper) 1960), but while it was widely used, it did not have a major impact on New Testament studies. Most scholars proceeded under the assumption that Bornkamm had pretty much said all that could be said and that it did not amount to much.

The real change came in the '80s with the advent of the Jesus Seminar. This project was the brainstorm of Robert W. Funk, a New Testament scholar who for years had been testing the waters on this subject with a series of groundbreaking essays. Funk was convinced that the quest for the historical Jesus was a valid and necessary project for New Testament research, that the methods were in place to accomplish that task, and that if a seminar of scholars could be gathered to take it on, then it could be done with dispatch, rigor, and clarity.

Funk had always been known to be an individual who pushed the envelope in scholarship. Yet even Funk could not have fully anticipated the firestorm created by the Jesus Seminar. Since he insisted that the project should not only be collegial, but that it should also be public and take the responsibility to report its findings to the public, the seminar soon became a known entity in the popular mind and associated with all that is radical about biblical scholarship. Yet the controversy had a laudable effect, because it forced the historical Jesus question to the front burner of New Testament research. Whereas in the '70s there was basically one book on the historical Jesus in the pastor's library, namely Bornkamm's, we have now witnessed an explosion of Jesus books with no end in sight.

Thus it is clear that the issue of the historical Jesus has moved to the forefront of New Testament scholarly debate. It seems as if everyone now has an opinion on the subject, and as if every scholar has a Jesus book somewhere in his or her vita or publishing plans. Yet it is not as easy to do Jesus research today as some would think. The scholarship produced since the early '80s has been immense, and has caused this field of research to become a virtual sub-specialty in its own right. Historical Jesus scholarship has become a complex, sophisticated arena of research. That research begins with an analysis of the sources.

The Sources for the Jesus Story

The Gospels

Our basic sources for the Jesus story are the gospels, primarily the canonical gospels, although the noncanonical gospels should not be excluded out of hand for historical research. A gospel is a hybrid type of ancient literature. As a genre, it is related to ancient biography, but it is more than a biography. Gospels were written to serve faith communities and in that sense represent a form of religious literature. Each gospel writer can be understood as a type of "preacher" whose gospel represents a type of "sermon."

A gospel is, of course, a rather peculiar form of "sermon" since the community it addresses is nowhere directly named. Yet when we read between the lines, we can draw conclusions about what kind of audience a gospel was written to address, whether a Jewish or Gentile Christian audience, and what kinds of issues it was written to address.

The gospels tell stories about Jesus and quote sayings of Jesus, and in doing so, they draw upon materials available in the "tradition." Some of this was in oral form, some in written form. It is not clear in any of the gospels exactly what individuals might lie behind these Jesus traditions. When the gospels tell their stories they speak with the voice of an anonymous third person. Where the information came from is not part of the tradition; this is apparent because the stories are told without reference to sources.

The gospels are a form of narrative literature. That means that they follow standard rules and contain standard features of narrative literature. Like other narrative literature, the gospels have plot, character development, and utilize literary forms and symbols. Notice, for example, how often the narrator provides necessary information to make a story make sense. In Mark's gospel, when Jesus says, "Do you not see that whatever goes into a person from outside cannot defile, since it enters, not the heart but the stomach, and goes out into the sewer?" it is the narrator who tells us, "Thus he declared all foods clean" (Mk. 7:18–19). Gospel writers often tell us what someone is thinking. For example, on an occasion when Jesus dines at the home of a Pharisee, we the listeners to the story are privy to the Pharisee's thoughts to himself: "When the Pharisee who had invited him saw it, he said to himself, 'If this man were a prophet, he would have known who and what kind of woman this is who is touching him—that she is a sinner'" (Lk. 7:39). A narrator may tell us what happens when Jesus is alone and no one else is there to witness it, such as when Jesus prays alone in Gethsemane (Mk. 14:32–42; Mt. 26:36–46; Lk. 22:39–46). Or the narrator may utilize the privileged vantage point of the storyteller to describe events that happen simultaneously in two different locations, so that, for example, the reader or listener of the story is able to relate what is happening during Jesus' trial to what is happening at the same time elsewhere in the courtyard when Peter denies Jesus (Mk. 14:53–72; Mt. 26:57–75; Lk. 22:54–71; Jn. 18:12–27).

The Relationship of the Gospels

Students of the gospels have long noticed their similarities as well as differences. Three of the gospels–Matthew, Mark, and Luke–appear to be especially closely related to one another, while the fourth, John, stands apart. The first three are called the synoptic gospels by scholars, in reference to the fact that when their texts are laid side by side in a "synopsis" they can be seen to have a word-for-word relationship with one another.

As an example of gospel relationships, let us compare the different versions of the baptism of Jesus:

MATTHEW 3:13–17

[13]Then Jesus came from Galilee to John at the Jordan, to be baptized by him. [14]John would have prevented him, saying, "I need to be baptized by you, and do you come to me?" [15]But Jesus answered him, "Let it be so now; for it is proper for us in this way to fulfill all righteousness." Then he consented. [16]And when Jesus had been baptized, just as he came up from the water, suddenly the heavens were opened to him and he saw the Spirit of God descending like a dove and alighting on him. [17]And a voice from heaven said, "This is my Son, the Beloved, with whom I am well pleased.'"

MARK 1:9–12

[9]In those days Jesus came from Nazareth of Galilee and was baptized by John in the Jordan. [10]And just as he was coming up out of the water, he saw the heavens torn apart and the Spirit descending like a dove on him. [11]And a voice came from heaven,"You are my Son, the Beloved; with you I am well pleased." [12]And the Spirit immediately drove him out into the wilderness.

LUKE 3:21–22

[21]Now when all the people were baptized, and when Jesus also had been baptized and was praying, the heaven was opened, [22]and the Holy Spirit descended upon him in bodily form like a dove. And a voice came from heaven, "You are my Son, the Beloved; with you I am well pleased."

The Priority of Mark

The first issue raised by this comparison of texts is the question of sources. How did the three gospels come to have such similar material? The similarities between these gospels cannot be explained by simply positing that they are independent versions of the same story. Rather their word-for-word relationship makes it clear that they must have a written source in common. It is like two students trying to explain to their teacher how the two of them got answers to an exam that are the same word for word. Clearly somebody has to be copying somebody else. Such a word-for-word relationship has to be a literary one.

The same is true with the gospels. For example, notice in the various versions of the baptism story in the *Revised Standard Version Bible* the basic word-for-word aspect of this brief segment (with only minor variations):

Matthew: "behold, the heavens were opened and he saw the Spirit of God descending like a dove and alighting on him; and lo, a voice from heaven, saying..."

Mark: "immediately he saw the heavens opened and the Spirit descending upon him like a dove; and a voice came from heaven..."

Luke: "the heaven was opened, and the Holy Spirit descended upon him in bodily form, as a dove, and a voice came from heaven..."

Different theories have been proposed as to who was copying whom. Some scholars have proposed that Luke was the first gospel, and Matthew and Mark copied it. Others have proposed that Matthew was the first gospel and that Luke and Mark copied it. But by far the majority of scholars accept the thesis that Mark was the first gospel and Matthew and Luke copied it. The theory of the priority of Mark explains more of the data than either the priority of Luke or the priority of Matthew. For example, Matthew and Luke are seen to have in common Mark's outline of the story, and contain over 90 percent of the content of Mark. Most scholars today accept the theory of the priority of Mark, and that is the theory we will be utilizing in this book.

The Source "Q"

While Matthew and Luke used Mark as their basic source, they also enlarged Mark's story, and in doing so they used another source that they shared in common. This other source is only known to us through the traces it left in Matthew's and Luke's use of it. We identify it at those points where Matthew and Luke show word-for-word similarities in materials that are not found in Mark. The source for this material is called "Q" after the German word *Quelle,* which means "source." Based on what we can reconstruct from Matthew's and Luke's use of this source, it consisted almost entirely of sayings of Jesus with no overall narrative structure and, especially, no account of the death of Jesus. Although we have never found a copy of "Q", we have found a copy of another gospel that looked a lot like it, the *Gospel of Thomas.* This "gospel," like "Q," consists of a collection of sayings of Jesus and anecdotes about Jesus with no underlying narrative structure and no story of Jesus' death. Scholars call this type of gospel a "sayings gospel" to distinguish it from a narrative gospel.

For an example of Q, note that immediately after the baptism story, Mark mentions a temptation of Jesus by Satan in the wilderness, but gives no details (Mk. 1:12–13). Matthew and Luke give an elaborated version of the temptation, consisting of three questions by "the devil," each followed by Jesus' answer (Mt. 4:1–11; Lk. 4:1–13). The questions and answers are exactly the same in Matthew and Luke, though the orders differ, indicating that they share a common source for this data, namely Q, but use it in their own ways. Other examples of Q can be found in Matthew's "Sermon on the Mount" and Luke's "Sermon on the Plain," in which large sections of Matthew's sermon are also found in Luke's sermon (Mt. 5:1–7:28; Lk. 6:17–7:1). This indicates that Q must have already had a "sermon" section, which Matthew and Luke both use but edit in their own ways. Matthew's sermon is larger and contains material that Luke has placed elsewhere in his gospel. For example, Matthew includes the Lord's Prayer in the Sermon on the Mount (6:9–15) whereas Luke places it later in another context in his gospel (11:1–4). The best explanation for such a phenomenon is that both are using the same source, Q, and that many of the sayings in Q were given without a context, so that it was up to the individual gospel writer to choose a context for the sayings.

The Sources "M" and "L"

Matthew and Luke also each have material found only in their gospels. Each has an independent version of a birth narrative of Jesus, for example. This material came from sources used only by these individual authors, or it represents their own creative adaptation of the tradition. It is conventional in scholarship to refer to Matthew's special material as "M" and to Luke's special material as "L." However, the use of these labels does not mean that scholars assume that all of "M" or "L" comes from a source. It may simply represent the author's creative input to the tradition.

The Theology of the Gospels

As storytellers and preachers, the gospel writers are only marginally historians. Certainly "what really happened" is part of what they are after, but they may not know the facts for certain. In any case, they place their emphasis on "what it really means" and they tell their stories accordingly.

For example, notice how something so simple as choosing a context for the sayings material represented an interpretation. Consider the saying of Jesus, "Is a lamp brought in to be put under the bushel basket, or under the bed, and not on the lampstand?" (Mk. 4:21). Mark locates this saying in the context of a discussion about the meaning of the parables (4:21), and follows it with the saying, "there is nothing hidden, except to be disclosed;

nor is anything secret, except to come to light" (4:22). The implied meaning of the "light under a bushel" image, then, is that though the kingdom is a mystery now, its meaning will eventually be fully revealed. Matthew locates the "lamp under a bushel" saying in the following context:

> You are the light of the world. A city set on a hill cannot be hid. Nor do men light a lamp and put it under a bushel, but on a stand, and it gives light to all in the house. Let your light so shine before men, that they may see your good works and give glory to your Father who is in heaven. (Mt. 5:14–16, RSV)

Here the image of the "lamp" refers to the mission of the disciples, with an emphasis on the exhortation not to hide the "light" that they bear. Luke uses the saying twice, once in the same context as Mark's, and a second time paired with the following saying: "Your eye is the lamp of the body. If your eye is healthy, your whole body is full of light; but if it is not healthy, your body is full of darkness" (Lk. 11:34). Here the meaning of the saying is applied to the issue of spiritual health, with the image of the "light" representing an inner light within the individual. Each of the gospel writers had to choose a context for sayings that lacked a context in the tradition. They did so because they had no choice, since they were placing the sayings in a narrative context. The choices they made were based on their interpretations of the meanings of the sayings.

The gospel writers also edited their stories to fit their theologies. For example, in the story of the baptism of Jesus quoted above, notice how the different versions represent different interpretations of the basic story. In Mark's version, it is only Jesus who is said to see the heavens open ("he saw") and the "voice...from heaven" speaks specifically to him: "*You are* my Son, the Beloved; with you I am well pleased (emphasis mine)." The story therefore tells of a personal epiphany to Jesus and functions as a commissioning story for the beginning of his ministry. Matthew interprets the story differently, however, and so inserts a conversation between Jesus and John the Baptist concerning the appropriateness of Jesus being baptized in the first place. The reason given echoes a theme emphasized throughout Matthew: it is in order "to fulfill all righteousness" (see also Mt. 5:17, 20). Consistent with this perspective, when Jesus is baptized the voice from heaven speaks not to Jesus but to those who are present at his baptism, "*This is* my Son, the Beloved, with whom I am well pleased" (emphasis mine). Rather than providing information to Jesus, the voice in Matthew provides a witness to others. Luke edits Mark also. First, by mentioning the arrest of John prior to the baptism (Lk. 3:18–20) rather than after the baptism (as in Mk. 1:14), Luke rather oddly leaves indistinct in his story exactly who baptized Jesus. Second, while Luke has the voice from heaven speak to Jesus just as it does in Mark ("You are..."), he edits the description of the event so as to suggest it was a phenomenon to be seen by all: "the heaven was opened, and the Holy Spirit descended upon him in bodily form like a dove." Like Matthew, Luke downplays the implication found in the source text, Mark, that the event is a private revelation to Jesus; rather he makes it a public event.

As they told their stories, the gospel writers were compelled to edit them as well, for the stories had to make sense as "sermons" to their individual congregations. The gospel writers were therefore more than storytellers, they were also theologians.

The Pre-Gospel Jesus Tradition

When the gospel writers wrote their gospels, they utilized a variety of sources, some of which we have identified above. But the earliest traditions about Jesus must have been in oral form. Preachers in the early Christian communities most likely utilized traditional sayings of Jesus or stories about Jesus in their sermons as they had been passed on to them. As oral tradition was passed on, it was subject to a variety of versions as each teller would tell the story just a bit differently. That is one reason why there is such variety in the Jesus tradition.

From Gospel Traditions to the Historical Jesus

As has been argued above, the Jesus story comes to us in a variety of versions that exhibit a process of transmission and editing by a variety of early Christian preachers over a period of several generations. There was but one historical Jesus, but we have many versions of Jesus in the tradition. In order to get back to the reality that was the historical Jesus, then, we have to get back beyond the tradition to its earliest layers. To a certain extent, this process resembles the task of archaeology, in which later layers of the material remains are peeled back, so to speak, so as to expose the earliest layer.

Distinguishing Between Sayings and Deeds

The Jesus tradition can be divided into two types: sayings and deeds. The sayings of Jesus traditionally have greater force in the historical analysis, since they can potentially come from Jesus himself. Deeds or stories about Jesus are potentially less reliable, since they cannot come from Jesus himself but can only be transmitted by someone else who describes what he or she witnesses. As we all know, witnesses to the same event can describe it in widely varying ways.

Issues in the Growth of the Tradition

We begin our study of the Jesus tradition with the assumption that some of the data is likely to be historical. But even historical data gets edited as it is transmitted and retold. We have given some examples of this process above. But editing of historical data is only part of the story. It is also the case that stories about Jesus get created. In fact, this is a point that is clear to all students of the Jesus tradition, because all can agree that at least the noncanonical literature is full of created materials. In some of the noncanonical gospels, we find, for example, a thoroughly gnostic Jesus, a far cry from the Jesus of the canonical gospel tradition. So we have clear evidence that Jesus sayings and stories were created in Jesus communities. The question is how much of the canonical data may fall into the "created" category, even though it, too, might be created within pious communities of faith.

Criteria for Historical Jesus Analysis

To analyze the data with as much objectivity as possible, most scholars work with a set of criteria by which one can draw probable conclusions about historicity of the Jesus data. It should be said from the outset that everyone who plays this game, that is to say, everyone who works from a scholarly perspective, must play by the same rules. All scholars therefore have to make judgments as to which data is historical and which is not, and in doing so, have to make available the basis of their judgments for scrutiny by others. No scholar can successfully argue that everything in the gospels is historical, because there are too many contradictions in the gospels. Even the most conservative of scholars will be forced to make such judgments. What the careful reader must look for is the method being applied. It is easy to overlook bad methodology if the results are comforting; that is to say, if a scholar paints a picture of Jesus that we find comfortable, we may not hold that scholar to as high a standard as we would one who painted a picture of Jesus that was not appealing. But in actuality, the argument must be based on good evidence and defensible criteria no matter what the conclusions are. The following criteria are adapted from the list developed by Steve Patterson in his book *The God of Jesus*. They are representative of the methods used by most scholars.

THE CRITERION OF MULTIPLE ATTESTATION.

This criterion provides a means for identifying the earliest materials in the Jesus tradition. It is based on the principle that data found in more than one independent source predates the sources in question. But in order for this principle to work, the sources must be independent. Thus the same data found in Mark and Q, for example, could be surmised to predate both of these, since Mark and Q seem to be independent of one another. But the same data found in Matthew, Mark, and Luke would not qualify under this criterion, because in that case there would really only be one source, namely Mark. Besides Mark and Q, another potentially early and independent source is the noncanonical *Gospel of Thomas*. Although in its present form it dates from the third century C.E., it often appears to have preserved an early form of certain Jesus sayings that is independent of the synoptic tradition. This is a debatable issue among scholars, with some arguing for the presence of early independent data in *Thomas* and others arguing that *Thomas* was not independent of the synoptics but is derived from them. If *Thomas* is used as a valid source, however, the result is that it enhances rather than undermines the arguments for historicity of canonical data. Thus the parable of the great feast, which is attested in both Q and *Thomas*, becomes a prime candidate to be included in the historical Jesus database on the basis of multiple attestation (see Mt. 22:1–10; Lk. 14:16–24; *Gospel of Thomas*, 64). It should be noted, however, that the weakness of this criterion is that it identifies only the earliest layers of the tradition. It cannot in and of itself verify that an early layer also derived from Jesus and not from his followers. It therefore functions best when used in conjunction with other criteria.

THE CRITERION OF DISTINCTIVENESS.

This criterion provides a means to identify Jesus sayings that appear to be unique to Jesus. It is also known as the criterion of dissimilarity. It is one of the most widely used and reliable of criteria, but it has its problems as well. It derives from the principle that data that is distinct in the tradition, that lacks any similarity to the preaching of the early church, most likely derived from Jesus. The strength of this criterion is that it identifies data in the Jesus tradition that cannot easily be accounted for in any other way except as having come from Jesus. It therefore identifies that which was distinctive about Jesus. Its weakness is that it is blind to those aspects about Jesus that may not have been distinctive or that may have been shared with his culture. Those aspects about Jesus must be identified by means of other criteria. A significant example of the use of the criterion of distinctiveness is the claim by Brandon Scott that all of the parables as a whole should be included in the historical Jesus data base (*Hear Then the Parable*). His point is that the parable is a distinctive form of metaphorical speech and is found to occur in the tradition only on the lips of Jesus. Based on the criterion of distinctiveness, whereby all of the parables as a group qualify as distinctive to Jesus, the parable of the prodigal son, which is attested only in one source, Luke, can be included in the historical Jesus database.

THE CRITERION OF EMBARRASSMENT.

This criterion provides a means to identify sayings that seem unlikely to have originated in the church because they would appear to have been an embarrassment. Thus their appearance in the Jesus tradition would seem more likely to derive from the historical layer. One of the most widely cited examples of this criterion is the charge that Jesus was "a glutton and a drunkard, a friend of tax collectors and sinners!" (Q: Mt. 11:18–19; Lk. 7:33–34). The argument is that the church is not likely to have originated such a charge; therefore it is thought to derive from the historical Jesus level itself. But once this data is placed in the historical Jesus database, the challenge then becomes how to interpret it, a challenge that has been met in a variety of ways by scholars. Some scholars think it represents a truth about Jesus. Others think it represents an untrue scurrilous charge about Jesus.

THE CRITERION OF COHERENCE.

This criterion allows one to include data because it coheres with data already identified by other criteria. It functions whenever a coherent profile of Jesus begins to emerge from the data already amassed. Based on that profile, other data that is consistent with it can be included. For example, based on the charge that Jesus was "a glutton and a drunkard, a friend of tax collectors and sinners," many scholars would include the story of Jesus dining with tax collectors and sinners in the historical Jesus database (Mt. 9:10–13; Mk. 2:15–17; Lk. 5:29–32) as a story that coheres with the saying. The interpretive question that then emerges is what Jesus might have meant by such dining practices. Consequently, even after identifying data as historical, it still falls to the interpreter to propose what it might mean. It is when all of the historical data is considered together that one paints the most credible picture.

THE CRITERION OF EARLY CHRISTIAN HISTORY AND INTERPRETATION.

This is a negative criterion. It provides a means for identifying material that derives from the period after Jesus. It is based on the observation that sometimes the gospel data reflect issues, events, and interpretations that derive not from the time of Jesus but from the time of the church that arose after Jesus' death. This is not surprising since the Jesus tradition was transmitted and developed in the context of early Christian preaching and worship. There would be a natural tendency to make the tradition relevant to the context in which it was used. For example, in Matthew, and Matthew alone, Jesus refers to the church as an institution and teaches about disciplinary rules within the church (16:18–19; 18:15–22). Yet the church did not exist in this form in Jesus' lifetime, nor is it probable that either Jesus or his disciples envisioned that the "church" would evolve out of the Jesus movement. Consequently, these sayings in Matthew are judged by this criterion not to have derived from the historical Jesus but from the preaching of the early church, in which instrustions about how leadership in the post-Easter church was to be exercised would be placed in the mouth of Jesus.

CRITERIA FOR THE DEEDS OF JESUS.

The criteria above have their greatest clarity when applied to sayings of Jesus. Sayings are distinct because they can derive from Jesus himself.

Stories, however, are a different matter. Stories about the deeds or actions of Jesus by their very nature must derive from someone other than Jesus. Different observers could obviously have different ways of describing the same event. And, just as in the case of the sayings tradition, stories about Jesus could easily be generated in the period after his death when he would have become a legendary figure in the imagination of the people. When judging stories, then, the issue is not the credibility of Jesus but the credibility of the one telling the story. One way to classify Jesus stories is to view them as typifications. That is to say, while the individual details of a story might be questionable, the story itself may be judged to be a typification of a historical detail about Jesus. In this way, the deeds can be evaluated according to the same criteria as the sayings as listed above. Thus the story about Jesus eating with tax collectors and sinners (Mk. 2:15–17), which was evaluated under the criterion of coherence above, may not, in fact, qualify as a record of a specific historical event. Notice, for example, how vague the story is about how the Pharisees, who were not at the table, could challenge those who were at the table. It is difficult to place the scene in a real dining room in the ancient world. On the other hand, the story can easily be seen as a typification, as a way of saying, "Jesus is the kind of person who would do something like this." The story even lends itself to such an interpretation, because it concludes with a saying of Jesus that interprets the event as a symbol for his entire ministry: "I have come to call [or invite to the table] not the righteous but sinners" (Mk. 2:17). That which it typifies about Jesus, that Jesus centered his ministry in some way on social outcasts, could then qualify to be included in the historical Jesus database. Similarly, the Jesus Seminar has concluded that the individual stories about Jesus, exorcising demons are difficult to affirm as specific historical events, but that which they typify, namely that Jesus was an exorcist, *can* be affirmed as historical (*Acts of Jesus* 33).

Issues in the Historical Jesus Debate

The use of the criteria outlined above can be seen as a preliminary gathering of data. It is when those data are put together and interpreted that a credible profile of Jesus can emerge. Of course, scholars differ in their assessment of the data. And so today we have a plethora of distinct interpretations of the historical Jesus. Yet in the midst of this debate, there are some key points that can determine how the data is to be assessed.

SETTING–RURAL OR URBAN?

Jesus was from Nazareth, a small village in Galilee. Many of his parables speak of the rural life, with references to farming and farm workers. Some scholars have therefore assumed that the setting for Jesus' ministry was a rural one, in a backwater region of Galilee. Recent excavations in Galilee have suggested a different scenario, however. Just four miles from Nazareth was the bustling city of Sepphoris, which was a richly multicultural center with as many Greek and Roman characteristics as Jewish. With such an urban center as this nearby, Jesus must have been much more familiar with the Greek and Roman world than we used to think. It is even possible that he might have known Greek, since multilingualism was common in his world, though most scholars still hold out for Aramaic as the language in which he preached. Nevertheless, once we envision Jesus in a bustling urban world, rather than in a backwater village, it can change how we interpret the data about Jesus.

SOCIAL STATUS—PEASANT OR "MIDDLE CLASS"?

The class system in the ancient world was not the same as ours; for example, there was no "middle class" as there is today. Yet it was a stratified society, and at the bottom of the ladder were the peasants. These were the menial workers, generally assumed to be rural farm laborers. The problem is that we know very little about such a class in Jesus' day; they leave no records in the historical data. There is even some doubt whether we are assuming too much when we attempt to profile a peasant class for that time and place when our categories are based on studies of feudal societies of a much later period. Yet scholars such as Dominic Crossan and Brandon Scott argue that Jesus was in fact a peasant. Scott points out that the subject matter and point of view of the parables suggests someone from the peasant class. An example is the parable of the workers in the field, which is told from the point of view of the hired farm laborers and therefore posits farm laborers as metaphorical types for the hearers of the parable (Mt. 20:1–15). But other evidence suggests a nonpeasant Jesus, such as the saying contrasting Jesus with John the Baptist. Whereas John is characterized as an ascetic prophet from a rural area ("eating no bread and drinking no wine"), Jesus is characterized as one who frequents banquets of the urban world ("a glutton and a drunkard, a friend of tax collectors and sinners," Mt. 11:18–19; Lk. 7:33–34).

CENTRAL MESSAGE: KINGDOM OF GOD.

The message of Jesus centered on the "kingdom of God." The parables, for example, characteristically begin "the kingdom of God is like..." However, the meaning of this concept is elusive. "Kingdom" is the standard translation of the Greek term used here, *basileia*, which can be seen as a political term to refer to a realm where God rules. Note, for example, that is the central image in the passion narrative the cross on which Jesus died was labeled "king of the Jews." Since crucifixion was a form of punishment reserved for political prisoners, this would strongly suggest that Jesus was perceived as a political upstart. Of course, he could be perceived as a political rabble-rouser whether he was one or not. But the language "kingdom of God" could be heard as a challenge to the current "kingdom," namely

Rome. On the other hand, the term *basileia* could also be translated "rule." Following this translation, one could then propose a meaning that spoke not of political boundaries but rather of religious or ethical allegiance. Such a meaning could also imply a critique of the prevailing political rule, but it could also just as easily be seen as apolitical. The saying, "The kingdom of God is among [or within] you" (Lk. 17:21) would fit the latter interpretation.

RELIGIOUS ORIENTATION—WISDOM OR APOCALYPTIC?

The options in the "kingdom of God" debate have been sharpened by the debate over the central religious orientation of Jesus. Was he an apocalyptic preacher who spoke of the coming end of the age? Or was he a wisdom teacher who spoke of the abundant life now? These two opposite poles in religious thinking are both part of the Jewish religious background and both can be evidenced in the Jesus tradition. The question, however, is whether they could have coexisted in the same individual and his message, or whether one of these was the central theme of Jesus, and the other became a part of the Jesus tradition as it grew in later generations.

This has now become a defining debate in historical Jesus studies. The more traditional view, and the one that many leading scholars still hold to today, is that Jesus was an apocalyptic prophet. In favor of this view is the fact that Jesus started out as a disciple of John the Baptist, and John was certainly an apocalyptic prophet. Representing this view of Jesus would be a group of sayings that proclaim the imminent coming of the Lord, such as this text from Mark:

> From the fig tree learn its lesson: as soon as its branch becomes tender and puts forth its leaves, you know that summer is near. So also, when you see these things taking place, you know that he is near, at the very gates. Truly I tell you, this generation will not pass away until all these things have taken place. (Mk. 13:28–30; see also Mt. 24:32–34; Lk. 21:29–32)

The problem with the apocalyptic Jesus, however, is that such a message has little relevance today, a problem recognized by Albert Schweitzer nearly a century ago. This message speaks of an imminent second coming, a belief that was common in the first generation of early Christianity but one that now, of course, has been discredited simply because it did not happen then and has not happened since.

The alternative view, that Jesus was primarily a wisdom teacher rather than apocalyptic prophet, has developed in scholarship more recently. It takes its cue from texts such as this:

> The kingdom of God is not coming with things that can be observed; nor will they say, "Look, here it is!" or "There it is!" For, in fact, the kingdom of God is among you. (Lk. 17:20–21)

According to this view, the parables would be read as metaphors, so that when they begin, "The kingdom of God is like ..." what follows is a description of the world as it can be. The weakness of this view is the apparent disconnect between Jesus and John the Baptist, at one end, and, at the other end, Jesus and earliest Christianity, which was imbued with apocalyptic thinking.

THE DEATH OF JESUS–WHAT DO WE KNOW AND WHAT IS ITS MEANING?

Scholars rarely if ever debate the basic facts of Jesus' death. The basic datum that Jesus died by crucifixion in Jerusalem during the rule of Pontius Pilate is generally accepted by all. But the details of his death are subject to a wide range of interpretations. These differing interpretations begin in the gospels themselves. On the one hand, there is disagreement as to when Jesus died. The synoptic gospels, following Mark, locate the arrest of Jesus on the night of Passover, just after the Last Supper, which was a passover meal, with his death following the next day (Mk. 14:12; Mt. 26:17; Lk. 22:7–8). The gospel of John also locates the arrest of Jesus on the night after his last meal, but this is a meal eaten prior to the Passover. Jesus dies the next afternoon at the same time that the lambs are being slain for the passover meal, which will follow that evening (Jn. 13:1; 18:28; 19:28–31). Scholars still debate which of these two chronologies for the death of Jesus is the more probable.

The gospels also vary in their interpretations of the meaning of Jesus' death. Mark, followed for the most part by Matthew, interprets Jesus' death as a "ransom for many" and emphasizes the forsakenness and suffering on the cross (Mk. 10:45; Mt. 20:28). Luke omits the reference to ransom and plays down the theme of suffering in favor of a story in which Jesus dies the model death of a martyr who even from the cross forgives those responsible for his death (23:34). John emphasizes the divinity of Jesus in his version of the passion narrative. Thus in his story Jesus is in charge of the sequence of events, from orchestrating his arrest (18:4–8), to willingly accepting the "cup" (18:11), to proclaiming his kingship even during his trial (18:36; 19:11), to carrying his own cross (19:17), and, finally, he chooses when to die and then, and only then, "gave up his spirit" (19:28–30). John tells his story of the death of Jesus in a form consistent with an interpretation presented earlier in his narrative, that "no one takes it [my life] from me, but I lay it down of my own accord" (10:18). To these interpretations, one can add Paul's. Paul did not recount a story of human responsibility for the death of Jesus, but put all the emphasis on the idea that God "gave him up for all of us" (Rom. 8:32).

But these interpretations do not get at the heart of the historical questions. Today scholars agree that the death of Jesus clearly took place as an act of Roman oppression. Indeed, crucifixion was an especially cruel form of capital punishment used by the Romans for the most heinous of criminals. It was the preferred form of punishment for political prisoners, and the very act of leaving the individual hanging there in full view of all to die a slow, painful, and ignominious death was seen as a warning message to the populace not to engage in any suspicious acts against Rome. Clearly Jesus was crucified as a political rabble-rouser, with the sign on the cross sarcastically identifying him as "king of the Jews," as a pretender to the throne. But how was that decision actually made by Roman authorities? Did Jesus actually preach a revolutionary message? Or was he misread by Rome? In the final analysis, to what extent was the death of Jesus consistent with his ministry and message? These are intriguing questions for scholars today.

The Historical Jesus for the Twenty-first Century

The current quest for the historical Jesus is one of the most exciting ventures in New Testament scholarship today. The conclusions that can be drawn from this research are striking and often contradictory. But the process of discussion and debate is a valuable one, for in this way the historical Jesus can emerge with a reality and immediacy akin to that he had in his own lifetime.

Among the interpretive options that have emerged, the following are representative: (a) Jesus as peasant revolutionary–this option sees Jesus as a peasant holy man with a revolutionary vision of justice in a world of injustice. This Jesus takes the side of the oppressed versus the oppressive rule of Rome. (b) Jesus as apocalyptic prophet–this interpretation also sees Jesus as opposing the oppressive rule of Rome, but preaching an ultimate victory by God. Consequently, his message is not so much one of revolution as it is one of repentance. (c) Jesus as teacher of alternative wisdom–this phrase, coined by Marcus Borg, describes the teaching program of a wisdom Jesus, one who opposed the oppression of Rome with an appeal to an alternative vision, one in which renewal would come not by revolution but by transforming human society.

Jesus preached, "Blessed are the poor, for theirs is the kingdom of God." On this all are in agreement. But what did he mean by this? Did he mean that the poor should rise up and claim that which is theirs? Or did he mean that the poor may have it badly now, but they will rejoice in the new age? Or did he mean to inspire a new way of thinking about human society in which even those people at the short end of the stick are to be valued and cared for? That is what we debate today. And how we read Jesus on such a fundamental issue can affect how we view the entire ministry and message of Jesus.

The historical Jesus matters because it gives attention to the human side of the Jesus story. While canon and tradition clearly affirm the human

Jesus, popular theology often overlooks this concept. In our popular theology of today, we tend more toward a docetic christology, one in which Christ is God from beginning to end of the story. But orthodox Christianity long ago rejected a christology that did not affirm that Jesus came "in the flesh." This affirmation is even more relevant today, for it provides a means to take seriously the reality of the Jesus story in terms that do justice to history, theology, and faith.

Suggested Resources for the Pastor's Library

Allison, Dale C. *Jesus of Nazareth: Millenarian Prophet.* Minneapolis: Fortress Press, 1999.

Borg, Marcus J. *Meeting Jesus Again for the First Time.* San Francisco: Harper SanFrancisco, 1994.

Crossan, John Dominic. *The Essential Jesus: Original Sayings and Earliest Images.* San Francisco: Harper SanFrancisco, 1994.

_____. *The Historical Jesus: The Life of a Mediterranean Jewish Peasant.* San Francisco: Harper SanFrancisco, 1991.

_____, and Jonathan L. Reed. *Excavating Jesus: Beneath the Stones, Behind the Text.* San Francisco: Harper SanFrancisco, 2001.

Funk, Robert W., *Honest to Jesus: Jesus for a New Millenium.* San Francisco: HarperCollins, 1996.

_____, and the Jesus Seminar. *The Acts of Jesus: What Did Jesus Really Do?* San Francisco: Harper SanFrancisco, 1998.

_____, Roy Hoover, and the Jesus Seminar. *The Five Gospels: What Did Jesus Really Say?* New York: Macmillan, 1993.

Meier, John P. *A Marginal Jew: Rethinking the Historical Jesus.* Three volumes. New York: Doubleday, 1991, 1994, 2001.

Miller, Robert J., ed. *The Apocalyptic Jesus: A Debate.* Santa Rosa, Calif.: Polebridge Press, 2001.

Patterson, Stephen J. *The God of Jesus: The Historical Jesus and the Search for Meaning.* Harrisburg, Pa.: Trinity Press International, 1998.

Sanders, E. P. *The Historical Figure of Jesus.* Harmondsworth: Penguin, 1993.

Scott, Bernard Brandon. *Hear Then the Parable: A Commentary on the Parables of Jesus.* Minneapolis: Fortress Press, 1989.

7

The Birth of Narrative Theology
The Gospel of Mark

M. Eugene Boring

A New Beginning: The Gospel as Narrative about Jesus

The gospel of Mark represents a radical new departure in the way the early church expressed and communicated its faith. Since modern readers are usually aware of the gospels before reading the letters, it may seem natural to us to think that the church has always expressed its faith by telling the story of "the life and teachings of Jesus," and that this means of communicating the Christian message was widespread in early Christianity. The fact is, for at least a generation after the death and resurrection of Jesus there was no connected narrative of Jesus' life, and when the Christian community did create or adopt the narrative mode of confessing its faith, this happened at first only in narrow circles.

Mark is considered by the vast majority of scholars to be the earliest gospel. This means that Mark was the first to express the gospel from and about Jesus in narrative form. All earlier Christian documents that became canonical are in the letter form. To be sure, the letters of the New Testament are also a kind of narrative literature, in a two-fold sense: they imply the series of events in which the writer and readers are involved (e.g. Paul's relations with the Corinthians), and they point to the story of God's saving acts in history, focused in the Christ event. The narrative christology of the epistles, however, points to the cosmic story of the preexistent Christ who became a human being, suffered, died, and was raised, with a bare minimum of reference to the life and teaching of Jesus of Nazareth. Mark is the first New Testament author to express Christian faith as the narrative or story of the earthly Jesus.

Hearing Mark's Story

Mark's potent story cannot be summarized; it must be experienced. Before proceeding further with this introduction, the reader is advised to cease and desist from reading all secondary literature (including this introduction) and to read the Markan narrative itself—or better yet, to listen as the story is read aloud by someone else. This requires about an hour and a quarter, the length of a good movie. (Audio tapes are available from a number of sources.) The following sketch is provided as an aid to analysis and appreciation.

An Analysis of Mark's Story

The author's opening words are a titular statement (1:1) informing the reader that the following story is about Jesus Christ the Son of God. The reader first hears an off-stage voice in which God is the speaker addressing the off-stage Christ in the words of scripture, declaring that Christ has a "way" that will be prepared by God's messenger (1:2–3). When the narrative curtain opens, the reader sees the strange figure of John the baptizer, preaching repentance and baptism for the forgiveness of sins, and announcing the future advent of a powerful figure who will baptize with the Holy Spirit (1:4–8). Jesus appears and is baptized without another word from John, but the heavenly voice speaks to Jesus (and the reader) declaring him to be God's Son, and the Holy Spirit descends on him (1:9–11). The Spirit drives Jesus into the wilderness, where he is tested by Satan (1:12–13; not "tempted," in the moral sense, in Mark). John is arrested and Jesus begins to preach the good news of the kingdom of God (1:14–15).

The first words the reader hears Jesus speak are "Follow me," addressed to the fishermen whom he calls to be his disciples (1:17; 1:15 is indirect speech, the author's summary). With his few disciples, Jesus begins a vigorous ministry of preaching, teaching with authority, casting out demons, feeding the hungry, healing the sick, cleansing lepers, giving sight to the blind, and raising the dead (1:21–8:26). His mighty works include power over nature: he calms the storm (4:35–41) and walks on the water (6:45–51). While God and the demons (and the reader) know Jesus' identity, despite his mighty works the characters in the narrative do not recognize him.

The story takes a dramatic turn in the episode pictured in 8:27–9:1. Jesus asks his disciples, "Who do people say that I am?" and receives a variety of impressive answers. Jesus then directs his question to the disciples themselves, and Peter answers for the group: "You are the Messiah." Jesus' response is not to congratulate Peter (contrast Mt. 16:17–19), but to command silence. For the first time, Jesus states that the Son of Man is to go to Jerusalem where he will be killed, but will rise from the dead (8:31). This pattern is repeated three times, so that there are two further "passion predictions" (9:31; 10:33–34). Through it all, the disciples remain uncomprehending, despite their witnessing the dramatic transformation of Jesus when Moses and Elijah appear to him on the mountain, and the voice that spoke to Jesus at the beginning ("You are my beloved son," 1:11, TLB) now addresses the disciples directly ("This is my beloved son," 9:7, TLB).

In Mark, Jesus makes one trip to Jerusalem (10:1–52). His arrival is hailed by the crowds as the "one who comes in the name of the Lord" who will bring in "the coming kingdom of our ancestor David" (11:1–10). Jesus' response is to drive the money changers from the temple, which sharpens his conflicts with the Jewish leaders (11:15–33). The debates Jesus had had with Jewish scribes in Galilee (2:1–3:6) intensify in Jerusalem (12:1–40). Jesus leaves the temple, takes four of his disciples to the Mount of Olives, and delivers the longest discourse in Mark, announcing the destruction of the temple, future persecution of his disciples, and the coming of the Son of Man in clouds with great power and glory (13:1–37).

On his fourth day in Jerusalem, at a dinner party in Bethany at the house of Simon the leper, Jesus is anointed by a woman who does understand that he is going to die (14:3–9). The next evening Jesus celebrates the Passover with his disciples, institutes the Lord's supper, and departs with them to pray in Gethsemane (14:12–42). With the help of Judas, one of his disciples, a crowd from the Jewish leaders apprehends him in Gethsemane. Verses 43–62 tell of Jesus' being brought to the house of the high priest, where he is interrogated and confesses himself to be the Christ, the Son of God, and promises that they will see him as the Son of Man seated at God's right hand ("the right hand of the Power") and "coming with the clouds of heaven" (14:62). The Jewish leaders turn Jesus over to Pilate, who has him crucified as one who claims to be "King of the Jews" (15:1–41). His disciples having disappeared, Jesus is buried by a friendly member of the Jewish governing council in a tomb cut from the solid rock (15:42–46).

Even in the early Galilean part of the story, while Jesus appeared to be having great success, people begin to reject and abandon him. Early on, the Pharisees and Herodians conspire to put him to death (3:6). Jesus' mother, brothers, and sisters fail to understand him, consider him deranged, and attempt to bring him back home (3:21, 31–35). When Jesus returns to preach in his hometown, the people of Nazareth are scandalized by him (6:1–6). In the latter part of the story, the misunderstanding and rejection of Jesus gains momentum: the crowds that welcome him to Jerusalem turn on him and call for his life (11:1–10; 12:37; 14:43; 15:11–15). One of the twelve betrays him to the authorities (14:1–2, 10–11, 43–45). Another denies with a curse that he knew him (14:66–72). In Gethsemane at the arrest, they all forsook him and fled (14:50–52). The story that had begun with men leaving all to become Jesus' disciples (1:16–20; cf. 10:28) concludes with a young man literally leaving everything to avoid being a disciple (14:51–52). The next day, from the cross Jesus will utter only one coherent word, "My God, my God, why have *you* forsaken me?" (15:34, emphasis mine).

Late in the story, Mark mentions that there were women who had followed him in Galilee, had supported his mission, had come to Jerusalem with him, and had observed the crucifixion and burial from a distance when the other disciples had fled (15:40–41, 47). They are the only exception to the almost unmitigated misunderstanding and rejection of Jesus, and only they come to the tomb on Sunday morning (16:1–4). There they find the empty tomb, and are told by a young man in a white robe to go and tell the others that Christ is risen and goes before them. All others have misunderstood, rejected, betrayed, denied, and failed. These women are the only hope that the message from and about Jesus will endure. Mark concludes his narrative with a sentence that breaks off in the middle, "And they said nothing to anyone, for they were afraid…"

The most ancient manuscripts of Mark end at 16:8, with the Greek word *gar* ("for"), which, like the English word "and" cannot normally end a sentence. Some later scribes were so convinced that this could not be the ending of Mark that at least three different "endings" were added. Most scholars believe Mark intended to end at 16:8.

Here the consummate skill and reserve of Mark the storyteller makes its impact. In the plotted narrative, the women were the last hope, but as it turned out they were the last to fail. Everyone in the story fails. But there were others who heard, and they understood from the beginning. The reader knows from 1:1 on who Jesus really is. When John and the crowds miss the divine voice from heaven, the reader hears (1:11). When the hometown folk at Nazareth reject Jesus, the reader stands by him and continues through the story (6:1–3). When the disciples fail to understand, who gets the message (8:14–21)? When the disciples sleep in Gethsemane, who is still awake and hears Jesus' prayer (14:32–40)? When all the disciples forsook him and fled, who stayed, and accompanied him to the cross (14:50–52)? The family and disciples of Jesus were not at the cross to hear Jesus' cry of abandonment, but the reader hears (15:34). The reader accompanies the women to the tomb, and when they too finally fail, it is as though Mark looks up from the page from the incomplete sentence of 16:8 with the unexpressed question, "What about you, dear reader?"

Literary Features

Mark is a carefully composed literary composition. This does not mean that the author was striving for literary elegance, or that he was capable of doing so. (Since the identity of the author is unknown I will use the conventional term "Mark" and the corresponding "he" to refer to the author, whoever he or she may have been. The generally positive portrayal of women in Mark [e.g. 5:21–34; 7:24–30; 12:41–44; 14:3–9; 15:40–41; 16:1–3; but 3:31–34; 6:17–28] suggests that Mark's church included strong women leaders as role models.) The level of Mark's Greek does not measure up to classical literary standards and is less elegant than any of the other gospels. But Mark's powerful story is neither accurate reporting of facts nor random collection of anecdotes. It is the thoughtful composition of an author who had reflected on what he wanted to say and on the strategy for communicating it. Mark inherited traditional materials from and about Jesus (see below on form criticism), but he selected, arranged, interpreted, and amplified them, giving the story the shape appropriate to what he wanted to say. Mark constructed the story, that is, he *fabricated* it. This does not mean he invented it or that it is false. Mark stands in a tradition of Jesus' life and message that extends back to the historical Jesus. But when Mark's story is called "fiction" or "fictive," Bible scholars are adopting the language of literary criticism to indicate that the story per se is Mark's construction.

Some of the features that reflect Mark's composition are as follows:

1.   Jesus' ministry is portrayed as lasting less than one year. Readers who blend all the gospels together may not notice that Mark's story begins in Galilee, that there is only one Passover, only one trip to Jerusalem, and that all Mark has to narrate fits within one year. (Contrast the gospel of John, which has three Passovers, with Jesus making several trips back and forth from Judea to Galilee). We do not know how many times Jesus was actually in Jerusalem. This historical information is irrelevant for Mark's *story*, in which the one trip to Jerusalem is important for the plot. This portrayal is Mark's construction.

2.   Likewise, in Mark's story the first part of Jesus' ministry (Galilee) is filled with miraculous power by which he brings God's salvation to the sick and hungry, the lepers and the demon possessed. In the second half of Mark (which takes place in Jerusalem), Jesus does not manifest such divine power except in the puzzling story of withering the fig tree (11:12–14, 20–25). The picture of Jesus as powerful in Galilee but weak in Jerusalem does not reflect the actual history but is a Markan construction. Presumably if Jesus could work miracles at all, his power was not subject to geographical limitation. The other gospels note this incongruity and do picture Jesus as performing miracles in Jerusalem and Judea.

3.   Another feature of Markan composition is that of intercalation, a literary device in which one story is inserted within another ("Markan sandwiches"). This framing technique results in units with the pattern A-B-A: one story is begun, another story originally independent is inserted, then the original story is completed. This technique can be utilized to create a powerful effect fraught with theological meaning. For instance, in 14:54 Mark relates that after Jesus' arrest Peter followed him at a distance, into the courtyard of the high priest. The narrative camera then switches to

Jesus, who for the first time in the story boldly confesses that he is the Christ, and is then beaten by the guards (14:55–65). Then the camera returns to Peter in the courtyard, where he denies with an oath that he knows who Jesus is (14:66–72). The narrator need say nothing to point out the contrast between Jesus who boldly confesses his identity and Peter who denies it; his literary construction gives the reader the picture. This technique is typically Markan (cf. 3:22–30; 5:21–43; 6:14–29; 11:11–25; 14:1–11; 53–72).

4.   Mark, like all story tellers, must choose what kind of narrator will tell the story to the reader. The readers can only hear what the narrator tells them. An author may tell the story through a narrator who is a character in the story (e.g., Huckleberry Finn in Mark's Twain's novel; some later apocryphal gospels such as the *Gospel of Peter* adopt this kind of narrator). Mark chooses the guise of an omniscient narrator who stands outside the story. Such a narrator knows, and lets the reader know, what the scribes are thinking in their hearts (2:6–7), what went on at Herod's birthday party (6:17–29), what transpired in Gethsemane when all were asleep (14:32–42), what was said at Jesus' hearing and trial (14:53–65; 15:1–3). To ask "where did the author get this information" is to misconstrue the genre of the gospel as if it is the kind of document produced by investigative reporting.

5.   Mark composes on the basis of and in response to tradition. The early Church between Jesus and Mark had handed on a large quantity of materials from and about Jesus, individual units of tradition that functioned in the teaching, preaching, worship, and debates of the early Christian community. The scholarly discipline concerned with studying this oral tradition that bridges the gap between Jesus and Mark is called *form criticism.* While many details of the analysis of form criticism remain disputed, one of the major achievements of form criticism was in showing that while much of the material used by the evangelists was church tradition from and about Jesus ("the beads"), the framework of the gospel stories was constructed by the evangelists themselves ("the string"). The material itself represents what the church had found useful in its ministry of preaching and teaching. When we teach and preach from texts in the gospels, we are thus not imposing something alien upon them. They already represent the proclamation and instruction of the early Christian community. Mark is not merely a collector or editor, but a composer. But unlike the authors of novels, Mark is not free to create his story from whole cloth. He struggles with a tradition that he affirms, modifies, amplifies, and interprets.

6.   A final illustration of Mark as composer is that he controls the narrative clock. The author controls how the story is told, regardless of how the events themselves occurred. Forty days can be compressed into a sentence (1:13), while one evening can take several pages (14:17–72). In Mark, the narrative clock slows down as one approaches the crucifixion.

All Jesus' ministry in Galilee takes about half the book, with hardly any temporal indicators—the reader can't tell what day or month of Jesus' ministry it is (chaps. 1–9); the trip to Jerusalem takes one chapter (10); the six days in Jerusalem, triumphal entry to burial, then take five chapters and are clearly delineated (11–15). On the day of the crucifixion, the clock slows down so that for the first time the hours themselves become markers (15:25, 33–34). All such decisions are in the hands of the author. This is what is meant by referring to the "fictive" world of Mark, or referring to the gospel as "fabricated."

Theological Features

Mark's story is a theological narrative. While it reflects real people and real events—Jesus, Mary, and Peter are not fictional characters who existed only in a story world, and the crucifixion is something that *happened*—Mark's narrative is not the account of a reporter who is attempting to recount "just the facts." This is clear from peculiar features of the narrative itself. Jesus raises a little girl from the dead while the funeral is in progress (5:35–42), but the people are commanded to keep the matter strictly secret (5:42). In the presence of his disciples Jesus stills a storm on the Galilean lake (4:35–40) and walks on the water (6:45–51), yet they do not understand who he is (4:41; contrast Mt. 14:33)—though the demons recognize him as the Son of God (1:24, 34; 3:11–12; 5:7).

Mark uses his literary skill to present a christology; the gospel of Mark is essentially narrative christology. The formation, genre, and function of the first gospel is a complex and disputed topic that must not be oversimplified. I do not here intend to disregard or minimize that complexity by reducing it to one factor or by imposing a single template on Mark's multidimensional story, but surely one of the principal generative factors in Mark's composition, if not the primary one, was his intention to present a narrative christology that combined the best elements in the conflicting christologies of his tradition. By this I do not mean that Mark elaborates a speculative essay on the nature of Jesus, but that he puts his narrative together in such a way as to communicate the meaning of the Christ event for Christian faith and discipleship.

The faith Mark represents can be stated abstractly in the proposition "the one true God has acted for the salvation of humanity in the truly human Jesus of Nazareth, an event that calls human beings to responsive obedience to God as disciples of Jesus Christ." Of course, neither Mark nor any other New Testament author presented the faith in terms of such abstract propositions. A wide variety of images and metaphors were adopted and adapted by the earliest Christians to express the meaning of this event: from the law court (justification); from the slave market (ransom, redemption); from the sacrificial cult (sacrifice, expiation, propitiation); from everyday life (salvation = wholeness, health, waking up, putting on new clothes, getting cleaned up, being reconciled, getting invited to a banquet when one is an outsider, etc.). Prior to Mark, faith in the saving efficacy of the Christ event was presented in a variety of literary forms, such as songs (e.g., Phil. 2:5–11), creedal statements (e.g., 1 Cor. 3:3–5), miracle stories (such as are now found for example in Mk. 5:21–42), individual sayings of Jesus and collections of such sayings (such as are now found for example in Lk. 6:20–49), liturgical materials (e.g., 1 Cor. 11:23–26), and the story of Jesus' death (such as now found in Mk. 14:12–15:39). Beginning with Paul, individual elements of such imagery and materials were woven into early Christian letters. Mark was the first to express the meaning of God's act in Jesus by composing a narrative of the life, death, and resurrection of Jesus.

Prior to Mark, Jesus' life had been presented in Christian teaching in two conflicting sets of images. (1) Some christological images pictured the life of the earthly Jesus as weak and victimized (*kenosis* christology that portrayed Jesus as "truly human"). Christology that focuses on Jesus' sharing the human condition devoid of divine power is called "kenosis" ("emptying") christology. The term is taken from Phil. 2:7 in which the preexistent divine Christ divested himself of divine power in the incarnation. (2) Other christological images pictured the life of the earthly Jesus as a manifestation of the power of God (*epiphany* christology that portrayed Jesus as "truly divine"). Christology that focuses on the earthly life of Jesus as itself a manifestation ("epiphany") of God's miraculous saving power is thus called epiphany ("manifestation") christology.

1. In the first set of images, Jesus is identified with the weakness of human existence. "Weakness" here does not refer to the character of Jesus' personality, but to his full participation in the human situation (cf. 2 Cor. 13:4 "crucified in weakness"). This christology is reflected in several streams of Christian tradition prior to Mark. In the whole Pauline tradition and the epistolary tradition derived from him, there are no stories or other indications that the earthly Jesus worked miracles or was filled with the divine power. In this tradition, pictures of Jesus' deity are all pre-incarnation or post-resurrection (cf. e.g., Rom. 1:3–4, Phil. 2:5–11; 2 Cor. 13:4, Col. 1:15–20; Heb. 2:5–11; 5:1–10; Rev. 5:1–14). Not only the epistles, but also elements of the gospel tradition, when regarded as individual units of tradition prior to their incorporation into their present gospel framework, portray Jesus in terms of kenosis christology (cf. e.g., Lk. 4:1–13, in which changing stones to bread and leaping from the temple are considered demonic temptations; Mk. 8:11–13, in which Jesus categorically declares that no sign will be given to his generation; and the pre-Markan passion story now found in Mk. 14–15, in which Jesus suffers passively).

2. In the second set of images, Jesus is portrayed as an epiphany of the saving power of God, as doing what only God can do. This is essentially the christology of the miracle stories, which circulated as individual units

(and clusters) in the pre-Markan tradition. In this tradition, Jesus forgives sins (Mk. 2:5–7); frees people from demonic power (1:21–28), hunger (6:30–44), sickness (1:29–31), and death (5:35–42); calms storms (4:35–39); and walks on water (6:45–51). In the Old Testament and Jewish tradition, all these acts are attributed to God. Though he affirms the Jewish credo of the one God (12:28–31), Mark affirms this christology.

These two ways of picturing the earthly Jesus were both vehicles of Christian theology, each representing one aspect of the Christian proclamation that *God* had acted in *Jesus* for human salvation. The two sets of images used to mediate this faith clashed with each other, and seemed to be mutually exclusive: if the earthly Jesus had been filled with the divine power and able to do what only God does, then he could not *also* be a truly human being who gets tired and sleepy (4:38), does not work miracles (6:5a; 8:11–12), who agonizes and trembles before death (14:32–38), and who is "crucified in weakness" (2 Cor. 13:4; Mk. 15:21–37) with only a despairing cry on his lips (15:34). Prior to Mark, the advocates of each christology considered the advocates of the other to be opponents of the faith. In the 50s, Paul, for instance, was an exponent of the theology of the cross (e.g., 1 Cor. 1:26–2:5), never recounts a miracle story about Jesus, and considers those who preach "another Jesus" to advocate a "different gospel" (2 Cor 11:4) and to be "enemies of the cross of Christ" (Phil. 3:18). In 2 Cor. 10–13 we have Paul's side of the argument. We do not have the writings of Paul's opponents, but presumably they advocated an epiphany christology, gloried in the miracles Jesus had done, and considered their own ministry to be a continuation of it.

Each of these two ways of picturing Jesus has theological advantages and disadvantages—there is no one christology that is adequate to its subject matter. Mark stands within a Christian tradition in which each of these views had its proponents, and he saw the value (and liabilities) of each. But how could they be combined? What was needed was a way of presenting God's act in Jesus that valued the way of proclaiming the gospel that told stories from Jesus' earthly life in which the saving power of God was manifest *and* that did justice to the cross and resurrection of Jesus, that is, to the reality that no one, not even Jesus' family or disciples, had recognized him as God's decisive act and definitive revelation during his earthly life, but only from the later perspective of the crucifixion and resurrection. This was Mark's christological problem. Mark wanted to affirm both the deity and humanity of Christ. He did not write an essay in order to "solve" it, but constructed a narrative, a distinctive literary form that juxtaposed these two images of Jesus and their theological meaning. This means, of course, that Mark's intention was not to tell "how it really was" in the life of Jesus, for Jesus' life was in fact either filled with the divine power or it was not; in Markan terms, he either could come down from the cross or he couldn't

(Mk. 15:29–32). Rather, Mark wanted to devise a narrative in which these two ways of thinking and talking about God's act in Jesus could be held together in one story. (I remind the reader that "thinking and talking about God's act in Jesus" *is* Christian theology.) Narrative can do this in a way that discursive logic cannot; it is a part of Mark's genius to adopt and adapt this insight of Jewish tradition and to implement it as Christian theology.

How can these two images of God's act in Jesus be held together in one story? Mark's response to this problem was to take the elements of secrecy and misunderstanding that were already resident in various elements of the stories about Jesus and to develop them into a comprehensive means of presenting the whole story of the Christ event: Jesus had done the miraculous saving acts during his earthly life as pictured in the epiphany christology, *and* these had not been recognized until after the story was over, as called for by the kenosis christology. Jesus commands secrecy (e.g., 1:34, 44; 3:7–12; 5:43; 8:26), the disciples misunderstand and are not able to do otherwise (4:41; 6:48–52), and even Jesus' teaching is not intended to be understood during his earthly life (4:10–12, 34). Only at the end of Jesus' life can it be recognized that "Truly this *man* was the Son of *God*" (Mk. 15:39, RSV, emphasis mine). Mark devised a literary means by which the story of Jesus' mighty acts could be told in such a way that the post-Easter reader could perceive them as representing God's saving act in the whole Christ event, but the people in the story could not perceive Jesus' identity until the story was over. This "Messianic secret" in its comprehensive form is Mark's creation as the literary means that facilitates the presentation of his truly human/truly divine christology within one narrative. Some form of the "Messianic secret" is found in all four gospels, and is an essential element in the gospel genre, distinguishing it from typical Hellenistic biographies.

The Markan emphasis on christology is not an alternative or competitor to Mark's focus on discipleship. In the Markan understanding, christology and discipleship are two sides of the same coin. Jesus' first act is to call disciples (1:16–20); their immediate response is as much a miracle as anything in the story. They do not volunteer, but are called; they are what they are by the divine initiative. Jesus' own ministry concentrates on teaching and preparing disciples for mission (4:33–34). While the gospel form as devised by Mark means that during Jesus' earthly life they must be pictured as obtuse and uncomprehending (see above), Mark's story points ahead to a post-resurrection picture of the disciples as faithful witnesses. In Mark 13:9–13, Jesus is portrayed as looking ahead to the time after Easter in which the disciples will be courageous witnesses, guided by the Holy Spirit, extending the Christian mission to all nations.

In both his christology and his picture of discipleship, Mark's emphasis falls on the cross. Mark affirms the images of both Jesus and the disciples as those who work miracles, but just as the narrative about Jesus leads to and emphasizes his suffering and death, so the essence of being a disciple is to take up one's cross and follow Jesus (8:27–9:1; 10:35–45). The story that begins with the announcement that the Son of God has a "way" (1:2–4) finally discloses that this way leads to the cross. To be a disciple is to have one's blindness healed and to follow Jesus in this way of self-giving (10:46–52). This is the Markan understanding of "Christian ethics." Even though Jesus emphasizes love as the supreme command (12:28–34), for Mark being obedient to God is not finally obedience to rules but following a person. For Mark, Christian faith and ethics do not mean the affirmation of a set of principles or ideals, not even love, justice, or inclusiveness, but to accept God's call to be one of Jesus' disciples as set forth in this story, and to follow Jesus "on the way" (8:27; 10:32; 10:52).

Genre

The most important issue for interpreting a gospel is the decision about its genre. A moment's reflection indicates that the same words will be understood in radically different ways depending on whether they are taken to be, for instance, a joke, a poem, an AP bulletin, an editorial comment, a song, or advertising copy. So also gospel texts will be understood differently depending on whether they are taken as, for example, accurate historical reports, theological interpretation of a historical event, historical novel, drama, legend, fiction, allegory, or "gospel" in the sense of a distinctive new genre created in early Christianity for the propagation of its faith.

Until recently, the dominant scholarly view was that the gospels are not biographies, but a new kerygmatic (or preaching) genre devised by Mark. It is still universally accepted that the gospels are not biographies in the modern sense, but there is currently a growing movement to regard the gospels as *bioi*, biographies in the ancient Hellenistic sense. However this scholarly dispute may be resolved, it is important to see Mark as having written a distinctive narrative that fits only awkwardly (if at all) into the literary categories already available to him. Though there are points of contact with the genre of Hellenistic biography, and though many readers might have (at least initially) categorized it within a genre with which they were already familiar, it is not the case that Mark simply adopts an available pattern and composes a "life of Jesus" on this basis. The tensive juxtaposition of pictures of Jesus as truly human and truly divine, the telling of the story as the definitive segment of universal history directed by God the creator, the presentation of the main character as both a figure of past history and the present Lord of the community who will come again in glory, the composition of the narrative on the basis of individual units of tradition that had themselves been utilized in preaching and teaching the gospel—all these set Mark apart from other Hellenistic authors and sets his narrative in a distinctive category.

Authorship

Who composed *such* a narrative as discussed above? The question of authorship cannot be discussed intelligently as the first issue; one must first get as clear an understanding as possible of the nature of the document one is discussing before asking the question of authorship. The preceding discussion has already made clear that, while it contains materials that go back to the time of Jesus, the gospel of Mark is not composed reporter-like on the basis of either personal or second-hand reminiscences. The materials available to Mark come through the experienced faith of the Christian community in its teaching, preaching, worship, and debates, not via a chain of individual eyewitnesses.

The title "The Gospel according to Mark" is not from the original author, but was added in the second century by the church when the four canonical gospels were combined as the fourfold witness to the one gospel. The gospel of Mark, like the other canonical gospels, is anonymous. The author does not give his or her name, nor speak in the first person. Yet the second-century Christian community considered it important to designate the gospel as from "Mark." Who was this Mark, why did the church attribute the gospel to him, and was the church historically correct in doing so?

A certain "Mark" first appears in the New Testament in Philemon 24 as among those with Paul who send greetings from his imprisonment. Philemon has traditionally been regarded as written from Rome in the early 60s, but both location and date are disputed; many scholars regard the letter as having been written from Ephesus in the 50s. A similar, but elaborated, list of greetings appears in Col. 4:10–14, adding the additional information that Mark is the "cousin of Barnabas." Colossians was probably not written directly by Paul, but takes up the tradition from Philemon that Paul had a coworker named Mark. The same is true of the only other reference to Mark in the Pauline tradition, 2 Tim. 4:11, which pictures Paul as (again) in prison, this time in Rome, asking Timothy to come to him and bring Mark. Near the end of the first century, a member of the Petrine school in Rome ("Babylon") wrote 1 Peter, indicating that Mark is now Peter's "son" (1 Pet. 5:13). About the same time, the author of Acts refers three times to a "John Mark" who was a member of the Jerusalem church who had contacts with both Peter and Paul (Acts 12:12, 25; 13:5, 13; 15:37, 39). The only one of these references that is historically certain is Philemon 24: there was a historical figure named Mark who was Paul's coworker in the mid-50s. The other references point to a developing picture of "Mark" in early Christianity as one who first worked with Paul, and later was Peter's coworker in Rome. Unless Philemon was written in Rome, the earliest connection between Mark and Rome is in 1 Peter, or sometime between 80 and 100 C.E.

This developing tradition continued in post-biblical literature, attributing the authorship of the gospel of Mark to this Mark who had been the companion of both Paul and Peter. Sometimes the composition of the document is set within Peter's lifetime, sometimes with and sometimes without his knowledge, permission, supervision, or approval of the final product; and sometimes it is located after his death. In the various forms of this tradition it is clear that the church's interest was in theological legitimization of Mark as representing the apostolic faith, not the historical accuracy of the claim that John Mark, resident of Jerusalem and disciple of Simon Peter, was the actual author, though the first generations of the church did not distinguish these two aspects of the claim to Markan authorship. The ancient tradition makes clear that Mark's gospel was accepted and valued in the church not because of its historical accuracy, but because it represented Peter's apostolic authority. Though the gospel of Mark may have been written by a person named Mark—it was a common enough name—the evidence is that this attribution was only made late and for theological reasons. Though it contains materials that go back to eyewitnesses of Jesus' ministry, these materials bear the marks of having been mediated to the author not by an individual, but by generations of community teaching, preaching, and worship. The gospel of Mark itself makes no claim to have been written by an eyewitness, and gives no evidence of such authorship.

Date

On the one hand, the gospel must have been written late enough to allow for the development of the oral tradition on which it is based, which would be about a generation, and, on the other hand, must have been written early enough to have been used by Matthew and Luke by about 90 C.E. These general considerations would locate Mark roughly between 60 and 80 C.E. This period is narrowed somewhat by the apocalyptic discourse of chapter 13, with its prediction of the temple's destruction, which seems to reflect the tumultuous times of the war in Judea 66–73, but it is not clear whether Mark was written during, just before, or just after the war. The reference to the death of James and John in 10:39 is also relevant. In the story line all these events are still in the future and predicted by Jesus; the question is whether the narrative itself reflects that they have already happened. Thus practically all scholars date Mark in the period 65–75, with the major issue being whether or not Mark 13 is understood to reflect the destruction of Jerusalem as something that has already occurred.

Provenance

The question of the place where Mark was written is important not only for understanding it in its historical setting, but for understanding the development of early Christian literature. Was the narrative mode of communicating the faith widespread in early Christianity, or was it at first only a limited (and somewhat late) development?

The tradition that Mark was written at Rome is not based on data from the gospel itself, but on patristic traditions regarding authorship. The allusions to suffering and persecution (e.g., 8:34–38; 13:9–13) may well reflect Nero's persecution of Roman Christians in 64 C.E., but this would have affected Christian self-understanding throughout the Roman world, and while it is compatible with a Roman location, is not evidence for composition in Rome. Likewise, the number of Latinized words is sometimes taken as evidence of a Roman origin, but the influence of the language of the Romans was not restricted to the city of Rome or to Italy, but pervaded the Empire.

Against the tradition of Roman provenance is the fact that Mark does not reflect Paul's *Letter to the Romans* written fourteen years previously. Not only are key words of Pauline theology in general and Romans in particular missing from Mark (e.g., "law," "the righteousness of God"), but the general christological perspective of the gospel is different from Paul's, who never communicated his christology by telling stories of the earthly Jesus, but concentrated everything on the death and resurrection. Neither is there any internal evidence that links the contents of Mark to the preaching of Peter. The Markan negative picture of Peter and all the disciples argues against this connection. Likewise, the gospel of Mark is not reflected in the earliest Christian writings emanating from Rome. First Peter and 1 Clement both come from Rome near the end of the first century; neither indicate directly or indirectly any awareness of the gospel of Mark, and neither has the gospel type of narrative christology, but only the Pauline cosmic christology. So also the Old Roman Creed, ancestor of the Apostles' Creed, represents the confession of the Roman Church at the end of the second century C.E., and has the Pauline christology that goes directly from the birth of Jesus to "crucified under Pontius Pilate," with no place for the kind of Markan narrative christology portraying the ministry of Jesus. Though the gospel of Mark was certainly accepted and current in Rome at the end of the *second* century, the creed was apparently formulated in Rome before narrative christology became the accepted norm. This creed is compatible with 1 Peter and 1 Clement, but not with Mark, which suggests that the gospel of Mark came to Rome from someplace else, some time after the death of Peter.

The actual geographical setting for the composition of Mark is thus unknown. The author's imprecise knowledge of Palestinian geography points to a setting outside Palestine (compare, e.g., 7:31 with a map!). A Syrian provenance is often suggested, but it is not possible to be more precise than this.

Some implications for the social and religious setting of Mark may be inferred from the text itself. That Aramaic terms and Jewish customs are translated or explained (cf. e.g., 5:41; 7:1–4, 11, 34; 14:36; 15:34) indicates that it was directed to a Greek-speaking church composed primarily of

Gentiles, but the debate with Jewish scribes and traditions (e.g., 7:1–23; 11:27–12:40) points to a community that is seriously engaged with Jewish tradition and synagogue leadership. The lack of reference to large cities (except Jerusalem), the primarily agrarian imagery, the lack of urban metaphors, the preponderance of situations in which poor people play leading roles, and the limitation of reference to monetary units to small-denomination coins suggest that the community from which Mark came belonged to the lower socio-economic strata. The community is not undergoing direct persecution, yet stands in tension with its environment and may be being harassed by both Jewish and Gentile authorities (13:9). The community knows the phenomena of charismatic gifts of the Spirit in its midst (13:11; cf. 1:8; 3:28–29), including prophets who speak in the name of the risen Lord (13:6), as in the Pauline churches (e.g., 1 Cor. 14) and those pictured in Acts (e.g., Acts 11:27–29), but Mark is suspicious of them (13:22). The Markan church was an apocalyptic community that expected the end to come soon (9:1; 13:28–30). It is not entirely clear whether Mark is promoting this apocalypticism, whether he is attempting to provide an alternative way of articulating the faith for a community that has already experienced some disappointment at the delay of the parousia, or whether he affirms that the end will indeed come within his generation, but that there is still time for the church to carry on its mission to the world (13:10).

Importance for the Church of the Twenty-first Century

Mark was written to a church prior to Christendom, a church tempted to "be ashamed" of Christ and his cross because it was not to one's advantage politically, economically, or socially to be a disciple of Jesus. Some in Mark's church were fascinated with miracles and found no place for talk of self-sacrifice and the cross. Others could not fit stories about a miracle-working Jesus into their view of the world and Christian discipleship. Some in Mark's church believed that the End was coming in the near future, which gave no time for mission and social responsibility and made these concerns irrelevant to the Christian life. Most in Mark's world, and many in Mark's church, believed that ethics was a matter of individual conscience and general principles rather than discipleship to the crucified and risen Lord. Mark addressed these concerns not by writing an essay but by retelling the Christian story. We who live not only in a post-denominational age, but after the age of Christendom as the established and privileged religion rewarded by the culture may find ourselves addressed by Mark's narrative of the saving act of God in Christ and the meaning of Christian ethics as discipleship to God's Son.

Suggested Resources for the Pastor's Library

Achtemeier, Paul J. *Mark.* Proclamation Commentaries. Second Edition. Philadelphia: Fortress Press, 1986.

Best, Ernest. *Following Jesus: Discipleship in the Gospel of Mark.* Journal for the Study of the New Testament, Supplement Series, 4. Sheffield, England: University of Sheffield, 1981.

Boring, M. Eugene. *Truly Human/Truly Divine: Christological Language and the Gospel Form.* St. Louis: CBP Press, 1984, 1996.

Cook, Michael C. *Christology as Narrative Quest.* Collegeville, Minn.: Liturgical Press, 1997.

Gundry, Robert H. *Mark: A Commentary on His Apology for the Cross.* Grand Rapids: Eerdmans, 1993.

Hooker, Morna D. *The Gospel According to Saint Mark.* Black's New Testament Commentary. Peabody, Mass.: Hendrickson, 1991.

Myers, Ched. *Binding the Strong Man: A Political Reading of Mark's Story of Jesus.* Maryknoll, N.Y.: Orbis Books, 1988.

Nineham, D. E. *Saint Mark.* Baltimore: Penguin, 1969.

Painter, John. *Mark's Gospel.* New Testament Readings. New York: Routledge, 1997.

Perkins, Pheme, "The Gospel of Mark," in *The New Interpreter's Bible.* Volume 8. Edited by Leander Keck. Nashville: Abingdon Press, 1995.

Rhoads, David, Joanna Dewey, and Donald Michie. *Mark as Story: An Introduction to the Narrative of a Gospel.* Second Edition. Minneapolis: Fortress Press, 1999.

Stock, Augustine. *Call to Discipleship. A Literary Study of Mark's Gospel.* Good News Studies, Volume 1. Wilmington, Del.: Michael Glazier, Inc., 1982.

Telford, W. R. *The Theology of the Gospel of Mark.* New Testament Theology. Cambridge: Cambridge University Press, 1999.

Tolbert, Mary Ann. *Sowing the Gospel: Mark's World in Literary-Historical Perspective.* Minneapolis: Fortress Press, 1989.

8

A Jewish-Christian Gospel
The Gospel of Matthew

STEPHANIE BUCKHANON CROWDER
DENNIS E. SMITH

Basic Data

While Papias, bishop of Hierapolis, (110–125 C.E.), as recorded by Christian historian, Eusebius, makes one of the earliest references to a gospel called "Matthew," there is little definite evidence to ascertain its exact origin. Many scholars maintain that the gospel of Matthew was written between 80–90 C.E. Because the author makes reference to the destruction of the Jewish temple in Jerusalem in 70 C.E.(24:2), and because he uses as a source a gospel written about that time, namely the gospel of Mark, such a date of origin is quite plausible. The city of Antioch is the setting often suggested for this work, primarily because it had the earliest Christian community outside of Palestine, a community that was founded by Hellenistic Jewish Christians. In addition, its heritage as a Greek-speaking city and site of anti-Jewish riots during 40 C.E. and the Jewish Wars of 66–70 C.E. also make it a prime candidate. However, the Greco-Roman city of Sepphoris, not far from Nazareth, with its prevalence of rabbinic Judaism is also plausible.

Regarding the authorship, the gospel mentions a tax collector named Matthew (9:9; 10:3). Tradition, most notably Papias as mentioned above, equates this Matthew with the author of the work. Yet the gospel itself makes no such claim and never specifically identifies its author. Indeed, it is most likely that the Matthew of the text was dead by the time the gospel writer recorded his work. Consequently, most scholars today do not consider this Matthew to be the author of the work. Whether there is sufficient data to determine the actual identity of the author of the gospel, his Jewish heritage cannot be denied. This is indicated by his familiarity with the Torah, the Jewish Law (5:17; 9:1–8; 12:1–8; 15:1–20)–as well as Jewish practices, such as hand washing (15:1) and phylacteries and fringes (23:5)–and Jewish sects, such as the Pharisees (5:20; 16:11–12; 23:1–36).

Just as the Jewish ancestry of the author of the gospel of Matthew comes to the surface throughout the work, so does the ethnic background of those in his community. The strong connections with Jewish traditions exhibited throughout the work suggest that they were predominately a Jewish Christian community, although it is likely that Gentiles were beginning to join the group as well (8:11–12; 12:21). It was a community that lived under the auspices of the Roman Empire. Thus they were not completely politically, socially, or religiously free. These persons were displaced or diaspora Jews living most likely in Syria and having to pay homage and obeisance to Roman potentates. Jack Dean Kingsbury maintains, nonetheless, that the members of Matthew's community were urban and prosperous. Matthew writes not only to those familiar with Jewish customs but also to those for whom such rituals were in themselves foreign, namely Gentiles.

In the opinion of many scholars, the author wrote to give a Christian response to Jamnia, the place where Judaism was reformed. After the destruction of the temple in 70 C.E., Jewish leaders gathered in Jamnia, a Judean village on the Mediterranean shore, and began a reorganization of Judaism based in the synagogue instead of the temple. Competition quickly developed between the traditional Jewish leaders, primarily Pharisees, and the upstart Jewish Christians, and the battleground was the synagogue. In Matthew, the author makes a point to refer to "their synagogues" (9:35; 10:17; 12:9) in reference to the opponents of Jesus, suggesting that there was a distinction between the synagogues of the traditional Jews and the synagogues of the Matthean community. Indeed, Matthew's community may have suffered from expulsion from the synagogue. Thus they needed to define their own religious stance and find a means to survive their having been thrust into a Gentile world. They saw Jesus as the new Moses who gave a new law to help people in transition who had been estranged from the official keepers of the law. For those on the outside like Matthew, the purpose of recording the acts and sayings of Jesus the Messiah was to bolster faith, explain present conditions, such as the destruction of the temple (24: 2), and to prepare for any future crises (chap. 24). Matthew's opponents were the scribes and Pharisees who aided in establishing rabbinic Judaism after the destruction of the temple in 70 C.E., yet who did not see Jesus as the messiah (9:11, 34; 12:2; 27:62–63). Matthew refers to these groups as hypocrites (chap. 23).

One can surmise that the gospel of Matthew is indeed a document written in response to crisis. The book speaks of conflict among fellow Jews as well as turmoil due to living in a colonial Roman environment.

While Matthew's community struggles to establish its Jewish Christian identity as different from and the fulfillment of traditional Judaism, it also seeks to maintain peace with the Roman Empire.

Methodology

There are various methodological approaches to studying biblical texts like Matthew. Each method depends on the desired focus and outcome of the interpreter. Historical criticism, literary criticism, socio-scientific criticism, and cultural studies are considered the four umbrella models for biblical study. Each is distinct in that each emphasizes differently the sender (author), message (text), receiver (audience/reader), and context (setting) of a particular work, such as a gospel. Whereas historical critics are more concerned with the sender and context, literary and social-scientific critics pay more attention to the message and context. On the other hand, those who employ cultural studies are more concerned with the receiver and the personal meaning the receiver acquires from the text. The two most often engaged approaches to the gospel of Matthew are historical criticism and literary criticism.

The most prominent and long-standing entry into discovering biblical meaning has been historical criticism. From the early nineteenth century until the 1970s this approach to the Bible dominated the religious academic arena. Such a methodology places primary emphasis on the setting of a biblical work and on the author who produced it. In regard to the study of Matthew, scholars who use this paradigm tend to concentrate on the social, political, and religious world of Matthew at the time of his writing; who the author Matthew was—his or her religious, cultural, and political background; and the actual historicity of such a person. In addition the author as redactor or editor is key. Thus, redaction criticism, which examines how sources are put together or adapted, falls under any historical-critical approach to Matthew. Questions regarding Matthew's deviations from and similarities to the other synoptic writers, Mark and Luke, come to the forefront using this critical method.

A well-used approach to Matthew is literary criticism. As earlier stated, this method of study centers on the message (text) and the context that produced it. A branch of literary criticism is narrative criticism. As the word "narrative" suggests, this paradigm centers on the gospel of Matthew as a story with plot, characters, setting, rising action, irony, and denouement or conclusion. This gospel as a story has a beginning with a genealogy and birth (chaps. 1–2), a middle filled with discourses and conflict (3–26), and an ending with a crucifixion, resurrection, and commissioning (27–28). Such a structure and all persons who participate in it assist in "telling the tale." The main character in the gospel of Matthew is Jesus the Messiah, with the supporting cast of disciples. Pharisees and scribes serve as foils and/or opponents to create dramatic tension. The gospel contains the actions and sayings of Jesus to support his claim as the Messiah who is rejected by his own, received by "the other" (i.e. Gentiles, and some Jews), and who is crucified, yet raised as the True One of Israel. Matthew's story centers on the character Jesus as the Messianic Fulfillment of Israel.

Social Context

The evangelist recorded his work during a time when Judaism was recovering from a period of turmoil and belligerence. The destruction of the temple in 70 C.E. after war with Rome marked this gospel, and this background assists the reader in understanding its social background. The reader must see Matthew's community as a colonial group residing under the all-seeing eye of the Roman Empire. The presence of client king Herod (2:1), his son Archelaus (2:22), a centurion (8:5), Herod Antipas (14:1), Herodians (22:16), legions (26:53), Pilate (27:2), and a cohort (27:27) as mentioned in the gospel clue the reader to the power of Rome within the Matthean context. Because the Jews suffered defeat at the hands of Roman soldiers and lost their temple in the process, reading the gospel of Matthew through the lens of persons who have been socially demoted and marginalized is appropriate.

If the 80–90 C.E. date for the origin of the gospel is accurate, then by the time of the document's composition, Christian Jews adhering to Matthew's proclamation about Jesus were being forced to deal with their own survival under Roman emperor Domitian who was known for persecuting Christians. Rome was still a dominant political and military force during this time. The client kings in Judea and surrounding areas paid homage and allegiance to Roman officials, and those under the sovereignty of these kings had to do likewise. Furthermore, the issue of taxes (22:17–21) and fiscal obligation pervaded this community's way of life.

Not only does the gospel of Matthew call attention to the dominant Roman presence in the community's everyday life, but the evangelist gives the reader information on how people within the community interacted with each other. First, the writer clearly shows an intra-Jewish conflict. Some believe Jesus is the Christ; others do not. The most profound opponents of Jesus are the scribes and Pharisees (chap. 23). From an historical perspective Pharisees were the primary retainers of the Jewish law heritage after the fall of the Temple. Through their ability to regroup after such devastation, the Pharisees spearheaded what was later termed "rabbinic Judaism." The gospel contains frequent references to the importance of the law of Moses and disagreements over Jesus' relationship to it (e.g., 5:17–20).

Matthew also describes communal social concerns regarding the rich and money (6:19–34; 13:22; 19:16–22; 23:25; 28:11). The role of women receives a positive twist with them taking active, not passive roles in the life of the community and as followers of Jesus (8:14–17;

9:20–22; 15:21–28; 27:55–56; 28:1–10). In addition, ministry to the sick and weak as present in the community pervade this story of Jesus (chap. 8; 15:29–39; 17:14–20; 20:29–34).

Finally, while the mission of Jesus is initially to the Jews (10:5–6, 15:24), Matthew the evangelist informs the reader of the receptivity of the Gentiles to the message (e.g., 8:5–13; 15:21–28). Thus the relationship to non-Jews who share a political, de-centered status similar to that of Matthew's Jewish Christian community comes to the surface. Initially the Gentiles are excluded from the mission of Jesus and the disciples (10:5–6; 15:24). But in the end the message of Jesus must go even to them. After falling among deaf ears among the chosen of Israel, the gospel must next be preached to the "nations," the Gentiles (28:19).

Religious Context

The religious context of the gospel of Matthew was connected to its social context. You cannot examine one without the other. Because Matthew's community was a Jewish community living in a society that was under the rule of Roman law, its practice of religion was intermingled with its existence in an oppressive social world. The way in which the Matthean community tied the religious with the social can be seen in several ways.

First, the evangelist situates his work in Judaic socio-salvific history. What Matthew records of his community does not occur haphazardly or separate from the history of Israel. For Matthew all that he relates about Jesus and his relationship with the Jews, those who believe in him and those who do not, must be understood in light of Jewish history centuries prior to Jesus' presence on earth. Matthew's genealogy (1:1–16) and his constant references to Elijah (11:14; 16:14; 17:10–12), Moses (7:12; 17:3) and the law and the prophets (3:3; 5:17–20) are present to remind the Jewish Christian of history, ancestry, and heritage. Furthermore, Jesus is the Messiah and the one for whom Jewish fore-parents and prophets long waited. He is the one who has finally come and whose way John the Baptist prepared (3:3). Donald Senior notes that, according to Matthew, Jesus came to inaugurate a new day, a new age. He came to establish a new community of believers including both Jews and Gentiles. In this way Matthew joins the present situation with on-going sacred history and the imminent future.

The socio-religious tie in Matthew can also be seen through the prevalence of the law in this gospel. The Pharisees as scholars of the law insisted upon strict allegiance and obedience to it. Adherence to it as the word of God was of utmost importance. Yet, Matthew clues the reader into a degree of conflict over its place with followers of Jesus Christ. While arguing that he does not desire to abolish the law (5:17), Matthew's Jesus still comes into conflict with Jewish leaders over the law's place among those who believe in him, particularly as seen through some of their practices (5:21–45; 12:1–8). The author of Matthew further heightens this tension by describing the synagogue as not belonging to his community, but rather being the worship place of the Pharisees, "their synagogue" (9:35; 10:17; 12:9).

Matthew presents his gospel as an apologetic, a defense of what his Jewish community believes. Such pretext is not only designed to provide an outline of belief for those in his group, but it also serves to buffer them from any Roman danger or persecution. So that the Jesus of Matthew's community does not conflict with any worship of Roman deities, the author does not separate the presence of Rome from this work. The writer even maintains that while there are some allegiances that belong to Jesus, there are those that must be granted to the emperor (22:20–22). For Matthew's community to continue practicing their religious creeds, they must appear socially safe and religiously acceptable. While the author's ultimate focus is on religious righteousness, care must be taken to practice such without offending the socio-political powers-that-be.

There was little to separate the religious from the social aspect of the Matthean community. As a group enamored with salvation history yet that existed in the present social circumstance, Matthew's fellow believers, while newly joined to one Jesus the Messiah, were also connected to the society into which he entered and in which they followed him.

A Synopsis of the Gospel

For the most part, Matthew follows the outline of Mark, his primary source. Indeed, Matthew can be seen as a revision of Mark. In his revision, he adds a new beginning, namely a birth and infancy narrative, and a new ending, a resurrection appearance and commissioning of the disciples. He also adds additional teachings of Jesus, mostly from his other primary source, Q. He arranges the teachings of Jesus in a set of five major discourses (chapters 5–7; 10; 13; 18; and 24–25).

1) FROM BIRTH TO BAPTISM (1:1–4:11)

a. Birth and Infancy (1:1–2:23). Matthew begins his story by establishing the Jewish lineage of Jesus through an extensive genealogy beginning with Abraham (1:1) and continuing to Jesus' earthly father Joseph, a descendant of the line of King David (1:16). The genealogy traces the male lineage of Jesus, as was the custom, but, surprisingly, also includes references to four women. All four of these women are of questionable background–two were prostitutes (Tamar and Rahab), two were Gentiles (Rahab and Ruth), two became pregnant out of wedlock (Tamar and Bathsheba). They set the stage for the last woman in the list, Mary, who is also a disgraced woman (1:19), and serve to make the point that God's ways can be surprising and subversive.

Matthew's birth and infancy narrative has many features in common with Luke's, such as an angelic announcement of the birth of the child, the divine impregnation of Mary, the birth of Jesus in Bethlehem, a visit to the newborn child by a group of worshipers, and the subsequent settlement of the family in Nazareth. But Matthew and Luke developed their stories independently of one another and actually tell different stories. It is only by conflating them that we get the common Christmas story that we tell today. Such a conflation results in a story that neither Matthew nor Luke told. Only by letting Matthew tell his story in his own way can we fully appreciate his interpretation of the birth of Jesus.

Mathew's birth and infancy narrative is arranged in five scenes, each of which is punctuated by fulfillment of a specific biblical text, a standard device found throughout Matthew's gospel. In scene one, when Mary was "found to be with child from the Holy Spirit" and Joseph was planning "to dismiss her quietly" rather than exposing her "to public disgrace," an angel stepped in and announced to Joseph in a dream that he should, in fact, take Mary as his wife (1:18–25). The child she carries is "from the Holy Spirit," the angel says, and instructs that Joseph is to name the child Jesus, "for he will save his people from their sins" (1:20–21). The narrator then informs us that this took place to fulfill Isaiah 7:14, which announces the conception of a virgin and the birth of a son to be called "Emmanuel" which the narrator translates for the reader as "God with us" (1:22–23, RSV). The theme of "God with us" is programmatic for the story of Jesus throughout Matthew's gospel and rounds out the story at its close when the risen Lord says to the disciples, "I am with you always, to the end of the age" (28:20).

Scene two (2:1–12) presents the visit of the "wise men from the East," who first contact King Herod about the birth of a king in Bethlehem, as foretold by scripture (Mic. 5:2 and 2 Sam. 5:2) and announced by a heavenly portent. Herod feigns interest in the child, but the wise men, after visiting the child and paying homage, are "warned in a dream not to return to Herod" (2:12). Here, consistent with the genealogy, Jesus is presented as a new David, king of the Jews, who is given kingly homage by noblemen from the East.

In scene three (2:13–15), upon being warned in a dream once more, the parents flee to Egypt to escape Herod and his plan to kill the child. In this way, the story of Jesus will be seen to follow the pattern of the story of Israel, for, like Israel, of Jesus it will now be said, "Out of Egypt I have called my son" (2:15, quoting Hosea 11:1). Meanwhile, in scene four (2:16–18), Herod begins to slaughter the newborn children, thus fulfilling scripture (Jer. 31:15) and paralleling the story of Jesus with the story of Moses. Jesus is also presented as a new Moses elsewhere in the gospel, most notably at the Sermon on the Mount (chaps. 5–7). In scene five (2:19–23), after the death of Herod the Great, the family returns from Egypt and seemingly intends to return to Bethlehem. But once again a divine message comes in the form of a dream and directs them to go instead to Galilee where it is safer. So it is that they settle in Nazareth, fulfilling a "scripture" that Matthew has cobbled together out of traditions no longer clear to us that Jesus "will be called a Nazorean" (2:23).

b. Baptism and Temptation of Jesus (3:1–4:11). Following the birth and infancy narrative, Matthew then takes up the story of Jesus where Mark begins, with the baptism of John. Like Mark, Matthew presents John the Baptist as one who prepares the way for the Messiah according to scripture (3:1–3). Here he also introduces the inevitable conflict with the scribes and Pharisees who will continue to oppose Jesus throughout the story (3:7–9). Since, unlike Mark, Matthew with his birth story established the divine origin of Jesus, he tells the story of the baptism itself a bit differently. First Matthew adds a dialogue between Jesus and John (3:13–15) in which John raises what in Matthew would seem to be an obvious question. Given who Jesus is, why should he be baptized? Matthew's answer, in the words of Jesus, is that Jesus is baptized "to fulfill all righteousness" (3:15), combining two key theological themes in Matthew, "fulfillment" and "righteousness." Then, when Jesus is baptized, the voice from heaven speaks not to him (as it does in Mark 1:11) but to the crowd as a witness to the identity of Jesus, "this is my Son" (3:17).

Following Jesus' baptism, Mark has a brief reference to a wilderness temptation, but Matthew actually recounts a temptation story. His source here is Q, since Luke has the same three temptations, though in a different order. In Matthew, the last of the three temptations takes place on a high mountain where Jesus is promised the kingdoms of the world. But Jesus has already been affirmed as a king at his birth, so he resists Satan and dismisses him. More than once in Matthew key events in the ministry of Jesus will take place on a mountain (see, e.g., chaps. 5–7; 17:1–8; 28:16–20). By including these forty days of testing, Matthew also draws parallels with Moses and Elijah, parallels that will become an integral part of his program to connect Jesus to Israel's history.

2) Ministry in Galilee (4:12–10:42)

a. The Call of the First Disciples (4:12–25). John the Baptist, as a supporting character, now fades into the background (4:12) and Jesus comes to the forefront by beginning his ministry in Galilee, once again in fulfillment of scripture (4:12–16). After announcing his basic message, "repent, for the kingdom of heaven has come near" (4:17), he then calls his first disciples, Peter and Andrew, then James and John, all fishermen at the Sea of Galilee. They respond to the simple command, "follow me," and the commissioning "I will make you fish for people" (4:19), and they leave behind their former lives and families in order to follow. They, and the other disciples who will be added to their number, will be with Jesus until the end of the story witnessing all he will say and do. The first actions they witness are a variety of miracles of healing (4:23–25). Then they form the core group of disciples to whom Jesus preaches the Sermon on the Mount (5:1). Along with the "disciples," Jesus has also begun to attract a "crowd" (4:25–5:1), and, as the story proceeds, the crowd will vacillate from following him to, at the end of the story, turning on him.

b. Discourse One: The Sermon on the Mount (5:1–7:27). The Sermon on the Mount is often considered a literary work of art. It is made up of sayings of Jesus from Q as edited, organized, and expanded by Matthew. Q must have originally contained a collection of sayings of Jesus in a sermon form, because Luke also has a briefer version of the sermon, which he locates not on a mountain but on a "plain."

This is the first of five discourses of Jesus in Matthew and plays a pivotal role in Matthew's story and theology. It is the first extended teaching by Jesus in the gospel. It is set up by the call of the first disciples and a summary statement about miracles of Jesus. Now, with the disciples gathered around as "pupils" of Jesus the teacher, he first instructs them in detail here in the sermon, after which he will provide further teachings in his miracles (chaps. 8–9). The sermon thus functions as a call to discipleship.

Three themes may be utilized as keys to understanding the sermon: eschatology, ethics, and the social setting of Matthew. The first two, eschatology and ethics, can be defined by an analysis of the Lord's Prayer, which is located centrally in the sermon and offers a key to its overall vision (6:9–13). The first petitions of the prayer, given in parallel phrases in Greek, are "may your name be sanctified, may your kingdom come, may your will be done, as in heaven so also upon earth." These petitions represent a prayer that the characteristics of the dwelling place of God, the place where God rules, may also be found on earth. It is thus an eschatological prayer, signified especially by the characteristic phrase, "may your kingdom come."

The last three petitions present ethics to correspond to the eschatology of the first three petitions. They interpret what it would mean in human community if the first three were fulfilled. Following chiastic style, they are presented in reverse order to parallel the first three. Thus "may your will be done" is paralleled by "give us today our daily bread." The idea is that where God's will is done, there will be found bread enough for all. "May your kingdom come" is paralleled by "forgive us our debts, as we forgive our debtors," indicating that where God rules there will be found forgiveness and a forgiving community. "May your name be sanctified" is paralleled by "do not lead us into temptation but rescue us from the evil one," indicating that where God's name is invoked there will be found a sanctuary from the all-pervading evil of this world. The Lord's Prayer thus presents a vision of the community of God as empowered by the eschatological coming of the kingdom. The rest of the Sermon on the Mount operates out of this same vision.

The Beatitudes define the kingdom of heaven as belonging to those who are persecuted, as befits an eschatological vision (5:10). They are also those who "hunger and thirst for righteousness" (5:6), that is, who attend to the teachings of Jesus. It is the Matthean community and its social situation that are being identified here. The Matthean community understands itself in contrast to the Pharisees; indeed, their "righteousness exceeds that of the scribes and Pharisees" (5:20). They share with the Pharisees a reverence for the law; therefore Jesus is understood to have come not to "abolish" the law but rather to "fulfill" it (5:17). The difference is defined by their belief that Jesus is the Messiah and that he teaches with an authority greater than that of the scribes and Pharisees (7:28–29).

Jesus then proceeds to give specific examples of his "fulfillment" of the law by taking broad restrictions and narrowing them to more specific requirements in the so-called "antitheses" ("you have heard that it was said … but I say to you," 5:21–48). Teaching in the manner of an ancient rabbi, Jesus here gets to the root of what would cause one to disobey the law. It is not enough not to commit murder, rather not to become angry gets at the essence of the law (5:21–22). It is not enough to keep from swearing falsely, but not swearing at all diminishes the temptation to do so unjustly (5:33–37).

Following his mini discourse on the law, Jesus reiterates the righteousness concept introduced in chapter 5. Again the importance is on a righteousness of conduct or doing. Righteousness or piety must be practiced with humility and without expectation of receiving (6:1–6). As an extension of pious living, praying must be done with sincerity. Fasting is also a component of righteous living (6:16–18). Having established prayer and fasting as vital to the pious life, Jesus discusses how such religiosity translates into everyday life. The disciple or believer in Jesus does not concern him- or herself with money, is strictly devoted to God, not human relationships and does not worry about food, clothing, or drink (6:19–34). The believer is not to judge others, but must treat all as he or she desires to be treated (7:12). Matthew ends this first discourse with warnings about those who pretend to come in Jesus' name and those who do not receive the word of God (7:13–27).

The "righteousness" of the community is consistently defined over against others, such as the "hypocrites in the synagogues and in the streets" (6:2, 5, 16) or the "Gentiles" (6:7). In short, discipleship in Matthew is rooted in the reality of the social situation of the Matthean community. It is a community in transition, still defining themselves as heirs to the Jewish tradition, but forced by their circumstances to distinguish themselves from the dominant Jewish leadership of their day, represented in Matthew's story by the scribes and Pharisees and from those who call on the name of the Lord, but do not do [the Lord's] will (7:21–23), namely other Christian groups in Matthew's world who were not as Torah observant as was Matthew's community.

c. Miracle and Mission (8:1–9:34). Chapters 8 and 9 present a collection of miracles of Jesus that serve to address the continuing themes of Matthew's story. Just as the Sermon on the Mount was seen as a demonstration of his "authority" (7:29) so also his miracles are demonstrations of his divine power (8:27) and serve to fulfill scripture (8:17). They evoke responses ranging from the amazement of the disciples ("What sort of man is this, that even the winds and the sea obey him?" [8:27]) and the crowd ("Never has anything like this been seen in Israel" [9:33]), to the rejection of the Pharisees ("By the ruler of the demons he casts out the demons" [9:34]). As in all the gospels, the miracles in Matthew tend to be interpreted metaphorically. Thus when the leper is "cleansed" (8:3) and the bleeding woman is healed (9:22), both of them receive more than just physical healing–they are also freed of the "uncleanness" that separated them from God.

This section also introduces the theme of the Gentile mission. Though Jesus is primarily occupied with the healing of Israel (8:4, 17; 9:18, 33), he also extends his healing ministry beyond Israel and its borders. The centurion who asks Jesus to heal his servant is complimented by Jesus as having faith greater than any in Israel (8:10). So it is, Jesus says, that "many will come from east and west and will eat with Abraham and Isaac and Jacob in the kingdom of heaven, while the heirs of the kingdom will be thrown into the outer darkness" (8:11–12). This is a reference to the eschatological banquet, the great celebration at the end of the age when all the Gentile nations ("from east and west") will gather at the table of God (as in, for example, Isaiah 25:6–8), while the "heirs," namely Israel, will find themselves cast out. This is a message that resonated with Matthew's community, which found itself increasingly estranged from its Jewish heritage and confronted with the growing importance of a Gentile mission.

Several mini sermons on discipleship are also embedded in this section. One such sermon is found in 8:18–9:1. Immediately after the notation that the miracles of Jesus represented the healing of Israel (8:17), Jesus changed his focus by giving "orders to go over to the other side" (8:18), introducing the journey motif that binds together this entire section. Jesus' command is met with several pledges to follow Jesus, all of which seem to fall short because they fail to count the cost of discipleship (8:19–22). But when Jesus gets into the boat, his disciples follow him (8:23) and thus take up the call to discipleship. The journey in the boat takes on metaphorical significance as a symbol for the journey of the community of faith. which is buffeted by storms, cries out in despair, and is kept from danger by the Lord (8:24–27). Their destination is "the country of the Gadarenes," namely Gentile country, which Jesus symbolically cleanses by casting the demons into a herd of unclean animals who then destroy themselves (8:28–32). Having accomplished this symbolic mission, Jesus then returns to "his own town" to continue his mission among his own people (9:1). It will remain for the church to take up the Gentile mission, as they are commissioned to do as the last command given by the risen Lord ("make disciples of all nations," 28:19).

Another mini sermon on discipleship is embedded in the story at 9:9–13. After Matthew the tax collector responds to the simple command of Jesus to "follow me" (9:9), he finds himself at a meal with the other disciples and with a motley group of "tax collectors and sinners" (9:10). The Pharisees are scandalized by this, but address their question to the disciples: "Why does your teacher eat with tax collectors and sinners?" It is Jesus who answers the question, and who thereby presents another lesson on discipleship. "I have come to call [Greek: invite to the table] not the righteous but sinners," he says. The meal has become a symbol for the eschatological kingdom of God when not only all of the nations will gather at God's table (as in 8:11–12), but also the most hated of outcasts, namely "tax collectors and sinners."

To those who oppose him, represented especially by scribes and Pharisees (9:3, 11, 34), Jesus responds by noting that the "new wine" of his teaching is no longer appropriate for the "old wineskins" represented by the teachings of the Pharisees (9:14–17).

d. Discourse Two: The Mission Discourse (9:35–10:42). Because the needs of the people are great ("the harvest is plentiful") but their current religious leadership is ineffective (the people "were harassed and helpless, like sheep without a shepherd"), Jesus has compassion on them and urges his disciples to pray to the "Lord of the harvest to send out laborers into his harvest" (9:36–38). He then sends out the twelve, who are here named in Matthew for the first time (10:2–4). They are commissioned to go only to Israel (10:5–6) and carry out the same healing ministry that Jesus has been engaged in (10:1, 7–8); only after his resurrection will Jesus commission them to go to the nations (28:19). They are also to test the hospitality of the people (10:11–14), much as Abraham's hospitality was tested at the oaks of Mamre (see Gen. 18:1–15), and if the people fail the test, they will suffer as did Sodom and Gomorrah (10:15), which are cities that, in contrast to Abraham, failed the test of hospitality (Gen. 18:16–19:29). The mission instructions here, though given to the twelve, are meant for the church to whom this gospel was written. It is they who will face the most severe forms of inhospitality even to the point of persecution (10:16–23, 26–31, 34–39). Yet those who welcome them will, in effect, be welcoming Jesus (10:40–41). And just as Jesus extended his hospitality to the most extreme of outcasts (9:10–13), so his followers are to give "a cup of cold water to one of these little ones in the name of a disciple" (10:42).

3) RESPONSE AND REJECTION (11:1–16:12)

a. Jesus, John, and Wisdom (11:1–30). A comparison of Jesus and John the Baptist sets the tone for the next phase of Matthew's story. Jesus and John are defined over against "this generation" (11:16), a generation that, like fickle "children setting in the marketplaces," responds to neither messenger (11:16–19). Jesus and John are here characterized by images from the Jewish wisdom tradition: "Wisdom is vindicated by her deeds"

(11:19; see e.g. Prov. 8–9). Like personified Wisdom in Jewish tradition, which, incidentally, is a female figure, Jesus is known for extravagant table celebration–thus he is vilified as a "glutton and drunkard" and a "friend [i.e. table companion] of tax collectors and sinners" (11:19; see also 9:10–13; compare Prov. 9:1–6). Also like Wisdom (Sirach 24:19), Jesus extends an invitation to "Come to me" (11:28–30) for divine instruction that will make the "yoke" of the law (as in Jer. 5:5) a burden easy to bear.

b. Rising Tensions and Conflict (12:1–50). Conflicts with the Pharisees deepen over sabbath law (12:2, 10) and, ominously, when Jesus heals on the Sabbath in "their synagogue" (12:9), the Pharisees for the first time in Matthew's story initiate a plot to kill him (12:14). Jesus, for his part, becomes more insistent in defining those who are "against" him versus those who are for him (12:30). The harshness of the divide between this "evil generation" (12:45) and the followers of Jesus would have resonated with Matthew's community. They were apparently experiencing a severe estrangement from rival synagogues in their world (represented in the story by "their synagogue," namely the synagogue of the Pharisees). Such an experience was equivalent to breaking one's ties with one's own family (12:46–50).

c. Discourse Three: The Parables of the Kingdom (13:1–13:53). The metaphorical power of parables is now used to address the tragic social situation of Matthew's community. Like seed that grows in good soil, a true disciple is one who "hears the word and understands it, who indeed bears fruit" (13:23). Disciples are those who endure the onslaughts of the evil one and the persecutions that arise "on account of the word" (13:18–21). Though they live in a time of confusion and transition, in which weeds grow along with good seed, there will come a time of judgment when the weeds will be collected and "burned up with fire" (13:36–43, see also 13:47–50). The kingdom may seem hidden at present, but like a small mustard seed (13:31–32) or like yeast hidden in a large lump of dough (13:33) or like treasure hidden in a field (13:44) or like the one pearl of great value (13:45), it will eventually prevail.

d. The Conflict Continues (13:54–16:12). Two episodes follow that illustrate how great the opposition of this "evil generation" has become. In the first, Jesus is rejected by his own hometown in "their synagogue" (13:54–58). In the second, at a great banquet presided over by Herod, John the Baptist is beheaded (14:1–12). In direct contrast to the banquet of Herod, Jesus then convenes his own banquet far from the dangers of Herod in "a deserted place by himself" (14:13–21). This story, and the episode that follows, both provide exemplary accounts of discipleship. In the first, the disciples are taught how they are to care for the people. At first they balk at the task of feeding the people, but Jesus insists, and then he presides at the meal while they serve (14:13–21). His actions in blessing and breaking the loaves (14:19) prefigures the Last Supper at which Jesus will preside later in the story. In the second episode, when, once again, the disciples find themselves engaged in a metaphorical journey of faith on a troubled sea, Jesus walks on water, and the disciples learn, through the example of Peter, just how far one can go on faith (14:22–33).

Following this, there are two episodes that present in even more graphic detail the differences between the Matthean community between themselves and their antagonists. In the first, Jesus debates with the Pharisees about their interpretation of the purity laws, especially regarding hand washing before eating (15:1–9). He accuses them of being "hypocrites" (15:7) and "blind guides" (15:14), and reinterprets the purity laws to apply not to issues of eating per se, that is to the "mouth," but rather to the purity of the "heart" (15:10–20). In contrast to the "hypocrisy" of the Pharisees is the exemplary faith of the Canaanite woman, who, though a Gentile, still insists that Jesus must give attention to her needs (15:24–28). It is a remarkable story. Though Jesus first ignores her (15:23) and then twice rebukes her (15:24, 26), she, through her cleverness, shows the strength of her faith and understanding and is duly rewarded. The lesson is clear: It is the Gentiles who offer fertile ground for the sowing of the word.

This section closes with a second feeding story where once again Jesus presides and the disciples serve (15:32–38). Just as the first version of the banquet of Jesus was contrasted with the banquet of Herod (14:1–21), so this second version is contrasted with that of the Pharisees. The disciples are to serve the "bread" of Jesus and are to "beware the yeast of the Pharisees and Sadducees," namely their teachings (16:11–12).

4) The Journey to Jerusalem (16:13–20:34).

a) Confession and Call to Discipleship (16:13–28). Matthew inherits the journey to Jerusalem episode from Mark, but, once again, he has revised it to fit his own purposes. At this point Jesus turns his face toward Jerusalem and the suffering and death that await him there (16:21), which he predicts three times (16:21; 17:22–23; 20:17–19), just as in Mark's story (Mk. 8:31; 9:31; 10:33–34). Each disciple must "take up their cross and follow" (16:24) on what becomes for them a metaphorical journey of faith. While on the journey, Jesus will concentrate on teaching them about discipleship.

The journey begins at Caesarea Philippi with the confession of Peter. Unlike in Mark, where Peter's confession does not quite measure up, in Matthew Jesus compliments Peter on his faith and affirms that, in fact, Peter will become the foundational leader for the "church": "You are Peter [*Petros* or "rock"] and on this rock [*Petra*] I will build my church" (16:18). This sets the tone for the teachings on discipleship throughout the journey section. Though Jesus sometimes rebukes (16:23) and criticizes (17:20) when the disciples fall short, for the most part they are portrayed as students in training for leadership in the church.

b) Transfiguration (17:1–27). The transfiguration story represents a special revelation to the core leadership of the disciples, Peter, James, and

John. The scene is one in which Jesus is shown to be the successor to Moses and Elijah, as confirmed by a divine voice, just as at Jesus' baptism.

c) Fourth Discourse: Caring for the Community (18:1–35). This section is unique to Matthew and pictures Jesus explaining how Christian leaders are to care for the "church." The use of the term "church" in Matthew is anachronistic, since it refers to an institution that did not exist in the time of Jesus. Clearly Jesus' instructions here are intended for Matthew's community. The Christian leader is compared to a shepherd who cares for each stray sheep (18:12–14), namely the "little ones" who have been entrusted to their care (18:6–7, 10). The church is defined as a community that extravagantly practices forgiveness (18:15–19, 23–35), befitting the one in whose name they gather and who continues therefore to be "among them" (18:20; see also 1:23 and 28:20).

d) Further Teaching on Discipleship (19:1–20:34). As the journey continues from Galilee to Judea, Jesus presents further teachings for the church in which the values of the kingdom and the costs of discipleship are emphasized. His strict teaching on divorce is presented as another example of the difference between his understanding of the law and that of the Pharisees (19:3–12). His view of wealth is that it is a hindrance to discipleship unless generous almsgiving is practiced (19:16–30). To the question, "Then who can be saved?" (19:25), he replies "for God all things are possible" (19:26), then appends the parable of the laborers in the vineyard, which illustrates the extravagance of God's grace (20:1–16). When the disciples dispute among themselves about greatness, he responds, "whoever wishes to be great among you must be your servant…as the Son of Man came not to be served but to serve, and to give his life a ransom for many" (20:20–28). Thus as the journey comes to a close there is a repetition of the theme with which it began, that just as Jesus "must" journey to his death (16:21), so also the true disciple must "take up [his] cross" (16:24) and follow in the same kind of journey of faith.

5) Conflict and Death in Jerusalem (21:1–28:20)

a) Triumphal Entry and Cleansing of the Temple (21:1–22). When Jesus enters Jerusalem, it is as a king, as Son of David, and the crowds acclaim him as such (21:9). So intent is Matthew on strict fulfillment of scripture that he has Jesus sitting on two animals at once, both a donkey and a colt, corresponding to Matthew's interpretation of Zechariah 9:9 (21:2–7). Immediately on entering the city, he exercises his authority by cleansing the temple, indicated both by his casting out the vendors and money changers and by his healing the blind and the lame found within it (21:12–17). Jesus is here seen not as opposed to the temple cult, but rather as opposed to what he sees as its corruption under the influence of "this generation." Later Jesus will refer to the destruction of the temple (24:1–2), which is presented in Matthew's story world as a prediction by Jesus, but in Matthew's real world it was a past event and is thus interpreted as a judgment on Israel.

b) Conflict with Jewish Leadership (21:23–23:39). The conflict between Jesus and the leadership of the Jews now moves to the temple. There Jesus is confronted successively by chief priests and elders (21:23–27), Sadducees (22:23–33), and, most of all, Pharisees (21:45; 22:15–22; 34–46). Jesus responds with a succession of parables that present stark scenarios of the judgment against them. They are like the son who said he would do the work in the vineyard but did not (21:28–32), or like the tenants who killed every emissary of the landowner, including his son, in an attempt to wrest control of the vineyard (21:33–41), or like those invited to the wedding banquet who refuse to come, and even kill the messenger (22:1–14). Jesus' conclusions are stark and direct: "the tax collectors and the prostitutes are going into the kingdom of God ahead of you" (21:31) and "the kingdom of God will be taken away from you and given to a people that produces the fruits of the kingdom" (21:43). Meanwhile, the Pharisees continue to plot against Jesus (21:45–46; 22:15). These texts functioned to justify the claim of Matthew's community to be the true heirs of Israel. They also provide a window into Matthew's understanding of the mission of the church, that it is to be directed characteristically to "tax collectors and prostitutes" (21:31–32) and to "both good and bad" from the nations of the world (22:9–10), though the "bad" will eventually be found out because they will lack the proper "wedding robe" (22:11–13).

There follows an extended denunciation of the Pharisees (23:1–39). It begins with a revealing comment about what the Pharisees represent in Matthew's world, namely authoritative Jewish leadership, for they "sit on Moses' seat" (23:2). The debate with them is not over the law per se but over its interpretation, and the debate has turned vicious. Consequently, Jesus presents a series of "woes" to the Pharisees, castigating them for their hypocrisy, defined more specifically in terms of pride (23:6–7), the neglect of "justice and mercy and faith" (23:23), and "greed and self-indulgence" (23:25). Clearly these verses represent a polemic against the Jewish leadership of Matthew's day and is expressed with rhetorical overkill. Nevertheless there is an important message to be found in the kingdom values proclaimed here.

c) Fifth Discourse: The Eschatological Discourse (24:1–25:46). Matthew here expands on the eschatological discourse found in his source, Mark (Mk. 13). These sayings of Jesus are presented as predictions of the immediate future, when the signs of the end of the age will be accomplished. But they function in the gospel as an affirmation of the Matthean community, for they describe events with which that community is already familiar, particularly the conditions of the Jewish War against Rome, which resulted in the destruction of the temple (24:2) and the fleeing from Judea (24:16). They also seem to have experienced persecution for their faith (24:9). For Matthew the end is no longer seen as imminent, for first must come the proclamation of "the good news of the kingdom...throughout the world" (24:14); consequently, "the day and the hour no one knows" (24:36). So the community is urged to "keep awake" (24:42; 25:13) and go about their tasks as "wise and faithful" servants who will be blessed if the master comes and finds them at work, not like the "wicked" servant who interprets the delay of the master's coming as a license to treat others with injustice (24:45–51).

The work of the community of faith in this interim period is powerfully portrayed in the parable of the sheep and the goats (25:31–46). This is a retelling of the ancient story of the divine being who comes among the people in disguise to test their hospitality and reward those who show hospitality and punish those who do not (see, for example, Gen. 18–19). Here in Matthew the meaning of hospitality is spelled out in terms of justice and compassion for the unfortunate (25:35). It is a text that brings to focus what "righteousness" really means in Matthew's gospel (compare 25:37 with 5:6 and 5:20) and in what manner the presence of Jesus in the community is to be known (compare 18:20 and 28:20).

d) The Last Supper (26:1–46). The impending death of Jesus has overshadowed Matthew's story from early on (see especially 16:21). Now the time of teaching is over (26:1) and events move rapidly toward that foreordained conclusion. Matthew constructs the story so that the action moves quickly from one scene to another. Jesus seems to initiate the action by announcing that the time of his death is only two days away and will be at the time of Passover (26:2). In the next scene the chief priests and elders are seen plotting against him (26:3–5). Then we move to a scene in which Jesus' body is prepared for burial in advance by means of a moving, symbolic action by an unnamed woman at a meal in Bethany (26:6–13). Then we return once more to the plot against Jesus, this time to observe Judas agreeing to a price to betray him (26:14–16). All of this sets the stage for the somber last meal of Jesus.

The time for Passover has now come, and Jesus and his disciples, as pilgrims to Jerusalem, gather in borrowed quarters to take the meal together, a meal that, the reader now knows, will be his last (26:17–19). The entire meal is overshadowed by expectation of his death. The first scene is Jesus' announcement that he will be betrayed (26:20–25). The scene is made even more poignant by the fact that the one who will betray him is one who shares in the intimacy of table fellowship, "one who has dipped his hand into the bowl with me" (26:23). The next scene, in which, by implication, Judas also participates, includes the ceremonial bread and wine, which are interpreted in reference to the death of Jesus and its significance.

Matthew's version of the so-called "eucharistic words" of Jesus follows that of Mark, but with an important addition. To the saying over the cup, "this is my blood of the covenant, which is poured out for many" Matthew has added "for the forgiveness of sins" thus making more explicit how this gospel interprets the saving significance of the death of Jesus (26:28; see also 1:21).

In the next scene, which takes place after they have left the table and have arrived at the Mount of Olives, Jesus makes another prediction similar to the prediction of his betrayal. Now he predicts that all of his disciples will desert him and Peter will deny him three times (26:30–35). As if they have already begun to falter, Peter, James, and John are unable to stay awake with Jesus as he prays at Gethsemane (26:36–46). Though he prays that "this cup pass from me," namely the cup of suffering, he accepts his fate as foreordained, "yet not what I want but what you want" (26:39). The prayer evokes the theme of the suffering of Jesus, but it is balanced if not overshadowed by the divine foreknowledge Jesus has of all events about to take place, so that he announces the arrival of the betrayer just as he appears on the scene (26:46). Thus the story keeps in uneasy balance the dual nature of Jesus, both human and divine.

e) Arrest and Trial (26:47–27:31). The arrest of Jesus, inaugurated by the kiss of betrayal of Judas, takes place with Jesus' full cooperation and in accordance with fulfillment of scripture (26:47–56). So also, just as Jesus predicted, he is betrayed, deserted (26:56), and denied (26:69–75). Indeed, there is heavy irony in the fact that Jesus is mocked as a prophet in the house of the high priest (26:68) while at that same time in the courtyard a prophecy of his is coming true, namely his denial by Peter (26:69–75), a motif Matthew copies from Mark (14:53–72).

The stories of Judas and Peter are intentionally contrasted in Matthew's story. Judas' betrayal is predicted just before the meal, Peter's denial just after. Judas then betrays before the high priest's trial, Peter denies just after. So also Peter repents and weeps bitterly (26:75), while Judas repents and hangs himself (27:3–10).

Following a pattern that begins in Mark, Matthew constructs the trials of Jesus in such a way that responsibility is seen to rest especially on the Jewish leadership. Indeed, Matthew even enhances this aspect of the story. It is a group of ruffians from the chief priests and elders who apprehend Jesus in Gethsemane, and they carry him to the house of Caiaphas the high priest for a trial (26:47, 57). There he is judged guilty of blasphemy and given a sentence of death (26:65). So, in order to bring it about, they carry him to Pilate (27:1–2). Pilate is reluctant to pronounce judgment (27:15–18, 21–23). His wife even pronounces Jesus innocent because of a dream she has had (27:19). (Note that dreams in Matthew are divine portents.) Pilate tries to release Jesus, but "the chief priests and the elders persuaded the crowds to ask for Barabbas and to have Jesus killed" (27:20). Pilate finally washes his hands before the crowd and announces "I am innocent of this man's blood; see to it yourselves" in response to which the crowd calls out, "his blood be on us and on our children" (27:24–25).

In the context of Matthew's social setting and theology, this curse was carried out in the Jewish War of 66–70 C.E., when Judea suffered greatly at the hands of Rome and when the temple was destroyed. Such a point of view developed in a time of conflict between rival Jewish groups as each sought to claim the heritage of Israel for itself. The passionate rhetoric of Matthew against a rival Jewish group should therefore be understood in the context of a particular historical situation. Instead, much too often in Christian history the "curse" in Matthew 27:24–25 has been utilized as justification for anti-Semitism. This is a severe misinterpretation of Matthew, since the curse is specific to Matthew's social situation and should not to be understood as applying to Judaism in general. After all, Matthew's community itself is Jewish.

f) Death and Burial (27:32–66). Many of the themes that have been developing throughout Matthew's story come in to focus here at the death of Jesus. There is heavy irony in the fact that Jesus is mocked as "King of the Jews," for the reader of Matthew's gospel knows that this is, in fact, his true identity. Thus he is given a robe and a crown (27:27–31), acclaimed king by a sign on the cross (27:37), and mocked as king by passersby, by the bandits on adjacent crosses, and by Jewish leaders (27:39–44). The fact that his kingship is proclaimed in such ironic form, and reaches its highest moment when he is on the cross, means that the entire idea of king and kingship must be rethought, as Matthew has been doing throughout his story. Thus Jesus as "king" ironically takes on a role opposite to the norm, namely the role of a "servant" (20:25–28) therefore redefining the values of his kingdom in terms of servanthood, justice, and compassion instead of arrogance, greed, and hypocrisy (23:1–28; see also 25:31–46).

The story is also closely tied throughout to fulfillment themes as well as to miraculous portents. The theme of Jesus' opposition to Jewish leaders and openness to Gentiles comes in to focus when the narrator announces that upon his death the curtain of the temple was torn in two, thus symbolizing that God's presence was now available to all, not just in the holy of holies (27:51). This leads directly into the theme of the "great commission" in chapter 28.

The crucifixion story includes many villains, but it also includes stories of exemplary piety. Though the disciples have deserted Jesus, others are still there to give witness. The centurion and others with him, upon seeing the divine portents, confess, "Truly this man was God's Son!" (27:54). The women who follow Jesus observe the events from afar, and are present at the crucifixion, burial, and resurrection (27:55–56, 61; 28:1). Joseph of Arimathea, who is named as a disciple, takes on the dangerous task of asking Pilate for the body so that he can bury it. When his request is granted, he buries Jesus in "his own new tomb" (27:57–60).

6) THE RESURRECTION (28:1–20)

For the most part, Matthew follows Mark's version of the empty tomb story, but he has made some important changes. In Matthew, the empty tomb story is bracketed by the story of the guards at the tomb, a story not found in any other of the canonical gospels, and one that seems to represent an answer to a charge that was made in later anti-Christian polemic that Jesus' body had been stolen (27:62–66; 28:11–15). In Mark's story, the women arrive to find the tomb open and then enter to see an angel within (Mk. 16:3–5). In Matthew's story, when the women arrive, they witness the angel coming down from heaven to open the tomb (28:2–4). His purpose is to show them that it is empty and to announce that Jesus has been resurrected (28:5–6). He then tells the women that the risen Lord has gone before them to Galilee, so they are to go tell the disciples that he is resurrected and that they are to go to Galilee in order to see him (28:7). In Mark's gospel, the women fail to do this (Mk. 16:7–8). Such an ending is unsatisfying, however, so Matthew edits it. In Matthew's version, not only do the women go to tell (28:8), but they also actually see the risen Lord who repeats the command to go and tell (28:9–10). This makes Matthew's account one that especially affirms the importance of women as proclaimers of the good news.

In the final scene (28:16–20), the disciples have gathered in Galilee on a mountain, which is appropriate since Jesus characteristically teaches on mountains in Matthew's gospel (see especially chaps. 5–7). There they see the risen Lord and receive his commission. Now the new age has arrived, for Jesus commissions them to go to "all nations," that is, to the Gentiles. They are to make them into "disciples" and teach "them to obey everything that I have commanded you," phrases that refer back to the central teachings of this gospel. Finally, to bring the gospel of "Emmanuel" ("God is with us," 1:23) to a close he announces, "I am with you always, to the end of the age."

Discipleship: A Central Theological Theme

Through all of the parables, sayings, discourses, healings stories, and miracles, Matthew the evangelist wants the listeners, those in his community, to respond with the action of discipleship. The recipient of the message must become a student, a learner of Jesus Christ. The author notes that Jesus' first and last task was the call of disciples (5:18–22; 28:16–20). Jesus begins his ministry by summoning persons to follow him, and his final words involve making more disciples. The disciple who follows Jesus takes the path Jesus took, and takes up his cross to follow (16:24–26).

According to Matthew true discipleships entails obedience (8:18–22). It is sacrificial sometimes unto death (10:16–37; 16:24–27). Those who obey

Jesus are also prepared for his return. They are not unprepared or idle. The disciple is busy calling others into the kingdom of God (24:36–25:30). Finally, the true disciple of Jesus according to Matthew shares him with others. The need for Jesus is great; therefore the work of those who believe in Jesus must be as great (9:35–38; 10:1).

Those who follow Jesus learn to live like him. Living like him means imitating his actions and behavior, living the right life. Again, at the onset of his portrayal of Jesus, the gospel writer establishes his teaching on piety and godly conduct. This teaching outlines various nuances of the "right life." The student of Jesus prays sincerely and without pretense even when death is near at hand (6:9–13; 26:36–46). The learner who seeks to live a righteous life depends on the Teacher not for didactic purposes, but as a child would a parent or guardian for protection and care (19:13–15; 18:1–5). Those who would live like Christ are careful of teachings contrary to his (13:24–30) and are honest, above-board persons, unlike the opponents of Jesus (chap. 23). The follower of Jesus, in order to display conduct pleasing to him, must forgive those in the community who have wronged them (18:21–22). Above all, the true disciple practices hospitality, compassion, and justice. He or she is one who offers "a cup of cold water" in hospitality (10:42), tends to those in need (25:34–36), and is welcoming to the most scandalous of outcasts (9:11–13; 21:31).

Matthew also offers a primer on Christian leadership. Peter emerges as the exemplary Christian leader who, though he sometimes lacks faith (14:31) and eventually denies Jesus (26:69–75), is nevertheless the one who steps out in faith (14:29–30), who repents of his sins (26:75), and who is praised by Jesus for his exemplary role (16:17–19). The feeding stories define Christian leadership in terms of the care and feeding of the congregation (14:14–21; 15:32–38). Christian leaders are charged to care for the "little ones" in their midst, much as a shepherd cares for every sheep that goes astray (18:10–14).

Importance for the Church in the Twenty-first Century

Matthew's message is still relevant to the church as it enters a new millennium. The acts of violence in schools, churches, and neighborhoods, and the sheer disregard for humanity that permeate our world, indicate that the kind of discipleship described by Matthew is still needed. Discipleship as proclaimed by Matthew is a servant discipleship, one that gives attention to the most needy and marginalized in society. It is characterized by compassion and justice, and by its opposition to greed and injustice.

Furthermore, believers must continue to share the good news of Christ. Those who adhere to the word of God must not assume that evangelism is useless or not politically correct. In Matthew, the goal of evangelism is to "make disciples of all nations" (28:19). It is an idealistic view of evangelism, one that sees its purpose as changing the hearts of people rather than merely filling the churches. Thus as long as there is greed and injustice in the world, disciples are needed and evangelism must continue.

Matthew also emphasizes inclusion of all in the circle of humanity. Just as Matthew's Jesus affirmed the mission to Gentiles, to tax collectors, prostitutes, and other sinners, so also the church today is to minister to those who are not like us ethnically or racially. The church must also be more open to women and their various ministries just as Jesus affirmed them. Furthermore, those who are physically or mentally challenged must be deemed a part of God's creation and creative plan as Jesus too affirmed those who were unclean and not whole. Finally, the poor as well as the rich are given a place in the kingdom of God, a kingdom that is no respecter of economic standing or status.

Finally, Matthew reminds us of the importance and purpose of leadership in the churches. Without good leaders, the people are like sheep without a shepherd. Like a good shepherd, the Christian leader is to care for all of the flock, especially the marginalized or "little ones." And most importantly the Christian leader is to preside at a table that is inclusive of all, where all nations may come and be welcomed at God's feast.

Suggested Resources for the Pastor's Library

Boring, M. Eugene. "The Gospel of Matthew," in *The New Interpreter's Bible.* Volume 8. Edited by Leander Keck. Nashville: Abingdon Press, 1995.

Corley, Kathleen E. *Private Women, Public Meals: Social Conflict in the Synoptic Tradition.* Peabody, Mass.: Hendrickson Press, 1993.

Davies, W. D., and Dale C. Allison, Jr. *Matthew.* The International Critical Commentary. Three volumes. Edinburgh: T & T Clark, 1988, 1991, 1997.

Garland, David E. *Reading Matthew: A Literary and Theological Commentary on the First Gospel.* New York: Crossroad, 1993.

Hare, Douglas R. A. *Matthew.* Interpretation. Louisville: Westminster John Knox Press, 1993.

Kingsbury, Jack Dean. *Matthew as Story.* Philadelphia: Fortress Press, 1988.

Levine, Amy-Jill. "The Gospel of Matthew," in *The Women's Bible Commentary*, 339–49. Expanded edition. Edited by Carol A. Newsom and Sharon Ringe. Louisville: Westminster John Knox Press, 1998.

Luz, Ulrich. *The Theology of the Gospel of Matthew.* New Testament Theology. Cambridge: Cambridge University Press, 1995.

Overman, J. Andrew. *Church and Community in Crisis: The Gospel According to Matthew.* Valley Forge. Pa.: Trinity Press International, 1996.

Patte, Daniel M. *Discipleship According to the Sermon on the Mount.* Valley Forge, Pa.: Trinity Press International, 1996.

Senior, Donald. *The Gospel of Matthew*. Nashville: Abingdon Press, 1997.

Wainwright, Elaine. "The Gospel of Matthew," in *Searching the Scriptures, Volume 2: A Feminist Commentary*, 635–77. Edited by Elisabeth Schüssler Fiorenza. New York: Crossroad, 1994.

9

The Story of Jesus According to "Luke"
The Gospel of Luke

RONALD J. ALLEN

I often begin my class "Introduction to the New Testament" by asking participants to indicate their favorite passages from the New Testament. Typically, about half of the passages cited are from the gospel of Luke or its companion, the Acts of the Apostles. The following are among the most frequently mentioned: the Lukan parables, the shepherds at the birth of Jesus, the road to Emmaus, Pentecost, and the story of Paul. Indeed, the dominant image of Paul for many beginning students is less the apostle as revealed in the correspondence from his own quill, and more the great missionary traveler pictured in Acts.

I mention this phenomenon because it suggests that while the gospel of Luke and the Acts of the Apostles constitute a relatively small part of the New Testament, they play a large role in the church. A grounding in the interpretive issues surrounding these materials will help us assess the role of their images in the church.

Basic Data

We do not have definite answers to the questions of authorship, date and place of composition, the community addressed, or the specific issues addressed. As is the case with the gospels of Matthew, Mark, and John, Luke does not furnish this data directly.

The identification of Luke as the author does not occur in the body of either the gospel or Acts. This attribution, found only in the title, first appears in an ancient manuscript (named p75) that dates from 175–225 C.E. We can neither prove nor disprove that a person named Luke was the author. Even if we knew the writer's name, that fact alone would not necessarily help us interpret these books. However, I follow the universal scholarly convention of referring to the writer by the name Luke.

Some Christians believe that the author of Luke-Acts was Luke, a companion of Paul (Col. 4:14; Philem. 24; 2 Tim. 4:11). Most scholars (whose view I share) acknowledge that such an identification is unlikely, but not impossible. Even if we knew that the author of Luke-Acts was a companion of Paul, our ability to make sense of the gospel and Acts would not be significantly enriched.

Because Luke is described as "the beloved physician" in Col. 4:14, some earlier interpreters believed that Luke and Acts are filled with medical terminology. However, people in the ancient world did not have a distinctive medical vocabulary. The consensus today is that Luke's language does not reflect medical background.

More important is the fact that Luke has an intimate knowledge of Judaism and of the Septuagint—the translation of the Hebrew Bible into Greek. Luke-Acts is permeated with Septuagintalisms (phrases and allusions from the Septuagint). Hence, many scholars think that Luke may have been a Christian Jewish person; that is, someone of Jewish origin who recognized God at work through the ministry of Jesus and the church. Others think that Luke was a Gentile who learned Judaism after conversion to Christianity.

We are uncertain about the place of composition. Among the leading candidates for place of composition are Achaia, Antioch, Caesarea, Ephesus, and Rome. But we cannot find compelling evidence for any one of these settings.

Most scholars think that Luke made use of preexisting materials to write the gospel and Acts. The two-source theory, which proposes that Luke's primary sources were Mark and Q, is the most common source theory among scholars. However this theory does not account for material that is unique to this gospel, such as the story of the parent and the two children (Lk. 15:11–32). Luke may have drawn these unique materials from a third source, or may have composed them.

Neither the gospel nor Acts indicate the date they were written. Most scholars agree that these two books were written after Mark because the gospel of Luke appears to be based on Mark's outline. Many scholars also conclude that Luke wrote after the destruction of the temple in Jerusalem in 70 C.E. because Luke 13:33–35, 19:41–44, and 21:20–24 seem to presuppose this event. By the middle of the second century C.E., other Christian writers quote from both Luke and Acts, thus indicating that these volumes were written by that time. The scholarly consensus is that Luke wrote about 80–90 C.E.

Luke is a remarkable storyteller. Indeed, Luke's overall narrative style, as well as the telling of individual stories, places these two books among of the most engaging narrative theology in sacred scripture.

Luke-Acts addresses several basic, intertwined issues:

- Who is Jesus Christ and what does he offer and require?
- What are God's purposes through Christ and the church, and in history? In particular, what is the reign (kingdom) of God? How will it be manifest? When? How can the community join it?
- What is the church? What is its mission, and among whom?
- How are Jesus Christ, and the church, related to the God of Israel and to Judaism?

To these fundamental themes, we can add many others. Among them: the nature and sources of authority in the church, the work of the Holy Spirit, the purposes and practices of discipleship, the relationship between persons of Jewish and Gentile origin within the Christian community, the role of women in the Christian community, the relationship of the rich and the poor in the church, attitudes toward and uses of material goods, the relationship of the church to persons who are outside of conventional social circles, the meaning of prayer and other important religious practices (e.g., baptism, breaking of bread, laying on of hands), the role of religious ecstasy in Christian life, the relationship of Luke's picture of Paul with the Paul of the undisputed letters, and Christian attitudes toward various forms of civil government.

Methods Important for Interpretation

Three methods of interpretation are most significant for the interpretation of the gospel and Acts: historical criticism, literary criticism, and rhetorical criticism.

Until the last two generations of scholarship, *historical criticism* was the reigning method by which scholars examined the gospel. Historical criticism attempts to understand a document against the background of the document's historical context. How would persons in the first century hear the gospel of Luke and the Acts of the Apostles? For instance, when hearing that Jesus eats with tax collectors and sinners (e.g., Luke 5:29–32), it is important to know the meaning of table fellowship in the time of Luke, as well as the historical details that tax collectors were Jewish persons who grew wealthy by collaborating with Rome to gouge the Jewish population for heavy taxes, and that the term "sinner" referred to those who flagrantly violated the desires of God.

Some historical critics attempt to go further by going behind the present text to reconstruct the historical circumstances to which Luke-Acts are addressed. However, many scholars recognize that these books do not yield the kind of information that allows us to describe the detailed situation of the congregation for which these books were written.

The most prominent approaches currently used in the study of the gospel of Luke and the book of Acts are *literary criticism*, and its kin, *rhetorical criticism.* Literary criticism is not a single method, but is a way of speaking of a wide range of approaches to the text that hold this feature in common: They attempt to interpret the gospel and Acts as literary works. Luke uses setting, plot, and characters to create a literary world. When we enter the narrative of Luke-Acts, we experience Luke's interpretation of the story of Jesus and the early church. When we emerge from that narrative, the story is a lens through which we can interpret our everyday worlds.

Reader-response criticism, a particular form of literary study, is especially helpful. The reader-response analysts seek to determine the responses elicited in the reader by the gospel and Acts. What response does a text seek to create through the interaction of genre, setting, plot, characters? For instance, when studying the healing of the bent-over woman (Lk. 13:10–17), the interpreter asks, What are the effects of this story in the listening community? What is evoked by the setting in a synagogue on the Sabbath? by the presence of a woman as a central character? by the conflict between Jesus and the leader of the synagogue? when Jesus calls the woman a "daughter of Abraham"? when Jesus put his opponents to shame while the wider crowd rejoices?

Literary criticism can help our understanding of the larger narrative of Luke-Acts by tracing how themes develop across the gospel and Acts. For instance, God's embrace of the Gentiles is introduced as a main theme of Jesus' ministry in Luke 1–2. This motif is developed in Jesus' initial sermon at Nazareth (4:16–30), and surfaces several times in the gospel. At the ascension, Jesus identifies this mission as a primary agenda for the church (Lk. 24:44–49; Acts 1:6–11). Following the chronology of Acts 1:8, Luke leads the reader to experience this story as its spreads from Judea (Acts 2:1–7:60) through Samaria (8:1, 4–25), and to the "ends of the earth" (Acts 9:1–28:31).

Rhetorical criticism takes its cue from the notion, prevailing in the ancient world, that texts and speeches are designed to persuade the listener or reader of a particular point of view. This mode of criticism intends to discover the styles (genre), goals, and methods of ancient approaches. Rhetorical analysis can apply both to written documents and to oral-aural events.

The rhetoric of antiquity contained specific genres, with their own conventions and intentions, that speakers and authors employed in connection with particular purposes. Rhetorical analysis can apply to a lengthy narrative such as Luke-Acts, or to specific passages within the larger narrative. By discovering the rhetorical genre of a text, an interpreter has an important window into the purpose of the text. Of course, the interpreting community must make sense of each text from the perspective of the overall purpose of the document.

In the materials that follow, I make use of an informal amalgam of literary (especially reader-response) methods and rhetorical criticism, supplemented by insights and data from historical criticism and sociological exegesis.

Social Context

Scholars assume the same social context for the gospel of Luke and the book of Acts. While Luke does not discuss the context directly, we can infer three aspects of it from these two documents: the relationship of the community to the wider Hellenistic world—especially to the Roman government, the relationship of the Lukan community to Judaism, and relationships within the community.

With respect to the community's *relationship to the wider Hellenistic world,* many scholars think that these writings encourage the listener to recognize that the Christian mission is at home in a Hellenistic environment. Luke and Acts indicate a familiarity with Hellenistic custom and settings that suggests they were composed outside of Palestine, perhaps in an urban environment. For instance, when the four friends bring the paralytic to Jesus in Mark 2:4, they dig through the thatch and mud roof of a modest Palestinian house. Luke changes this detail to indicate that the friends let down the paralytic's bed through a tile roof (Lk. 5:19). Tile roofs were characteristic of relatively more prosperous Hellenistic settings.

Some earlier interpreters thought that the social purpose of Luke-Acts was to defend the church to Roman civil officials by assuring Rome that the church did not represent a threat to its dominion. However, most scholars today think that the gospel of Luke and the book of Acts were written for a Christian community, and not for those outside. Luke encourages Christians to recognize ambiguity in the Roman presence. This ambiguity is represented in the figure of Pilate, Roman governor of Palestine. On the one hand, at the trial of Jesus, Luke's Pilate declares the Savior innocent. On the other hand, because Jesus is innocent, Pilate should release the Nazarene, but does not. At the insistence of the Jewish mob, Pilate releases Barabbas, a murderer, and allows Jesus to be crucified (23:13–24). This theme is more fully developed in Acts.

The *relationship of the Lukan community to Judaism* is complicated. Because this relationship is central to the religious context, I discuss it more fully in that section. With respect to social context, it is important to note that Luke wrote at a time when the church was still in the process of sorting out its relationship with Judaism. Jesus and the first followers were Jewish. The early Christian community existed as a subgroup within Judaism. We might even refer to these early witnesses as Christian Jews.

Yet alongside respect for Jewish tradition, both the gospel of Luke and the book of Acts report conflicts between selected Jewish authorities, and Jesus and the early church (e.g., Lk. 5:29–6:11; 12:1–11; 13:10–17; Acts 3:1–4:22; 5:17–42; 6:8–8:1). Most scholars think that, while genuine historical reminiscence is behind some of these incidents, their present form reflects conflict between the church and Judaism of Luke's day. The church reads elements of its conflict into the stories of Jesus and the earlier Christian communities. These stories, then, suggest that the Lukan social context was marked by tension between some traditional Jewish people (whom scholars sometimes call "the synagogue") and the Christian movement (sometimes called "the church").

We need to be careful not to oversimplify this aspect of Luke's social context by starkly contrasting "the" synagogue and "the" church. The basic issue is the degree to which the church—with its Gentile mission—can be regarded as an authentic expression of Judaism. Some people, represented by the Jewish opponents of Jesus and the church in Luke-Acts, believed that the church violated some of Judaism's deepest convictions. Still other Jewish people defended Jesus and the church without themselves becoming Christian (e.g., Gamaliel in Acts 5:38–39). Furthermore, the church was conflicted within itself as to how to relate to Judaism (Acts 15).

Luke's social context also involves *relationships within the Lukan community.* This aspect of the social setting has multiple dimensions.

The stress on the Gentile mission prompts many commentators to think that the gospel and Acts presume a social situation in which Christian Jews and Gentile Christians are in the process of learning how to be hospitable to one another. Which practices of Judaism must be retained as normative for all members of the church? Which customs should Christian Jews continue, while not regarding them as necessary for Gentile Christians? How can Jewish and Gentile persons live together within the church so that the community of the church witnesses to the eschatological unity of all peoples?

Jesus' repeated emphasis on discipleship as following the way of the cross, and Acts' portrayal of the social difficulties of many early Christians, leads some scholars to think that the Lukan church is suffering (e.g., Lk. 8:23–27; 21:7–24; Acts 4:1–22; 5:17–42: 6:8–8:1). Luke interprets this suffering as part of the tribulation—the suffering of the world prior to the apocalyptic cataclysm that ends the present age of history and inaugurates a new world. Some interpreters think that the church is in distress as a part of the general distress of Judaism in the wake of the destruction of the temple in 70 C.E. Other scholars think that the suffering of the church results from persecution by the synagogue. If the latter, the persecution would likely be a form of synagogue discipline.

The gospel and the early chapters of the book of Acts give much attention to poverty and wealth, and to the use of material goods in community (e.g., Lk. 6:24–38; 12:13–21; 16:19–31; 18:18–25; Acts 2:41–47; 4:32–39; 6:1–6). Consequently, many interpreters think that Luke's social context is one of economic disparity.

Soon after World War II, Hans Conzelmann, in his groundbreaking work *The Theology of St. Luke,* proposed that Luke divided history into three ages: the periods of Israel, of Jesus, and of the church. Conzelmann noticed that Luke envisioned the age of the church as a protracted delay before Jesus' return (e.g., Luke 12:38, 45; 19:11; 21:24). In that period, according to Conzelmann, Luke substituted the coming of the Spirit for the expectation of Jesus' apocalyptic return. Today, however, few Bible expositors subscribe completely to Conzelmann's thesis. The gospel and Acts are filled with references to the coming apocalyptic event (e.g., Luke 8:16–18; 10:13–15; 12:4–12, 13–21, 35–57; 13:1–9; 17:20–37; 19:11–27; esp. 21:5–38; Acts 1:10–11; 2:17–21; 10:42; 17:29–31; 24:15, 25). Instead, most scholars today think that Luke intends to lead the community to recognize the Spirit as God's gift to help the community make its way through the delay. Luke's repeated emphases on the Spirit as a source of power, and on the apocalypse as a day of judgment, suggest that some in the community are lethargic, and need to be called to account and action.

Luke develops a picture of Jesus as a teacher, and of the apostles as his authoritative successors. Some interpreters think that this pattern suggests that Luke's community is dealing with false teachers.

The gospel and Acts repeatedly call attention to the importance of women in the ministry of Jesus and in the early Christian communities. Some scholars take this emphasis to be a sign of disagreement within the Lukan church regarding the role of women in the Christian community.

Religious Context

The religious context of the gospel of Luke and the book of Acts is permeated by the notion that the reign of God is being manifested afresh through Jesus and the early church, and will reach its universal fulfillment when Jesus returns from heaven. This motif is more fully discussed later.

Beyond the reign of God, the religious context of Luke has other significant components: (a) the relationship among Judaism, Jesus, and the early Christian movement; (b) the relationship between Luke's religious vision, and the religions of the Gentiles; (c) the relationship between optimum response of the disciples to the reign of God and their actual faith and behavior. Concern for the first and last of these components of the religious context permeates both the gospel and Acts.

From the start of the gospel through the end of Acts, the narrative devotes considerable attention to tensions in *the relationship between traditional Jewish people, and Jesus and the early church.* On the one hand, Luke honors the God of Israel and many Jewish traditions. Luke-Acts is written in a Septuagintal style so that these books appear to extend the story of biblical Israel into Luke's own day. Luke never pictures Jesus or members of the early church asking Jewish persons to cease practicing Judaism. Luke pictures Jesus as a faithful Jewish person who is in conversation with other Jewish people regarding what it means to be faithful.

When Jesus and the early Christians criticize the Pharisees and other leaders of Judaism, they do so as those inside the Jewish community, much as the classical prophets criticized Israel (e.g., Lk. 4:24; 13:33–34; 24:19). However, there is a notable difference in purpose between the critique of Israel by the biblical prophets and the critique of Jewish leaders in Luke-Acts. The prophets direct their criticism toward Israel in the hope that the people will repent and return to God's ways. The critique of Judaism expressed in Luke-Acts is not intended to prompt repentance, but to help justify the growing separation between the non-Christian synagogue, and the church.

On the other hand, many passages picture Jesus and the early Christian witnesses in conflict with Jewish people who do not acknowledge the validity of the ministry of Jesus or the church. The high percentage and intensity of Luke-Acts devoted to this material intimates that Luke's community is in tension with some members of the Jewish community who do not recognize the genuineness of the Christian movement.

These tensions relate to the destruction of the temple by the Romans in 70 C.E. This event dominated the religious landscape of Judaism in the late first century C.E. Judaism asked enervating questions. Why has this tragedy come upon us? Where is the future of Judaism now that we can no longer be centered in the temple? Who, now, is the authentic interpreter of our sacred traditions? Responses to these questions were at the root of the tension between non-Christian Judaism and Christianity in Luke-Acts.

Some in the Jewish community laid part of the blame for the fall of the temple at the feet of the church. The church brought Gentiles into membership in the Christian community without initiating them into Judaism. Some leaders of Judaism regarded this practice as a violation of the deepest values of Judaism. In their view, such heresy contributed to the divine displeasure that resulted in the destruction of the temple. Eventually, the Pharisees finally became the leaders of a consensus that regarded the observance of Torah as the central mark of Jewish identity. Although the temple was gone, one could be faithful in any time and place by keeping Torah.

The gospel of Luke offers a different interpretation of the fall of the temple. This event came about because the Jewish community did not recognize "the time of your visitation from God" through Jesus (Lk. 19:44). Furthermore, the future of the church is in the Gentile mission (e.g., Lk. 24:47). However, as I point out in the discussion of the book of Acts in the next chapter, the Jerusalem Council concluded that Gentiles who came into the church should engage in several key Jewish practices (Acts 15:28–29), even though they did not become Jewish.

As noted in discussion of the social context (above) most scholars think that Luke retrojects elements of disagreement between Judaism and Luke's church regarding these matters into the conflict stories of

Luke and Acts. We can loosely say that the characters in the gospel and Acts bespeak attitudes that were typical of the Christian community in Luke's day.

With respect to *the relationship between Luke's religious vision, and the religions of the Gentiles,* we would expect Luke, as a person steeped in Judaism, to portray religions other than Judaism and Christianity as offering incomplete awareness of the Divine. This thinking proves to be true, especially in Acts. However, Luke does not engage in wholesale and absolute condemnation of other religious traditions. Luke manifests an ambiguity toward other religious traditions.

Luke acknowledges that God is at work in all times and places (e.g., Lk. 6:35; Acts 14:17). Persons outside of Judaism and the church can know something of God, can receive God's blessing, and can even make a faithful witness (e.g., Luke 4:25–27; 10:29–37; 23:47; Acts 8:26–40; 16:11–15). This spirit is consistent with the openness to Gentiles in elements of the Hebrew Bible, as well as the Gentile-friendliness of the Septuagint and diaspora Judaism. Luke regards religious contexts other than Judaism and Christianity as settings in which people can receive genuine religious insights that need to be refined and supplemented (e.g., Acts 17:22–34). Of course, the book of Acts makes it clear that such knowledge and behavior is not complete.

However, this perception does not apply unilaterally to all other religions. Other religions can lead to destructive behavior, and can even serve the purposes of the devil (e.g., Acts 16:16–24; 19:23–39). And the reverse is true as well. Indeed, Jewish people can be as contentious and unenlightened as pagans (e.g., Lk. 11:37–54; 12:1–12; Acts 4:1–22; 5:17–32; 6:8–8:1; 23:6–10, 12–15).

In connection with *the relationship between optimum response of the disciples to the reign of God and their actual faith and behavior,* Jesus' followers can lack religious insight and need to be instructed in the ways of God. For example, the disciples need to understand Jesus' messiahship and death, and to recognize these as the patterns for their own lives (e.g., Lk. 9:18–27, 43–45; 18:31–34). The disciples are not able to heal the convulsing child at the bottom of the mount of transfiguration (Lk. 9:37–43). They debate the question of which disciple is the greatest and try to stop the exorcist who casts out demons but does not follow them (Lk. 9:46–50; 22:24–28). They ask Jesus how to pray (Luke 11:1–13). They need to be warned against the Pharisees, and instructed in witness (Luke 12:4–57; 16:1–13; 17:1–10; 17:22–18:14). They need to be prepared for the delay between the resurrection and Jesus' return in glory, and for the coming apocalypse (Luke 19:11–27; 21:5–36). They need to be reminded of God's faithfulness, even when they are unfaithful (22:31–38, 54–62). The apostles need the women and the stranger on the road to kindle their awareness of the resurrection (24:1–35).

Literary Data

Writers and speakers in antiquity typically made use of conventional forms for written or oral-aural expression. Each form had its own style and purpose. Of course, writers and speakers could adapt conventional genres to the composer's particular purpose. Since Luke and Acts are intended to be heard together, it makes sense to consider them as two parts of a single genre. I join some other scholars in seeing these materials as an apology in the form of a narrative that offers a normative interpretation of the story of Jesus and the early Christian community.

In the Hellenistic world, the term "apology" referred to a justification of an interpretation of life. Apologies could have both external and internal foci. The external focus is directed to persons outside the community in the hope of persuading them to accept the claims of the apology.

Even more importantly, an apology could have an effect upon those inside the community. In the latter role, the apology helped reinforce and clarify a people's understanding of their identity and purpose. Some Jewish apologetic literature in the period of the composition of Luke-Acts performs this function. For example, Josephus, a Jewish leader who lived about the same time as Luke, wrote *The Jewish War* with the ostensible purpose of inviting readers to recognize Judaism as an old, established, and peaceful movement that represents no threat to the larger social good. However, the primary purpose of *The Jewish War* is to encourage the Jewish community to see *itself* in the way depicted in Josephus' text. Other Jewish literature of this period functions similarly, such as *The Letter of Aristeas*, several of the writings of great Alexandrian Jewish theologian and philosopher Philo (*Hypothetica, Against Flaccus, Embassy to Gaius*), and Josephus' *Against Apion* and *Antiquities of the Jews*. Though not technically apologies, the Wisdom of Solomon and Ecclesiasticus (also known as Sirach or Ben Sira) shore up the Jewish identity of Jewish persons living in the diaspora.

The gospel of Luke and the book of Acts move in this path. As Luke Timothy Johnson says, "To a possible outside Hellenistic reader, the Christian movement is presented as a philosophically enlightened, politically harmless, socially benevolent and philanthropic fellowship. But its more immediate purpose is to interpret the Gospel for insiders within the context of a pluralistic environment of both Jews and Gentile *(The Gospel of Luke)*, 9." The Christian community of Luke's day is to understand its mission to be that of enacting in its later time the identity and purpose revealed in the gospel and Acts.

Luke joins several other Jewish authors in casting his apology in the form of a narrative. A distinctive quality of the Lukan narrative is its Septuagintal style. Luke uses phrases, citations, allusions, and other stylistic features of the Septuagint to leave the impression that the story of Luke-Acts is a continuation of biblical history. This style suggests that the story of God of Israel is now extended through the stories of Jesus Christ and the Christian community.

Organization

Luke's apologetic history does not offer the listeners a series of propositions or arguments to shape their common life. Rather, Luke creates a narrative world that is organized by a journey motif. Indeed, the early church is known as "the Way" (Acts 9:2; 18:25, 26; 19:9, 23; 22:4; 24:14, 22). The listening community imaginatively experiences the journey of Jesus and the early church. In the process, we move not just geographically (from Bethlehem through Jerusalem to Rome) but theologically. We identify with the followers of Jesus in the gospel and in Acts, and we are moved to consider how we can make a witness in our own time and place that is in continuity with our ancestors.

Luke's geographical references and characters are often charged with theological meaning. When following the Way, we should always ask what is represented in each place and person. For instance, Jerusalem is a primary place of revelation; the journey to Jerusalem in the gospel is a journey to the knowledge of God that is decisive for the Christian community. The journey from Jerusalem in Acts is guided and empowered by the revelation that was given at Jerusalem.

The journey falls naturally into ten segments. The first five of these divisions occur in the gospel of Luke and are discussed in this chapter. The last five segments occur in Acts and are considered in Chapter 10.

LUKE 1:1–4.

The prologue is similar to the prologues of other historical works in Luke's period (e.g., Josephus' *Antiquities of the Jews*; cf. Lucian of Samosata, *How to Write History,* 23). Luke-Acts is addressed to "Theophilus." The name could refer to a specific person. In those days, wealthy benefactors often subsidized authors. Theophilus could have been such a person. However, because the name means "friend (*philos*) of God (*theos*)," some commentators think that "Theophilus" represents not a singular person but the Lukan community who are friends of God.

The prologue articulates Luke's apologetic intent. Luke draws upon preexisting sources, but interprets them so that we will "know the truth." Luke writes so that the listeners can be assured that this interpretation of Judaism, Christ, and the church are trustworthy.

LUKE 1:5–2:52.

This section establishes continuity between the promises of God to Israel and God's work through Jesus Christ and the Jesus movement. The ethos is thoroughly Jewish. Angels preside over the events, thus indicating that God directs them. The characters (Elizabeth and Zechariah, Mary and Joseph) are all faithful Jewish people. Jesus is born in Bethlehem, the birthplace of David, a leader through whom God worked powerfully. Jesus is circumcised and presented in the temple. Anna and Simeon, prophetess and prophet, indicate God's blessing. As this section concludes, the twelve-year-old Jesus clarifies his mission, and its relationship to Judaism by saying, "Wist ye not know that I must be about my Father's business?" (Luke 2:49, KJV).

Affinity between Jesus and Judaism is reinforced in this part of the gospel by the fact that many of the characters' speeches echo the style of the Septuagint. For instance, Luke 1:46–55 (the Magnificat) bears the imprint of 1 Samuel 2:1–10. The song of Zechariah (the Benedictus) has the qualities of a psalm (Luke 1:68–79).

These events continue the promises of God to Israel. Through Jesus, God honors the promises that God made to David to maintain Israel as a community (Lk. 1:32–33, 68–69; cf. 2 Sam. 7:16). However, Luke interprets the promises to David not as a national hope but as a part of the promises that God made to Sarah and Abraham (Lk. 1:54–55). The goal of the divine promise is to bless the Gentiles by means of Israel (Gen. 12:1–3). God is faithful to Judaism by blessing the Gentiles through Jesus Christ and the church (Lk. 1:29–32).

When Jesus and the disciples later come into conflict with Jewish leaders, the listener is led to conclude that the conflict is not between a dissident Jesus who is abrogating Judaism, but is between Jesus a faithful Jew and other Jewish people who do not live up to the best of their own tradition (Lk. 2:34–35).

LUKE 3:1–9:50.

This Galilean segment reveals that the mission of Jesus (in word and deed) is to manifest the reign of God in the latter days. Jesus calls apostles, and authorizes them to preach the reign of God and to work its signs. We see the complexity of Jewish responses to the mission of Jesus.

Galilee, about one hundred miles north of Jerusalem, was less prosperous than Jerusalem. Jewish and Gentile people related positively in Galilee. Galilee is outside the center of the Jewish religious, political, economic power in Jerusalem. By opening the ministry in Galilee, Luke indicates that the reign of God does not conform to conventional boundaries in the human community, but transforms them.

John the Baptist is a prophet who indicates that the last days of world history are near (Lk. 3:1–20). John cites Isaiah to establish the Gentile mission as an essential part of these days: "all flesh shall see the salvation of God" (3:6).

The baptism of Jesus shows that Jesus has received the Holy Spirit (Lk. 3:21–22). His life is the model of the spirit-filled witness to the reign of God. His baptism is also a model for the immersion of believers in Acts.

Virtually all scholars view Luke 4:16–30 as a paradigm that reveals the main lines of the ministry of Jesus and the church. Jesus was in the synagogue on the Sabbath. Jesus, a visiting rabbi, read from Isaiah 61:1–2 conflated with Isaiah 58:6. These materials use powerful symbols from Judaism to depict the restoration of the broken world in the reign of God. The poor receive the good news of God's abundance for all. Captives return home. The blind see. The oppressed are freed. The universal Jubilee (the year of God's favor) comes about. These qualities refer both to material conditions and to spiritual perception.

Jesus interprets the reading. "Today, this scripture has been fulfilled in your hearing" (Lk. 4:21b). The restoration is underway through Jesus and the church. Initially the crowd is receptive (4:22). However, their mood changes when Jesus uses two examples that indicate the breadth of the restoration (4:28–29). Elijah fed the Gentile widow in Zarephath (4:25–26, from 1 Kings 17:8–16), and Elisha healed Namaan, a Gentile general in the army of Syria (4:27, from 2 Kings 5:1–19). The synagogue crowd prefigures some Jewish reactions to the Jesus movement by trying to put Jesus to death. God intervenes, and Jesus passes through the midst of the crowd (4:30).

This pattern continues throughout the gospel and Acts. Jesus and the church announce and enact the restoration. Some people welcome it. Others resist. However, God always proves faithful to those who witness to the reign of God.

Most of the miracle stories in the gospel of Luke occur in 3:1–9:50. The miracles embody the rule of God by restoring people or situations that are broken. A miracle is a mini-instance of the eschaton. These miracle stories are also models for the miracle-working ministry of the church in the book of Acts.

The sermon on the plain, in Luke 6:17–49, which is Luke's version of the great sermon from Q (see also Matthew's sermon on the mount, Mt. 5:7), provides Jesus' first extensive teaching about the reign of God and about how to embody its restorative practices. Luke 6:20–26 indicates that in the rule of God, the poor are blessed while the rich are cursed. In Luke 6:27–49, Jesus articulates how the disciples are to witness to the restoration, such as "Love your enemies, do good to those who hate you." These instructions are a not a comprehensive manual on how the disciples are to embody the rule of God, but are examples of the effects of the reign of God.

Earlier Jesus has chosen twelve apostles (Lk. 5:1–11, 27–28; 6:12–16). In the sermon on the plain and in the next section of the gospel (9:51–19:27), Jesus instructs them more fully in the way of discipleship and apostleship.

Luke 9:18–27 adds a crucial nuance with regard to the reign of God. For Luke, the Messiah is the primary agent for manifesting the reign of

God. Luke 9:21–27 reveals that, as a part of the manifestation of the reign of God, the Messiah will be crucified. The cross (suffering) of the Messiah (9:21–22) is a pattern for the followers of Jesus who will take up their crosses daily (9:23–27). The notion that suffering accompanies faithful testimony derives from Judaism (e.g., Isa. 52:13–53:12; 4 Macc. 6:1–7:23; 8:1–18:5, esp. 17:17–22). Judaism remembers that many of the prophets suffered (e.g., Lk. 6:22–26; 11:45–52; 13:33–34; Acts 7:52). Apocalyptic theologians foresaw a period of suffering, sometimes called the tribulation, as a part of the transition from the old age to the new. During this time the rulers of the old age (e.g., Satan) would try to turn back God's reign.

Luke 9:18–27 interprets the meaning of the death of Jesus and the suffering of the early Christians in Acts. It alerts the listener to recognize that the reign of God often appears to be much less than it is; persons not steeped in Jewish tradition would hardly expect a crucifixion to be a part of the coming of the divine rule. This section implicitly contrasts the power of God with the powers of this world. God's self-giving love aims to restore, even when that self-giving leads to a cross; the rulers of the present age aim to preserve their own power, regardless of the suffering they cause others. So also the true disciples to give themselves completely.

LUKE 9:51–19:27.

This long section describes the journey of Jesus and the disciples from Galilee to Jerusalem. The representatives of the reign of God move from the boundaries of the Jewish social and religious world (Galilee) to the center (Jerusalem), where confrontation takes place in Luke 19:45–23:56. In 9:51–19:27, the listener is initiated further into the character of the reign of God. Along the way, we learn that the apostles and a wider group of missionaries have power to preach and to perform signs and wonders. We also learn that they need further instruction in the ways of God (10:1–11, 17–23). In fact, the teaching in the travel narrative seems designed to encourage a Lukan church that is weary.

Most of the Lukan parables are told along the journey to Jerusalem in response to incidents or challenges that arise in connection with Jewish leaders or the disciples. The parables create images that interpret the rule of God and its theological foundations. In order to understand them, the listener enters into their imaginative worlds. The meaning of a parable can never be fully expressed in a propositional point. The twin parables of the shepherd in search of the sheep and the woman searching for the lost coin reveal that Jesus and the church search for those who are lost because God's nature is to do that very thing (Lk. 15:1–10). The parable of the parent and the two children demonstrates that repentance makes it possible for all–even Gentiles–to be welcomed into God's dominion (15:11–32). As the story ends, the elder child has not joined the celebration. The listener must decide: Will I identify with the joy of God's coming or will I identify with the elder child? The story of the rich person and Lazarus calls the wealthy to avoid the fate of the rich person (Lk. 16:19–31); the story of the widow and the unjust judge (Lk. 18:1–8) moves from the lesser to the greater. In the same way that the widow received justice from the unjust judge (the lesser) so the community can be confident that God will one day bring the fullness of divine rule (the greater). The story of the Pharisee and the tax collector (Lk. 18:9–14) exposes the hypocrisy that is possible in the conventionally religious person (the Pharisee), and highlights the religious insight that can result from awareness of the need for God in the most surprising of individuals (the tax collector). The parable of the pounds stresses the importance of continuing to witness as the people await Jesus' return (Luke 19:11–27).

Luke often weaves together parables and propositions so that the conventional language states a clear idea while the parable creates an imaginative experience of the reality bespoken in conventional speech. In Luke 14:1ff., for instance, Jesus is at a banquet given by a Pharisee at which some guests are selecting the seats of honor. The banquet motif calls to mind the eschatological banquet that will occur in the afterlife. In 14:7–14, Jesus explains that in the rule of God, persons do not seek conventional social recognition, but manifest humility and invite the needy. The parable of the great banquet then creates a narrative world in which listeners realize that God invites persons from the margins of life to the divine reign (14:15–24).

Luke 19:28–24:53.

The narrative unit of this part of Luke-Acts should be Luke 19:29–Acts 1:26. For the events of Acts 1:1–26 are integral to the narrative complex that begins in Luke 19:29. To honor the fact that Acts is discussed in this textbook in Chapter 10, I take up Acts 1:1–26 in that chapter.

When Jesus enters Jerusalem (as noted previously, a definitive theological symbol), the crowd spread their cloaks before Jesus in a traditional gesture of welcoming royalty (19:29–40; 2 Kings 9:13). But Luke's crowd does not wave leafy branches (as in Mt. 21:8 and Mk. 11:8) or palm branches (as in Jn. 12:13). Such branches, used during the Maccabean revolt, were associated with military victory (2 Macc. 10:1–9). By omitting branches, Luke signals that Jesus does not sanction armed revolt and does nothing to deserve death.

In language that is reminiscent of prophetic oracles of judgment, Jesus declares that Jerusalem will be destroyed (19:41–44). When Jesus drives out those who are selling things in the temple, he does not cleanse it but makes a prophetic gesture that symbolizes its destruction (19:45–46). Later, Jesus explains that the destruction of the temple and Jerusalem are part of the tribulation events leading to the full institution of God's reign (21:5–36).

Immediately after entering the city, Jesus comes into conflict with Jewish leaders—mainly the chief priests and the scribes (19:45–20:47). However,

Jesus is also in tension with his own disciples as a dispute breaks out as to which disciples are the greatest (22:24–28). Some apostles fall asleep when Jesus needs them in the garden of Gethsemane (22:45). Peter denies Jesus (22:31–34, 54–63). Jesus' betrayer (Judas) is a disciple.

The Pharisees disappear from the story of Jesus' death, perhaps because the church of Luke's time is dealing primarily with Pharisees. Notice, for example, that Christian Pharisees are present at the Apostolic Council (Acts 15:5). Luke is more positive toward the Pharisees than the other gospels.

Jesus' betrayal and death takes place at Passover, a celebration of the archetypal event of Jewish liberation. Luke's telling of the institution of the Lord's supper makes it clear that the supper prefigures the eschatological banquet that celebrates the completion of the reign of God (22:7–23).

Luke knows that the Jewish magistrates did not have the authority to put people to death. In this gospel, as in the others, the Roman government sentences Jesus to death. The chief priests, scribes, and elders initiate the proceedings that carry Jesus to Pilate, the Roman magistrate. Luke tells the story of the Jewish legal proceedings against Jesus so as to cast the Jewish leaders in a slightly better light than in Matthew and Mark (Lk. 22:66–71). Luke devotes far less space to the trial before the Jewish assembly. Luke's trial honors more precepts of Jewish legal custom than the trials in Matthew and Mark. Nonetheless, we are painfully aware that the charges the Jewish leaders bring against Jesus are untrue (Lk. 23:2).

Pilate recognizes that the charges are without merit (23:3–5). When Pilate discovers that Jesus is a Galilean, the procurator refers Jesus to Herod, who concurs that Jesus is innocent (23:6–12). In order to establish proof, Jewish law called for the agreement of two witnesses. The listener is stunned when two people never agree that Jesus is guilty, but that does not stop Jesus' death.

Throughout the gospel, Luke emphasizes that the events in the story are directed by God. At the very beginning of the gospel, Mary modeled the proper response to the divine initiatives when she trusted in the angel's promise that she would bear the Savior. Now, Jesus exhibits the same quality when he dies obediently (23:46). Joseph of Arimathea (representing the faithful among the Jewish people) buries Jesus.

On the first day of the week, women go to the tomb to anoint Jesus' body in the Jewish way. However, two figures (signaling veracity) from heaven reveal that Jesus is risen (24:1–12). The resurrection confirms that the promises of God revealed through Jesus are trustworthy. The incident at Emmaus also reveals what happens each time the community breaks bread: they discover anew the presence of the risen Jesus with them (24:28–32).

The penultimate action in the gospel is Jesus' commissioning the church to preach repentance and forgiveness in Jesus' name to all nations, that is, among the Gentiles. To equip them, Jesus will send power (the Holy Spirit) from on high (24:44–49). As the gospel ends, Jesus ascends to the right hand of God, thus revealing that he can complete the manifestation of the rule of God, and certifying that he can send the Spirit. However, the story is incomplete. For the next chapters, we turn to the book of Acts.

Theological Themes

Luke's themes develop across the gospel and into Acts. A listener has a mature perspective on a Lukan theme by tracing it from the first book through the second. In this chapter, I focus on the reign of God, the Holy Spirit, and the tradition of authoritative interpretation. In Chapter 10, I will discuss the restoration of the human community, restoration of the role of women, poverty and abundance, and prayer.

The *reign of God* is a comprehensive lens through which to understand the gospel and Acts. According to this motif, since the fall (Gen. 3:9–17), the world has not manifested God's intentions. However, God promised to reestablish the fullness of divine rule. According to Luke, this latter intention is coming about through the ministry of Jesus Christ. Jesus calls to repentance those in Israel who do not recognize the reign of God or do not live according to its values. The distinctive mission of the church in Acts is to welcome Gentiles into the knowledge of the reign of God by repentance, baptism, receiving the Holy Spirit, and living by the ethical precepts of Judaism. The church extends the ministry of Israel. God's dominion will be fully established in every relationship and situation when Jesus returns in glory. In the meantime, the church is to be a sign of the reign of God.

The gospel and Acts interpret the divine rule. This theme is introduced as the way to understand Jesus' ministry in the birth narrative (e.g., 1:46–56, 68–79, esp. 78–79; 2:10–11, 29–32) and the preaching of John the Baptist (3:4–9, 15–17). It receives paradigmatic expression in 4:16–30. In the Galilean section of the gospel (3:1–9:50), Jesus teaches the values and practices of the rule of God, embodies them through the miracles, and interprets the cross and resurrection as revealing the way of the rule of God. On the journey to Jerusalem (9:51–19:27), these themes are intensified. The powers of the old world attempt to extinguish the manifestation of the divine rule through Jesus in Jerusalem (19:28–24:53). However, the resurrection confirms that the forward movement of this rule is relentless. The appearance of Jesus and the church are signs that this age is drawing to a close and that God's purposes are moving toward fulfillment.

Although Acts contains the phrase "reign of God," or the shorthand "reign," only eight times (Acts 1:3, 6; 8:12; 14:22; 19:8; 20:25; 28:23, 31), the gospel creates a literary perspective by which listeners understand the church to continue the ministry of Jesus in witnessing to the reign and its implications, especially for Gentiles.

All commentators call attention to the prominence of the *Holy Spirit* in Luke and Acts. In Judaism, the Spirit is an agent through whom God works in the world and through whom God empowers witness to God's ways. On occasion, the Spirit fills people with religious ecstasy that overflows into a phenomenon similar to speaking in tongues. The motif of the Spirit shows that the ministries of Jesus and the church are led by God. The preaching of John the Baptist is reliable because John is filled with the Spirit (1:15). The Spirit is responsible for the birth of Jesus (1:35, 41, 67). Simeon's interpretation of Jesus is of the Spirit (2:25–27). John the Baptist indicates that Jesus' purpose is to baptize the world with the Spirit and fire (3:16). The baptism of Jesus confirms that Jesus' ministry takes place at the impulse of the Spirit (3:21–22). The Spirit initiates Jesus' ministry, and leads Jesus into the temptation with the devil that steps up the apocalyptic struggle between God and the powers of the old age (4:1–13). Henceforth, Jesus is "filled with the power of the Spirit" (4:14). God will give the Spirit to those who seek the divine rule (11:1–13). Blasphemy against the Holy Spirit– denying that the ministry of Jesus and the church come from God (see Acts 7:51)–will not be forgiven (Lk. 12:10). When believers are brought to trial, the Holy Spirit will teach them what to say (12:12). The listener understands that all of Jesus actions and words are led by the Spirit.

In Acts, the Spirit continues the restoration demonstrated in the gospel. Jesus promises the Spirit to the disciples (Acts 1:5, 8). At Pentecost, this promise comes true as the Spirit fills believers with ecstasy, reverses the confusion of Babel, emboldens Christian witness, and creates a community of worship, study, prayer, and sharing all things in common (2:1–47). The Holy Spirit makes it possible for the church to witness to the reign of God in its worlds as Jesus did in the gospel. The Spirit leads Peter and Stephen to speak boldly (4:8; 6:10). The Spirit is the source of the teaching of the ancestors (4:25; 28:25) and of authoritative teaching in the community (e.g., 6:3, 5, 10; 11:24, 28; 20:28). The Spirit fills the community with ecstasy (e.g., 4:31; 13:52; 19:2–6). The Spirit exercises discipline (5:3, 9). The Spirit makes it possible for Stephen to die as Jesus does (7:55). Just as the Spirit led Jesus into the wilderness to confront the devil, so the Spirit leads early Christian witnesses to confront persecution (e.g., 20:22–23; 21:11). The Spirit directs the early Christian witness to specific places (8:29; 16:6–7; 20:22–23; 21:4), and even transports them from one place to another (8:39). Luke stresses that the Spirit is a source of the Gentile mission (9:17; 10:19; 11:12; 13:2–4; 20:22) and is proof of the authenticity of that mission (10:44–48; 11:15). The Holy Spirit continuously leads and teaches the church, and plays a leading role in the Apostolic Council that leads to the Apostolic Decree (15:8, 14). The possession of the Spirit is essential for mature Christian life (19:1–6).

Luke establishes a *tradition of authoritative interpretation and leadership* in the Christian community. Jesus is the model of the Spirit-filled leader who interprets the promises and commands of the Septuagint from the point of view of the manifestation of the divine rule. Jesus' life is the pattern for the disciples and the church—as Spirit-filled witness to the divine rule through teaching, working miracles, embracing the outcasts, disputing with Jewish officials, persecution and suffering, and resurrection (Lk. 5:1–11; 6:12–49; 8:19–21; 9:1–6, 10–17, esp. 18–27, 44; 10:1–20; 12:4–53; 13:32–33; 14:25–35; 17:1–10, 24–26; 18:31–34; 22:24–30; 24:44–52).

This pattern is the pattern for the apostles, and for the broader church. The apostles and Paul function in the narrative in Acts in ways that are similar to Jesus in the gospel. They announce the great restoration that is taking place through Jesus Christ (e.g., Acts 2:14–39; 3:1–10; 4:8–12; 8:26–40; 9:19–29; 13:16–41; 14:8–18; 17:22–33; 19:8–10; 22:3–20; 26:4–23; 28:23–24). They speak and act in the power of the Spirit (for occurrences, see the preceding paragraph). They interpret their witness through the lens of the Septuagint (e.g., Acts 2:17–35; 3:13–14, 22–26; 4:11, 23–26; 7:2–53; 8:29–35; 9:15; 13:16–41; 15:16–17; 18:14–18; 28:26–27). They embody the reign of God through miracles, even raising the dead (e.g., 3:1–10; 5:12–16; 9:32–43; 14:8–10; 19:11–20; 20:7–12; 28:1–10), and through common life that mediates divine providence (e.g., Acts 2:42–47; 4:32; 5:1–11; 6:1–7 cf. 11:27–29). They are faithful in bold witness in persecution, and even in death (e.g., 4:1–22; 5:17–42; 6:8–8:8; 9:23–31; 12:1–19; 13:4–12; 14:19–20; 16:16–40; 17:1–7; 18:5–17; 19:23–40; 21:27–36; 22:30–23:10; 23:12–35; 24:1–9; 25:1–12; 26:4–23; 28:17–31). God faithfully delivers most of them from distress (e.g., Acts 5:17–26; 12:6–17; 16:25–40; the many instances of deliverance after the arrest of Paul in 20:27–36). Their community is a reunion of Jewish people with Samaritans, and others outside the Jewish community (e.g., 8:4–25; 10:1–11:18; 13:46–51; 14:27; 15:1–19, esp. 3, 7, 12, 14, 17, 19; 18:6; 21:17–25; 22:3–21; 26:4–23; 28:30). Acts 20:17–35 describes the role of the authoritative leader in the Christian community. The Lukan church can apply this pattern to its own time.

I have commented extensively on other theological themes that are important in Luke-Acts. These include the *return of Jesus in glory* (see "Social Context" above), the *relationship of Israel, Jesus, and the church* (see "Social Context" and "Religious Context") as well as *Lukan attitudes toward civil authorities* ("Social Context").

Importance for the Church of the Twenty-first Century

I comment now on several motifs in the gospel of Luke and the book of Acts that are important for preaching and teaching in the church in the twenty-first century. In this chapter, I discuss the manifestation of the reign of God, the Holy Spirit, the delay in the return of Jesus, the importance of the First Testament for the church, and the importance of thinking critically about Christian attitudes concerning Judaism. Chapter 10 takes up a model for helping the church interpret the divine leading, the welcome of outsiders, the use of material goods, the restoration of women, the relationship of the church and state, and prayer.

A common way that Christian preachers and teachers seek to *relate the gospel of Luke to the world today is by finding analogies between the two worlds.* This approach assumes both difference and continuity between the time of Luke and today. Many aspects of culture differ between Luke and us, such as dress, foods, housing, transportation, geography, climate, language, cultural assumptions, forms of government, philosophies. However, beneath such differences are basic similarities of experience. While forms may differ between Luke's world and ours, underlying experiences are frequently analogous. A simple way to use this approach is to ask, "What are the setting, characters, events, and values in the text? What settings, persons, events, and values in our world function similarly to those in the text?"

Luke-Acts urges us to look for the *manifestation of the reign of God.* The gospel invites the church to believe that aspects of the emerging world of the twenty-first century—brokenness, idolatries, falsehood, exploitation, violence, and death—are not congenial with the world that God wants. Through the Spirit, God is ever present and seeking to restore the broken world so that all relationships and situations conform to the purposes of God. The preacher and the congregation can identify distortions of God's desires for situations today, can point to relationships and circumstances in which God seeks for the divine reign to be manifest, and name agents through whom God is bringing about this manifestation. The book of Acts stresses that the Church is to embody the divine rule in its own life, and is to help the wider human community recognize the divine reign and respond through repentance, baptism, and the receiving of the Holy Spirit.

Luke-Acts prompts the church to recall that God is universally present with all people and in all situations and that God seeks the good of all (Acts 14:17). Acts thus encourages the church not to allow its theological vision to become too narrow. Since God is universally present, Luke's second volume also prompts today's church to ask what other religions might have in common with Jewish and Christian perspectives.

This material helps the church develop lenses to perceive manifestations of the divine rule. Israel was a tiny community in a relatively obscure place. Jesus was an itinerant preacher living from day to day who announced the final stages of the manifestation of the cosmic reign of God. In Acts, the church begins as a very small renewal movement within Judaism. Yet the church is called to help the world read the signs of the times that point towards social and cosmic transformation. In each case, God is powerfully present, but in ways that might miss the eye of the average onlooker.

The *presence and leading of the Holy Spirit* is a permeating theme in the gospel of Luke and the book of Acts, and is a perennial topic in Christian community. Luke portrays the Spirit as an agent of God who empowers Jesus and the Twelve for faithful witness, and who sustains the disciples during the delay of the return of Jesus. The church witnesses to the power of the Spirit to bring the reign of God into expression by restoring broken relationships and community. This emphasis challenges the church to be alert for the presence, leading, and empowerment of the Spirit.

From Acts, we deduce the following criteria to identify whether an experience or leading is of the Holy Spirit: The Spirit induces the energizing awareness of the God of Israel as interpreted through the Septuagint and Jesus Christ. The Spirit restores the divided human family by bringing together persons and groups who have been separated. The Spirit empowers the Gentile mission. The Spirit brings to life other modes of witnessing to the reign of God (e.g., providing for the poor, restoring the place of women in Christian community). Where these activities are taking place, the Spirit is the animating force.

Motifs related to the Holy Spirit are significant for the church today. On the one hand, congregations in the long-established denominations today are sometimes diminished in spiritual power. The book of Acts invites such congregations to recognize that the Holy Spirit is attempting to stir the community to vital religious life and to mission beyond the congregation. On the other hand, some contemporary congregations in the Pentecostal and charismatic wings of the church have a dramatic awareness of the Holy Spirit that results in vital interior religious experience, but without full-bodied witness to God's intent to restore the social divisions of the human family. Of course, some contemporary Pentecostal and charismatic congregations manifest precisely the quality of life that the book of Acts portends. Acts calls all churches to recognize and respond to the full work of the Holy Spirit.

The *delay of the return of Jesus* is an aspect of Luke's theology that requires reflection. The early Christians believed that Jesus had ascended to heaven, from which he would return in order to complete the manifestation of the divine rule. His return would interrupt history, and reconstitute history according to God's designs. Many Christians continue to believe that Jesus will return in this way. However, they must explain theologically why Jesus has not come back as promised, especially given the continuation of widespread brokenness and evil. Other Christians conclude that the motif of the return of Jesus is a mythological way of speaking that was at home in the first century but that depends upon a cosmology that we no longer accept. Since we live in an infinitely expanding universe, this line of reasoning goes, we no longer think of "heaven" as a place that is literally "above" to which Jesus could ascend and from which he could return. Some of these Christians think that the language of the second coming of Jesus continues to be useful because, even though we no longer believe that Christ will come from a place that is "above," God can still send Christ to interrupt the course of this world a second time. Other Christians approach this motif in a third way. They reason that if God has the power to return Jesus, to end evil, and to install the reign of God in all aspects of cosmic life, but does not do so, then God is not trustworthy. These Christians conclude that while God has more power than any other entity, God is not omnipotent in the sense of being able to do whatever God wants whenever God chooses. Instead of anticipating a singular event in which Jesus returns from heaven and interrupts history, they think of God as constantly present, doing all that God can do to help the world conform to God's purposes. These Christians do not expect a second, interruptive event, but take the image of the second coming to mean that God is not satisfied with the world the way it is, and a promise that God will continue working to help the world conform to the divine purposes.

The gospel of Luke and the book of Acts also help the church remember that *the First Testament is essential to the identity and self-understanding of the Christian community.* Luke interprets God, Jesus Christ, the Spirit, and the church in categories drawn from the Septuagint. A central purpose of the Christian community was to extend the story of the Septugint into Luke's own day. Jesus Christ and the Christian community are means whereby God keeps the promise that God made to Abram and Sarai that through them, all the families of the earth might be blessed (Gen. 12:1–3).

This conviction vividly corrects a tendency toward Marcionism in many congregations. Marcion lived in the second century C.E. and taught that the God of the Old Testament was an inferior deity who was legalistic, inconsistent, despotic, even wrathful. He also taught that Judaism was a superstitious, outdated, legalistic religion that was superseded by Christianity. Christianity, according to Marcion, taught that God is love. Marcion concluded that the only writings that could provide the Christian community with proper guidance were the gospel of Luke (revised to highlight Marcion's teaching) and selected writings of the apostle Paul. Other Christian writings were despoiled by remnants of Judaism. Marcion was declared a heretic by the church. However, viewpoints similar to his can still be found in the Christian world. But, from the perspective of Luke-Acts, Marcion is fundamentally mistaken.

The gospel of Luke and the book of Acts also call the church to think critically *about our attitudes and behavior toward the Jewish people and their institutions and practices.* Because of tension between the synagogue and the church in the first century, the gospel of Luke portrays some Jewish people in a negative way. Luke's caricature, along with others in the Second Testament, has been used to fuel anti-Judaism and anti-Semitism in the Christian community. In World War II, the Nazis—many of whom were Christians—murdered over six million Jewish people because of anti-Semitism.

Today's preacher or teacher can do three things to help the contemporary church understand and respond appropriately to this attitude and material. First, a leader can help the Christian community understand why antipathy developed between the synagogue and the church in the first centuries common to Judaism and Christianity. Second, the leader can help the church recognize that it is inappropriate for the church to think or act as if God no longer loves the Jewish people (or Judaism). Third, since the reign of God is about restoring relationships in this world to conform more fully to God's purposes, the preacher can help the congregation imagine ways in which the contemporary Christian community can work with Judaism in common witness.

The *faithfulness of God* permeates all themes in Luke-Acts. These writings are designed to assure the listener that just as God was faithful to Israel, to Jesus, and to the early Christian community, so God will be trustworthy to the church of the period after the close of the Acts. Today's church is often anxious about matters ranging from wondering whether our ecclesiastical institutions can survive to the many forms of economic and social distress that beset North American societies today. A community nurtured in the faithfulness of God can witness boldly in an uncertain time to the divine restoration of all things that is signaled through the stories of Jesus and the early church.

Suggested Resources for the Pastor's Library

Allen, Ronald J. *Preaching Luke-Acts.* Preaching Classic Texts. St. Louis: Chalice Press, 2000.

Cadbury, Henry J. *The Making of Luke-Acts.* New York: Macmillan, 1927.

Conzelmann, Hans. *The Theology of St. Luke.* Translated by Geoffrey Buswell. New York: Harper, 1960.

Craddock, Fred B. *Luke.* Interpretation. Louisville: John Knox Press, 1990.

Fitzmyer, Joseph. *The Gospel According to Luke.* Anchor Bible 28 and 28A. Garden City, N.Y.: Doubleday & Co., Inc. 1980, 1985.

Johnson, Luke Timothy. *The Gospel of Luke.* Sacra Pagina Series. Collegeville, Minn.: The Liturgical Press, 1991.

Neyrey, Jerome H., ed. *The Social World of Luke-Acts: Models for Interpretation.* Peabody, Mass.: Hendrickson Publishers, 1991.

Nolland, John. *Luke 1–9:20, 9:21–18:34, 18:35–24:52.* Word Biblical Commentary. Three volumes. Dallas: Word Publishing Co., 1989, 1993.

Talbert, Charles. *Reading Luke: A Literary and Theological Commentary on the Third Gospel.* New York: Crossroad, 1982.

Tannehill, Robert C. *The Narrative Unity of Luke-Acts: A Literary Interpretation. Volume 1: The Gospel According to Luke.* Philadelphia: Fortress Press, 1986.

10

The Story of the Church According to "Luke"

The Acts of the Apostles

RONALD J. ALLEN

Throughout its history, the church has turned to the Acts of the Apostles for guidance and theological precedence. For instance, many Christian leaders have looked to the book of Acts as early Christian history. Some churches use Acts to locate traditions in the period of the New Testament in order to validate the continuation of those traditions in the present. Christian movements seeking to restore the New Testament church often use the book of Acts as a blueprint. Many charismatic churches regard the work of the Holy Spirit in Acts as paradigmatic for the work of the Spirit today. Many Christians imagine Paul as described in Acts, rather than as the Paul of the letters. On the Sundays after Easter, the Revised Common Lectionary omits readings from the Old Testament and replaces them with passages from Acts.

The gospel of Luke and the Acts of the Apostles are from the same author. They are one narrative. The story that begins in the first volume continues in the second. Consequently, I have not reproduced in this chapter all the material already written about the gospel of Luke (in chapter 9). I summarize those materials and highlight considerations that are particular to Acts.

Basic Data

Much of the basic data for Acts are the same as for the gospel of Luke and are not repeated in this chapter. Here I discuss only matters that are unique to understanding Acts.

We do not have the original title to this volume. By mid to late second century C.E., the designation "The Acts of the Apostles" appeared in the writings of Clement of Alexandria, Irenaeus, and the Muratorian Canon. Scholars sometimes lament the title "The Acts of the Apostles," since only a handful of apostles have a prominent place, and since many people other than the apostles take leading roles. After the Apostolic Council (Acts 15), Paul—who is not formally one of the twelve apostles—becomes the central character who carries the gospel into the heart of the Gentile world.

Very likely, Luke used sources when writing the Acts of the Apostles. However, we cannot identify these sources. They are not available in an external form. Nor can we identify passages within Acts in which the vocabulary, grammar, or style demonstrate that Luke is drawing on a source. Characteristic of many authors in the Hellenistic age, Luke thoroughly rewrites sources and brings them into a single authorial style.

Luke writes several passages in the first person plural, such as, "We set sail from Troas" (Acts16:11; cf. 16:11–17; 20:5–15; 21:1–18; 27:1–28:16). Some Christians think that these "we passages" are eyewitness accounts from Luke or from another traveling companion. I join other interpreters in regarding the "we passages" as a literary device that Luke draws from other writers. The Septuagint sometimes shifts from third person to first person (e.g., Ezra 8:23–31; 8:35–9:15). Hellenistic writers sometimes narrated journeys in the first person in order to heighten the dramatic effect.

Two main versions of the Acts of the Apostles circulated in ancient manuscripts. (1) The Alexandrian text is very much like the one that is in our Bible. Scholars who specialize in the study of ancient manuscripts conclude that the Alexandrian version is closer to the original. (2) The Western text is about 10 percent longer than the Alexandrian version. It does not contain any material that is missing in the Alexandrian version, but develops the material in the Alexandrian text at greater length. The Western text portrays the Jewish leaders much more negatively than does the Alexandrian text.

The Acts of the Apostles addresses the same basic issues as the gospel of Luke, though the focus changes somewhat:

- Who is Jesus Christ? The gospel reveals the identity and purpose of Jesus Christ as divine agent through whom the reign of God is manifest. Acts draws out the implications of this perception.
- What are God's purposes through Christ and the church, and in history? The gospel interprets the reign of God as the restoration of all things, so that all relationships and situations will embody God's purposes in all ways. Acts shows that this restoration is taking place, and will culminate when Jesus returns. In the divine rule, Gentiles honor and serve the God of Israel. The Acts of the Apostles tells the

story of how the church witnesses to the fulfillment of this divine promise.

• What is the church, and what is its mission? The relationship and mission of Jesus and the apostles prefigure the nature and purpose of the church. In Acts, the church is the Spirit-filled community whose life embodies God's restoration and witnesses to it through common life, preaching, and other forms of testimony.

• How are Jesus Christ and the church related to the God of Israel and to Judaism? Acts repeatedly stresses the theme that the God of Israel is the God of Jesus Christ and the church. The narrative of Acts continues the story of the God of Israel that begins in the Septuagint. Acts shows that God's restoring purposes are being made known in Jewish and Gentile settings through Jesus Christ and the church.

Other issues are important for understanding Acts. This book traces lines of authority in the church, and provides a paradigm within which the church can make decisions. In this second volume, Luke details the nature, signs, and purposes of the Holy Spirit. The story of Acts gives us a vivid memory of the church as a community of God's restoration. The church welcomes women, cares for them, and acknowledges their leadership. The Christian community is a divine means of providing for the poor and relieving the dangers of wealth for the rich. In the church, persons of Jewish and Gentile origin live together in common service of the God of Israel. Acts narratively portrays the significance of key religious practices—prayer, the laying on of hands, baptism, the breaking of bread. Along the way, Acts considers the ambiguities of civil authorities. The story of Paul dominates over half of Acts, and it raises the issue of the relationship of the Lukan Paul to Paul as known through his letters.

Methods Important for Interpretation

The three methods of interpretation most important for interpreting the gospel are also important for understanding Acts: historical, literary, and rhetorical criticism. Since these have already been discussed in detail in chapter 9, here I will merely summarize their importance.

Historical criticism attempts to explain Luke-Acts from the perspective of its first-century setting. Historical criticism also helps us identify how people in antiquity understood objects, places, words, phrases, ideas, characters, and literary genres. For instance, Paul calls upon his Roman citizenship to prevent being flogged (Acts 22:22–29). Historical criticism helps us understand this story by supplying information about the meaning of Roman citizenship in antiquity.

Literary criticism is the most widely used approach to the book of Acts today. It is a method that recognizes that Acts is, first, a story or narrative and must be appreciated as such. Literary critics study how Luke uses setting, characters, plot, and atmosphere to generate a literary world. Literary criticism of Acts follows the narrative that begins in the gospel and develops in Acts.

Reader-response criticism is a dimension of literary criticism. This mode identifies the responses evoked in the reader by Acts. Reader-response analysis can be applied to the overall narratives, and to individual passages. For instance, reader-response analysis leads us to conclude that Paul's instructions to the Ephesian elders are intended to spark the reader to realize that the functions of the elders in Ephesus are also the functions of the leadership of the church in Luke's day (Acts 20:25–35).

Rhetorical criticism is similar to literary analysis, especially reader-response criticism. It differs by paying greater attention to the rhetorical conventions of antiquity, as manifested (and transformed) in Luke-Acts. I discuss the overall rhetorical purposes of Acts in connection with "Literary Data" below.

In the interpretation of Acts in this chapter, I use an informal alliance of literary criticism and rhetorical methods, in conjunction with insights from historical criticism.

Social Context

The gospel and Acts were written for the same social setting. Luke does not mention the social situation directly, but scholars surmise this context from indirect clues within the text.

In Acts, as in the gospel, the *relationship between the church and the wider Hellenistic world* is ambiguous. Luke reports typical Hellenistic customs and practices with easy familiarity. Virtually all the stories in Acts take place in cities, thus reinforcing the notion that the gospel and Acts presuppose an urban milieu.

Some aspects of the Hellenistic world facilitate the Christian mission in Acts. For instance, Paul was able to journey widely and frequently because sea travel was available to many people. Roman officials sometimes protect Paul from angry crowds and ultimately make it possible for him to carry the gospel to Rome (e.g., 19:35–41; 22:22–29).

However, as the narrative develops, we realize that Luke is also critical of Hellenism. When Jesus returns from heaven, all people will be judged (Acts 17:29–31; cf. 1:10–11; 2:17–21; 10:42). While some officials befriend early Christians, other officials harass Christian agents (e.g., 16:19–24; 18:12–17; 24:22–27). The Hellenistic world is one of misunderstanding, idolatry, and violence (e.g., 14:8–18; 18:23–40).

Some scholars have viewed Luke-Acts as a political apologetic designed to assure the Roman government that the church did not represent a threat. However, few interpreters hold this view today. Luke portrays civil authorities in Luke-Acts as neither altogether benign nor altogether evil. The community can learn to make its way through the world in which Rome holds sway. Yet the unfaithful behavior of some officials makes it clear that they are not ultimately benevolent or trustworthy (e.g., Lk. 23:13–24; 16:19–24; 18:10–14; Acts 24:24–27; 25:9–12; 26:30–32; 27:24–32).

In these regards, Luke implies a theme from the Septuagint. God uses governments (and other agencies) that do not honor God to serve the divine purposes, even when those governments may not be aware of their holy work. For instance, God used Cyrus the Persian to liberate Israel from exile (Isa. 45:1–8).

The *relationship of the Lukan community to Judaism* is complex. Because this relationship is fundamental to the religious context of Luke-Acts, I take it up in more detail in that discussion (following). For now I note that, on the one hand, the Acts of the Apostles asserts basic continuities between Judaism and the early Christian community. The God of Jesus and the church is the God of Israel. The Septuagint is a preeminent authority to help interpret the meaning of Jesus Christ and the church. The apostles act as faithful Jewish people. Some Jewish people affirm the validity of the Christian witness. On the other hand, the social context of the Acts of the Apostles contains tension between the church and Judaism. The church had existed as a group within Judaism, as a group of Christian Jews. However, in the narrative of Acts, representatives of the church and the traditional synagogue are often in conflict. Luke tells these stories to justify the parting of the ways of church and synagogue in Luke's own day.

While historical actuality may lie behind some of the conflicts between the primitive Christians and conventional Jewish folk in the Acts, the present form of these stories reflects conflict between the church and synagogue of Luke's day. The church reads elements of its contemporary difficulties with Judaism into the narratives of Jesus and the early church. Acts is written to help the Christian community of Luke's day understand why a movement with Jewish roots is in tension with some Jewish people.

Relationships within the Lukan community are also an important part of the social context of Acts. The church is conflicted within itself as to how to relate to Judaism. As we see from the controversies leading to Acts 15, the church is divided on whether to require Gentiles who come into the church to be initiated into Judaism, or whether Gentiles can now serve the God of Israel while remaining Gentiles. This stress, permeating Acts, suggests that persons of Jewish and Gentile background in the Lukan church are having difficulty living in community.

In the gospel, Jesus announces that the Christ and the disciples will suffer (Lk. 9:18–27). Many of the early Christian witnesses in the book of Acts do suffer (e.g., 4:1–22; 5:17–42; 6:8–8:1; 9:23–30; 12:1–5; 13:44–52; 14:1–7, 19–20; 16:19–24; 18:12–17; 19:23–41; 20:1–6, 17–24; 21:17–36; 22:22–29; 23:12–35; 24:6; 27:13–44). This persistent emphasis causes some scholars to think that the Lukan community perceived itself as suffering. We cannot specify the nature of the suffering. From the gospel, we learn that Luke understands such suffering to be a part of the pre-apocalyptic tribulation of the last days.

The early chapters of Acts tell of several events in which the Christian community cares for the poor in their midst (2:42–47; 4:32–5:11; 6:1–7; 11:12–30). These passages suggest that the Lukan social context was plagued by disparity between the rich and the poor within the church. Perhaps the poor are neglected.

The social context of Acts includes questions in the community about the end of history. A generation ago, Hans Conzelmann proposed that Luke wanted the church to believe that that the second coming of Jesus was being delayed. Jesus came "in the middle of time" rather than toward the end of history. Consequently Luke wrote to prepare the church to live as an institution for an indeterminately long time. Few scholars today follow Conzelmann in detail. Most interpreters think that Luke alerts people to a delay (e.g., Lk. 12:38, 45; 19:11; 21:24). However, Luke calls hearers to recognize that an end is coming for which they need to prepare (e.g., Lk. 8:16–18; 10:13–15; 12:4–12, 13–21, 35–56; 13:1–9; 17:20–37; 19:11–27; esp. 21:5–36; Acts 1:10–11; 2:17–21; 10:42; 17:29–31; 24:15, 25) Some people in Luke's social context may have given up hope in the second coming. They may have languished in witness.

Acts emphasizes the Spirit. This emphasis may be for the purpose of kindling hope in the midst of the delay. Others think that the prominence assigned to the Holy Spirit is partly the result of lack of awareness of the Spirit.

The gospel pictures Jesus as an authoritative interpreter of the traditions of Israel and of the reign of God. In the gospel, Jesus prepares the apostles to become authorities in the community. In Acts, the Holy Spirit empowers the apostles in leadership. Perhaps the Lukan church had questions about authority in community.

The gospel and Acts present women as models of belief, as recipients of healing and teaching, as faithful disciples, and even as teachers. This positive characterization leads some interpreters to think that the Lukan community may have been struggling with the role and function of women in the early Christian community.

Religious Context

The religious context of Acts presumes that the reign of God as manifest through the ministry of Jesus in the gospel is now moving in history afresh. This reign will be fully manifest only when Jesus returns from heaven.

With respect to *the relationship between non-Christian Judaism and the Church*, Luke underscores the Jewish character of Jesus and the early Christian movement (see "Social Context," above). The apostles are faithful Jewish people. The Spirit comes to them in Jerusalem, the spiritual center of Judaism, on Pentecost, a Jewish holy day. They frequent the temple. Paul never forsakes his Jewish identity and behavior. In his missionary travels, Paul habitually preaches in synagogues. Neither Paul nor the apostles routinely suggest that the Jewish people should leave the synagogue or forsake Jewish practice. We might think of the early churches as Christian synagogues whose vocation is to testify that the reign of God makes it possible for Gentiles to serve the God of Israel.

Jesus is the Jewish agent through whom God is manifesting this rule. The connection of Jesus, the Jewish people, and the Gentile mission is compactly represented in Acts 3:17–26. When Jesus comes from heaven, God will complete the "universal restoration" and thereby keep the promise to Abraham and Sarah (cf. Gen. 12:1–3; 22:18; 26:4).

When Peter invites a Jewish audience to repent, be baptized, and receive the gift of the Holy Spirit (Acts 2:38), the call is not to abandon Judaism, but to become a part of the community of witness to the reign of God. Repentance in Judaism is not turning from one religion to another, but is turning from betraying God to serving God.

Luke casts approving attention on Gamaliel, a respected Pharisee, a teacher of the law, who defuses the urge of the high priest and Sadducees to kill the apostles. "I tell you, keep away from these [apostles] and let them alone; because if this plan or this undertaking is of human origin, it will fail; but if it is of God, you will not be able to overthrow them—in that case, you may even be found fighting against God!" (Acts 5:38-39).

While making a defense before the council, Peter says, in reference in Jesus Christ, "There is salvation in no one else, for there is no other name under heaven given among mortals by which we must be saved" (Acts 4:12). Salvation refers to participating in the universal restoration. Christians frequently take Acts 4:12 to mean that Jewish people must leave Judaism and become Christian in order to be saved. However, this passage can be interpreted as a statement of the instrument by which the reign of God is becoming manifest: Jesus Christ. If so, the passage does not inherently deny salvation to persons who are not Christian. The Acts identifies Jesus Christ as means whereby the God of Israel completes the cosmic regeneration. Jewish people already acknowledge the universal God. For them, the fundamental call is not to leave the religion of Judaism and join Christianity. Rather their call is to honor the movement toward the reign of God that includes the reunion of Jewish and Gentile communities.

As a part of the renewal of the cosmos, Jesus Christ makes it possible for Gentiles to join the distinctively Jewish act of repentance by turning from idols and other forms of evil (e.g., Acts 11:13 ; 17:29-30; 20:21; 26:20). By repentance, baptism, and the Holy Spirit, Gentiles can be included in the divine restoration. The Jerusalem Council settles the question of whether Gentiles must become Jewish (Acts 15:28–29; cf. 15:20; 21:25).

However, after Pentecost, the early Christian witnesses begin a series of confrontations that continue throughout Acts (e.g., 4:1–22; 5:17–42; 6:8–8:1; 11:19; 12:1–19, esp. 1–5; 13:44–52; 14:1–7, 8–20, esp. 19–20; 17:1–9; 21:7–14; 21:27–22:22; 22:30–23:35; 24:9; 25:1–12; 28:24–27). As already indicated ("Social Context") these narratives justify the growing distance between the non-Christian elements in the traditional synagogues, and the church of Luke's time.

In these confrontations in Acts, Jewish leaders typically accuse the representatives of the church of violating some aspect of Jewish law. Luke repeatedly emphasizes that this Jewish objection is groundless. The Jewish people who disrupt the Christian mission are in league with their ancestors who rejected the prophets (e.g., 7:52; 28:25–29). They are condemned (e.g., Acts 3:23) not because they are Jewish, but because they do not respect the ministry of Jesus and the church.

In regard to *the relationship between Luke's religious vision and the religions of the Gentiles,* Luke keeps faith with Judaism by stating that God is universal and impartial (Acts 10:34; cf. Ex. 15:11; Deut. 10:17–18; 1 Kings 8:41–43; 2 Kings 5:1–19; Ps. 47:2; Dan. 2:47; *Wisdom of Solomon* 5:18; *Ecclesiasticus* 35:1). Paul and Barnabas declare, "In past generations [God] allowed all the nations to follow their own ways; yet [God] has not left himself without a witness in doing good–giving you rains from heaven and fruitful seasons, and filling you with food and your hearts with joy" (Acts 14:16–17). In Acts 17:22–34, Gentiles have positive knowledge of God through nature and through Greek philosophers and religions. Paul is consistent with the Jewish tradition of Wisdom of Solomon 13:1–9 by preaching on the Areopagus that some Gentiles seek for God, even if they cannot name the Divine. They intuit an "unknown god." Paul cites the Greek poet Epimenides as an authority (Acts 17:28a).

However, the knowledge of God that comes through nature and Greek religion is insufficient. Gentiles are called to Jewish repentance (Acts 17:28b–31). Gentile religion typically results in idolatry (e.g., Acts 14:8–18; 20:23–40). Some Gentiles resist the gospel as forcefully as Jewish leaders (14:1–6; 16:16–40). Gentiles collude with Jewish people in rejection of the gospel messengers (e.g., Acts 4:27–28; 14:5–6).

The *relationship between optimum Christian vision and the actual faith and behavior of the church* is also ambiguous. At times the early Christians are models of piety. However, some Christians in Acts forsake the best of their tradition and need correction. For instance, the disciples in Jerusalem do not initially accept Paul as truly a disciple (9:26). The circumcised believers in Judea think that Peter should not fraternize with uncircumcised Christians (11:1–18). The Apostolic Council is called to resolve the relationship of Christian Jews and Gentile believers (15:1–29). Apollos knew the baptism of John and spoke, but Priscilla and Aquila "took him aside and explained the Way of God to him more accurately" (18:24–28). The church at Jerusalem needs to know that Paul is not teaching Jewish people to forsake the customs of Moses (21:17–28).

Literary Data

In antiquity, authors and orators usually expressed themselves in conventional forms of communication. Because the gospel and Acts tell a single story, it is logical to think of them as the same genre. As noted in chapter 9, I share the view of some other interpreters that Luke-Acts is an apology in the genre of a narrative that offers a normative interpretation of the story of Jesus and the early church for the sake of shoring up the community's identity in the face of threat. The Acts of the Apostles offers its hearers a memory of the past that can shape their identity and behavior in the present.

Another approach to the genre of Acts is to regard it as a Hellenistic novel, sometimes called a romance, whose purpose was to instruct its readers while it entertained them. Borrowing a phrase from the Roman author Horace, the narrative is written so that its readers can receive "profit with delight." From this perspective, while Acts contains some genuine historical reminiscences, its present form is similar to that of historical fiction in that Luke has created the tale to teach its morals while delighting its readers. This viewpoint founders on two difficulties. For one, it concludes that the gospel and Acts are different genres, whereas the two books tell a continuous story in one ongoing style. Second, the Septuagintal style of this book suggests that Luke intends the narrative of Acts to continue the story of biblical Israel.

Organization

Jesus states the organizational pattern of Acts. "You will be my witnesses in Jerusalem, in all Judea and Samaria, and to the ends of the earth" (Acts 1:8). The narrative follows the movement of the Christian mission from Jerusalem and Judea (Acts 1:1–8:3), through Samaria (8:4–40), to the ends of the earth (9:1–28:31).

THE GOSPEL IN JERUSALEM AND JUDEA (1:1–8:4).

The Acts of the Apostles does not have a prologue. However, Acts 1:1 calls to mind the prologue to the gospel.

At the ascension, Jesus is raised to the right hand of God (a place of authority) in heaven (1:6–11; 2:34; 7:56). Jesus' authority thus exceeds all earthly figures, including high priest and Caesar. The apostles are reconstituted from eleven to the eschatological twelve (1:12–26).

Pentecost, a Jewish harvest festival, is the occasion of the pivotal event of this era (2:1–41). The manifestation of the Spirit signals the eschatological harvest. Just as Jesus received the Spirit at his baptism (Lk. 3:21–22), so the

Spirit falls upon the church. The Holy Spirit reverses the confusion of languages that began at Babel (Gen. 11:1–9).

Peter's reference in his sermon to "the last days" (Acts 2:17; not found in Joel 2:28–32) interprets Pentecost and the story of the church (Acts 2:22–36) as eschatological. People are restored to the roles God intended from the beginning–sons *and daughters* prophesy. People become participants in the community that witnesses to the restoration (the church) by means of repentance, baptism, and receiving the Holy Spirit (2:38). The community develops a common life (2:42–47; cf. 4:32–5:11; 6:1–7 cf. 11:27–29).

Chapters 3–4 develop a pattern that is typical in Acts. The apostles embody the reign of God by working a miracle (3:1–9) and preaching (3:10–26). The miracle is a mini-demonstration of the universal restoration. The sermon interprets the significance of Jesus Christ, his rejection by Jewish leaders, concluding with the point that, through Christ, God is completing the promises to Abraham and Sarah to bless Gentiles. Some Jewish authorities arrest Peter and John (4:1–22). The apostles make a defense. The Jewish leaders threaten the apostles. God protects the disciples in the same way that God led Jesus to safety after the synagogue crowd tried to throw him off a cliff (Lk. 4:29–30).

The behavior of the community of believers in Acts 4:32–37 is a reverse image of the leadership of the Jewish community in 4:1–22. However, Ananias and Sapphira remind Christian readers that the church contains corrosive elements (Acts 5:1–11).

The pattern of Acts 3:1–4:22 recurs on a smaller scale in 5:17–42. The apostles are imprisoned by Jewish authorities (as Jesus said: Lk. 21:12–19). An angel frees the disciples and thus demonstrates the providence that attends the church's witness. Luke tells a version of this story three times (5:17–21; 12:6–11; 16:23–29), thus reiterating its importance.

The respected Jewish leader Gamaliel exhorts the Jewish people not to condemn the Christian movement, but to leave the church alone to determine whether the Christian movement is of God (5:33–39).

The intra-church conflict between the Hebrew-speaking widows and the Greek-speaking Jewish widows (Hellenists) allows Luke to show that offices evolved in the early church in order to adapt to fresh circumstances (6:1–7). It also underscores the positive care for women in this community (who are among the poor of Lk. 4:18).

Acts tells the story of the arrest, trial, and death of Stephen in parallel with similar events in the life of Jesus: a false charge, false witnesses, a crowd stirred up by Jewish leaders, and a violent death in which Stephen models faith in God by yielding his spirit (Acts 6:8–8:1; cf. Lk. 22:47–23:49). Stephen invokes the prophetic tradition of Jewish self-criticism to explain the attitudes of Jewish people who reject the Christian witness to the realm of God (Acts 7:51–52; cf. Ex. 32:9; 33:3–5; 34:9; Lev. 26:41; Deut. 9:6, 13; 10:16; 31:27; Jer. 4:4; 6:10; 9:26; 17:23; 19:15).

Paul was present at the death of Stephen, and persecuted the church (8:1–3). Listeners are able to contrast Paul before and after the encounter with the risen Jesus on the way to Damascus.

CHRISTIAN WITNESS MAKES ITS WAY THROUGH SAMARIA (8:4–25).

Samaritans were descendants of the Jewish people who stayed in Palestine when Jewish leaders were exiled to Babylonia. Samaritans recognized only the books of Moses as scripture, and worshiped on Mt. Gerizim. Tension persisted between Samaritans and the Jewish people, and Acts references this tension in its story. The rule of God anticipates the reunion of the Jewish and Samaritan communities. This reunion begins in Acts 8:4–25. The baptism of the Ethiopian eunuch is a further step in the movement of the Christian witness to the end of the earth (Acts 8:26–40; cf. Acts 2:39).

THE AUTHORIZATION, AND INITIAL MOVEMENT OF THE MISSION INTO THE EASTERN MEDITERRANEAN WORLD BEGINS (9:1–15:35).

This phase begins with the call of Paul (9:1–19) and takes the gospel as far west as Attalia, about a fourth of the way from Jerusalem to Rome. In 9:1–19, Luke describes the new vocation of Paul in language reminiscent of the calls of the prophets (compare Acts 9:15 with Isa. 49:1–6 and Jer. 1:4–10). Jesus calls Paul to bring the news of the universal restoration to Gentiles (Isa. 42:1–7; 49:1–6; Lk. 2:29–30; 3:4–6; 4:16–30, esp. 25–27; 24:47; Acts 1:8; 2:39). Like Jesus, Paul will suffer (Acts 9:16). Luke tells the story of Paul's call three times to stress its importance (9:1–16; 22:1–21; 26:2–23).

The picture of Paul in Acts and the impression of Paul in the undisputed letters contain similarities. Most importantly, both portray Paul as witness to the Gentiles. However, there are also differences in these two portraits. Acts never refers to Paul's letter writing. There are discrepancies in chronology between the two bodies of literature. For example, according to Acts, after his call Paul immediately goes to Damascus, and soon to Jerusalem, whereas Paul in Galatians indicates that he went to Arabia for three years (Gal. 1:17–20). According to Acts, the Apostolic Council takes place on Paul's third visit to Jerusalem, whereas Galatians leaves the impression that it takes place during Paul's second visit (Gal. 2:1–10). Paul in Acts is a great speaker, whereas Paul describes himself as a weak public presence (2 Cor. 10:10). Paul works miracles in the Acts, whereas the letters make no mention of this ministry. In Acts, Paul agrees to the Apostolic Decree that calls for Gentiles to observe certain Jewish dietary behaviors (Acts 15:28–29; 21:25), but the historical Paul never refers to such a decree; Galatians 2:5 seems to resist such dietary practices. Most scholars think that Acts contains some reliable historical information about Paul, but we cannot always confidently separate that information from Lukan redaction.

Certification for the Gentile mission also comes from Peter (Acts 10:1–48). Cornelius, a Gentile, receives a vision to send for Peter (10:1–8). Peter, archetypal representative of Christian Judaism, receives a vision from God to eat foods that are unclean (10:9–16). The motif of two visions working together is a literary device that strengthens the hearer's awareness that the events are under the control of God. The apostle explains to Cornelius that "God shows no partiality" (10:34). Peter interprets the Gentiles' receipt of the Holy Spirit as a sign that the Gentile mission is of God (10:47).

The church experiences missionary success (Acts 11:19–29). However, the Christian mission continues to meet opposition (12:1–25). On the first missionary journey, the pattern is for the messengers to encounter curiosity that turns to hostility among Jewish persons and receptivity among Gentiles (e.g., Acts 13:4–12, 13–47, 48–51; 14:1–5, 8–20).

To this point, however, it is not clear how the Gentiles are to relate to the traditions of Judaism. This issue is clarified in the Apostolic Council in Acts 15:1–29. Some Christian Pharisees want to require that Gentiles "keep the law of Moses" (15:5). Peter and James do not agree (15:6–21). Their arguments are from revelation (Peter's vision), from experience (the Gentiles have received the Holy Spirit), from practice (the law is "a yoke that neither our ancestors nor we have been able to bear" [15:10]), from the confirmation of signs and wonders, and from scripture (15:16–17).

Under the impulse of the Holy Spirit, the council drafts the Apostolic Decree or Letter. "For it has seemed good to the Holy Spirit and to us to impose on you no further burden than these essentials: that you abstain from what has been sacrificed to idols and from blood and from what is strangled and from fornication. If you keep yourselves from these, you will do well" (Acts 15:28–29). These guidelines are similar to those for Gentiles who live in Israel (Lev. 17:3, 10–14; 18:6–30; cf. Ex. 34:15–16; Lev. 3:17; 19:26; Deut. 12:16, 23–27). They are also similar to the commandments that God gave to Noah for the whole human family, also called "no hide" laws (Gen. 9:3–4). Later rabbis thought that the so-called Noahide laws gave Gentiles the opportunity to live righteously (e.g., Babylonian Talmud, tractate Sanhedrin 56b). Some scholars call attention to the fact that these regulations particularly discourage Gentiles from continuing to traffic with idolatry (e.g., by eating food that had been sacrificed to idols). We might characterize this teaching as a form of de-paganizing and modest Judaizing of Gentiles

THE FURTHER EXPANSION OF THE GENTILE MISSION IN THE MIDDLE MEDITERRANEAN WORLD (15:36–21:16).

The Christian witness now moves as far west as Beroea and Corinth (about two thirds of the way from Jerusalem to Rome). The central character is Paul with new missionary partners Silas and Timothy. Paul receives the famous call to bring the gospel to Macedonia (Acts 16:6–10). Lydia, a leading businesswoman and a God-fearer, is baptized (16:11–15). In response to a confrontation, the missionaries are imprisoned, but delivered (16:16–40; cf. 5:19–21; 12:6–11).

In Thessalonica, the Jewish people in the synagogue become so angry with the Christian preaching that they collude with local ruffians to bring Paul and Silas to trial. The mob seizes Jason, a Christian sympathizer, accusing the church of claiming that "there is another king [besides Caesar] named Jesus" (17:7). The listener knows that accusation is both false and true–false in that the church does not seek to depose the emperor, but true in that the ascension reveals that Jesus is Earth's ruler. Paul then makes his way to Athens, a traditional symbol of the best of Greek philosophy and religion. On the Areopagus he preaches (see the discussion of Acts 17:22–34 in "Religious Setting").

When Paul arrives in Corinth, we learn that he is a tentmaker (i.e., someone who made tents and other goods out of leather). Paul works with Aquila and Priscilla, who had been expelled by emperor Claudias from Rome (18:1–3). The Alexandrian Jewish leader Apollos represents the need for proper teaching in the church (Acts 18:24–28). Paul baptizes disciples who had known only the baptism of John. Through the laying on of hands, they receive the Spirit, showing that they are fully initiated into the community (Acts 19:1–7).

The success of Paul's preaching prompts some Ephesian silversmiths who make shrines to the goddess Artemis to riot because Paul costs them business. A town clerk quiets the crowd to prevent them from being charged with rioting (Acts 19:23–41). Luke's reader knows that the Ephesians' anxiety is unnecessary since the Christian community provides materially for all who turn from idolatry (Acts 2:42–47; 4:32–5:11; 6:1–7; cf. 11:27–29).

Paul then journeys toward Jerusalem for a last visit (Acts 20:1–12; cf. Lk. 8:40–56). Along the way, Paul speaks with the elders (Acts 20:17–36–discussed earlier in "Methods of Interpretation"). The Spirit guides Paul to Jerusalem (21:1–6), where a prophet prepares listeners for Paul's arrest and for the suffering that awaits (21:7–16).

THE GOSPEL NOW JOURNEYS TO ROME BY MEANS OF PAUL'S IMPRISONMENT (21:17–28:31).

Arriving in Jerusalem Paul confronts the false rumor that he has been teaching Jewish people to forsake the law . When a mob tries to kill the missionary, Roman soldiers protect Paul (21:17–36).

With the tribune's permission, Paul begins to make a defense to the crowd by telling the story of his call on the road to Damascus (21:37–22:21; 9:1–19). After the crowd interrupts, the Romans violate their own legal practice by flogging without cause. The prisoner intervenes, "Is it legal for you to flog a Roman citizen who is uncondemned?" (22:22–29). Paul's Roman citizenship carries Paul to Rome. Maltreatment of a citizen (a special status in Rome) was forbidden.

The tribune releases the missionary to the Jewish Council. However, Paul speaks only one sentence when rancor breaks out, prompting the tribune to sequester Paul, again protecting Paul from Jewish violence (22:30–23:35). He then sends Paul to Felix the Governor.

When Felix conducts a hearing, Paul portrays himself as faithful in Jewish belief and practice (24:10–23). Felix reveals the corruption of Rome by longing for a bribe and, to curry Jewish favor, leaving Paul imprisoned for two years (24:24–27). When Felix is replaced by Festus, the new governor immediately attends to Paul's case. Acting on the right of citizen, Paul appeals to have his case heard by the supreme tribunal in Rome (25:1–12).

After hearing Paul, Festus and King Agrippa think that Paul is innocent (25:13–26:1). Paul tells the story of his call on the road to Damascus a third time (26:2–32).

On the long sea voyage to Rome, the passengers give up hope in a storm (27:1–20). An angel, signaling divine providence, reveals that the missionary must testify to the emperor. All are saved (27:21–44). This story shows (again) that God can be trusted through the storms that accompany Christian witness.

After a harmless viper bite (demonstrating Paul's innocence) and a healing on Malta (28:1–10), they arrive at Rome–powerful symbol of the Gentile world, especially idolatry. The gospel and Acts show the grace of God reaching toward Rome in order to restore the broken Gentile world.

When the Jewish community in Rome debates Paul's claim that the reign of God is at hand, Paul cites Isaiah 6:9–10, a passage that claims that God hardens Israel's heart so that they will not repent (28:26–27). Paul declares that "salvation of God has been sent to the Gentiles; they will listen" (28:28).

The last word we hear about Paul is that he is in Rome preaching and teaching (28:30–31). Acts does not recount the fate of Paul. However, Luke leaves a trail of clues that indicate that Paul's witness ended with death (after the pattern of Jesus). This conclusion pushes the reader to respond, "Will I continue to proclaim the reign of God and teach the Lord Jesus as boldly in my setting as Paul did in his?"

Theological Themes

Because Luke-Acts tells a single story, we must trace its theological themes from the gospel into Acts in order to understand their full development. In chapter 9, I discussed the themes of the reign of God, the Holy Spirit, the tradition of authoritative interpretation, and leadership. I now take up the restoration of the human community, the restoration of women, poverty and abundance, and prayer.

In the gospel and Acts, the human community is restored through the reunion in the realm of God of Jewish people with outcasts, marginalized, sinners, Samaritans, and Gentiles. In Luke's gospel Jesus does not interact with large numbers of Gentiles in the gospel, but Jesus does welcome outcasts and sinners in such a way as to anticipate the story in Acts of the inclusion of Gentiles as part of the eschatological ingathering. The first people to whom the angels bring the news of Jesus birth are shepherds–persons whom many people in the first century regarded as dishonest and nonreligious (Lk. 2:8–14). Jesus eats with tax collectors and sinners (e.g., 5:27–31; 7:29–30, 34; 15:1–10; 19:1–10), and holds up tax collectors as models of repentance (18:9–14; 19:1–10). Jesus' meals with tax collectors and sinners anticipate the eschatological banquet (e.g., 13:29; 14:7–24).

Jesus makes an initiative toward the Samaritans (9:51–56), and tells the parable of the good Samaritan to urge the community to recognize that Samaritans can witness to the rule of God while insiders (priest and Levite) can deny it (10:25–37). A Samaritan healed of leprosy returns to thank Jesus for healing (17:11–19). In Acts 8:4–25, Samaritans welcome the divine reign.

Gentiles are all who are not Jewish. A part of the vocation of Israel is to witness to the Gentiles, as in Genesis 12:1–3 when God says, "I will bless you [Abraham and Sarah]…and in you all the families of the earth shall be blessed." Through Isaiah, God declares, "I have given you [Israel] as…a light to the nations" (Isa. 42:6). As a part of the transformation from the old age to the new, the God of Israel is blessing Gentiles through Jesus Christ. The church invites Gentiles into the restoration.

The gospel anticipates the movement to the Gentiles (e.g., Lk. 2:10–11, 25–32; 3:4–6, 23–38; 4:16–30, esp. 25–27; 7:1–10; 13:29; 14:15–24, esp. 23; 15:1–32, esp. 11–24; 24:44–49). In Acts the news of God's ingathering reign goes from Jerusalem, through Samaria, to the ends of the earth, that is, to the Gentiles. Peter evokes the memory of the promises to Abraham as basis for this mission 3:25–26; cf. 3:13), as does Stephen (7:2–8, 16, esp. 17, 32). The God of Israel has always been the God of all peoples (e.g., Acts 7:49–50). The mission to the Gentiles begins directly when the risen Jesus calls Paul as missionary to the Gentiles (9:15; cf. 22:14–15, 21; 26:17–18, 23). Almost two-thirds of Acts tells the story of how Paul fulfills this prophetic vocation. Gentiles become full participants in the church's witness to the universal restoration by repentance, baptism, receiving the Holy Spirit, and living according to the essence of Judaism (15:1–29).

Women are restored to full participation in the community in the reign of God. According to Genesis 1:26–27, women and men were originally equal partners in life. After the first couple ate the forbidden fruit (Gen. 3:1–13), women fell under a curse that included being subordinate to men (Gen. 3:16). In the reign of God, relationships between women and men are restored in Jesus and Christian community.

In Luke-Acts, women are agents and models of the divine realm. Elizabeth immediately welcomes the birth of John, whereas Zechariah (a priest!) is struck mute (Lk. 1:5–25). Only after Zechariah accepts his spouse's instruction does his speech return (1:59–66). Scholars typically speak of Mary as the model believer (1:26–38). With Jesus still in her womb, Mary becomes the first preacher to interpret the significance of his ministry (1:46–55). Jesus uses the healing of a woman as a prime illustration in his inaugural sermon at Nazareth (4:25–26). Jesus forgives a woman who is a sinner (7:36–50). In 8:1–3 we learn that a group of women financed the mission of Jesus. Jesus visits the home of Mary and Martha, and instructs them as disciples in the reign of God (10:38–42). Jesus straightens a bent-over women and calls her "daughter of Abraham" thus refers Jesus to her as a full member of covenantal community (13:10–17). Luke calls attention to the faithfulness of the women to Jesus when he is crucified (23:26–31, 48–49, 54–55). Women are the first Christian preachers for they are the first to announce the resurrection (24:1–11).

Luke pictures women as a part of the community of prayer that selects Matthias to take Judas' place among the Twelve (Acts 1:12–14). On Pentecost, Peter draws from Joel 2:28–32 to indicate that the Spirit is being poured out on sons *and* daughters who shall prophesy, and on male *and* female slaves (Acts 2:17; cf., Acts 21:7–9). Women join men in following the pattern of the ministry of Jesus and other authoritative teachers of Israel.

God provides justice for women through the church when the office of deacon is instituted (Acts 6:1–6). Women are persecuted for their witness (8:3; 9:2; 22:4). Peter embodies the reign of God by raising Tabitha (Dorcas) from the dead (9:36–41). Like the women at the empty tomb who became the first to announce the resurrection (Lk. 24:1–11), Rhoda announces the release of Peter from prison (Acts 12:11–15). Luke gently reminds the reader that Judaism is matrilineal (Acts 16:1). Paul and Silas seek to preach to women who gather at the place of prayer in Philippi (16:13). Lydia is mentioned without connection to a male, and is apparently an independently functioning business woman (a dealer in expensive purple cloth) (16:11–15). Paul exorcises a young slave woman and suffers for it (16:16–40). Women (including some of high standing) respond positively to the gospel in Thessalonica, Beroea, and Athens (Acts 17:4, 12, 34). Priscilla joins her spouse Aquila in teaching (Acts 18:1–4, 24–28). However, Luke's picture of women is not romantic. For example, Sapphira is complicit with Ananias in lying to the Holy Spirit (Acts 5:1–11; cf. 13:50).

Interpreters stress themes relating to *poverty and abundance.* Expositors sometimes speak as if Luke presents a simple antithesis between the poor whom God favors, and the rich who fall under God's judgment. However, Luke's teaching is more complicated. The heart of Jewish thinking on these matters is that God wants all in the community to enjoy material blessing. Members of the community who are materially secure are to share with those who are not. Laws provide for the poor, the widow, and the orphan. Community sharing is a means of divine providence for the poor. The secure who do not share with the poor invite judgment. Wealth can corrupt self and community when its accumulation becomes an end in itself. The reign of God is an era of abundance. However, the end of the present age is accompanied by the condemnation of those who have not been faithful to the poor.

The theme of material possessions in the gospel and Acts develops along these lines. In the gospel, Luke demonstrates God's care for Jesus and the apostles. Jesus and the apostles are itinerant missionaries living from day to day. Through the faithful in community, God provides for them as the prototype of God's care for the poor in Acts. Jesus announces that good news for the poor is a component of the reign of God (Lk. 4:18–19; 6:20–21). Luke's references to the poor are multi-layered in that they include those who are destitute because of economic oppression, as well as those who make themselves voluntarily poor in the service of the reign of God. Jesus is the archetype of the poor (9:58). Likewise, the apostles "left everything and followed him" (5:11). God provides for the impoverished (12:22–33). Women and others in the community care for the needs of Jesus and the followers (e.g., 8:1–3; 9:3; 10:1–12; 22:35–38; 23:50–56). Jesus anticipates eschatological abundance by feeding the 5,000 in the wilderness (9:10–17), and assures the apostles of abundance in the eschatological fullness (11:1–13; esp. 18:28–30).

Voluntary poverty is not a requisite for participation in Christian community. However, many people in the first century regarded voluntary poverty as a sign of the trustworthiness of religious leaders. The poverty of Jesus and the apostles functions as a sign of their faithfulness rather than as a norm for all.

Luke sometimes appears categorically to condemn the rich (e.g. 1:46–55; 6:24–25). However, elsewhere, persons of means serve as sources of provision for the poor (e.g. 3:10–14; 19:1–10). Jesus offers a wealthy person the opportunity to participate in the reign of God by sharing possessions with the needy (18:18–27). Jesus warns the wealthy that if they seek to preserve their own lives by the accumulation of wealth while neglecting the needy they will fall under divine judgment (12:13–21; 16:19–31; cf. 12:41–47). Luke's difficulty is not with wealth as such, but with the ways in which it corrupts self and community. Jesus' condemnation of wealth is designed to awaken people to the need to repent and to use their material goods faithfully.

In Acts, God provides for the poor through community. This motif has two edges. (1) God cares for the poor through the sharing of the community, thus becoming a means whereby God's desire for the material needs of all in the community is satisfied. (2) Those who have material goods are freed from the dangers posed by wealth by putting their possessions at the service of the community.

Acts 2:42–47 and 4:32–37 depict the life of the incipient Jerusalem community as one in which they "had all things in common; they would sell their possessions and goods and distribute the proceeds to all, as any had need" (44b–45). Scholars take this notion in different ways. Some interpreters think that Luke implies that people maintained individual ownership, and sold their goods as members of the community had need. Other scholars conclude that Christians sold their possessions and put the money in a common treasury. Either way, the needs of the community have priority over individual ownership (as in Acts 11:27–30; 20:33–35; 24:17). The deacons are elected to see that all widows in the community receive a share of the community's goods (6:1–6).

The story of Ananias and Sapphira underscores the seriousness of sharing all things (5:1–11). This narrative is a pastoral warning: those who do not do put their goods at the service of the community face the fate of the couple. Judas sells Jesus for thirty pieces of silver, but his bowels break open as a consequence (Acts 1:18–20). Other stories reveal the corruption of self and social world that result from preoccupation with wealth (e.g., 8:14–24; 16:16–24; 24:26).

The gospel and Acts articulate a distinctive emphasis on *prayer*. Luke frequently adds the motif of prayer to incidents in which it is not mentioned in parallel accounts in Matthew and Mark. For Luke, prayer is the self-conscious opening of self and community to the divine leading, and especially to manifestation of the divine rule. The conception of John the Baptist is announced to Zechariah when "the whole assembly of the people was praying" (Lk. 1:10, 13). Anna's interpretation of Jesus arises from prayer and fasting (2:37). After baptism, Jesus is in prayer when he receives the Holy Spirit and hears the heavenly voice (3:21). Luke pictures Jesus as frequently in prayer (5:16). Jesus names the apostles after prayer (6:12–16). Jesus teaches the disciples to pray for those who abuse them (6:28). The revelation of suffering messiahship and discipleship takes place in the context of prayer (9:18–23), as does the prefiguration of Jesus' eschatological glory (9:28). Jesus teaches the disciples that the heart of Christian prayer is for the reign of God. The parable of the friend at midnight assures the disciples that God will disclose the divine rule and empower them with the Holy Spirit (11:1–13). The disciples are always to pray (18:1). Abuse of prayer subverts religiosity (18:9–14). The disciples are to pray that they will not face the eschatological tribulation (22:40–46).

In the Acts of the Apostles, prayer guides the community in the selection of leadership. The community elects Matthias to replace Judas in the apostolic circle in the context of prayer (Acts 1:12–26; 6:1–6; 14:23). Prayer is a constituent of the primordial Jerusalem community (2:42–47). The early community joins in Jewish patterns of prayer in the temple and in the home (3:1). Prayer releases powerful ecstatic experiences among the people (e.g., Acts 4:31). While dying, Stephen, like Jesus, prays for his persecutors (7:59). Through prayer, Samaritans receive the Holy Spirit (8:15). Peter admonishes a Samaritan who wants to buy the gift of the laying on of hands to pray for forgiveness (8:22–24). Through prayer, God guides Ananias to participate in the call of Paul (9:11; 22:17). Cornelius, the first Gentile convert, is a person of prayer (10:2). Peter is in prayer when he receives the vision to commence the Gentile mission by going to Cornelius (10:3–33, esp. 9, 30, 31; 11:5). Peter is delivered from prison after the church prays (12:5, 12). Paul and Barnabas are commissioned by prayer (13:3). Paul prays while in prison (16:25). Paul prays for the King Agrippa to receive the gospel (26:29). In the midst of the storm at sea, Paul prays, and all on the ship are saved (27:29); and he works miracles through prayer (Acts 28:8).

Among other themes that are important are *the relationship of Israel, Jesus, and the church* (see "Social Context" and "Religious Context") and *Lukan attitudes toward civil authorities* (see "Social Context").

Importance for the Church of the Twenty-first Century

When discussing the importance of the book of Acts for the twenty-first century, one feature deserves special consideration. Some Christians regard Acts as little more than a factual history of events that took place in the first century C.E. Using this approach, some Christian communities have attempted to find contemporary significance in Acts by thinking that Luke's second volume offers a blueprint for the structure of the church in all times and places. These groups attempt to restore the New Testament church by patterning themselves after the church in Acts. Other Christians conclude that Acts has little to say to the church since today's Christians do not experience the same kind of miraculous guidance for the church Acts pictures for the early church.

However, the approach to Acts taken in this chapter—an approach that is similar to most other scholarly views of Acts today—is that the book of Acts is less concerned with details of history than with interpreting God's reign for the sake of the world. In this sense, the book of Acts provides the church of the twenty-first century with a model of God's desire to restore the world of today to the purposes of the divine rule. The specific issues that we face may be different from those faced by the church in Acts, but the pattern of the church of Acts can help us wrestle with these issues.

The Apostolic Council in Acts 15 offers *a model for helping the church interpret the divine leading.* When faced with the question of whether to require the Gentile converts to convert to Judaism as a part of affiliating with the Christian community, the church comes together as a community and listens to several resources for resolving this issue: suggestions of the Christian Pharisees that the Gentiles should become Jewish, perspectives from the Bible, personal revelation to Peter, the experience of the Gentiles in receiving the Holy Spirit, the practice of being under the law, signs and wonders that have occurred among Gentiles, and the movement of the

Spirit in the council. The members of the council have a vigorous conversation in which they consider the contributions that these various points of view make to the discussion.

This conversational model can help the church in the twenty-first century deal with new issues or reconsider older issues by prompting us to listen to perspectives from the Bible, from tradition, from experience, and to bring them together through reason while being sensitive to the impulses of the Spirit. This conversational approach is a powerful antidote to tendencies toward idolizing a limited number of sources when trying to interpret God's purposes in the church and world.

The gospel of Luke and the book of Acts call the church to *witness to God's desire to welcome today's outcasts, sinners, Samaritans, and Gentiles into full participation in the renewed world.* The Christian mission includes welcoming persons who have been on the margins of our social worlds, and who may even have been a threat to it. Many Christian communities today are made up largely of persons who are similar in race, social class, philosophical and political viewpoint, other attitudes, and behaviors. Today's church sometimes reflects the same tensions that are found in the fractious wider world. The church is to embody the eschatological community by welcoming poor, rich, Samaritans, and Gentiles. Through the church, all receive God's providential care.

The gospel and Acts call the church *to engage in ministries that restore the place of woman to the fullness of divine purposes.* From Luke beginning the gospel with Mary as the model disciple to the end when women are the first preachers of the resurrection, Luke emphasizes that women enjoy full standing as leaders in the community that is spawned by the reign of God. On Pentecost, the Spirit falls equally on women and men, creating a community of prophets. Women in the book of Acts are recognized as independent beings, as leaders of the house churches, as teachers, and as representatives of the rule of God. To be consistent with this emphasis, today's church needs to be sure that women can witness and lead fully in today's Christian community.

Today's disciples of Jesus are *to use material goods to provide for the needs of the poor and to alleviate the dangers of material goods for the wealthy.* In the reign of God, all people have material goods in abundance, but no one regards material goods idolatrously. The poor will be freed from the anxiety of living from day to day, while the rich will be freed from the anxiety of worrying about the accumulation of wealth.

These motifs are important for the church at the beginning of the twenty-first century. On the one hand, poverty is a permeating feature of life in North America and throughout the world. Acts summons the church to share its goods with the poor as a means of demonstrating God's desire for all to know abundance and to be freed from the enervation of living from day to day. On the other hand, many Christians in North America are undermined by the insatiable desire to accumulate wealth. The quest for material wealth can become idolatrous. The gospel and Acts summon the church to recognize that real security, for both poor and rich, comes through sharing goods.

The gospel and Acts *prepare the Church of today for conflict with the rulers of the present age.* The ministry of Jesus led Jesus into disagreement with many of the leaders of his world. Disagreement became so severe that Jesus was put to death. Likewise, the church in Acts comes into conflict with both Jewish and Gentile authorities. Stephen and Paul are killed. Others are harassed and imprisoned.

This motif has a pastoral element: it warns Jesus' followers to expect difficulty when they offer the possibility of a new world to the residents of this old age. It also offers the figure of Jesus as a model. Jesus confronts the leaders of his day with the reign of God. However, even in death God proves faithful to Jesus. The resurrection validates the power of God to overcome the forces that reject the divine rule. At each instance of persecution, Acts says that the Holy Spirit is with believers to empower them. When today's church encounters resistance, Luke-Acts encourages the community to boldness in the confidence that the Holy Spirit is similarly active among us.

The writings of Luke encourage listeners *to reflect critically on the degree to which the values and practices of the state are consistent with the reign of God.* The state is presented ambiguously in Luke-Acts. At times, the representatives of the Roman state appear to act as unconscious agents of divine providence in protecting Christian witnesses from mobs, and in facilitating the movement of the gospel to Rome. Some representatives of the state demonstrate faith in God. Rome is the preeminent symbol in Acts of the Gentile world. By sending the gospel to Rome, Luke-Acts signals God's desire to restore that part of Gentile culture that is most idolatrous and violent. At other times, representatives of Caesar refuse to acknowledge the innocence of Jesus and Christian witnesses. Few representatives of the state repent, are baptized, or receive the Holy Spirit.

Luke-Acts implicitly reminds the Christian community that the authority of the state extends only until the return of Jesus from heaven. Government is a penultimate reality. Government violates the reign of God when it regards itself as imperial, absolute, and unquestionable. The attitudes and behavior of the state are to be judged by the degree to which they serve the purposes of the reign of God. These materials imply that the church can cooperate with the state when the purposes of the state are consistent with those of God. However, when the attitudes and behavior of the state are contrary to those of the reign of God, the church can call the state to repent in the manner of John the Baptist speaking to the soldiers in the wilderness (Lk. 3:7–10).

Luke-Acts encourages the listeners *to regard the heart of Christian prayer as praying for the full manifestation of the reign of God.* The gospel and Acts urge listeners to remember that the practice of prayer is essential to Christian identity. Furthermore, the heart of Christian prayer is seeking to be open to the complete manifestation of the divine rule. This emphasis implores the contemporary church to develop lives of personal and corporate prayer in which the community seeks to be open to the divine rule.

Acts reminds today's church of *the faithfulness of God.* The God of Israel who is faithful to the people Israel has now revealed the divine faithfulness to the Gentile world through Jesus Christ. Given the many uncertainties that are a part of today's Christian community, this theme is important for preaching and teaching, especially when churches seek to engage in ministries that are today's equivalents of the Gentile mission. A deep and abiding awareness of the faithfulness of God can help empower the church to be Jesus' witnesses from Jerusalem and Judea, through Samaria, and to the ends of the earth.

Suggested Resources for the Pastor's Library

Allen, Ronald J. *Preaching Luke-Acts.* Preaching Classic Texts. St. Louis: Chalice Press, 2000.

Barrett, C.K. *Acts.* The International Critical Commentary. Two volumes. Edinburgh: T & T Clark Publishing Co., 1994, 1998.

Cadbury, Henry J. *The Making of Luke-Acts.* New York: The Macmillan Publishing Co., 1927.

Conzelmann, Hans. *Acts of the Apostles.* Hermeneia. Philadelphia: Fortress Press, 1987.

Dunn, James D.G., *The Acts of the Apostles.* Epworth Commentaries. Valley Forge, Pa.: Trinity Press International, 1996.

Fitzmyer, Joseph. *The Acts of the Apostles.* Anchor Bible 31. New York: Doubleday, 1998.

Haenchen, Ernst. *The Acts of the Apostles: A Commentary.* Philadelphia: Westminster Press, 1971.

Johnson, Luke Timothy. *The Acts of the Apostles.* Sacra Pagina. Collegeville, Mn.: The Liturgical Press, 1992.

Neyrey, Jerome H., editor. *The Social World of Luke-Acts: Models for Interpretation.* Peabody, Mass.: Hendrickson Publishers, 1991.

Pervo, Richard. *Profit with Delight: The Literary Genre of the Acts of the Apostles.* Philadelphia: Fortress Press, 1987.

Smith, Dennis, and Michael Williams, ed. *The Storyteller's Companion to the Bible.* Volume 12. *The Acts of the Apostles.* Nashville: Abingdon Press, 1999.

Tannehill, Robert C. *The Narrative Unity of Luke-Acts: A Literary Interpretation.* Volume 2. *The Acts of the Apostles.* Minneapolis: Fortress Press, 1990.

11

Word Becomes Flesh
The Gospel of John

LARRY PAUL JONES

Basic Data

Although the name John appears in the narrative only in connection with John the Baptist and Simon, son of John, tradition claims that John, the son of Zebedee, wrote the Fourth Gospel while an old man living in Asia Minor. Some second-century manuscripts have the heading, "The Gospel According to John," but that reveals more about the church at that time than about the author of this work. Christian Gnostics linked the Fourth Gospel with the apostle John in order to give greater legitimacy to their use of it. Opponents of the Gnostics, who also claimed John as the authority for their point of view, attributed the text to John in order to refute the Gnostics' interpretation of this gospel. This intense debate over apostolic authorship seems out of place for a narrative that never refers to the disciples of Jesus as apostles and limits the Twelve to a minor role. As it identifies Jesus as the one "sent" by God, who in turn "sends" believers into the world, the Fourth Gospel defines "apostle" broadly rather than narrowly.

Many readers, again beginning in the second century, have considered a character in the narrative, the Beloved Disciple or the disciple whom Jesus loved, the cryptic "signature" of the author (see John 13:23; 19:26–27, 35; 20:2–20; 21:1–14, 20–24). The role of this disciple at the crucifixion and in the closing scene of the narrative plays no small part in this. Since the text never names this disciple, theories of his identity abound, but none of them proves he wrote the text. Given the lack of convincing evidence, it seems best to conclude that we do not know who wrote the book but that, whoever the author may have been, the Fourth Gospel nevertheless reflects early traditions and stories about Jesus.

When we attempt to date the text, we have greater clarity, if not consensus of opinion. In determining the latest possible date of composition, external evidence proves the most helpful. Since Heraclon and Irenaeus, among other church leaders, knew the text and debated its apostolic authorship, we know it existed early in the second century. The earliest manuscript evidence for the text of John, although fragmentary, indicates that the text arrived in Egypt early in the second century as well. This suggests completion of the work no later than 100–110 C.E.

In determining the earliest possible date of composition, internal evidence offers the most help. John 21:18–19 appears to refer to the martyrdom of Peter. That would require a date later than 64 C.E. More significant internal evidence comes from the appearance of the expression "put out of the synagogue" (*aposynagōgos* at three places in the narrative. Three decades ago J. Louis Martyn convincingly argued that this phrase reflects a practice within Judaism of excommunicating heretics from the synagogue not during the time of Jesus but late in the first century (*History and Theology in the Fourth Gospel*). At some point after the destruction of the Jerusalem temple in 70 C.E., Jewish leaders, fearing the disintegration of their faith or vying for control of it, found it necessary to ban Jewish Christians from the synagogue. They accomplished this formally through the Benediction Against Heretics (*Birkat ha-minim*). Recent scholarship suggests that this ban applied generally to all perceived heretics and not specifically to Christians, but it still appears to have been in place by the final two decades of the first century. If the gospel of John reflects the early stages of this conflict, we could date it as early as 80 C.E. If it reflects a stage when the strain between factions has become formalized, a date of 90 or 95 C.E. seems more plausible. The extremely polemical attitude of this narrative toward the Jews makes the later date preferable. The writing of the Fourth Gospel surely occurred between 80 and 100 C.E. and probably between 90 and 95 C.E.

The statement of purpose in John 20:30–31 declares that the author intended to help people to believe in Jesus and have life in his name. Textual variants of the verb "believe" (*pisteuō*) cloud the clarity of this purpose. If we accept the aorist tense of this verb found in some textual witnesses, we will translate it, "that you might come to believe," and conclude that the author writes to persuade non-Christians to believe. If we accept the present tense found in equally reliable witnesses, we will translate it, "that you may continue to believe," and conclude that the author intends to strengthen those who believe already. The Fourth Gospel certainly calls people to believe in Jesus. It presents Jesus as the only avenue to God and the most complete revelation of God. Given that depiction, the author probably wrote both to call nonbelievers to faith and to encourage believers in their faith. The Fourth Gospel tells the story of a life so significant that the world itself cannot contain all the books that could be written about it (21:25), the life of the Word that was with God and was God (1:1). Surely an author bold enough to tackle the task of telling a story that important could and would envision more than one type of intended reader.

Social and Religious Contexts

In John's story of Jesus, we find references to worldly conflict that seem more at home when the gospel was written than during the lifetime of Jesus. For example, during his words of farewell, the Johannine Jesus warns his disciples that the world hates them (15:18–19) and that a day will come when their opponents will equate killing them with worshiping God (16:2). Tension between Jesus and the Jews stands at the very heart of this conflict and appears throughout the narrative. On most occasions, Jesus himself initiates this conflict by challenging Jewish customs, violating the Sabbath, or making deliberately provocative statements about his nature and mission. At the festival of Tabernacles, Jesus enters a debate with some Jews "who had believed in him" (8:31) in which he refers to them as children of the devil (8:44). When we encounter this vehement polemic against the Jews, we may forget that Jesus is a Jew, that he observes Jewish festivals, that he declares that salvation comes from the Jews, and that most of those who follow him are Jews. How can we explain this intense animosity toward his own people and traditions?

As the Pauline epistles and the book of Acts illustrate, early believers in Jesus were predominantly Jewish. It is clear that the Johannine community was also Jewish; otherwise why was there concern about expulsion from the synagogue? These early Christians continued to observe parts of Jewish law, to debate (Jewish) scripture, to gather in synagogues, and to long to make a pilgrimage to the Jerusalem temple. Indeed, early Christianity could be called a sect of Judaism. Christian interest in spreading the gospel to Gentiles no doubt prompted controversy, but there was no immediate separation from Judaism. The Jewish War with Rome (66–70 C.E.) and the destruction of the temple (70 C.E.) altered that. Deprived of the temple they revered, Jews turned increasingly to the law, but Jewish and Gentile Christians turned with equal fervor to Jesus. As noted in the discussion of the date of the Fourth Gospel, some Jews eventually found it necessary to define themselves more narrowly and to excommunicate those whom they deemed heretics. The Fourth Gospel reflects and addresses this context. By blending the tensions between Jews and Christians in his world into the world of the narrative, the author defends his belief in Jesus and offers encouragement to believers who find themselves shunned by their Jewish friends. That allows the Johannine Jesus to address the specific needs and challenges of the Johannine community.

Despite this struggle, the Fourth Gospel relates positively to the Jewish milieu of first-century Palestine in many ways. Quotations and images from

Jewish scriptures appear frequently. The Johannine Jesus attends Jewish feasts and festivals, uses the divine name "I Am" to identify himself, and regularly employs symbols from Judaism in his speeches. The narrator interprets the actions of Jesus as the fulfillment of Jewish scripture, beginning with John the Baptist's presentation of Jesus as the Lamb of God (1:36) and running through Jesus' final words (19:28) and the treatment of his dead body (19:36–37).

The world of the gospel of John also has a great deal in common with the Qumran community, which produced the Dead Sea Scrolls and flourished in isolation near the Dead Sea from the second half of the second century B.C.E. until roughly 60 C.E. John's dualistic contrast of light and darkness and good and evil, despite belief in a supreme deity, echoes the same in the Qumran documents. This does not establish a direct relationship between the Johannine community and Qumran. Rather this shared language indicates the immersion of the Johannine community in the religious environment of first-century Palestine.

More than four decades ago, C. H. Dodd drew attention to the similarities between the Fourth Gospel and Hellenistic philosophy particularly as evidenced in the writings of Philo of Alexandria (*The Interpretation of the Fourth Gospel* [Cambridge, Eng.: Cambridge Univ. Press, 1953] 54–73). The narrator introduces the reader to the preexistent and divine Word (*logos*) sixteen verses before providing the name Jesus, and later depicts Jesus as the light (*phōs*) of the world. Philo uses both terms extensively. Jesus sounds very Platonic when he calls himself the "true food" and the "true vine" and insists that he came from above whereas his opponents are from the world. Such a dualistic view derives ultimately from Platonic thought. This dualism in John establishes no direct relationship with Philo, Stoic philosophers, or others, but it indicates the intellectual and philosophical milieu from which the text emerged. This also applies to the relationship between the Fourth Gospel and gnosticism. As second-century Gnostics observed, the Johannine vocabulary and worldview, with its radical dualism between this corruptible world and the incorruptible world above, certainly has affinities with gnosticism. That reflects the influence of gnostic thought in the first-century world, but does not indicate that either the author or the Johannine community were Gnostic.

Despite its dualism and the conflict behind and within it, the Fourth Gospel depicts Jesus attracting and accepting believers from a wide spectrum of society. An influential Pharisee, a Samaritan woman, a man born blind, followers of John the Baptist, Jewish pilgrims to Jerusalem, and a variety of other women and men have the opportunity to become believers. This probably reflects both the diversity present in first-century Palestine and the eclectic community to and for whom the author wrote.

The gospel of John was composed in and for a time of upheaval and conflict. It reflects and addresses a rapidly changing and exceedingly complex social and religious milieu that careful readers must take into account in their interpretations.

Methods of Interpretation and Literary Data

Prior to the 1970s, historical critical approaches dominated Johannine studies. Although these studies addressed theological and sociological concerns, they sought primarily to uncover and analyze the historical layers of the text. They dissected the gospel narrative into isolated and defined units of text in an attempt to discover the community (or communities) and meaning behind the text. In the past three decades, scholars have begun to experiment with literary critical studies that seek to examine the gospel narrative as a whole, investigating its literary structures and asking what those structures mean and how they give rise to meaning. Literary studies do not necessarily oppose historical critical approaches, but they ask a different set of questions of and about the text. Literary approaches investigate, for example, the plot of the narrative (how the story unfolds), the characterization (how characters are depicted and developed), the rhetorical strategies that affect the relationship between the narrator and the reader, and the use of metaphor, irony, and other literary conventions and devices. Instead of dissecting or digging into the text, literary studies seek to experience the text and to ponder how its component parts relate with each other and affect the reader. These studies still address theological, sociological, and ecclesiological concerns, but do so not by looking behind the text but by interacting with the text as we have received it.

The attention given to its literary structure and features has reopened debate about the genre of the Fourth Gospel. Not long ago a majority of scholars considered the canonical gospels *sui generis*, a new type of literature created by the church and without parallel in the ancient world. Comparison of the gospel narratives with literary works roughly contemporary with them has challenged that view. Recent scholarship typically identifies the Fourth Gospel as a form of either ancient drama or ancient biography. Both of those genres focus on the uniqueness of Jesus, particularly on how the portrayal of him affects the reader. Aristotle referred to this as *pathos*, a means of persuading hearers or readers through rousing their emotions so as to put them in a particular frame of mind (*Rhetoric*, 1.2.3–6). The author of John employs a variety of literary devices to exert this influence. We have room here only to survey a few of the most important of them.

Readers have often noted the Johannine use of irony. Irony is a literary device whereby the story seems to be saying one thing but the reader is led to understand it with a different meaning or, in this case, a deeper meaning. The narrator of the Fourth Gospel is stylistically an "omniscient narrator," one who always knows more than the characters and typically shares that perspective with the reader. Thus as we read the narrative we hear characters making derogatory statements about Jesus that we recognize as truer than they realize and we often overhear characters missing the deeper meaning of the words Jesus speaks. For example, as the woman at the well engages Jesus in dialogue she asks, "Are you greater than our ancestor Jacob, who gave us the well, and with his sons and his flocks drank from it?" (4:12). The reader, who has learned that Jesus is the Incarnate Word, who descended from heaven, smiles knowingly. Near the end of the narrative, the soldiers place a crown of thorns on Jesus' head, drape him with a purple cloak, and mockingly hail him as the king of the Jews (19:2–3). The reader knows the bitter irony that this *is* the king of the Jews and the savior of the world. The effect of the irony is not simply to allow readers to feel smug but rather to give them an opportunity to see and ponder the deeper meaning of the events narrated; the author employs irony to help the reader perceive the true identity of Jesus and to sense the tragedy of failing to have that perception.

The author also employs a closely related literary technique, misunderstanding or double entendre. This device typically comes into play when Jesus uses a word that has a double meaning or utters an easily misunderstood phrase. When his dialogue partner misses the point or becomes confused, he has the opportunity to explain himself more fully. The most noted example of this occurs in the dialogue with Nicodemus (3:1–15), when Jesus insists that only those who have been born "from above" (*anōthen*) can see the kingdom of God (3:3). Depending on the context, the adverb *anōthen* can mean "from above," "again," or even "from the beginning." When Nicodemus becomes confused because he has taken Jesus literally, Jesus responds with a lengthy discourse in which he reveals the nature of his ministry and identity (3:9–21). Several chapters later, Jesus tells a group of would-be followers that true disciples learn the truth and the truth makes them free (8:32). When his hearers interpret freedom as liberation from the power of another person, Jesus informs them that he offers freedom from sin and defines sin as failure to perceive his true identity (8:34–43). Such misunderstandings occur frequently, and the reader always benefits from the confusion or deficiency of Jesus' dialogue partners. As Jesus explains his true meaning, the narrator can develop the principal themes of the narrative and teach the reader to look more deeply than the literal and obvious meanings of words and actions. This also allows the reader to feel included among those who recognize Jesus' true identity and significance.

The narrative of the Fourth Gospel is also characterized by symbolism. Characteristic phrases such as "I am the light of the world" or "I am the bread of life" clearly use such categories as "light" and "bread" in a symbolic sense. Although many of these symbols have roots in the Hebrew Bible, most of them come from everyday life (e.g., water, bread, and gate). That makes them available to the widest possible audience in the Greco-Roman world and invites all readers to begin with what they know and build on that as the meaning of the symbol emerges. As a literary device, a symbol functions in two ways: it points toward something other than itself and it in some way represents that to which it points. Water, for example, symbolizes (points toward) the Spirit that Jesus offers to believers and, at the same time, represents the Spirit. The living water that Jesus offers the woman at the well ends all thirst and allows her to leave her bucket behind (4:10–15, 28). The bread in the story of the feeding of the five thousand symbolizes (points toward) the eternal life Jesus offers, while at the same time representing that eternal life because it cannot be bought or earned but can only be freely given to believers by God (6:1–14, 32–40).

All of the Johannine symbols eventually point to Jesus because they complete his revelation. As the net holding the fish that the risen Jesus instructed the disciples to catch is not torn despite the number of fish in it (21:11), so also Jesus promises not to lose any of those whom God gives him (e.g., 17:12). As a good shepherd risks his life on behalf of the sheep, so also Jesus gives up his life to die on the cross on behalf of his own (10:11–18). Yet, an element of mystery always remains when we interpret these symbols. As the Lamb of God (1:36), Jesus dies at the time when the Passover lambs are being slaughtered in the temple (18:28, 31). The narrator makes note of that, but offers no explanation. When Jesus washes the feet of his disciples he renders them clean, yet one of those with washed feet almost immediately leaves to betray him (13:1–30). Johannine symbols point to realities worth pondering, but do not reveal everything. Only Jesus can do that. Symbols entice readers to look for connections that do not immediately greet the eye, while reminding them of their absolute dependence on Jesus.

This brief survey of three of the literary devices found in John indicates how the narrator expects the reader to pay close attention to details and look beyond the surface for deeper meaning. In other words, the narrator challenges the reader to enter a relationship with the text. The Johannine narrator tells lively but relatively long stories that unfold slowly and contain frequent surprises. Those who jump to conclusions quickly will miss the message, but those who allow themselves to receive the message as it comes will find themselves led into faith and community.

Organization

The gospel of John narrates the journey of the Word of God as he enters the world, conducts an itinerate ministry in Palestine, accepts crucifixion and entombment in Jerusalem, and reappears to several of the faithful in Jerusalem and beside the Sea of Galilee. A reader following this journey may note along the way what C. K. Barrett calls "displacements," parts of the narrative that seem out of sequence (*The Gospel According to John,* 22). At the end of chapter fourteen, for example, Jesus appears to bring his words of farewell to a close with the command, "Rise, let us be on our way" (14:31). Jesus continues to speak and pray, however, and no one goes anywhere until chapter eighteen. In the farewell scene, Jesus complains that none of his disciples ask where he is going (16:5) despite the fact that Peter earlier questioned, "Lord, where are you going?" (13:36). The story of the woman caught in adultery (8:1–11) also seems misplaced. It interrupts Jesus' teachings during the Feast of Tabernacles and if it is removed the narrative moves without difficulty from 7:52 to 8:12, which is the way it appears in most ancient manuscripts.

These and other breaks and inconsistencies in the narrative have convinced many readers that the text we have received went through two and possibly more stages of composition. Perhaps the best reconstruction of the phases of development of the text and its community is Raymond Brown's *The Community of the Beloved Disciple.* Brown posits four phases ranging from the mid-first to the mid-second century C.E. and encompassing the Johannine epistles into the community's history. But not everyone agrees. All narratives have flaws and imperfections. Despite the often-noted displacements and inconsistencies, the narrative of the Fourth Gospel remains coherent, sound, and sensible just as we have it. Investigation of possible stages of composition of the text and of the sociological and ecclesiological changes that prompted them will continue and may yield fresh new insights for interpretation. That should not, however, thwart examination and interpretation of the narrative as it now exists.

Generations of Johannine scholars have separated the text into two primary parts: chapters 1–12, typically designated "the Book of Signs" or the public ministry; and chapters 13–20, usually called "the Book of Glory" or the private ministry. This division treats John 21 as an appendix or a later ending. The facts that the narrator announces the arrival of Jesus' "hour" in John 13:1 (thus indicating that the "hour" is the passion of Jesus) and that all of Jesus' signs or miracles occur in chapters 1–12 support this division. Brown modifies this only slightly and designates John 1:19–12:50 "The Book of Signs," in which Jesus reveals himself by sign and word, and John 13–20 "The Book of Glory," in which Jesus reveals his glory through his crucifixion, resurrection, and ascension. He surrounds these major units with a shorter prologue (Jn. 1:1–18) and epilogue (Jn. 21) (*The Gospel According to John*, 1.cxxxviii-cxxxix). Barrett distinguishes Jesus' passion from the time he spends alone with his disciples and offers this outline: Prologue (1:1–18); Narratives, Conversations, and Discourses (1:19–12:50); Jesus Alone with His Disciples (13:1–17:26); Passion and Resurrection (18:1–20:31); and Appendix (21:1–25) (Barrett, 11). Others have proposed similar outlines, each of which distinguishes Jesus' more public teachings and acts in the first half of the narrative from the time he spends in private and the events of his passion in the second half.

Scholars attempting to employ literary conventions of the ancient world in identifying the genre of the Fourth Gospel have proposed significantly different narrative plots. Nearly eighty years ago, F. R. M. Hitchcock

(*Theology* 7 [1923]: 307–17) suggested that Fourth Gospel resembles a Greek drama, with five acts surrounded by a prologue and an epilogue: Prologue (1:1–18); Act 1 (1:19–2:12); Act 2 (2:13–6:71); Act 3 (7:1–11:57); Act 4 (12:1–19:42); Act 5 (20:1–31); and epilogue (21:1–25). More recently, Mark Stibbe (*John's Gospel* [New York: Routledge, 1994], 35–36) has characterized the Fourth Gospel as a drama that leads to a climatic denouement when Thomas calls the risen Jesus his Lord and God (20:28). He separates the narrative into five stages: Prologue (chap. 1); Act 1 (2–4); Act 2 (5–10); Act 3 (11–12); Act 4 (13–19); Act 5 (20); and Epilogue (21). Both of these studies employ conventions of ancient literature in their interpretations and provide insights into how the author intended the narrative to affect the reader.

Nearly a decade before Hitchcock compared the Fourth Gospel with a drama, Clyde Webber Votaw (*American Journal of Theology* 19 [1915]: 45–73, 217–49) proposed that gospels in the New Testament resemble ancient biographies and, like them, seek to draw attention to their central figure in order to convince readers of his significance. More recently, Charles Talbert *(What Is a Gospel?* [Macon, Ga.: Mercer Univ. Press, 1985], 53–90) has explored similarities between the depiction of Jesus in the Fourth Gospel and the frequent appearance of a descending-ascending redeemer in ancient narratives. He emphasizes the fact that ancient biographies have less interest in tracing the development of their heroes from cradle to grave than in revealing their character in the hopes of affecting public opinion and behavior. After noting that ancient biographies typically include a narrative of origins, a central and extended narrative of public life, and narrative of death and lasting significance, Fernando F. Segovia *(Semeia* 53 [1991]: 23–33, 47, 50–51) finds a similar structure in the Fourth Gospel. His plot designates a Narrative of Origins (1:1–18), a Narrative of the Public Life or Career (1:19–17:26), and a Narrative of Death and Lasting Significance (18:1–21:25). The components of the second and third sections of this plot draw attention to Jesus' movement back and forth between Galilee and Jerusalem and to the stages of his journey through his arrest, trials, death, and resurrection. Segovia argues that the narrative arrangement of the Fourth Gospel has a strong polemical function, which forces readers to form an opinion and either accept or reject Jesus.

The strength of these studies lies in their examination of the text in light of ancient literary conventions and in their awareness of Jesus' movement in the text. Close attention to the narrator's presentation of Jesus and to his journeys allows readers to experience the text as it unfolds and not to attempt to confine it within some logical or thematic outline. As we note the way the narrator introduces Jesus to the reader and then follows his movements from his initial acts of ministry to his resurrection appearances, we can plot eight distinct stages in the narrative:

As expected in an ancient biography, the text begins by introducing its hero, whom the narrator first identifies as the Word of God and the only Son (1:1–18). In the second section of the opening stage, the testimony of John the Baptist, who identifies Jesus as the Lamb of God and Son of God, completes the introduction (1:19–34). This section focuses on theology more than history, immediately challenging the reader to ponder Jesus' nature and identity. That focus continues as these lofty titles and added descriptions of Jesus echo throughout the remaining narrative.

The second through the fifth stages of the narrative plot Jesus' journeys through Galilee, Samaria, and Judea, each one climaxing in a trip to Jerusalem to attend a Jewish festival and in increased discord between Jesus and the religious authorities. His first journey includes the call of his first disciples and his initial sign at Cana (1:35–2:11). He then travels to Jerusalem to observe the Passover (2:13). When some there express faith in him because of the signs he has performed, he curiously does not "entrust himself to them" (2:24), thus introducing a tension in the narrative between "signs faith" and true faith. His second journey takes him through Samaria and back to Galilee and Cana, before he departs again for the Holy City to attend an undesignated feast. At the end of this visit, he chides the crowds for failing to believe either Moses or him (5:45–47). The third journey begins with Jesus traveling back and forth across the Sea of Galilee before returning to Jerusalem for Tabernacles. Before this visit ends, the crowds attempt to stone him (8:59) and the authorities try to arrest him twice (7:30,

32). Jesus' final journey takes him first to Bethany, where the raising of Lazarus prompts another attempt to arrest him and plots to kill not only him but also Lazarus (11:45–53; 12:9–11). After reentering Jerusalem for Passover, Jesus predicts his death and quotes Isaiah to characterize those who refuse to believe in him as blind and hard-hearted (Jn. 12:37–40). As the relationship between Jesus and the religious authorities becomes more strained with each journey, the reader becomes caught up in it and must decide with whom to agree. Long before the passion narrative begins, all room for neutrality has disappeared.

For the first time since the beginning of the story, Jesus remains stationary during the sixth stage of the narrative. He speaks specifically to "his own" (13:1), preparing them for his return to God and for the ministry that they will conduct with the help of the Spirit. Even in this intimate setting, the animosity and controversy continue as he prays for God to protect those who have accepted his word against the world that hates them (17:14–15).

Stage seven of the narrative, Jesus' "hour," takes him first to the Kidron Valley, where he is arrested. He is then led to the home of the high priest, where he is questioned (18:12–14, 19–24), and to Pilate's headquarters, where the soldiers flog him, the crowds taunt him, and the governor condemns him (18:28–19:16). He carries his own cross to Golgotha (in contrast to Mark's story, compare John 19:17 with Mark 15:21) and, after relinquishing his spirit (19:30), is entombed in a nearby garden (19:38–42). Even when portraying Jesus' death, the narrator continues to exalt him. Despite the objections of the religious authorities, the Lamb of God dies beneath the inscription, "King of the Jews" (19:19), and fulfills scripture four times before being removed from the cross (19:24, 28, 36, 37).

In the final stage of the narrative, the risen Jesus appears first to Mary Magdalene (20:11–18), twice to the disciples in Jerusalem (20:19–23, 26–29), and one final time to the disciples beside the Sea of Galilee (21:1ff.). The story of the Son of God is complete. The reader must now accept this witness and believe in Jesus or reject both it and him. The narrator confesses that no number of books could tell the entire story (21:25), but this one contains sufficient testimony for the reader "to believe that Jesus is the Messiah, the Son of God, and…have life in his name" (20:31).

Primary Theological Teachings

On the surface, the gospel of John seems infatuated with Jesus. From its beginning to its end, Jesus stands at the center of the narrative. Every scene features him as a character or a topic of discussion. While that sounds appropriate for a biography, remember that ancient biographies emphasize not the cradle to grave history of their heroes but rather their lasting significance. When we focus solely on Jesus and treat the Fourth Gospel primarily as a christological work, we overlook the heart of its message.

Although clearly the hero, Jesus does not stand alone at the center of the narrative. The Fourth Gospel has a theological core because it seeks first and foremost to proclaim a message from God, a message that is Jesus and is revealed in Jesus.

The narrator makes this clear from the beginning, declaring in the introduction that Jesus came to make the unseen God known (1:18). This God has two primary appellations. God is the Father and the one who sent Jesus.

Jesus refers to God as his Father more than one hundred times. While this appellation can refer to God as the Father of all, it typically establishes the intimacy between God and Jesus. The Father loves Jesus (e.g., 5:20), commands and speaks to him (e.g., 14:31), draws followers to him (e.g., 6:37), and glorifies him (e.g., 8:54; 13:31–32; 17:1–5). Indeed, Jesus lives only because of the Father (6:57). The intimacy between God and Jesus could not be greater. Even though it incites the authorities to plot to kill him, Jesus insists that he and the Father are one (10:30). In his words of farewell to his disciples, he chides Philip for asking to see the Father and declares, "Whoever has seen me has seen the Father" (14:9). Jesus has a decidedly theological purpose and mission. The only Son comes to make the Father known.

Jesus has this purpose and mission only because the Father has sent him. He comes to do the will of the one who sent him (4:34) and to do that exclusively (5:30). What he teaches belongs not to him but to the one who sent him (7:16; 14:24). Even when he declares that he comes to bring eternal life, he defers to God: "And this is eternal life, that they may know you, the only true God, and Jesus Christ whom you have sent" (17:3). The Fourth Gospel cannot separate the story of Jesus from God. Indeed, if not for the one who sent Jesus, there would be no story to tell. This intimate relationship between God and Jesus reveals the nature of God and the nature of the relationship God envisions between believers and the world (17:20–23).

God can seem distant and aloof in the Fourth Gospel. The Father has a house with many dwelling places, but Jesus must make that ready and prepare the way for believers (14:1–6). The crowds can hear the voice of God (12:28–29), but cannot see God and no one except Jesus seems capable of knowing God (e.g., 8:55). Yet, this "distant" God takes fleshly form as the Word that comes to dwell with the people (1:14). The God of the Fourth Gospel is mysterious and awesome, but not detached and utterly unapproachable.

Without doubt the gospel of John has a high christology. Jesus knows more about people than they know about themselves (2:24–25), exists before Abraham (8:58), and claims divinity by referring to himself as "I am" (e.g., 8:24, 28, 58; 13:19), a phrase that echoes the Greek translation of the name of God in Exodus 3:13–14. The Johannine Jesus is no mere human. Unlike the synoptic Jesus, no one tempts him (John has no temptation story), and he utters no cry of dereliction from the cross. Yet, this same Jesus cries at the tomb of a friend (11:35), washes the feet of his disciples (13:5), and loves his own to end (13:1). Nothing removes the paradox. Jesus is the Word that is God, but is also Son of God. He is the vine, but God is the vinegrower (15:1). He does only what he sees the Father doing (5:19). He reveals himself in order to accomplish his primary purpose of making God known. The seemingly christocentric Fourth Gospel has a thoroughly theocentric Jesus. The theology of the one sent by God gives the narrative its theological core.

Jesus' theocentric mission shapes the ecclesiology of the Fourth Gospel. As the one sent from above to make God known, Jesus makes only two demands on would-be followers. He commands them to believe in him and to love one another. That alone determines and characterizes true disciples.

The introduction claims that all who believe in Jesus become children of God (1:12). The Johannine Jesus challenges everyone to do that. He calls to faith a wide array of people: an influential Pharisee named Nicodemus (3:1–21) and an unnamed woman of Samaria (4:1–42); crowds of Jews beside the Sea of Galilee (6:1–15) and pilgrims gathered for Tabernacles in Jerusalem (7:37–39); a man born blind (9:1–41) and close friends in Bethany (11:17–27); people struggling to understand him and those already identified as his disciples. For most of the narrative, believing alone distinguishes and identifies the faithful. Unfortunately, English translations cannot draw attention to an essential characteristic of this faith. Whereas the verb, "to believe" (*pisteuō*), appears ninety-eight times in the narrative, the noun, "faith" (*pistis*) never appears. The Fourth Gospel has interest not in the static content of faith but in the dynamic action of "faithing," which means nothing more and certainly nothing less than accepting God's self-revelation in Jesus. Just as Jesus does not exist outside his purpose of making God known, so also the act of believing is the essential and determining characteristic of true disciples.

Jesus commands those who believe to love one another (13:34–35). This action reflects the nature of God and the mission of Jesus. God sends the only Son because God loves the world (3:16) and Jesus completes his mission because he loves God and his own (13:1; 14:31). Four times during his words of farewell, Jesus commands his disciples to follow this example and to love one another (13:34, 35; 15:12, 17). They become children of God by believing (1:12). Others will recognize them as children of God by their love for one another (13:34–35). This love surpasses syrupy sentimentality. Those who believe in Jesus face intense persecution and find themselves expelled from the synagogue. The man born blind, for example, loses his community and family as he comes to faith (9:34). When Jesus commands believers to love one another, he calls attention to the fact that genuine love requires laying down one's life for one's friends (15:12–13).

This refers not only to his offering up himself for them, but also to what awaits them. In the next chapter he warns of a time to come when their opponents will consider killing them an act of worship (16:2).

These demanding commandments, to believe in Jesus and to love one another, apply to all disciples. This alone distinguishes them from others and forges their fundamental identity. The Fourth Gospel has no hierarchy among believers. The Twelve appear in only two scenes and have no place of primacy (6:66–71; 20:24). Jesus offers his acts and words of farewell to an undetermined number of disciples, who represent all believers. At the end of his third resurrection appearance, his words to Thomas put those who believe without seeing him on equal footing with believers who have seen him (20:29). A narrow gate leads to the community of the faithful. Only those who believe in Jesus may pass through it. At the same time, however, that community has wide arms of acceptance. All who believe in Jesus, regardless of other characteristics, may enter. No one in the Fourth Gospel escapes the need to make one crucial decision, the decision whether or not to accept the message of God that Jesus is and brings to the world.

The decision placed before humanity by God's self-revelation in Jesus shapes Johannine soteriology and eschatology. God sends the Son into the world to save it, to offer people the opportunity to believe in him and thus to have life. Those who reject this opportunity pass judgment on themselves (3:18–21). Their refusal to believe separates them from God and eternal life. Those who believe avoid this judgment and pass from death into life (5:24). For the gospel of John, this passage takes place immediately.

The Johannine Jesus does at times look toward the future for the fulfillment of God's designs and promises. He occasionally refers to a "last day" (6:39, 40, 44, 54), he speaks of a heavenly home that he will prepare for the faithful (14:2), and he prays that believers eventually will become one as he and God are one (17:20–23). Most of the time, however, Jesus focuses on the present. He tells the woman at well that those who drink the living water he offers will never again thirst (4:14) and he identifies himself to the crowds outside Capernaum as the living bread that enables those who eat it to live forever (6:51). When confronted in Jerusalem for healing on the Sabbath, he avows, "anyone who hears my word and believes him who sent me has eternal life, and does not come under judgment, but has passed from death to life" (5:24). He repeats this in even stronger terms when Martha assures him that she knows that her brother will rise from the grave on the last day. Jesus challenges her to consider that last day already present: "I am the resurrection and the life. Those who believe in me, even though they die, will live, and everyone who lives and believes in me will never die. Do you believe this?" (11:25–26). Those who believe in Jesus conquer death here and now. Just as Jesus existed before Abraham was (8:58), those who believe in Jesus become one with him and enter eternal life in the present. The Word became flesh for that very reason: to offer humanity the opportunity to move out of the darkness of death into the light of life (1:1–14). While the Fourth Gospel denies neither the danger of living in the world nor the risks of believing in Jesus, it passionately insists that the denouement for every individual is determined by that individual's response to God's self-revelation in Jesus. Those who do not believe indicate their preference for darkness (3:19). Those who believe do not have to hope or wait for eternal life; they enter it immediately. The future, like the present, may bring oppression, persecution, and even death; but nothing will change the fact that believers already live resurrection life and eternal life. Like Nicodemus, readers may ask, "How can these things be?" (3:9). As the introduction advises, accepting the Word and becoming a child of God do not result from "the will of the flesh or of the will of man" (1:13). God alone makes this possible. It is a wonderful and life-changing paradox, a revelation from God to be accepted and believed.

Importance of the Fourth Gospel for the Church of the Twenty-first Century

As the gospel of John enters its twentieth century of use, it poses two potential problems and two areas of particular promise for readers. The problems, although formidable, will not allow us to avoid the text. The areas of promise lie so close to the heart of the faith that they make it imperative that we engage the text.

The gospel of John declares that the Word of God became flesh. Those who take that metaphor seriously will take the words spoken by this Word of God seriously as well. Twenty-first-century readers may find two words in the Johannine vocabulary especially disturbing: the "Jews" and the "Father."

The Jews oppose Jesus in the Fourth Gospel. They challenge his authority (5:10–18), charge him with blasphemy (10:33), attempt to stone him (8:59; 10:31–33), plot to kill him (5:18; 7:1; 8:37–40; 11:45–53), and demand that the Roman governor crucify him (19:14–16). The Johannine Jesus, on the other hand, claims to predate Abraham (8:58), declares that those who do not eat his flesh and drink his blood have no life in them (6:53), dares to use the divine "I Am" in reference to himself (e.g., 8:24, 28, 58; 13:19), and calls a group of Jews children of the devil (8:44). Unfortunately, instead of leaving this animosity in the narrative, some have used it to justify heinous acts and attitudes of anti-Semitism. Given that history, how can we continue to use a text that has fueled such sinful behavior?

Some help comes from studies that make a distinction between the religious authorities and the Jewish people in general as they appear in the narrative. Even before using such studies, however, we must distinguish any historical group of Jews, past or present, from the literary character, "the Jews," in the gospel of John. Characters in a narrative may represent or reflect historical persons, but they are not those persons. In the gospel of

Mark, for example, Jesus' disciples fail in nearly everything they do. That does not indicate that Jesus surrounded himself with incompetent bunglers. Rather the disciples' blunders function as a literary device that advances the narrative. As they make mistakes, Jesus clarifies and explains his teachings for the reader. The opposition of the Jews functions in a similar fashion in the Fourth Gospel. Their challenges to his claim to be the bread of heaven give Jesus an opportunity to clarify his identity and mission. Their insistence that they know his parents and from whence he comes allows the narrator to stress Jesus' divine origin. Their opposition helps to reveal what it costs and means to believe in Jesus. As characters in the narrative, the Jews help the narrator to indicate how and why some people refuse to believe.

Earlier we dated the gospel of John near the end of the first century, a time of intense struggle within Judaism. The Johannine community found itself in the midst of that struggle. Jewish members of the community found themselves opposed and cast out of the synagogue by their neighbors, friends, and family members. The Fourth Gospel addresses that situation. When the narrator or Jesus warns the disciples about the threat of expulsion from the synagogue (9:22; 12:42; 16:2), that admonition speaks both to the characters in the narrative and to the contemporaries of the author. This means that they themselves were embedded in Judaism. The pain of parting at least partially accounts for the harshness of the rhetoric. We should no more consider the gospel of John the definitive word about the Jews of the first or any century than we allow those with whom we struggle to speak the definitive word about us.

Finally, we must remember that the Johannine Jesus is a Jew. Jesus affirms that salvation is from the Jews (4:22), attends Jewish festivals (2:13; 7:2, 10; 10:22–23; 12:12), fulfills Jewish scripture (7:37–38; 12:14–15, 38–41; 19:24, 28, 33–37), and dies on the cross as the King of the Jews (19:19). Any misguided condemnation of either ancient or modern Judaism assails him as well. The function of the Jews in the Fourth Gospel may embarrass us, but we need not jettison the narrative. We will derive far greater benefit from lamenting abuses of this characterization, confessing to God how readily we stereotype those with whom we disagree, and praying for forgiveness and grace.

As the church struggles to find names and titles for God that faithfully reflect the breadth of Christian tradition without limiting its members to patriarchal language, John's use of the name, "Father," in reference to God may prove as problematic as its characterization of the Jews. This appellation for God appears more than one hundred times in the narrative. We can do nothing to alter that fact or to change the harm and pain inflicted when the church or parts of it define God in solely patriarchal terms. Nor can we remove this central image from the narrative. We can, however, explore what this name implies and represents.

As noted earlier, the Fourth Gospel refers to God as Father primarily to establish and underscore the intimacy between God and Jesus. The narrative identifies God as the one who sends Jesus nearly as often as it calls God the Father. This makes it patently clear that God alone stands behind and is revealed in the ministry of Jesus. Neither the author of the Fourth Gospel nor we can find an entirely adequate metaphor for God. Human language cannot stretch far enough to express the ineffable. By identifying God as the Father who sent Jesus, the narrative proclaims that God alone gives Jesus his unique character and mission and that God resides in Jesus as completely as possible without violating his distinct identity. As "Father," the unseen God draws recognizably near and becomes self-revealed in Jesus.

Many readers will find the Johannine use of Father problematic, but before we close and seal the book, let us remember that it was written long before our concerns. We can balance the Johannine imagery when we use the text in worship and study. We can also admit the limitations of its primary image of God, yet still learn from it and be moved by it as we ponder what it proclaims about the nature of God.

Johannine use of "the Jews" and "the Father" presents challenges for modern readers. We do not serve God or the church well by ignoring that. But neither do we serve them by casting the narrative aside because of these limitations. Faithfulness to the One self-revealed in Jesus calls for informed interpretation of Johannine language, coupled with prayer that God will use and transcend the limits of our language as well.

We turn now to two areas of promise in Johannine studies. We will begin with the way that the narrative calls readers to a decision. Every character in the Fourth Gospel is in large measure defined by her or his response to Jesus. Nicodemus and the woman of Samaria have extensive dialogues with Jesus. Whereas readers feel ambivalent about the prominent leader of the Jews, who fades away without distinction (3:1–10), they heartily applaud the unnamed woman, who invites an entire village to come to Jesus (4:28–30). Although Jesus heals both a lame man at the pool in Jerusalem and a man born blind, the effect on the reader differs sharply. Readers question the once lame man because he seems to lack interest in a relationship with Jesus (5:13–16), whereas they celebrate the once blind man as a hero because he defies the authorities and worships Jesus (9:30–38). Every character that encounters Jesus faces the crucial decision of whether or not to believe in him. Believing in Jesus does not mean simply acknowledging that he has power, that he can work wonders, or that he speaks for God. Rather, believing means fully entering discipleship. Illustrations of this include the man born blind who risks his place in the family in the community to follow and worship Jesus (9:1–41), the sheep who hear the voice of the Good Shepherd and follow him (10:1–3), and the disciples who follow Jesus even at the risk of expulsion from the synagogue and death (16:1–3). Every character in the narrative that believes in Jesus actively enters discipleship and becomes recognizably different in and from the world.

The Fourth Gospel confronts its readers with that same decision. After declaring that all who believe in Jesus become children of God (1:12), the narrative provides what it considers sufficient testimony for readers to accept its witness, believe in Jesus, and have life in his name (20:31). The narrative considers this decision life-changing and absolutely imperative. God has become fully revealed in the Word made flesh. Jesus is the resurrection, the way, the truth, the life, and the means of access to God. The Fourth Gospel does not attempt to prove that as much as it solemnly avows it.

Does this render the gospel of John passé in an increasingly pluralistic world? Should we consider it fit for the archives but not for daily use? Absolutely not! When we call ourselves Christian, we declare that we are not neutral or unbiased about Jesus. We confess Jesus as Lord and Savior. We have vigorous and significant disagreements about what those roles and titles mean, but we accept no other Lord and seek no other Savior. Christians believe that there is something peculiar, distinct, and definitive about Jesus. The Fourth Gospel believes that, proclaims that, and challenges others to believe and proclaim it. We may want to debate the particulars of Johannine christology, but this narrative will not let us ignore the question. The gospel of John demands that believers state with conviction what they believe about Jesus and that believers make any convictions that they have recognizable in the world.

That does not confine use of this text to the intolerant. We cannot enter dialog with others about God, faith, and salvation unless we have some idea where we stand and why we stand there. Unless being Christian makes us distinct, we have no identity and nothing to bring to the dialog. The Fourth Gospel first addressed people who knew well the risks involved with believing in Jesus. It does not apologize for those risks, but instead insists that people take them. When we scratch the surface of our faith, will we find similar conviction?

The Fourth Gospel insists that believing in God's self-revelation in Jesus makes a difference in who we are and how we live. As a people who believe that God responds to the world primarily out of love, we must take issue with public policies and majority opinions that violate those loved by God. As a people who believe that God is defined by relationship, we must challenge practices and assumptions that elevate what we earn or what we do above whose we are and how we relate with one another. Christians claim to live by a set of standards other than those of the world and to be guided by a reality and truth that transcend earthly powers and preferences. The gospel of John challenges us to identify those standards and that reality as clearly as we can and to live in relationship with them. The aim is not to become smug, self-centered, and detached, but to allow ourselves to live what we believe because we believe that we cannot otherwise have life. Unless we come to faith solely for the comforts that it provides, believing in Jesus means living a relationship with God in which we risk being identifiably different. May God protect us all from misplaced hubris that denies the worth or integrity of others, but may God use whatever means necessary, including the Fourth Gospel, to call us to the life that faithfulness alone makes possible.

The second area of promise from study of the gospel of John relates closely to this call to decision. The Johannine call to faith applies to all. The Fourth Gospel attempts to address a wide audience and to call an eclectic group of readers to faith. As previously noted, Jewish followers of John the Baptist, Jewish authorities, Samaritans, Gentiles, the powerful, and the powerless all respond positively to Jesus and enter the group of believers. According to the Fourth Gospel, only those who believe in Jesus have life, but no one who becomes a believer remains on the outside.

The content of that faith is left open. As those who experienced Jesus during his first Passover in Jerusalem (2:23–25) and Nicodemus (3:1–10) illustrate, it is not enough to marvel at Jesus because of the signs he performs. One must believe in him, that he came from God and reveals God. Since that is the sole criterion for faith prescribed by the narrative, the Johannine community of believers can be and is incredibly heterogeneous. Jesus does not ask the woman of Samaria to stop being a woman or a Samaritan. He challenges her to believe him and to worship in spirit and truth. On the last day of Tabernacles, Jesus does not ask the worshipers to stop being Jews. He invites them to believe in him and drink (7:37–38). Believing alone determines whether or not one belongs. The Fourth Gospel knows no other criteria for "membership."

Given the historical context of the narrative, this is an amazingly broad appeal. The gospel of John challenges a community experiencing rejection to define sharply what they believe and hold to that conviction, while keeping their arms open to all who believe it. Although it often sounds sectarian, the gospel of John calls believers not to withdraw from the world but to be visibly present to it. John offers all who sit in outposts of rejection (of which there were and are many) an invitation to a community formed by faith and known by its love. As we ponder how to be the church in the twenty-first century, the Fourth Gospel has a voice worth hearing.

Suggested Resources for the Pastor's Library

Barrett, C. K. *The Gospel According to John.* Second edition. London: SPCK, 1956.

Brown, Raymond E. *The Gospel According to John*, Anchor Bible 29 and 29A. Garden City, N. Y.: Doubleday and Company, 1966, 1970.

Culpepper, R. Alan. *Anatomy of the Fourth Gospel.* Philadelphia: Fortress Press, 1983.

_____. *The Gospel and Letters of John,* Interpreting Biblical Texts. Nashville: Abingdon Press, 1998.

Kysar, Robert. *John the Maverick Gospel.* Revised edition. Louisville: Westminster John Knox Press, 1993.

Martyn, J. Louis. *History and Theology in the Fourth Gospel.* Second edition. Nashville: Abingdon Press, 1979.

Schnackenburg, Rudolf. *The Gospel According to St. John.* Three volumes. New York: Crossroad, 1987.

O'Day, Gail R. "The Gospel of John," in *The New Interpreter's Bible.* Volume 9. Nashville: Abingdon Press, 1995.

Smith, Dennis E. & Michael Williams, eds. *The Storyteller's Companion to the Bible, Volume 10: John.* Nashville: Abingdon Press, 1996.

Smith, D. Moody. *The Theology of the Gospel of John.* Cambridge: Cambridge University Press, 1995.

Resnsberger, David. *Johannine Faith and Liberating Community.* Philadelphia: Westminster Press, 1988.

Talbert, Charles H. *Reading John: A Literary and Theological Commentary on the Fourth Gospel and the Johannine Letters.* New York: Crossroad, 1992.

12

The Domestication of Paul
The Pastoral Epistles

BONNIE B. THURSTON

The pastoral epistles represent the culmination of the development of Paul's thought. Probably documents from the late first or early second century, their primary concern is "how one ought to behave in the household of God, which is the church of the living God" (1 Tim. 3:15). First and secong Timothy and Titus depict the church as it moves toward institutionalization. The letters are usually treated as a unit, as I shall do, except in the section on "Organization," which discusses each separately.

Basic Data

The pastoral epistles represent the last phase of New Testament history. Their preoccupation is with the emerging institutional church. In the period from roughly 100 to 140 C.E. the church was settling down to its task of "living in the world." Founded religions face two major crises: the death of the founder, and the death of his/her associates. In response to the second, Christianity began to develop authoritative documents, creedal orthodoxy, and a structure of authority. We see all three interests in the pastoral epistles.

The term "Pastoral Epistles" was given to 1 and 2 Timothy and Titus by Paul Anton in the eighteenth century because the letters purport to be from a pastor to a pastor; Paul the shepherd gives guidance to his "sons" Timothy and Titus. The letters appear to be from Paul to Timothy in Ephesus (1 Tim. 1:3; 2 Tim. 1:18) and Titus in Crete (Titus 1:5). Timothy figures prominently in the Pauline mission. He was from Lystra; his mother was Jewish and his father Greek (Acts 16:1); he traveled extensively with Paul (1 Cor. 4:17; Rom. 16:21), was important in the apostle's work at Corinth and Philippi, and apparently coauthored 1 and 2 Thessalonians, 2 Corinthians, Philippians, and Colossians. Titus was a Greek who attended the Jerusalem Council (Gal. 2:1–3), helped reconcile Paul to the church at Corinth (2 Cor. 2:13; 7:6–16), and was instrumental in gathering the collection of support from Greek churches for "the poor among the saints at Jerusalem" (2 Cor. 8:6–23; Rom. 15:26).

It is unlikely that Paul wrote 1 Timothy or Titus, although 2 Timothy has more claim to Pauline authorship. Those who view the pastoral epistles as Pauline think they were written after his Roman imprisonment. They argue that Paul was released, returned to the East and then was imprisoned a second time in Rome and before his martyrdom wrote the pastoral epistles around 60 C.E. The problem with this reconstruction is that the only evidence for a second Roman imprisonment comes from the pastoral epistles themselves.

The question of authorship is like that for Colossians and Ephesians. The pastoral epistles use Pauline words but with different meanings. For example, in uncontested Pauline letters, "faith" is a verb, trust in God with reference to what has been accomplished in Jesus; but in the pastoral epistles "faith" is a noun, a body of beliefs that are to be guarded and preserved intact (as in 1 Tim. 3:9; 4:1; 6:10). Furthermore, about twenty percent of the vocabulary in the pastoral epistles is not found in the rest of the New Testament and thirty percent not in Pauline letters. Of the 306 words in the pastoral epistles that are not in the Pauline corpus, two-thirds of them are used by second-century Christian authors (especially Ignatius and Polycarp). The language and style of the letters are not Paul's.

It is more difficult to find attestation of the pastoral epistles in the early church than it is for others of Paul's letters, although from the second century they were considered Pauline. The pastoral epistles do not appear in Chester Beatty P46 or in Marcion's canon ca. 160 C.E., two early sources for collections of Paul's letters. Finally, as the discussion that follows indicates, the historical circumstances surrounding the pastoral epistles are quite different from those of Paul's churches.

In my view the pastoral epistles are pseudonymous documents written in the first quarter of the second century, probably in Asia Minor, by a follower of the apostle Paul. Attributing Paul's authority to these documents is especially important because the writer is interested in the preservation of correct doctrine and apostolic tradition. The writer views himself as a defender of the faith delivered to the apostle Paul and transmitted to the church. Attributing the letters to Paul gives veracity to the ideas presented.

Paul did not "make up" his gospel; he received it by direct revelation from Jesus (Gal. 1:11–12), learned some of the tradition from the apostles in his visits to Jerusalem and his contact with other missionaries (Gal. 1:18), and had extensive knowledge of Hebrew scripture (and perhaps Christian documents). He says as much in 1 Corinthians 15:3, "for I delivered to you as of first importance what I also received" (RSV). This is technical language for the process of transmission. Paul uses the Greek verb *paradidōmi,* which means to pass on what is received. It is almost the exact equivalent of the Latin *traditio* from which we get "tradition." The correlative verb *paralambanō* meant receiving the tradition from those who passed it on.

The writer of the pastoral epistles is anxious to preserve this "passed on and received tradition," but with an important difference. In the pastoral epistles the "handed on" verb becomes *parathēkē,* which means "what is deposited" or "what is entrusted to one's care" (see 1 Tim. 4:11; 6:20; 2 Tim. 1:12–14). Paul's dynamic tradition is replaced by a static one, a fixed deposit once laid down and now to be preserved. The word *doctrine* appears 15 times in the pastoral epistles, usually with the adjective *sound* (and note the formula emphasizing that the words can be trusted [1 Tim. 1:15, 4:9, 2 Tim. 2:11, etc.]). In the pastoral epistles the tradition of the apostle Paul is becoming a fixed body of doctrine that, guaranteed by the authority of the apostle, is to be preserved by the church. The rhetorical strategy by which this is done is to portray Paul at the end of his career offering advice to those who will maintain his normative tradition. The primary issue in the letters, certainly in 1 Timothy and Titus, is the maintenance or preservation of "sound doctrine" and the structures of authority by which that will be accomplished.

Methods of Interpretation

The historical-critical disciplines have been well employed in analysis of the lexical and stylistic aspects of the pastoral epistles, their textual history, and their historical circumstances. Two other methods have proved especially illuminating: rhetorical analysis and sociological analysis.

In his groundbreaking work "The Background and Significance of the Polemic of the Pastoral Epistles" *(Journal of Biblical Literature* 92 [1973]: 549–564), Robert Karris has pointed out the traditional schema behind the polemic of the pastoral epistles. In attacking his opponents (with whom he never enters into direct theological debate), the writer of the pastoral epistles employs conventional criticisms borrowed from popular philosophic discourse. He calls his opponents names: greedy, deceivers, unable to practice what they preach, quibblers, full of vice, and quick to prey on women. To cause aversion for the opponents' view and sympathy for his own, he paints the opponents in as unsavory a light a possible (see, for example, 1 Tim. 1: 3–11; 4:1–7; 6:3–5.) Rhetorically the pastoral author presents himself as the ideal teacher who alone has authority to teach.

Sociological analyses, such as those of David C. Verner and M. Y. MacDonald, have shed immense light on the situation of the pastoral epistles. Verner suggests that in this early period the household was the basic unit of the church, and the church was modeled on the household. Tensions in the church related to the changing position of women in society and in the household. Traditional patriarchal household structures and traditional sex/gender roles were associated on a symbolic level with the preservation of orderly society. Thus to defy the social order was to be subject to charges of subversion.

Christianity, Verner argues, confronted social norms on two important fronts: its attitude toward women and its attitude toward slaves. The theoretical equality seen in Galatians 3:28, or the marital reciprocity in 1 Corinthians 7, or the implied treatment of slaves in Philemon flew in the face of Greco-Roman practice. Flaunting these conventions opened the church to charges of subversion. In order to preserve itself in society, the church gradually began to conform to the norms of society at large. In the pastoral epistles we see this in concern for "good citizenship" and in teaching acceptable behavior for men and women.

Social Context

The pastoral epistles depict the church moving from its primitive simplicity to a defined body of doctrine and system of organization. It did so in response to real, practical problems. Chief among them was "social acceptability." At the end of the first and the beginning of the second century, the church faced difficulties on two fronts. From the outside there was conflict with the state. Christians were a minority group, an illegal religion, a group vulnerable to social ostracism and political disfavor, as evidenced by the persecutions of Domitian, who was emperor from 81–96 C.E. Therefore, it was necessary to make a good impression on outsiders. This is seen in the concern the pastoral epistles show for what outsiders think (see, for example, 1 Tim. 2:2; 5:14; 6:1–2; Titus 2:1–10). From the inside, the church faced the danger of false teaching (see 1 Tim. 1:3–7; 4:1–16; 2 Tim. 3:6–9; Titus 1:10–15; 3:8–11). At this early stage there was no orthodoxy because there was nothing to maintain it. (In spite of the possible reference to the gospels in 1 Tim. 5:18, there was yet no canon of scripture, for example.) So it became necessary to stress "sound" (i.e. Pauline) teaching and church organization. The pastoral epistles are preoccupied with the church's social standing in the world, with "respectability" and with "sound doctrine."

Religious Context

It is thought that the false teaching against which the pastoral epistles writer rails is related to gnosticism. What is known about gnosticism as a movement comes largely from a later period and derives from the Church Fathers who opposed it. Gnostic ideas first appeared in the late Hellenistic or the early Imperial period among speculative or syncretistic Jews. The Nag Hammadi documents testify to a widespread gnostic movement in the second and third centuries C.E.

In gnosticism, central importance was attached to the origin and destiny of humanity and to revealed knowledge of God by means of which the spiritual element in humans could be redeemed. Gnosis distinguished between the "Demiurge" or "Creator God" and the supreme, remote, unknowable Divine Being. A spark of the Divine substance was believed to be in some persons and through certain rites, often involving an ascetic, celibate lifestyle, this divine element could be rescued from its evil, material environment, namely the physical body. Some gnostic groups advocated radical egalitarianism and permitted women equal rank with men. Some form of gnosticism that included an ascetic lifestyle and promoted the equality of women seems to be the object of attack in the pastoral epistles, particularly when the writer opposes asceticism or limits the authority of women.

The pastoral epistles also exhibit an extraordinary number of terms from popular Hellenistic philosophy (see, for example, "godliness" or "piety" [*eusebeia*] in Titus 1:1; "lover of goodness" [*philagathos*], "prudent" [*sophron*], "self-controlled" [*egkrates*] in Titus 1:8). Like the Ephesian writer (but in my view not so successfully), the writer of the pastoral epistles attempts to use the language of popular philosophy to describe Christianity and the church. The purpose of the writer is to describe Christianity in terms that would be familiar to its Hellenistic-Roman converts and congenial with popular culture.

Literary Data

The pastoral epistles are probably pseudonymous documents. They appear to be letters, but exhibit many deviations from Paul's use of the form. It is worth noting that one scholar, James D. Miller, has suggested that the pastoral epistles are a compilation by one person of many fragments of genuine Pauline material. In fact the documents read more like church orders from the later second-century period. (Church orders were "manuals" for leadership and worship in the church.) *The Didache*, a church order roughly contemporary with the pastoral epistles, is a good point of comparison. Like other deutero-Pauline letters, the pastoral epistles reflect the incorporation of many traditional forms. Chief among them are hymn fragments, household codes, vice and virtue lists, polemical remarks (see "Methods of Interpretation" earlier), and a "trustworthy saying" formula. (As much as 46 percent of Titus is "traditional materials.")

As was the case in Philippians 2:6–11 and Colossians 1:15–20, the writer of the pastoral epistles inserts what appear to be fragments of hymns to illustrate his points. The following texts may be hymn fragments: 1 Timothy 2:5–6a; 3:16; 2 Timothy 2:11–13; Titus 3:4–7. Three things about this practice are noteworthy. First, it is a familiar homiletical technique still used by preachers today: illustrate a difficult point with a well-known and loved hymn. Second, the existence of hymnody suggests the development of Christian liturgy. The church had developed enough to *have* hymnody and "set pieces" for worship. Third, each fragment is about Jesus Christ. This is consistent with other hymn texts of the New Testament. The earliest hymns of the church not only praised Jesus, but are our earliest record of christology, of what the early church thought and taught about him.

The household code form was discussed in connection with Colossians. It has been noted that the basic structure of all three pastoral epistles is the household code. 1 Timothy addresses men (2:8), women (2:9–15), bishops (3:1–7), deacons (both male and female, 3:8–13), widows (5:3–16), elders (5:17–22), and slaves (6:1–2). The "cast" includes both members of the Hellenistic household and the "household of God." Second Timothy, while not exhibiting the code so directly, employs many household/family references and metaphors including the "sonship" of Timothy (1:2; 2:1), mention of his biological family (1:5), and the metaphor of a house (2:20–22). Titus is explicitly structured as a household code for God's household as it describes elders (1:5–6), bishops (1:7–9), older men, older women, young women, young men, and slaves (2:1–10). The letters literally reflect the "domestication of Paul," as his teachings are applied in the context of the Greco-Roman household.

Since the pastoral epistles have as their particular interest proper behavior that issues forth from authentic teaching, it is not surprising that they would make use of the common Hellenistic form of vice/virtue lists (See, for example, 1 Tim. 1:9–10; 3:2–3; 6:4–5; 2 Tim. 2:22; 3:2–4; Titus 1:7–10). The instructions given to various groups within the household usually come in the form of a vice or virtue list, and the vices to be avoided and the virtues to be cultivated are usually not specifically "Christian," but those generally accepted by the culture. Note, too, the especially sharp, polemical tone (see "Literary Data" earlier) of the vice lists. The writer of the pastoral epistles undercuts the teaching authority of his opponents by pointing out their moral failures.

Finally, the pastoral epistles employ a "faithful sayings" formula that precedes material about Christ or Christian living (see 1 Tim. 1:15; 3:1; 4:9; 2 Tim. 2:11; Titus 3:8). This is not surprising in material that, first, seeks to oppose false teaching and, second, sets forth the authoritative, apostolic word. The concern for false teaching, "myths," "genealogy," and speculation is also evident in the writer's frequent use of the terms "godliness" and "soundness." In the attempt to set forth the "doctrine of God our Savior" (Titus 2:10), faithfulness and soundness are of utmost importance. To do so the writer may be using traditional creedal fragments (compare Titus 2:11–14 and 1 Pet. 1:13b–19).

Organization: 1 Timothy

First Timothy exhibits notable departures from the Pauline letter form. It has the standard salutation (1:1–2), but before the thanksgiving prayer (1:12–17) there is an attack on false teaching (1:3–11), which Timothy is then charged to avoid (1:18–20). The body of the letter (2–6:19) is made up of instructions on prayer and worship (2:1–15) of the sort that Paul might put in an exhortation section at the end of a letter, a church order (or rules for church leadership; 3:1–13; 5:1–19), which is interrupted with more material on false teaching (3:14–4:16), and a section of general parenesis or exhortation (5:20–6:19). The closing section contains further exhortation to Timothy (6:20–21).

The salutation (1:1–2) provides the usual information about authorship and the recipient of the letter. That Timothy is a "loyal child" may be an allusion to disloyal or untrue "children" of Paul. To the standard "grace and peace" wish, the author has added mercy. Instead of proceeding to the thanksgiving, the letter opens with an attack on false teachers (1:3–11). Their doctrines are characterized in terms that might allude to gnosticism: "myths and endless genealogies that promote speculations" (v. 4), and "meaningless talk...without understanding" (vv. 6–7). In contrast is the "divine training that is known by faith" which aims at love (vv. 4–5). Verses 8–11, which sound Pauline, suggest that the different doctrine of which the writer disapproves may include antinomianism (or opposition to law). Timothy's own "prophecies" (i.e., divinely inspired utterances) are in sharp contrast to the false teachings of Hymenaeus and Alexander (vv. 18–20; note that it is characteristic of the pastoral writer to name his adversaries). The thanksgiving (1:12–17) is basically an expression of gratitude to God "because he judged me faithful and appointed me to his service" (v. 12). It has a Pauline ring, reflects the apostle's biography, and contains the first example of the "faithful saying" formula in the pastoral epistles (1:15) (compare the doxologies of 1:17 and 6:15–16).

Chapter 2, an extended instruction on prayer and worship, has three parts: a command to pray for secular leaders (2:1–7), a command to men (2:8), and commands to women (2:9–15). These worship instructions reflect larger themes in the letter. The instruction that Christians should pray for "kings and all who are in high positions"(v. 2) reflects the concern with "social acceptability" of the church in the Empire. Embedded therein is a hymn fragment, vv. 5–6a, stressing the salvific activity of Jesus Christ. While men are simply enjoined to pray with uplifted hands and a peaceful attitude (v. 8), extensive instructions are given to women, suggesting they are a special problem for the writer.

First Timothy 2:9–13 is a "terrible text" for modern women. Those interpreting it should note that it appears in the context of teaching on appropriate worship, which is its primary concern. The adornment of women in v. 9 is an indication of the wealth of some members of the pastoral epistles' community (cf. 1 Tim. 6:17–19), and reflects the theme in the pastoral epistles of the danger of riches. The "good deeds" suggested in v. 10 (RSV) are part of a larger pattern of acceptable behavior for Greco-Roman women reflected in vv. 11–12. Verse 15 is theologically problematic; it implies that Christ's sacrifice on the cross was not sufficient for woman's salvation, but that she must perform a "deed," bearing children. While the command to bear children may be in response to the false teacher's rejection of marriage (4:3), the statement is both non-Pauline and poor theology.

First Timothy has two major concerns, false teaching and the appropriate leadership in the church that is intended to prevent it. First Timothy 3:1–13 and 5:1–20 is a "church order," a description of qualifications for church officers. The order is punctuated by another section on teaching, 3:14–4:16. The church of the pastoral epistles was moving from a loose organization toward a more structured institution. Undoubtedly the problems with heresy contributed to this move. It was hoped that having legitimated authorities would preserve the "deposit" of the apostolic tradition against opponents. The church order section of 1 Timothy reveals less about the duties of the offices and more about qualifications for the holders of the offices. Basically, church officials were to avoid vices frowned upon by Greco-Roman society and exhibit virtues of which it approved.

The word "bishop" or "overseer" or "guardian" (*episkopos*) is a term for an administrative officer in civic and cultic societies. The "deacon" (*diakonos*) or "servant" was, according to Acts 6:1–6, to see to the outward needs of the church, what we now call "social service." There were both male and female deacons. The term "elder" (*presbuteros*) is hard to trace, but is probably from Jewish tradition and referred to a respected member of the community who functioned as a teacher. Widows were older women without other means of support who were enrolled in an order that served the church through prayer and work with women. First Timothy 5:1–20 and 6:1–2, in addition to describing in detail the widows' order, regulates relations among older men, older women, and younger women, and between slaves and masters within the household of faith.

The excursus on false teaching in 3:14–4:16 begins with the author's travel plans. In case he is delayed, he is sending the letter with his instructions about how "to behave in the household of God" (3:15). He introduces the matter of false teaching with a hymn fragment (3:16) describing the work of Jesus Christ. The hymn's view of Jesus is consistent with what other New Testament sources suggest. His vindication "by the Spirit" (3:16) probably leads to the citation of the Spirit's authority in 4:1. The author attacks the asceticism of "teachings of demons" in 4:1–5, 7–8 and, against a gnostic view of the material world, argues for the goodness of God's creation. This is what Timothy, in spite of his youth, is to teach. The false teaching, deceit, hypocrisy, profane myths, and old wives tales of the false teachers are to be combatted with reading of scripture, and the gift of prophecy that Timothy received when he was commissioned for service (4:13–14).

The final section of 1 Timothy, 5:21–6:19, again alternates general parenesis with attacks on false teaching. A series of miscellaneous instructions (on the rebuke of sinners, 5:20–21; on ordination, 5:22; on health, 5:23; and on sins, 5:24–25) is framed by references to "sins." After a brief command on the relation of slaves and masters in 6:1–2 (which is part of the household order) the author returns to false teaching (6:2b–10), which "does not agree with the sound words of our Lord Jesus Christ and the teaching that is in accordance with godliness" (6:3). The behavior of the false teachers (6:4–5) apparently includes the expectation that they will get rich from their teaching (6:5b–10). Contrasted to them is Timothy, the "man of God" who is charged to "keep the commandment...of our Lord Jesus Christ" (6:11–14), the mention of whose name leads to a doxology (6:15–16). Probably as an implicit attack on the false teachers who hope to have monetary gain from their teaching (and certainly as an allusion to 2:9–10), the writer ends with a reflection on the difficulty of riches and his own preference for being "rich in good works" (6:17–19). The letter closes with an exhortation to Timothy contrasting the deposit that has been entrusted to him with the "profane chatter" and gnosis of the false teaching (6:20–21a) and with a grace wish (which may be in the plural, 6:21b).

First Timothy is not an easy letter to outline. The author's apparent distress at the false teaching causes him to move erratically from one subject to another, always circling back to polemical attack. However, the careful reader observes that blocks of material in the letter alternate between instructions to God's household (including Timothy, one of its leaders) and polemical attacks on false teaching.

Organization: 2 Timothy

Second Timothy is the most personal of the pastoral epistles and has the greatest claim to Pauline authorship. It addresses Timothy, who, while youthful, was in charge of several churches that needed to be defended from false teaching. The form of the letter is more closely Pauline with its salutation (1:1–2), thanksgiving (1:3–7), body (1:8–4:5), personal conclusion and greetings (4:6–21), and grace wish (4:22). The salutation (1:1–2) is in standard Pauline form, but adds to the "grace wish" "mercy" (as does 1 Tim. 1:2). The thanksgiving (1:3–7) is basically an expression of gratitude for Timothy's ministry and faith, a faith he learned from his grandmother and mother (1:5, cf. 3:14–15).

The body of the letter opens, as does 1 Timothy (and Galatians and Colossians) with an exhortation based on the author's/Paul's biography (1:8–18). The exhortation is framed by references to the author's life: 1:8–18 and 4:6–18. Several of the churches of Asia Minor apparently found Paul's imprisonment an embarrassment. "Paul" reminds Timothy and his churches of why he is imprisoned: for the "testimony about our Lord" (1:8) "who saved us and called us...not according to our works but according to his own purpose and grace" (1:9; cf. 1:11–12). This rehearsal of the Pauline gospel is followed by vv. 9b–10, which sound like Ephesians' rhetoric. The issue is "sound teaching that you have heard from me" (1:13), which is to be "guarded." The author mentions a general turning away of the churches in Asia Minor and two false teachers, Phygelus and Hermogenes, and he blesses Onesiphorus who has aided him.

Most of the body of the letter, 2:1–4:5 is exhortation to Timothy. The masculine metaphors of soldier, athlete, and farmer depict the strength that Timothy is to exhibit as he entrusts the Pauline gospel to "faithful people" who will teach others (2:1–7). The substance of that gospel is Jesus Christ, whom Timothy is to "remember" and whose sufferings and vindication are shared by believers (2:8–13). False teaching is to be avoided; it is polemically characterized as "wrangling over words" (2:14), "profane chatter" (2:16), and "gangrene" (2:17). Again, the author names names, charging that Hymenaeus and Philetus spread falsity in teaching "that the resurrection has already taken place" (2:17–18), a theological position compatible with gnosticism.

The exhortation to Timothy about his personal behavior (2:20–26) employs the Pauline metaphors of the church as a house and of different "vessels" (2 Cor. 4). That there are many utensils for various work echoes the "many gifts, one spirit" idea in Paul (see 1 Cor. 12; Rom. 12). Timothy's own life is to be characterized by faith, love, and peace and is to avoid not only "youthful passions" (2:22), but "stupid and senseless controversies" (2:23) of the sort just criticized in 2:16–18. The characteristics of the "Lord's servant" (2:24) echo qualifications for office in 1 Timothy and Titus.

Mention of the "snare of the devil" in 2:26 apparently leads the writer to reflect on the "last days" in 3:1–9. The vice list in vv. 2–5 characterizes behavior in those days. "Weak women" (RSV) are especially at risk from false teachers like Jannes and Jambres, men who "oppose the truth" and are "of corrupt mind and counterfeit faith" (3:6–8). Paul's charge to Timothy (3:10–4:5) implicitly compares him to these false teachers.

The author/Paul reminds Timothy of his own sufferings (a theme in the letter), which are the lot of "all who want to live a godly life in Christ" (3:12) and commands him to hold fast to what he has learned, presumably from Paul, but also from his mother and grandmother, women who were sources of authoritative tradition (3:14–15; cf. 1:5). The scripture that is commended in 3:16–17 was the Septuagint (the Greek translation of the Old Testament); no Christian canon existed. Timothy is charged "in the presence of God and of Jesus Christ" (4:1) to "proclaim the message" (4:2) and to be "sober, endure suffering, do the work of an evangelist, carry out your ministry fully" (4:5), all this in the face of people who will not want to hear (4:3–4, cf. 3:1–9).

Second Timothy closes with a moving description of Paul's impending death (4:6–8); with extensive personal instructions (4:9–18; note v. 11 says, "only Luke is with me," but three men and a woman send greetings), including confidence in God's ability to deliver, and a doxology (4:17–18); and with the standard greetings and benediction of a Hellenistic letter (4:19–22).

Organization: Titus

As do the other two pastoral epistles, Titus follows the pattern of a Hellenistic letter: opening formula (1:1–4), body (1:5–3:14), closing (3:15b). The extended salutation in 1:1–4 is reminiscent of Romans 1:1–7, but there is no thanksgiving that might suggest that, as in Galatians, the author is not pleased with the community to which he writes.

The body of the letter has three units. The first 1:5–2:10 is basically a household code for the *oikos* ("household") of the church (elders 1:5–6; bishops 1:7–9; older men 2:2; older women 2:3; younger women 2:4-5; younger men 2:6; slaves 2:9). These instructions to the household are broken by an excursus on the disobedient, indicated by an inclusion formed by reference to sound doctrine at 1:9 and 2:1. The reference to the "sound doctrine" taught by the bishop (1:9) leads the writer to think of false teachers (1:10–2:1). Again, their position is treated polemically; they are "idle talkers and deceivers" (1:10), "liars, vicious brutes, lazy gluttons" (1:12, a quotation from the Cretan poet Epimenides), taken up with "Jewish myths" (1:14), and "detestable, disobedient, unfit for any good work" (1:16).

The second section of the body, 2:11–3:11, alternates material on christology with imperatives for action: 2:11–14 christology; 2:15–3:3 exhortation; 3:4–8a christology; 3:8b–11 exhortation. The christology sections are clear not only from content, but from a carefully repeated structure. Each begins with a form of the phrase "when God appeared," with emphases on the grace of God and God as Savior (2:11; 3:4), and closes with a clause explaining what God has done (2:14; 3:7). The function of the christology is to provide authority for the practical exhortations. The main focus of Titus' theology is christology, and the main focus of the christology is soteriology, the saving role Jesus played in God's plan.

The final section of the body of the letter follows Pauline precedent in setting forth the author's/Paul's travel plans and giving instructions to colleagues (3:12–13). There follows in 3:14 a final imperative on "good works" (a theme in the letter: 2:7, 14; 3:1, 8, 14) and an unusually brief closing formula, 3:15b, which omits any reference to Jesus Christ. (Only in Colossians and the pastoral epistles does "grace" appear without Jesus Christ.)

Theological Themes

The pastoral epistles are largely interested in ethical instruction. They insist that the gospel, properly understood, issues forth in changed behavior in the lives of believers. The theology of the pastoral epistles revolves around three foci: that of false teaching/heresy; that of church order/ministry; and that of christology. The first two foci are related to the circumstances of the church at the end of the first and the beginning of the second centuries. Throughout the pastoral epistles the author worries about false teaching and its effects on his communities. As noted, the precise nature of this false teaching is not clear, although it was probably influenced by gnosticism and, in the author's mind, was particularly attractive to women. Instead of entering into open debate with the opponent's positions, the writer of the pastoral epistles engages in polemic against the teachers themselves. While this may cause aversion for the teachers, it does not give us a clear picture of their "heresy."

The development of church order/offices of ministry is to be the primary defense against false teaching. The church is developing from loose, local congregations toward a hierarchy of offices with the bishop as "head." The primary function of this structure was to keep doctrine pure; it was the "insurance" for the preserved "deposit" of "the faith." Authoritative leaders were to maintain pure doctrine, which they had received from authoritative sources. The lists of offices, however, reveal less about the duties of the offices than they do of the qualities required of holders of the office. Clearly the church was organized like a Hellenistic/Roman family with fathers, mothers, and siblings, and with both a public and private life. As structures shifted away from the household model and became more public and reflective of the structures of Roman Imperial rule, the "lower rungs" of the hierarchy were "squeezed out" of positions of authority.

What we find in the pastoral epistles has been characterized as the emerging *institutional* church. It relied on the idea of a "golden age" of apostolic tradition from which pure doctrine is derived. Rather than being expressed as a verb, "faith" became a noun, an "object" that could be expressed in propositional form, handed on, and preserved. The pastoral epistles evince a high view of the written deposit of scripture, the use of the epistolary form for dissemination of doctrine, and the use of pseudonymity to confer authority. The movement toward what became ordained ministry is in evidence, and there is considerable concern for what those outside the church think of it.

While "heresy" and church order may be matters of practical theology, the pastoral epistles also reflect important developments in christology. As do Philippians and Colossians, the pastoral epistles use hymn fragments to illustrate practical instruction (see "Literary Data" earlier). Those fragments focus on who Jesus Christ is and what he accomplished. They are particularly concerned with his role as mediator and "ransomer," that is, with soteriology. It is characteristic of the pastoral epistles to call God "savior;" six of eight occurrences of that phrase occur in the pastoral epistles. The hymn in 2 Timothy 2:11–13 is an eloquent statement of the identification of Christ and the believer, and the christology in Titus explicitly equates God and Jesus Christ (2:13; 3:4). The "justification" that Christ provides by his "grace" is thoroughly Pauline.

Importance for the Church of the Twenty-first Century

The polemical nature of the pastoral epistles and their deep-rootedness in Greco-Roman social norms makes it hard for many modern readers to feel comfortable with them. That discomfort points to one of the important issues that the pastoral epistles raise, the issue of conformity to contemporary morays and norms. The writer of the pastoral epistles is concerned with what "outsiders" think of the church. It is a fair concern; "outsiders" in Roman officialdom had the power to persecute and destroy a *religio illicita* ("illegal religion") like Christianity. But the question for us becomes how much accommodation is too much? For example, we see the writer of the pastoral epistles compromising the gender equality of earliest Christianity (reflected in the gospel witness and in Pauline letters) to preserve Christian respectability. "Good Christian women" were taught to act like good Roman matrons. Was that God's intention or a compromise with culture? How do we as Christians stay "in" the world without being "of" the world?

Second, the pastoral epistles emphasize the importance of strong teaching rooted in the received traditions of the faith. While we do not want to be paranoid about rooting out heresy, we do need to be aware that not every new teaching is a good teaching. We, like those second-century Christians, need to be careful about "speculations" and "meaningless talk." It is perfectly appropriate for us to inquire about the "pedigree" of those who preach and teach (2 Tim. 3:14–15). Furthermore, Christians of today will also feel comforted by the pastoral epistles' understanding that the "sacred writings…are able to instruct…for salvation through faith in Christ Jesus" (2 Tim. 3:15).

Suggested Resources for the Pastor's Library

Arichea, Daniel C. & Howard A. Hatton. *A Handbook on Paul's Letters to Timothy and to Titus.* New York: United Bible Societies, 1995.

Barrett, C. K. *The Pastoral Epistles in the New English Bible.* Oxford: Clarendon Press, 1963.

Beker, J. Christiaan. *Heirs of Paul: Paul's Legacy in the New Testament and in the Church Today.* Minneapolis: Fortress Press, 1991.

Collins, Raymond F. *1 & 2 Timothy and Titus: A Commentary.* New Testament Library. Louisville: Westminster John Knox Press, 2002.

Dibelius, Martin & Hans Conzelmann. *The Pastoral Epistles.* Hermeneia. Philadelphia: Fortress Press, 1972.

Knight, George W. *The Pastoral Epistles: A Commentary on the Greek Text.* Grand Rapids: Eerdmans, 1992.

MacDonald, Margaret Y. *The Pauline Churches: A Socio-Historical Study of Institutionalization in the Pauline and Deutero-Pauline Writings.* Cambridge: Cambridge University Press, 1988.

Miller, James D. *The Pastoral Letters as Composite Documents.* Cambridge: Cambridge University Press, 1997.

Verner, David C. *The Household of God: The Social World of the Pastoral Epistles.* SBL Dissertation Series 71. Chico, Calif.: Scholars Press, 1983.

Young, Frances M. *The Theology of the Pastoral Letters.* New Testament Theology. Cambridge: Cambridge University Press, 1994.

13

The Epistolary Tradition
The Letters of James, 1–2 Peter, 1–3 John, and Jude

NANCY CLAIRE PITTMAN

Long after Paul and his immediate successors had died, Christians in the first few centuries C.E. continued to write letters to one another about their common faith in Jesus and the lifestyle demanded by that faith. Over nine thousand of these letters have survived the centuries, suggesting that Christianity was a movement that was developed and promoted by letter writers. The letters to be discussed in this chapter, the letter of James, the first and second letters of Peter, the first, second, and third Letters of John, and the letter of Jude, represent this movement in the last quarter of the first century and the first decade of the second.

The church historian Eusebius classified these seven texts together and called them the "general" or "catholic" epistles (Ecclesiastical History 2.23.25). This designation, which has endured through the centuries, refers to the fact that these letters, with the exceptions of 2 and 3 John, were not explicitly addressed to an individual, a single church, or a group of congregations within one city. James and 1 Peter do not even reflect particular concerns about specific events or issues within the communities to which they were directed. The other letters, while speaking more directly to theological and ethical problems within Christian communities, describe the perpetrators of these problems so vaguely and address issues so central to the faith and life of all churches that the "catholic" label remains appropriate. It is the universal appeal of these letters that led to their use throughout the Greco-Roman world in the years leading up to their acceptance in the canon.

Beyond their general applicability to a variety of situations, these letters share at least six other similarities. First, all except 1 John have an epistolary opening or closing or both. In the Greco-Roman world these elements were often quite stylized. The opening typically consisted of a reference to the author and his audience and a blessing or greeting. For Christians this blessing invoked God and Christ Jesus. The closing statement, if there was one, offered benedictory words to the recipients or doxological words to God.

Second, all of these letters contain *paraenesis,* that is, moral and religious exhortation, although the concerns within each vary widely. Through the medium of the letter, the authors urge their audiences to adopt the perspectives and behaviors described within and to reject those of the surrounding culture or of an opposing group within their communities. They typically ground their exhortations for right behavior in theological and christological proclamation.

To argue their cases, the authors of these letters often employ forms of Greco-Roman rhetoric, an approach to public speaking and to education itself that was widely used throughout the ancient Mediterranean world. Thus, many scholars today make use of rhetorical criticism to study the ways in which the arguments of the letters are constructed and the effects such arguments might have had on their original readers. Scholars attempt to identify the kinds of rhetoric—judicial, deliberative, or demonstrative *(epideictic)*—that appear within each letter and to analyze the way in which each part of the letter is arranged into a persuasive whole. However, such an approach must be used cautiously because Greco-Roman letter-writing style and paraenesis itself remained largely independent of such a discipline primarily designed for the oral delivery of speeches.

Third, these letters reflect Christian interaction with many of the values that pervaded their common cultural Greco-Roman context. Honor and shame, praise and blame, the importance of the group or family and the unimportance of the individual, purity and corruption—all of these issues were extremely significant in the societies that comprised the Hellenistic world. And each ethnic, religious, or social grouping, including the emerging Christian communities, appropriated these and other ubiquitous cultural beliefs and reconstituted them in relation to their own overarching worldviews and needs. In order to understand these values within their sociohistorical milieu, many biblical scholars utilize social-scientific methods and perspectives as they interpret these letters in their original context.

Fourth, while these writings exhibit encounters with the surrounding pagan cultural worldviews, these writings are also distinctively engaged with Jewish literature and theology. They resound with allusion to and quotation from the Hebrew scriptures; they absorb and then transform Jewish ritual and extra-biblical tradition. Most of this material is filtered through the lens of Hellenistic Judaism; the Septuagint is the most widely quoted version of the Hebrew Bible. And though none of the letters show any interest in the conflict between Christians and Jews that characterizes other New Testament literature, they manifest, both implicitly and explicitly, the belief that this nascent Christian movement stands in firm continuity with its Jewish antecedents.

The general epistles share a fifth characteristic in that the authorship of each one is impossible to establish with any certainty. Throughout the twentieth century most scholars have doubted that their "inscribed authors," that is, the names given in the epistolary openings of the letters of James, 1 and 2 Peter, and Jude, are the actual authors. Instead they have theorized that these letters are pseudonymous, written in the names of famous heroes of the faith by later Christians. Perhaps these people were students or disciples of the earlier apostles; perhaps they sought authority for the exhortations and affirmations they were communicating in their letters. A few scholars, of course, have continued to argue that each letter was indeed written by the person named in each opening. Although in each case I will examine the evidence for authorship, I offer no definitive solution. Nonetheless, these names do communicate significant information. They locate the letters in particular theological traditions that trace their roots and their authority back to the apostles who first proclaimed God's salvation in Jesus Christ.

The final similarity concerns the letters' place in the historical development of the early Christian movement and their continuing contribution to the church's theology and ethics. Earlier in the twentieth century, scholars often viewed these letters as "catholic" in two senses of the word. The one, discussed above, had to do with the lack of specific address for these letters. The other sense represented a "proto-Catholic" form of Christianity that was said to be emerging in the last years of the first century and the first decades of the second. At that time, so it was argued, the churches were challenged to do three things: to speak more doctrinally in light of ascendant heresies, to order themselves more firmly in light of growing challenges to their leadership, and to reorder their priorities more resolutely in light of the delay of the parousia. Thus scholars often assumed that the theology, christology, and ecclesiology found in these letters had somehow regressed from the spiritual heights reached in the genuine Pauline letters.

Scholars today have rightly questioned this view of the development of the Christian movement and the concomitant devaluation of these letters as important for the transmission of the faith. In fact, these letters display few of the qualities hypothesized for a proto-Catholic movement. None of them, for example, mandate or even discuss specific forms of hierarchical leadership that all churches must institute. And several of them manifest belief in an imminent return of Christ. As interpreters discard the outdated presuppositions and comparisons of a previous generation of scholars, they have begun a fresh quest for the theological and ethical significance of these letters. In fact, they are showing us ways in which these late first-century, early second-century documents can speak to Christians in the late twentieth and early twenty-first centuries.

The Letter of James: Making Friends with God
Introductory Issues

The letter of James presents its readers with a stark choice: choose to be either a friend of God, as Abraham was, or a friend of the world (1:8; 2:23; 4:4). The one who seeks friendship with God must seek wisdom from God, resist temptation, practice self-control and patience, treat fellow Christians and neighbors with impartiality, and "be doers of the word" (1:22). But the one who seeks friendship with the world lives in enmity with God, has a heart full of desire, envy, and ambition, flatters the rich and ignores the poor, boasts with arrogance, judges in ignorance, and displays a faith that is dead.

This letter, so long on ethical exhortation and short on sustained theological and christological reflection, has strong affinities with Jewish wisdom traditions. The association is clearly seen in the presentation of the choice between good and evil paths, but it is also found in the practical advice for daily living that characterizes much wisdom literature, especially Proverbs. Yet James also draws upon the covenant themes of Torah, particularly those aspects dealing with appropriate actions toward others (2:8–13), and prophetic themes that emphasize compassion for the poor (2:1–7) and the dangers of idolatry (4:4). At the same time, the letter also makes use of common Hellenistic themes like the necessity for discipline and the quest for perfection in the moral life, and rhetorical forms like diatribe.

Throughout the centuries James has been much maligned and misunderstood. It was somewhat slower than other New Testament writings to gain acceptance as canonical because, according to Eusebius, it was counted among the "Disputed Books" *(Ecclesiastical History* 3.25.3; Eusebius also included Jude, 2 Peter, and 2 and 3 John in this group). Furthermore, although it was ultimately included in the canon by the end of the fourth century, many Protestant Christians since the sixteenth century have been disturbed by it. To a large extent this discomfort can be traced to Martin Luther, its most famous critic. He referred to the letter as an "epistle of straw" for two reasons: the life, death, and resurrection of Christ is mentioned nowhere, and Luther's own understanding of justification by faith as found in the Pauline corpus is apparently contradicted in James, especially in 1:22–25 and 2:14–26.

Luther's characterization of a theologically incorrect James versus a theologically correct Paul has been quite influential both in the interpretation of James and in the issues of authorship and date. Until fairly recently most scholars have continued to follow Luther, arguing that James makes justification dependent upon works, not faith (1:22–25; 2:14–26). In fact, they explained, this letter may well have been a response to a misinterpretation of Paul's discussion of justification in the epistles to the Galatians and Romans. In this case James would necessarily have been written by someone familiar with the theologies of Paul and his more extreme interpreters. Thus the letter may have been written as late as the early second century in the name of Paul's opponent in Jerusalem, James.

However, recently Luke Timothy Johnson *(The Letter of James,* 111–14) has suggested that this perceived connection between James and Paul be loosened. After all, according to both Paul (Gal. 2:9) and the author of the Acts of the Apostles (Acts 15:12–21; 21:17–25) James and Paul were never diametrically opposed to one other. Because it is quite possible that there was no real conflict between the two leaders or their followers, a comparison of their texts based on supposed opposition does not result in an adequate or appropriate interpretation. It is much better to read the letter of James concerning the matter of faith and works on its own terms.

Without the speculative reconstruction of a relationship between Paul's letters and this one, we lose a popular, if problematic, argument concerning author and date. The problems are compounded by the lack of any other concrete evidence upon which to build a case. Within the epistle the author simply calls himself "James, a servant of God and of the Lord Jesus Christ." Although the author makes no attempt to establish his leadership or apostolicity, interpreters widely agree that the name refers to James the brother of the Lord and a leader of the Jerusalem church mentioned in Acts 12:17; 15:13–21; 21:18; 1 Cor. 15:7; and Gal. 1:19; 2:9, 12.

There is no consensus, however, concerning the actual author. Most scholars believe the writing is pseudonymous for the following reasons: an uneducated Galilean craftsman probably could not have employed the Greek language and Hellenistic rhetorical devices so skillfully; Eusebius and other early Christians cast doubt on James' authorship; and, as I just discussed, the author knew and responded to issues raised by Paul and his later interpreters. If this is the case, then the epistle can be dated in the last two decades of the first century. And, in spite of the fact that a few recent scholars have pointed out that the third argument is quite speculative and the other two can be contested, most scholars continue to suggest tentatively that James the brother of Jesus did not write this letter. At the same time, they recognize that the use of the name James places this epistle within a theological tradition that traces its roots to James the brother of Jesus and represents an older form of Jewish Christianity. An answer to the question of date is equally elusive; the best guess may be the mid-70s to the mid-80s.

The identity and social location of the original recipients are also difficult to determine. The epistolary opening offers only one explicit clue, "to the twelve tribes in the Dispersion" (1:1), which is undoubtedly not a literal reference to the twelve tribes of Israel who were scattered throughout the Mediterranean world. "The twelve tribes" as a common metaphor for Israel may point to the Jewishness of the audience; "Dispersion" may simply indicate an audience outside Palestine. We cannot determine a more precise geographical location. The appeals to Torah, wisdom, and other Jewish traditions throughout the letter support the traditional understanding of the audience as Jewish Christians, as does its connection to James their leader. We should not discount, however, the possibility that these words may also carry theological weight. In other parts of the New Testament, similar phrases indicate the new community of God's people constituted by Jesus Christ. And "Dispersion" may reflect a situation of spiritual exile and alienation from the dominant culture (see 1 Pet. 1:1–2).

Within the body of the letter, we can garner a few more clues about the social location of the original recipients of this letter. Like its author they were probably quite familiar with the Hebrew Bible. From the strong language used against wealthy people, we can deduce that the majority were also poor. In fact, the trials and suffering that are mentioned in 1:2 or 5:10–11 may be a result not simply of their material poverty but also of unjust treatment at the hands of rich landowners. There is no evidence that they were experiencing severe state-sponsored persecution. Once again, however, we should remember that "poverty" in this letter may also be a metaphor for a mode of spirituality in which riches and status are eschewed.

Another troublesome problem in the study of the letter of James is the discernment of principles of unifying order and composition. Themes are often stated and then amplified later in varying length; statements are made with no apparent connection to other parts of the letter. In his influential 1921 commentary on James, Martin Dibelius declared that there is no principle or "continuity in thought" other than a random combination of points of advice resulting from the paraenetic character of the writing as a whole. More recently scholars have attempted to identify complex organizational schemes based on rhetorical strategy, comparison with other texts or external traditions, or thematic patterns. None of these theories have received full acceptance in the scholarly community.

For our purposes, the simplest strategy may be to recognize that the letter consists of short essays on a variety of topics. Thus we can see that there are major shifts in the organization of the letter as a whole that occur when a new theme is taken up and discussed. Many times, but not always, those shifts are marked by a call for the attention of the readers with the address, "brothers and sisters" or "beloved." The following discussion of the contents of James is based on such a strategy.

Contents of the Letter

1:1. EPISTOLARY OPENING

1:2–27. SYNOPSIS

The following verses, marked by a direct appeal to the readers, comprise a catena of ethical aphorisms and exhortations, most of which the author discusses later in the letter. For example, the wisdom that comes from God in 1:5–8 is elaborated in 3:13–4:10; the exhortation to act out one's faith in 1:22–25 is enlarged in 2:14–26; the problem of the gossiping tongue mentioned in 1:26 is described fully in 3:1–12.

2:1–13. Practice Impartiality

The first extended essay is a call to practice impartiality toward others without regard for wealth or status. Showing favoritism is a transgression not only of the commandment of Lev. 19:18, but of the whole law, which must be followed in all its particulars.

2:14–26. Show Faith through Works

In this section believers are urged to show their faith through compassionate action on behalf of those in need and through loyal service to God. The perfect example of such an active faith is Abraham's sacrifice of Isaac; in fact, by this action Abraham showed himself to be the true friend of God. Rahab the prostitute, who welcomed the messengers from Joshua, is another example of one who is justified by her works.

Because this passage has garnered so much attention, it requires closer examination. Throughout this passage the author employs Pauline-sounding words like "faith," "justification," and "works," and, like Paul in Gal. 3:6 and Rom. 4:3, 9, quotes Gen. 15:6: "Abraham believed God, and it was reckoned to him as righteousness" (2:23). It is these factors in particular that have led numerous scholars to posit the connection between this letter and the Pauline corpus. However, there are good reasons to challenge this connection, as Luke Johnson has noted *(The Letter of James,* 58–64, 245–50). On the one hand, this shared vocabulary and appeal to Abraham does not have to imply a literary relationship between the Pauline epistles and James or a struggle between two early Christian leaders. These factors may simply indicate different uses of common traditions from Torah and the early Jesus movement. On the other hand, Paul and the author of James use this language very differently. For example, in James the word "works" never appears in the phrase "works of the law" and always denotes moral actions on behalf of others. But in Romans 4 and Galatians 3 "works of the law" refers to circumcision and other ritual laws. Thus James' argument is actually closer to Paul's statement in Gal. 5:6: "For in Christ Jesus neither circumcision nor uncircumcision counts for anything; the only thing that counts is faith working through love."

3:1–12. Tame the Tongue

This essay exhorts the readers to guard their tongues. Tame this "restless evil," urges the author. Refuse to allow foul things to pour out of the mouth and let only that which is fresh and good come forth.

3:13–4:10. Walk the Way of God; Shun the Way of the World

These verses are the heart of the letter. In them the author outlines two ways that never cross, two friendships that are mutually incompatible: the way of wisdom from above and the way of the world. The former "is first pure, then peaceable, gentle, willing to yield, full of mercy and good fruits, without a trace of partiality or hypocrisy" (3:17). This is the way of righteousness and it is walked by those who are humble, who submit to God and resist evil, and who purify their hearts. All these things should produce works "done with gentleness born of wisdom" (3:13). Only by living this kind of life can we make friends with God, in a friendship that is completely contrary to the way of friendship with the world.

4:11–5:6. Do Not Judge One Another, Boast, or Oppress the Righteous

Two prohibitions and a warning follow the discussion of the two ways. Do not speak evil or judge one another for only God is the judge (4:11–12); and do not boast about plans for the future (4:13–17). Be warned, "you rich people," for no gold and silver will be able to save you when your abuse and oppression of the laborers and righteous ones is revealed (5:1–6). All three of these pericopes contain striking similarities to sayings of Jesus preserved in Matthew's Sermon on the Mount and Luke's Sermon on the Plain.

5:7–18. Pray with Patience

In the face of suffering the author implores the readers to be patient. Though the coming of the Lord is near (5:8), until it arrives they should endure steadfastly and avoid grumbling and swearing. Pray in suffering and sickness, sing in joy, confess sins.

5:19–20. Final Admonition

These last two verses, again marked off by a direct appeal to the readers, serve as a final encouragement to seek after those who wander from the way of God and bring them back. This exhortation sums up the concern for others that permeates the entire writing. No other conclusion is offered.

Importance for the Church of the Twenty-first Century

The exhortatory mood that pervades this letter distances it from a modern audience. It also obscures the theological convictions that support and brace these ethical commandments. God gives wisdom and every other good gift generously and ungrudgingly (1:5, 17). God does not tempt us capriciously or entice us into failure (1:13), but acts righteously and compassionately (1:20; 2:13; 5:11). God chooses the poor, opposes the proud, gives grace to the humble (2:5; 4:6). God responds faithfully to prayer (5:15). And Jesus, about whom admittedly very little is said, is our example for impartiality (2:1), our teacher (4:11–5:6), our final judge (5:9). By attending to these underlying affirmations, we can recover the power of its ethical message.

So how do we make friends with this God, according to the letter of James? We do it by making friends with others, especially with those who are poor and without status in the world. This kind of friendship is founded on genuine love of neighbor and not the advancement of one's own interests over another's. It is built on the steady, daily exercise of the ordinary virtues of self-control, steadiness, honesty, and impartiality, and the avoidance of selfish desire, envy, or ambition. It is completed by the willingness to listen for the wisdom of God and to practice it in our relationships with the people around us. If we live this way we may encounter enmity from the world, but our friendship with God will endure.

The First Letter of Peter: The Holy Nation of God

Introductory Issues

"But you are a chosen race, a royal priesthood, a holy nation, God's own people, in order that you may proclaim the mighty acts of him who called you out of darkness into his marvelous light" (2:9). So avers the author of 1 Peter to an audience comprised of "aliens and exiles" in Asia Minor. Through Jesus' death and resurrection God has made these people God's own; for that reason they have hope even in the face of suffering and harassment. And regardless of the circumstances in which they find themselves, they are called to live lives of holiness, virtue, and obedience in witness to God's gracious action in Jesus Christ.

This elegantly crafted letter transfers imagery for Israel used throughout the Old Testament to the new community established in Jesus Christ. The readers are addressed at the beginning of the letter as "the exiles of the Dispersion" (1:1; cf. James 1:1)–a metaphor that recalls the people of Judah banished to Babylon. They are chosen by God, as the ancient Israelites where chosen (1:2), and redeemed not by the blood of a lamb on the doorpost but by the blood of Christ (1:19; cf. 1:2)–images that evoke the Hebrew slaves' exodus from Egypt and their foundational covenant with God. The readers are also a "spiritual house" (2:5) and a "house of God" (4:17 KJV; the NRSV says "household of God," but the same Greek word *oikos* is used in both places)–language that points both toward the temple as the appropriate setting for sacrifice to Israel's God as well as toward the actual people of God who are worthy to carry out those sacrifices.

So thoroughly Jewish is this letter and so completely is imagery for Israel applied to its Christian audience that it is surprising to realize that the actual recipients were Gentiles. We know this because the author says they "were ransomed from the futile ways inherited from [their] ancestors"

(1:18) and they "have already spent enough time in doing what the Gentiles like to do" (4:3). In fact, the transfer of imagery for Israel is so total that the word *Gentile* in this letter does not indicate a racial or ethnic identity but a theological identity as unbeliever.

The salutation tells us the locations of the audience, various regions in Asia Minor, and indicates that its members are "exiles of the Dispersion." In 2:11 they are called "aliens and exiles." Both phrases primarily convey theological meaning, referring to people who by virtue of their new birth in Christ (1:3, 23) no longer belonged to the larger Greco-Roman culture in which they physically dwell. They were like foreign sojourners living in the societies of Asia Minor, just as the inhabitants of Judah were exiles in Babylon, and just as Abraham was a foreign sojourner in the societies he visited. Based on the kind of advice that is given regarding participation in the larger society (2:11–17; 4:3) and the regulation of large households (2:18–3:7), we can surmise that the addressees were from a variety of socio-economic backgrounds.

Finally, this group does not appear to have been experiencing internal conflict or division. Instead, these Christians faced another kind of dilemma: how could they maintain their group's identity and cohesion and at the same time minimize their foreignness and any threat perceived by the larger society, which could react to them with hostility? Should they withdraw completely from that society or find ways to be in but not of it? As I will discuss below, exactly what this letter recommends in this situation is a subject of some debate.

Because the suffering of believers is a major theme in this letter, it is easy to assume that the audience was being persecuted in some serious way. However, there is little external evidence that Christians in Asia Minor in the first century were systematically persecuted by the imperial government of Rome or its local representatives. If the audience was being persecuted by such officials, we might expect to find evidence within the letter of hostility directed at them. But in fact the letter speaks positively of the role of government in God's world (2:13–17). Thus while its members may have experienced harassment initiated by the local population in reaction to their lifestyle and radical commitment to one Lord, their suffering was not the result of state-sponsored oppression.

Questions regarding author and date, just as in the case of the other general epistles, cannot be answered with any confidence. Although the salutation clearly says that "Peter, an apostle of Jesus Christ" is writing this letter, most scholars do not believe that the disciple Simon Peter actually wrote it. Several arguments weigh heavily against his authorship. The Greek language in which it is written is too educated for a Galilean fisherman to produce (see Acts 4:13). The life and teachings of Jesus are not mentioned as might be expected from a close friend and follower. The reference to Rome as Babylon in 5:13 suggests a date after 70 C.E., after Peter had already died, because Rome is only called Babylon in Jewish and other Christian literature after the fall of Jerusalem. Further appeals to perceptions of a more developed christology than a first-generation Christian might have held or to a dependence upon the Pauline corpus have also been made. Although these arguments have been rebutted with varying degrees of success, it remains unlikely that this letter was written by Peter himself. Again we should remember that the name Peter carries not only historical but theological meaning. Probably an individual or group eager to pass on traditions and authority associated with Peter wrote the letter some time between 80 and 100 C.E. in Rome.

Earlier in this century a number of scholars argued that the first part of the book, 1:3–4:11, was an early Christian baptismal homily and that the remainder, 4:12–5:14, was appended as a word of comfort to persecuted Christians. This claim was supported by several references to baptism in the first part and by the clear break after 4:11, which concludes with a doxology and amen. These theories have largely been rejected in recent years and scholars now prefer to look at the letter as a unity. Beyond this supposition there is little consensus regarding the composition of the letter or its structural indicators.

Contents of 1 Peter

1:1–2. EPISTOLARY OPENING

The greeting of 1 Peter is unusual in that the identification of the audience is more important than that of the author. These "exiles" have been chosen by God and made holy by the Spirit so that they can be obedient to Christ and "sprinkled with his blood" (1:2). They may be aliens in a foreign land, a humble status to be sure, but they are also God's favored ones. Their true identity is actually quite exalted. And they are exalted for a purpose: obedience to Christ. All these themes will be spelled out more fully in the body of the letter.

1:3–2:10. THE FOUNDATION FOR A LIVING HOPE

This first section of the body of 1 Peter sets out the basis for Christian hope even in the midst of the suffering to be described later. Before the readers became Christian, they were ignorant and hopeless, pursuing futile things and purposes (1:14; 18); they were "not a people" (2:10). But they also had already been chosen by God for grace (1:10; see also 1:2). In the time of conversion and initiation they were born anew through the gospel of Christ (1:3, 23), were redeemed by his blood (1:18–19), and were transformed into God's people (2:10). Thus their present situation is marked by joy, love, and faith even in the face of trials and suffering (1:5–7, 22). After all, the foundation of the community of faith is Christ Jesus himself. He is the rock upon which the audience is built into a "spiritual house." Thus who Jesus is and what he does indicate who the church is and what it does.

2:11–3:12. Submission to Human Authorities

The second major section begins with a direct address to the audience, "beloved," and a first-person appeal, "I urge you...to abstain from the desires of the flesh" (2:11). This is followed by another imperative that serves as the theme statement of this section: "Conduct yourselves honorably among the Gentiles, so that, though they malign you as evildoers, they may see your honorable deeds and glorify God when he comes to judge" (2:12). Further, the author exhorts the audience to submit in particular situations: Everyone should accept the authority of the emperor and other human leaders (2:13–17), slaves should accept the authority of their masters even if they suffer unjustly (2:16–25), and wives should accept the authority of their husbands (3:1–6). Appended to this last unit are words urging husbands to care for their wives (3:7).

These latter two situations have engendered one of the most interesting scholarly debates regarding 1 Peter. On the one hand, David Balch argues that these texts on submission are drawn from Hellenistic household codes that can be traced to Aristotle. They are inserted in this letter as part of an ongoing process of acculturation in which this group of Christians tried to make themselves more acceptable and less threatening to the surrounding Greco-Roman society by borrowing certain behavioral standards from it and encouraging its members to adopt them. According to this view, these members were largely slaves in non-Christian households or women married to nonbelieving husbands. By acting out the values of the dominant culture, these people minimized the risk of offending their social superiors.

On the other hand, John H. Elliot claims that these household codes were mediated through Hellenistic Judaism and incorporated in 1 Peter as illustrations of appropriate Christian relations, regardless of their general acceptance in the larger society. In this letter they are based on an appeal to Jesus' own example of humility and unjust suffering which in turn is related to Isaiah 53 (2:22–25). These codes, therefore, were not used in service to some kind of program of assimilation, but as reinforcement of a Christian ethic of subservience that has "God's approval" (2:20). Their usage also supports the overall purpose of the letter, which is to strengthen communal solidarity in resistance to pressure to conform to the culture in which they live.

3:13–4:19. Endurance in Suffering for Doing What Is Good

A rhetorical question, "Now who will harm you if you are eager to do what is good?" opens the third major section of the body of the letter. The author already knows the answer: There are people who will harm even those who do good. But he is not going to focus on the causes of unjust suffering or on those who perpetrate it. Rather, throughout these verses he offers encouragement, even incentives, to endure affliction even if administered unfairly. Although a doxology and amen are found at the end of 4:11, they do not necessarily serve as a conclusion. Section 4:12–19 actually continues the discussion of Christian suffering.

Although suffering may characterize the present life of Christians, it is not a value in and of itself. Only when it is the result of doing good is suffering worthwhile (3:14; 4:15–16). If believers receive ill treatment for doing what is right, they should count themselves blessed (3:14; 4:14). The model for such suffering service is Christ, who "suffered for sins once for all, the righteous for the unrighteous, in order to bring you to God" (3:18). Furthermore, the end of all this suffering is quite near (4:7), and with the end comes a time of judgment in which everyone, including the unrighteous, must give an accounting to the One "who stands ready to judge the living and the dead" (4:5).

5:1–11. FINAL INSTRUCTIONS TO THE COMMUNITY

The author now addresses the elders, probably the leaders of the churches, giving them specific instructions for tending the flock of God. They are advised to give willing and appropriate oversight; younger people are encouraged to accept their leadership. Finally, the whole community is called to humble themselves to one another, cast their cares upon God, resist the devil, and depend upon the support and strength of Christ.

5:12–14. EPISTOLARY CLOSING

The closing formula includes a reference to Silvanus, the letter carrier, and to the purpose of the letter, to encourage the audience and to remind it that these things are "the true grace of God" (5:12). The Christians in "Babylon" and Mark, whose identity can only be guessed, send their greetings. After encouraging everyone to practice the liturgical kiss, the author wishes peace for all believers.

Importance for the Church of the Twenty-first Century

In the letter of 1 Peter the audience is exhorted to be the holy nation of God that it was called to be through the grace of Jesus Christ. With Christ as its foundation and its example, the Christian community is urged to live in peace with one another and with the surrounding Greco-Roman society, to keep itself unstained by corruption while bearing witness to its non-Christian neighborhood, to submit to authority no matter how unjust it may be, no matter how much suffering must be endured. Christ himself is the model for such submission and the church must be his willing followers.

The exhortatory tone of the letter, the emphasis upon the endurance of suffering, and specific instructions like those regarding slaves' submission to masters and wives' submission to husbands are troubling to many modern Christians and are often difficult to preach. One way to approach these difficulties is to help listeners understand the socio-historical context of the letter; another is to balance them with other texts in the canon. Balch, for example, emphasizes the discontinuity between 1 Peter's hierarchical view of relationships and more egalitarian views of relationships among Jesus' early followers in the gospel of Luke or among the Israelites in the Torah.

However, we may gain a deeper appreciation for, if not agreement with, this text if we listen to our fellow believers in non-Christian societies. These believers often face the same problem that 1 Peter's original audience faced: how to maintain Christian identity and values in an indifferent, unaware, or even hostile environment while at the same time trying to maintain friendly relations with non-Christians in such an environment. Often viewed by others as sectarian or as a danger to the dominant social order, these Christians must occasionally endure harassment in various forms, from daily threat against house or church building to loss of opportunities for schooling or careers. Their leaders must find ways to comfort and encourage them. In such contexts 1 Peter's strategy of endurance and compromise often seems the better part of wisdom.

The Second Letter of Peter: Waiting for the Eternal Kingdom of Our Lord

Introductory Issues

The promise that the Lord is coming is trustworthy and true, claims the author of the second letter of Peter, but the time of waiting will be filled with false teaching and temptation. More than any other letter among the catholic epistles, this one is concerned with the parousia of Christ, or more accurately, the delay of the parousia. It serves as a response to people who did not believe that he would come again, who did not trust the apostolic witness to that effect, and who did not want to lead lives of holiness and godliness (3:11).

This letter, with a standard epistolary opening but no closing, is also a testament, an ancient Jewish "farewell speech" of a hero of the faith. This literary form is usually pseudepigraphal and contains both ethical exhortation and revelation of the future. By adopting this well-known form, the author of 2 Peter purports to write the apostle Peter's "Last Will and Testament" to his spiritual heirs. Furthermore, although there are a few paraenetic passages in this text (e.g., 1:5–11; 3:11–18), the overall character is apologetic and polemical. Using strongly argumentative rhetoric, the author defends what he takes to be the apostolic faith against a group of opponents.

Even fewer scholars than in the case of 1 Peter would argue that this letter/testament was actually written by the Galilean fisherman. Again the use of a high form of Greek and Hellenistic rhetoric counts against his authorship. But two other factors also make it improbable. First, 2 Peter makes reference to or is dependent upon several other texts within the

New Testament. A previous letter from Peter is mentioned (3:1), probably an allusion to 1 Peter. (The two letters are so different stylistically that they are surely not from the same hand.) A collection of Paul's letters is also noted and authority is attributed to it (3:15–16). In addition, 2 Peter and Jude obviously share a literary relationship which is seen in the resemblances between Jude 4–13, 16–18 and 2 Peter 2:1–18; 3:1–3. Most scholars now agree that 2 Peter is dependent upon Jude.

This leads to the second factor, the probable date of 2 Peter. The literary relationships just mentioned suggest that this letter was produced after 1 Peter and Jude and after Paul's letters had begun to be circulated together. Moreover, the phrase " ever since our ancestors died" in 3:4 is a reference to the death of the first generation of Christians, most of whom must have died before 80 C.E. Thus the letter should be dated around the end of the first century. Of course, this is long after Peter was killed in the Neronian persecution of the mid-60s, making his authorship impossible. Although the author was not Peter or the author of 1 Peter, it may still have been someone connected to a Petrine circle in Rome.

Second Peter is addressed to "those who have received a faith as precious as ours through the righteousness of our God and Savior Jesus Christ" (1:1). We can ascertain very little about the geographical or social location of these people, but from the text itself we can learn something about the character of the communities to which it was sent. Unlike the situation of the churches to which 1 Peter and James were sent, this one was marked by conflict. The author claims that there were teachers within these communities who taught false doctrine and "destructive opinions" (2:1). Most importantly, they denied that the Lord will ever return in judgment (1:16; 3:4) and declared themselves free to act according to their own desires (2:18–19).

Earlier in this century scholars believed that these opponents to the apostolic doctrine of 2 Peter were Gnostics or proto-Gnostic Christians. However, the lack of a pronounced dualism between spirit and flesh, a hallmark of gnosticism, and the growing recognition that it did not really develop as a religious system until the second century has led most scholars to abandon this claim. Jerome Neyrey (122–28) has recently argued that the opponents were Epicureans. As followers of the Greek philosopher Epicurus, these people denied divine justice, postmortem retribution, and indeed any kind of existence at all after death. However, while this philosophy was so pervasive in the Hellenistic world that Christians may have encountered it and made use of various aspects of it, 2 Peter itself does not mention it by name. In fact, 2 Peter 2:1–2, 21 seem to indicate intra-community conflict, not friction between Christianity and a wholly external religio-philosophical system.

Contents of 2 Peter

1:1–2. EPISTOLARY OPENING

1:3–11. INTRODUCTION

These verses offer a summary of the author's teaching and preaching and serve as a way of establishing common ground between himself and his recipients. Through the power of God the community has already been given both great promises and everything it needs to live in godliness. Exhortation to "make every effort to support your faith with goodness" leads to a chain of virtues, which culminates in love (1:5–7; cf. Rom. 5:1–5). This in turn guarantees entrance into "the eternal kingdom of our Lord and Savior Jesus Christ" (1:11).

1:12–15. THE FAREWELL OF THE APOSTLE

This small section makes clear the testamentary occasion of the letter. Because the apostle will be dying very soon, he wants to be sure that his readers will remember God's promises to the Christian community and the call to live a moral life that is built on these promises.

1:16–3:10. REFUTATION OF THE OPPONENTS

The main section of 2 Peter is a response to the objections leveled by the opponents against the apostolic witness of the expected return of Jesus. Because these problems are never stated outright, the interpreter must pay careful attention to the way in which arguments are made against them in order to ferret them out. There appear to be four primary objections made by the opponents: the author and his supporters based their expectation of Christ's parousia upon "cleverly devised myths" (1:16); the prophecies in the Hebrew Bible and the Petrine interpretations were not divinely inspired (1:20–21); there will be no final divine judgment (2:3b–10); and, the delay of this judgment makes it even more unlikely (3:4).

The author employs a number of strategies to respond to these criticisms. He recalls Peter's experience of the transfiguration (1:17–18) and affirms the inspiration not only of the Hebrew scriptures (1:21), but also the Pauline letters (3:16). He appeals to various accounts of the judgment of God in the Hebrew Bible, and reminds his readers that throughout these events God not only punished the wicked, God also rescued the righteous ones (2:4–10). Finally, he offers two explanations for the delay: on the one hand, one day for God is like a thousand years (3:8; cf. Ps. 90:4); on the other hand, God delays to give everyone the opportunity for repentance (3:9).

In the middle of this tightly woven section is an extended discourse against the false prophets and teachers who will mislead members of the churches into all kinds of licentious behavior (2:1–22). Not only is the third objection refuted here, but the sins of these deceptive leaders are enumerated in strong, graphic language. So great will be the judgment upon them that it would have been better for them never to have "known the way of righteousness" (2:21).

3:11–18. EXHORTATION AND DOXOLOGY

While the recipients of this letter wait for "new heavens and a new earth, where righteousness is at home" (3:13), they are exhorted to lead lives of godliness and purity. And they should wait with patience for the day of God, regarding "the patience of our Lord as salvation" (3:15).

Importance for the Church of the Twenty-first Century

Obviously today we are still struggling with the delay of an event that is discussed so much, not just in 2 Peter but throughout the New Testament. We continue to use many of the same arguments to defend its delay. And we still wrestle with an even more profound expectation that also lies beneath much of the polemic in 2 Peter: surely the quality of our actions today, the choices we make for holiness and godliness or for desire and the pleasures of the day, will have some consequence beyond the moment. With our brothers and sisters in the late first-century world we also depend upon the promise that our lives are directed toward a future that is replete with the grace and glory of God, be it a future that lurks just beyond death or one that ushers in the renewal of all creation and all creatures. Along the road to that future we make choices that lead toward our participation in it and away from it. We ourselves may never use the strong language of 2 Peter against those who oppose us, at least not in public. And the categories of honor and shame, purity and corruption, which so imbue this and the other letters we have been discussing, may have little meaning for us. Yet the hope that our small and great denials of immorality and unrighteousness will lead to God's justice and mercy still pervades our lives.

The First, Second, and Third Letters of John: Abiding in the Love of God

Introductory Issues

God requires only two things of believers, according to the Johannine epistles: belief in Jesus Christ, the Son of God; and love for one another. If we follow these commandments, we abide in God and God abides in us (1 Jn. 3:23–24). Although they sound simple to understand and easy to accomplish, elaboration upon these two commandments throughout 1, 2, and 3 John makes clear that the recipients must believe in the true understanding of Jesus Christ and practice love in the correct way to fulfill them. If they do not get these things right, they are revealed as "children of the devil" (1 Jn. 3:10), "deceivers [who] have gone out into the world" (2 Jn. 7), and people who have done evil and therefore not seen God (3 Jn. 11).

The vocabulary and themes of these letters are very similar to those of the gospel of John, leading both ancient and modern commentators to agree that surely some kind of relationship exists between them. That relationship is probably not a result of the authorship of one person, especially of John the son of Zebedee to whom these writings were often attributed by ancient historians. Neither the letters nor the gospel contain such an identification within their texts. Moreover, these letters, unlike the other general epistles, do not give an authorial name; 2 and 3 John only mention the enigmatic "elder" within their salutations. Most modern scholars now concur that the letters were written by someone who participated in a community or school that was associated with the author of the gospel of John.

The letters were probably written after the gospel, although interpreters have proposed other sequences of writing. While this issue cannot be settled conclusively, many argue that 1 John attempts to clarify theological and christological issues raised in the gospel that became problematic as the Johannine community developed. For example, the specific form of christological confession in 1 John ("Every spirit that confesses that Jesus Christ has come in the flesh is from God [4:2]) may be seen as a correction of a possible docetic interpretation of the gospel of John. This explains why 1 John seems more intelligible to many people when it is read in light of the gospel.

It is also impossible to determine which of the three letters was written first. Again, because 2 and 3 John seem to make more sense when read after 1 John, we can presuppose that they were written in the order in which they appear in the canon. Yet another question can also not be resolved with any certainty: were the three texts produced by the same person or different persons? Since both 2 and 3 John state that they were written by "the elder," we can assume that they were written by one person. Similarities in language and occasion between 1 and 2 John suggest that the same person also wrote them.

Before a date can be tentatively fixed, we should consider the situations in which they were written. The gospel of John shows evidence of conflict between early Christian and Jewish communities (e.g., Jn. 9:13–34), but there is no trace of this kind of crisis in the Johannine letters. Instead, the difficulties seem to be within the Johannine community itself. In 1 John harsh words are directed toward a group who "went out from us" (2:19) and who had apparently been teaching that Jesus had not come in the flesh (see 2:18–27; 4:1–6). Although this group cannot be precisely identified, we can surmise that its members somehow rejected the idea of a fully human, fully physical Jesus. Perhaps they believed in an incipient form of docetic christology. But the author is not addressing these people directly; rather, he is talking to a group for whom he feels some affinity and responsibility, addressing them as "little children" and "beloved." This suggests that 1 John is primarily an effort to reassure the remaining group and to explain a more faithful understanding of Christ and of the love required to follow him.

The occasion of 2 John appears quite similar; the elder repeats his concerns about deceivers "who do not confess that Jesus Christ has come in the flesh" (7). In contrast, because nothing is said about the christological issues of the first two letters and the love commandment is not repeated, 3 John reflects a different occasion. The rebuke of the unknown leader Diotrephes also indicates some kind of intra-community struggle over authority.

If we say that these letters were written after the Fourth Gospel, obviously any dates we propose for their writing would depend upon its date. According to Raymond Brown *(The Epistles of John,* 100–101), the gospel was written around 90 C.E. Since 1 John was written in response to controversy over primarily christological issues, time for these problems to develop would have to elapse. Brown suggests that maybe ten years passed, dating 1 John around 100 C.E. Because 2 John arises out of a similar occasion, we can infer that it was also written around the same time. 3 John was probably produced somewhat later, perhaps between 100 and 110 C.E. Ephesus is the traditional locale for these texts.

Throughout the foregoing discussion, I have referred to 1, 2, and 3 John as letters. This is undoubtedly an appropriate generic description for 2 and 3 John since they contain the usual elements. But in spite of the fact that 1 John is customarily referred to as a letter or epistle, interpreters are well aware that it has no opening or closing salutation or any other feature that would suggest that it should be categorized as a letter. Thus it has been called a homily, an essay, or a circular letter, but none of these options have received widespread acceptance. At the most basic level we can say that it is a written communication, but one that was probably read aloud to first-century Christian communities just as a letter would have been.

It is fairly easy to see how 2 and 3 John are structured, not the least because they are so brief, but the compositional indicators for 1 John are practically invisible. In fact, there are almost as many outlines for this text as there are commentators who have outlined it. Difficulties arise because deceptively simple themes are stated, and then restated in a slightly different way, and then stated once again in yet another way. As C. Clifton Black says, "the First Epistle is more like Ravel's vertiginous Bolero, which repeats a few themes with increasingly complex orchestration" *(New Interpreter's Bible,* 371).

Contents of 1 John

1:1–10. Prologue

In the prologue the author announces what he and his co-believers have heard and seen and touched from the beginning. In 1:1–4 he repeats familiar themes from the prologue of the Fourth Gospel, John 1:1–18, and emphasizes the physicality of what was revealed to them, that is, the life of Jesus Christ. He also speaks of the circle of intimacy that binds together God as Father and Jesus as Son and those who accept this witness into a *koinonia* (Greek) or "fellowship" (NRSV). In vv. 5–10 the author states with greater clarity the message he is handing on to his listeners that God is truth and light. He also elaborates the idea of *koinonia* with God in a series of alternating positive and negative conditional clauses.

2:1–14. Reasons for Writing

A sequence of explanations for writing this message is begun at 2:1, but the topic of sin and forgiveness is not forgotten. In fact, the first reason for writing is "so that you may not sin" (2:1). But of course since all people sin, the author assures his readers that we have an "advocate" in Jesus who is "the atoning sacrifice for our sins, and not for ours only but also for the sins of the whole world" (2:2; cf. 1:7). In the gospel of John the Holy Spirit is called the "Advocate"; here it is Jesus "the righteous" who now stands in God's court and pleads on behalf of the faithful. The image of Jesus as "atoning sacrifice" shifts the metaphoric setting from court to temple. Here Jesus is like a sacrificial lamb (cf. Jn. 1:29). At 2:3 the author introduces a new theme, the commandments of God, with which he will continue to work throughout the remainder of the letter. More specifically, albeit indirectly, he is talking about the injunction to love.

2:15–3:10. The Last Hour

Because the members of this community are now living in the last hour, warns the author, they must not love the world and the desires of the world that are passing away (2:15–17). They must also recognize that the presence of the antichrists, people who do not believe that Jesus is the Christ and the Son of God, is a sign of the last times.

Throughout this text familiar Johannine motifs such as love, sin and lawlessness, abiding in God, rejecting and being rejected by the world, continue to reverberate. The echoes of an important christological theme also resound. God and Jesus are so close to one another, so intimate, that in 1 John they become practically interchangeable.

As the believers wait for the coming of Christ (2:28; the text simply says "his coming") they must continue to abide in God and to live as children of God. This is their present reality; their future reality, which is inextricably linked with Jesus, has yet to be revealed (3:2). This section concludes with a disquisition on the differences between the children of God and the children of the devil.

3:11–4:21. Love One Another

This section deals with the two commandments that comprise the centerpiece of 1 John. The first is the commandment to love that has been hinted at before (2:9–11), but not so clearly or imperatively expressed. At 3:11, the author finally states explicitly that the believers must love one another, and underscores its importance with the phrase, "this is the message" (cf. 1:5). As in the letter of James, the faithful are told that love must be exhibited through concrete action on behalf of others; but unlike James, no specifics are given.

The second commandment is given in 3:23, "that we should believe in the name of his Son Jesus Christ." This belief must take a particular form now made explicit: that the man Jesus who came in the flesh is from God (4:3). Those who do not acknowledge this participate in the spirit of the antichrist come from the world (4:5), the place or state in which Christ is rejected.

In 4:7–21 we find a vibrant recapitulation of all that has been said in this text concerning love. We must love because God is love. We must love because God loves us enough to send God's Son to take away our sins. We must love because only then will we abide in God. Through love we have no fear on the day of judgment or any other day because "perfect love casts out fear" (4:18). And through love we have no hatred for our brothers and sisters.

5:1–12. Believe that Jesus Is the Christ

The first unit in this section, 5:1–5, is a reiteration of themes that have already been discussed in the letter and revolves around the second commandment concerning belief in Jesus. Those who believe are "born of God" and have conquered the world through this faith. In the second unit, 5:6–12, the very unusual phrase "the water and the blood" appears, words so opaque that scholars have wrestled with their meanings for centuries. They may contain sacramental overtones–water pointing to baptism, blood to the Lord's supper. Or they may be an allusion to the death of Jesus as it is described in John 19:34 in which blood and water poured from Jesus' side. It is also quite likely that the way in which blood is stressed in 5:6, "not with the water only but with the water and the blood," underscores a central christological claim of 1 John that the Christ is the very human, very real Jesus. Thus, the testimony of the "Spirit and the water and the blood" in 5:8 is a spiritual, liturgical, physical, and finally very christological testimony.

5:13–21. Epilogue

These last verses contain a jumble of repeated or related exhortations and affirmations. No doxology or closing salutation brings this writing to an appropriate end; perhaps there is no good way to end such a sonorous and solemn paean to belief in Jesus Christ and love of one another.

Contents of 2 John

Second John, a true letter with an epistolary opening and closing, is written to "the elect lady and her children," a metaphor for the church.

The elder is pleased to hear that some in this community are "walking in the truth" (4); apparently others are not. After repeating the love commandment (5), he turns his attention once again to the "deceivers" who do not believe that Jesus came into the world in fully human form (7–9). In contrast to 1 John, he also gives them a specific command not to receive these people into their community (10–11). In the epistolary closing (12–13) the elder expresses the hope that he will soon come to see the recipients and sends the greetings of others in his own community.

Contents of 3 John

In the epistolary greeting of this letter, the elder addresses himself to an individual named Gaius who, like some of the children of the "elect lady" of 2 John, "walks in the truth" (3). He then urges Gaius to continue to show hospitality to Christian travelers. His approval of Gaius contrasts sharply with his disapproval of someone named Diotrephes. This unknown member of the church is ignoring the authority of the elder, spreading lies about him, and not offering hospitality to the same Christians that Gaius has welcomed so warmly (9–10).

Though brief, this letter offers a fascinating glimpse into first-century church politics. Diotrephes may very well have been host of the church that met in his house, and he was attempting to limit the guest list. But as the elder reminds Gaius, the church should be a place of hospitality to all; no single individual has the right to close the church doors to those who would enter. Yet at the same time, the elder seems to reverse the instruction found in 2 John 10 that those who come to the church with false doctrine should be denied entrance. Thus, in 3 John hospitality is a virtue that should define the church. But in 2 John hospitality has its limits, especially when heresy threatens to enter. Such a quandary has often faced the church in its long history.

Importance for the Church of the Twenty-first Century

Hauntingly beautiful phrases and statements in these letters may mask too easily the conflict that threatened the unity, possibly even the existence, of the Johannine community. The commandment to love echoes from the end of the first century down to the end of the present century, but it reaches us in a minor key. For it was first repeated in a community that was torn apart not merely by doctrinal differences but by angry name-calling and resentful rejection of personal integrity and authority. Too many Christians know too well the pain of such a situation; too many of us have seen it acted out in our own churches.

The elder offered no explicit recommendations for how we should express the love that he has commanded in these circumstances, beyond the encouragement to offer hospitality to those of whom he approved. But those words are practically negated by the admonition to refuse it to those with whom he did not agree. The truth is that speaking of love for one another is so easy in the general sense, but when we are forced to be specific about it, things become more difficult. How can we love the people who have insisted only on their own way? How can we love the people with whose opinions we are in the deepest disagreement?

We can do this only by clinging to the love of God that is fully expressed in Jesus–that is the answer given by the elder even in the midst of his own struggle with hatred and anger. And he reminds us that this very human Jesus loved the people around him in completely visible, wholly audible, fully tangible ways. There is nothing ethereal about the love of Jesus, nothing general and vague. He was more than spirit; he was a man who lived among us, who sacrificed himself for us, who continues to abide with us even after his death. Little children, says the elder to all of us who are arguing among ourselves about the great theological issues of our day, let us find ways to love each other as concretely, as specifically, as Jesus loves.

The Letter of Jude: Contending for the Faith of the Saints
Introductory Issues

Intruders have entered the community and are threatening the faith upon which it is built with their ungodliness and licentiousness, warns the author of the letter of Jude. These people are as brazen as the angels who left heaven to mate with humans, as wicked as the citizens of Sodom and Gomorrah, as apostate as Cain and Balaam. They will indeed meet the judgment of God as all their evil predecessors did, but in the meantime, the pious ones, beloved of God, must resist their machinations, snatch the weak from their clutches, and hold fast to the love of God.

Like 2 Peter this letter is addressed to a community that was experiencing serious division over doctrinal and ethical issues. And as in 2 Peter, the author takes a side in this problematic situation, arguing vehemently against people characterized as "dreamers," "scoffers," "grumblers and malcontents." But exactly what these people were doing or saying to attract such negative language is difficult to piece together. They were probably itinerant Christian teachers or prophets who disavowed the authority of the Law and a final judgment of God and thus preached greater freedom from ethical and moral responsibilities. In their antinomianism they denied the lordship of Jesus and the faith that had been transmitted through the apostles. While this group probably did not represent some kind of early gnostic movement, it is impossible to determine whether or not they were associated with some other early Christian heresy known to us today.

The identity of the author is equally difficult to determine. The inscribed author is Jude the brother of James. Because the only two brothers named James and Jude in the New Testament are also in Jesus' immediate family (Mt. 13:55; Mk. 6:3), we can say that he was also the brother of Jesus. But did this Jude actually write the letter or is it pseudonymous? On the one hand, the fact that his status as Jesus' brother is not announced counts toward its authenticity. If an unknown author had really wanted to gain respect and authority for his writing he would have called attention to his more important relationship to Jesus. In addition, the letter is steeped in Jewish traditions, which may indicate the author's proximity to, if not residence in, Palestine. On the other hand, the beautiful Greek and the skillful use of Hellenistic rhetorical forms and devices of the letter weigh heavily against the authorship of a Galilean peasant, just as in the case of the letters of James and 1 and 2 Peter. The author also speaks of "the apostles" as if he were not among this earlier, more authoritative generation of leaders (17).

Appeals to location and date do not assist us in solving this dilemma. The letter itself offers very little information about location beyond the knowledge of Jewish traditions, which, noted above, might suggest Palestine. But we must acknowledge that such learning could be obtained throughout the diaspora. Equally useless are appeals to a hypothesis concerning the gradual de-emphasis on eschatological hope in the last years of the first century that earlier scholars used to date various New Testament texts. The eschatological expectation found in Jude, reasoned these scholars, indicates a more primitive form of Christian faith. However, since hope in the imminent parousia of Christ and subsequent judgment is found in New Testament texts (e.g., the Revelation to John) that can be confidently dated much later in the first century, this hypothesis has been largely rejected. Therefore, we have two alternatives regarding authorship and date, neither of which is supported by overwhelming evidence. Either this letter was written by Jude in the middle of the first century or by a pseudonymous author sometime in its last quarter. A convincing method for choosing between the two has yet to be established. The location of the author or recipients also cannot be determined.

To make his case against his opponents the author draws upon a broad range of Jewish material including texts from the Hebrew Bible and from extra-canonical sources like *1 Enoch* and the *Testament of Moses*. He also skillfully employs the argumentation of deliberative rhetoric while at the same time conforming to the conventions of Greco-Roman epistolary style. The result is a very compact and elegant letter that effectively defends the apostolic faith and persuasively argues against the deleterious beliefs and actions of the intruders.

Contents of the Letter

1–2. Epistolary Opening

3–4. Occasion and Purpose

The author was preparing to write a letter to these Christians about their common salvation when he received news about the problems they were experiencing with intruders. So he laid aside the plans for the original letter and wrote this one instead. His purpose is to encourage the faithful in the community "to contend for the faith that was once for all entrusted to the saints" (3). Although many interpreters maintain that "the faith" refers to a set of doctrines, it is more likely that it is synonymous with Paul's use of the word *gospel,* which is rooted in the confession that Jesus is Lord.

5–16. Judgment against the Intruders

In this section, the body of the letter, the author attempts to prove that the people who have infiltrated the community are ungodly and that certain judgment awaits them. He does this by making comparisons between them and various unrighteous groups found in Jewish tradition. All of them received God's severest condemnation (5–7); by implication, so will the false teachers of Jude's community.

The comparisons continue in verses 8–11 as the author alleges that his opponents "defile the flesh, reject authority, and slander the glorious ones," probably a name for angels. Furthermore, because they feast without reverence, these people are "blemishes" upon the eucharistic celebrations of the community (12a). They are also as unproductive as rainless clouds or fruitless trees, as aimless as waves of the sea and stars wandering through the heavens (12b–13). In short, these intruders are the "ungodly sinners" mentioned in *1 Enoch* 1:9 and their activity signals the last days.

17–23. Final Exhortations

This prophecy is confirmed by warnings of the apostles about "scoffers" who will appear at the end. In light of this fulfillment of prophecy, the beloved ones are called to edify themselves, to pray, to keep themselves in the love of God, and to look forward to Christ's mercy. They are also urged to take care of those who are attracted to the ideas of the intruders.

24–25. Concluding Doxology

An affirmation of God's power and grace concludes this brief letter. God can keep the faithful from falling and make them stand "without blemish" in God's presence—no doubt an allusion to the positive form of God's judgment that the true believers will receive. And to the One who can do these things is ascribed the highest forms of honor and praise.

Importance for the Church of the Twenty-first Century

Like the names that are hurled against the opponents in the Johannine epistles, the name-calling here may seem vituperative and vindictive. It offends our modern North American sensibilities and impedes our appreciation for this letter. And in Jude it is not softened by the repeated commandment to love. Once again, we must move beyond initial impressions and look for the more profound theological and ethical affirmations that caused early Christians to preserve and eventually canonize this letter. There is the same expectation we encountered in 2 Peter that what we believe and how we behave matters to God. We also meet in Jude genuine commitment to the centrality of Jesus Christ in all of human life. What we say about him affects what we do, and what we do has cosmic consequences. Those of us in the late twentieth century and the early twenty-first perhaps know that better than our fellow believers of Jude's time, for we have seen the damage done to the environment in the name of stewardship to God and heard the cries of those oppressed in the name of Jesus. We are experiencing in these things a foretaste of divine judgment. And yet, as we show compassion through our actions of love and service and as we depend upon the mercy of Christ, we also can be kept by God in safety and placed in God's presence without spot or blemish. So with Jude we can join in praise: to the Holy One be "glory, majesty, power, and authority, before all time and now and forever. Amen" (25).

Suggested Resources for the Pastor's Library

Achtemeier, Paul J. *1 Peter.* Hermeneia. Minneapolis: Fortress Press, 1996.

Bauckham, Richard J. *Jude, 2 Peter.* Word Biblical Commentary. Waco, Tex.: Word Books, 1983.

Brown, Raymond E. *The Epistles of John.* Anchor Bible 30. New York: Doubleday, 1982.

Chester, Andrew, and Ralph P. Martin. *The Theology of the Letters of James, Peter, and Jude.* New Testament Theology. Cambridge: Cambridge University Press, 1994.

Craddock, Fred B. *First and Second Peter and Jude.* Westminster Bible Companion. Louisville: Westminster John Knox Press, 1995.

Johnson, Luke Timothy. *The Letter of James.* Anchor Bible 37A. New York: Doubleday, 1995.

Keck, Leander, ed. *The New Interpreter's Bible.* Volume 12. Nashville: Abingdon Press, 1998.

Lieu, Judith M. *The Theology of the Johannine Epistles.* New Testament Theology. Cambridge: Cambridge University Press, 1991.

Michaels, J. Ramsey. *1 Peter.* Word Biblical Commentary. Waco, Tex.: Word Books, 1988.

Neyrey, Jerome H. *2 Peter, Jude.* Anchor Bible 37C. New York: Doubleday, 1993.

Perkins, Pheme. *First and Second Peter, James, and Jude.* Interpretation. Louisville: Westminster John Knox Press, 1995.

Rensberger, David. *1 John, 2 John, 3 John.* Abingdon New Testament Commentaries. Nashville: Abingdon Press, 1997.

Sleeper, C. Freeman. *James.* Abingdon New Testament Commentaries. Nashville: Abingdon Press, 1998.

Smith, D. Moody. *First, Second, and Third John.* Interpretation. Louisville: Westminster John Knox Press, 1991.

Wall, Robert W. *Community of the Wise: The Letter of James.* The New Testament in Context. Valley Forge, Pa.: Trinity Press International, 1997.

14

An Exhortation to Faithfulness
Hebrews

Judith Hoch Wray

Hebrews begins with one of the most carefully written sentences in the New Testament. The first four verses encapsulate most of the themes of the homily. In translation, much of the rhetorical artistry is lost, since English translation seems unable to reproduce the alliteration and assonance of the Greek of this opening verse. However, the christological focus remains.

From the beginning, the careful rhetoric of the text, most obvious in its oral manifestation, establishes Hebrews, not as an "epistle," but as an early Christian homily. The power of its exhortation to faithful Christian living is unparalleled in the New Testament. The contents of Hebrews include both some of the most quoted texts in Christian proclamation and some of the most enigmatic.

Basic Data

Authorship

In its earliest attested form (Chester Beatty papyrus, p[46], about 200 C.E.), Hebrews is included among the Pauline epistles after Romans. However, even Clement of Alexandria (ca. 150–215) and Origen (ca. 185–253) recognized that the style in "To the Hebrews" differed significantly from the rest of the Pauline corpus.

The author identifies himself, not as an eyewitness to the ministry of Jesus, but as a second-generation Christian who never claims the direct revelation or authority claimed by Paul (Heb. 2:3; contrast Gal. 1:11–24). Few scholars today defend the theory of Pauline authorship; and speculation about other possible authors bears little fruit.

We can, however, infer a few things from the text. This elusive preacher was obviously well-educated, having benefitted from rhetorical training, was somewhat acquainted with Greek philosophical categories, and was well-versed in the exegesis of Jewish scriptures in a Greek form and familiar with standard Christian homiletic practices of his time. He was probably of Jewish ancestry, but standing within a Gentile-oriented wing of early Christianity. This pro-Gentile theological emphasis and the reference to Timothy in Hebrews 13:23 may suggest at least some interaction or acquaintance with Paul.

The author stands within the philosophical and religious thought-world of his time and yet presents a unique perspective on the ministry of Christ and the nature of the salvation provided by the incarnation. Parallels between Hebrews and Philo suggest that the two authors are indebted to similar traditions of Greek-speaking and -thinking Judaism, but Hebrews does not use the same kind of allegorical exegetical techniques or even similar philosophical interpretation of Jewish tradition as does Philo. Later Gnostic writers adapted much that they found in "To the Hebrews," but charges of gnosticism in Hebrews are unjustified.

Origen finally concluded that "who wrote the epistle, in truth, no one knows" (Eusebius, *Ecclesiastical History* 6.25.14). Hebrews is, like Melchizedek, "without father, without mother, without genealogy, having neither beginning of days nor end of life" (7:3).

Date

The original date of composition is also elusive. We can only establish a general date range. Based on the development of some traditions evident in the text, on the stated dependence on the transmission of the word of salvation from others (2:3), and on the remark that some had been believers for some time (5:12), we conclude that the date of composition was several decades after the beginning of the Christian movement.

Hebrews makes no reference to the destruction of the temple, an observation which might, on the surface, require a pre-70 date, but arguments from silence are always questionable. Hebrews seems more concerned with the prototypical wilderness tabernacle and its cultic activities than with the Herodian temple and contemporary high priests. The preacher, focusing on encouragement to faithfulness by comparing Christ's efficacy with the efficacy of the archetypal wilderness tabernacle and cult, probably avoids mention of the destruction of the Herodian temple because it would distract from his argument. The fact that the preacher feels a need to provide a Christian identity for this community apart from Judaism suggests a post-70 date.

We know little of the social and religious context beyond that which we can glean from the text. The hearers have been Christians for some time (5:11–14), have faced some persecution (10:32–33), are now faltering in their involvement in their Christian community (cf. 10:23–25, 34), are in danger of regression (10:26–27), and are of diminished confidence in their confession of Christ (10:35–39). This is a second-generation Christian community showing signs of weariness and apathy, a scenario not easily imagined before the late 80s or 90s. Obvious literary dependence of *1 Clement* 36:2–6 on the text of Hebrews sets the upper limits for a date of composition of Hebrews at 90–120 C.E.

Addressees

The title, "To the Hebrews," appears at the head of the earliest extant form of the text (p^{46}). The manuscript seems to have been known by that name among most early Christian writers. Since the title may be an editorial label attached in order to include it, by analogy, to "To the Romans," etc., among the Pauline epistles, we cannot rely on the title for clues about the original audience to which this sermon was preached.

The author is addressing a specific congregation with whom he is acquainted. (Note the personal nature of Heb. 10:32–34.) The sermon is quite pastoral, urging growth toward maturity that seems to include the preacher along with the hearers (6:1–3). The preacher belongs, in some way, to this community. The eloquent rhetoric of Hebrews surely presupposes a congregation that will understand and respond to the rhetorical subtleties and flourishes, as well as a congregation well versed in the Septuagint, and conversant with the foundational biblical stories of faith and Jewish cultic practices as depicted in Torah.

We may then posit an educated, Jewish Christian community, with access to quality Greek education and philosophies, or an educated Gentile Christian community that, as a part of its Christian catechism, has been steeped in the foundational biblical stories of faith and Jewish cultic practices as depicted in Torah, or–and this is most likely–a mixed Jewish and Gentile Christian community with the above characteristics. This identification points to a venue in or near a major city but outside of Jerusalem. Rome, or its environs, certainly would be a likely candidate and would be consistent with the final greeting when, as a letter, the sermon is sent elsewhere: "Those from Italy send you greetings" (13:24b). In the final analysis, however, we do not have enough information to know to whom Hebrews, in sermon and/or epistle form, was addressed.

Use of Scripture in Hebrews

Every section of the well-orchestrated argument asserts that God has spoken. Those appeals to the authority of the scripture echo and elaborate on the opening declaration of Hebrews:

> Long ago God spoke to our ancestors in many and various ways
> by the prophets, but in these last days he has spoken to us by a

Son, whom he appointed heir of all things, through whom he also created the worlds. (Heb. 1:1–2)

The author of Hebrews quotes only what he identifies as "God's words," such as Psalms. He never quotes biblical narrative as if it were from God, although he tells his own version of narrative stories and appropriates narrative vocabulary to argue a point at hand.

The author of Hebrews, who relies heavily on proof-texts from the First Testament, selectively reappropriates the First Testament for his own Christian and christological purposes. The author was using as his Bible the Septuagint (abbreviated LXX), the Greek translation of the Hebrew Bible. He uses scriptural proof-texts to argue against the continuation of traditional religious practice contained in scripture. A few verses from Jeremiah and the Psalms serve as God's testimony against dozens of chapters from the Pentateuch.

Hebrews retells the biblical story in a way that diminishes events and institutions connected with the national distinctiveness of Israel. For example, Joshua is said to have failed to bring the people rest (4:8) and then is omitted from the heroes of faith list in chapter 11; the entering into Canaan narrative is omitted except for the fall of Jericho (without mention of Joshua) in Hebrews 11:30. And Moses is mentioned for his faith (11:23–28), not for leading the people of Israel out of Egypt, but for considering "abuse suffered for the Christ to be greater wealth than the treasures of Egypt" and for leaving Egypt (apparently a reference to his first escape to Midian in Ex. 2:11–15). For Hebrews, biblical history no longer focuses on the establishment and well-being of a nation. Rather, it culminates with the theological claims of the superiority of Christ.

Much of the argument is built around a platonic/allegorical method, one that is shared with many first-and second-century Jewish and Christian writers as a means for interpreting the Bible, namely the First Testament. The Platonic worldview distinguished between the "real world," where the true "forms" or ideal was to be found, and this world, which is only a shadow of the real world. When applied to an interpretation of an ancient text, this viewpoint allowed the interpreter to distinguish between the literal meaning of the text and its higher, idealized meaning. This method is called allegorical interpretation. Just as the Platonic worldview envisioned the real world as the world of the divine, so also allegorical interpretation was seen as closer to the divine message than the literal. This perspective is seen when the author refers to the Jewish temple as "a sanctuary that is a sketch and shadow of the heavenly one" (8:5), or to the temple/tabernacle of Jesus as "the greater and perfect tent (not made with hands, that is, not of this creation)…For Christ did not enter a sanctuary made by human hands, a mere copy of the true one, but he entered into heaven itself" (9:11, 24), or to the law as "only a shadow of the good things to come and not the true form of these realities" (10:1). Such an interpretive method allows the author to refer to Jesus as "high priest" even though that designation has nothing to do with Jesus as a historical figure.

The platonic/allegorical method of the author also buttressed the supercessionist theology that permeates this writing throughout. By downgrading literal meaning of scripture in favor of an allegorical meaning, the author was able to take the traditions and institutions of Israel and reinterpret them as all finding their fulfillment in Christ. The name given to this theology is supercessionism, a view that Judaism has been replaced by Christianity. This view developed in the early centuries of the Christian movement as it sought to define itself over against the Judaism out of which it sprang. It was a theology that developed in a polemical context, and, by definition, is an overstatement. It has spawned centuries of anti-Semitism in Christian theology. Consequently, Hebrews must be read by the careful student with a view to the historical circumstances that led to its overstated rhetoric. We can appreciate the gist of its message without repeating its excesses.

Method of Interpretation, Genre, and Structure of "To the Hebrews"

Hebrews, in its original form, was a carefully crafted sermon, designed for oral presentation within the context of worship. The quality of the oral dynamics in the Greek text suggest that this sermon was first preached in person to a congregation and then sent on to another or other congregations as well, with the epistolary ending added. (The ending is so clearly linked to the rest of the text that we have no reason to posit another hand's composition of the closing section.) Please note that I will not, at any time in this chapter, refer to "To the Hebrews" as an epistle. Titles that add the "Letter to..." or "Epistle to..." designation only serve to invite errors in interpretation based on misunderstanding of the genre.

"To the Hebrews" is the only New Testament document that, as a book, qualifies as a sermon. (Sermons are recorded within Acts; portions of Romans, 1 Corinthians, and 1 and 2 Peter were probably excerpted from sermons.) What difference does that make? Different genres, by nature, invite different methods of interpretation. Literature composed for oral speech will, of necessity, incorporate rhetorical clues to meaning in ways that a purely literary work need not. Repetition, with variation, facilitates comprehension. Poetry, word plays, alliteration, and assonance invite a joyous and attentive hearing of the content.

Various forms of persuasive rhetoric defined much of the content and goal of a Hellenistic education. Educated persons were expected to demonstrate effective use of certain rhetorical devices and were trained to recognize creative rhetorical skills in the speech of others. Given the carefully structured and clearly oral nature of the text we know as "To the Hebrews," rhetorical criticism is an essential and most helpful method of interpretation.

An introduction to "To the Hebrews" almost requires an introduction to first-century Hellenistic and Jewish rhetoric.

A helpful analysis of the rhetorical structure of this homily comes from Lawrence Wills ("The Form of the Sermon," 277–99), who identifies the discernible pattern of a "word of exhortation" that "quite likely...took on a fixed meaning as the sermon of the worship service in early Christianity." Wills notes that the pattern generally consists of (1) an indicative or exemplary section (hereafter referred to as "exempla") in the form of scriptural quotations, authoritative examples from past or present, or reasoned exposition of theological points; (2) a conclusion, based on the exempla and indicating their significance for those addressed; and (3) an exhortation.

Other early Christian texts that follow this "word of exhortation" form include *1 Clement;* Acts 2:14–40; Acts 3:12–26; Acts 20:17–35; 1 Cor. 10:1–14; 1 and 2 Peter. This sermonic form in Hebrews–exempla/conclusion/exhortation–provides the overall structure, as well as being repeated within smaller units, as building blocks for the larger sermon.

One popular rhetorical device was the chiasm, an arrangement in the form of a *chi* (X), by which thought development was ordered in ascending and descending order, such as A-B-C-D-C'-B'-A'. This structure is designed to highlight the *center* element of the chiasm, inviting the hearer/reader to look for the primary meaning in the *middle* of the discourse. For example, note in Heb. 9:18–22, this careful chiastic structure:

A "not even the first covenant was inaugurated without blood" (18)
B "in accordance with the law..."(19)
C "he took the blood..."(19)
D "sprinkled..."(19)
E "'This is the blood of the covenant that God has ordained for you.'" (20)
D' "sprinkled..."(21)
C' "with the blood..."(21)
B' "under the law..."(22)
A' "almost everything is purified with blood..."(22)

The focal point of the chiasm is item E, which is a "quote" from Exodus 24:8 and which, in this context, is undoubtedly intended to elicit memory of the communion liturgy (cf. 1 Cor. 11:25; Mk. 14:24; Mt. 26:28; Lk. 22:20).

Here is a master rhetorician at work, using sophisticated linguistic skills to persuade those who will hear. The well-educated hearers of this homily would have recognized much of the rhetorical emphasis that we, who have lost our sense of classical rhetoric, may miss apart from careful analysis of the written text. The summary commentary will provide details to the basic outline provided below.

Outline of "To the Hebrews"

Intro: Exordium (1:1–4)
  I. Christ superior to the angels and like us (1:5–2:18)
 II. Christ, faithful and merciful, for us (3:1–7:28 [8:6])
    A. Christ as faithful, worthy of more glory than Moses (3:1–6)
      Sermon illustration about faith, from the negative (3:7–4:13)
    B. Christ as merciful high priest
      Word of exhortation based on Psalm 110 (4:14–8:6)
III. Christ's ministry as superior:
      Word of exhortation based on Jer. 31:31–34 (8:1–10:39)
 IV. Final word of exhortation on the results of faith (11:1–12:29)
  V. Epistolary postscript (13:1–25)

Summary Commentary

1:1–4. Exordium

This opening exordium, quite literally the most carefully crafted sentence in the New Testament, introduces many of the themes for the entire sermon, asserts the speech of God as the authority for the proclamation, and establishes the christological nature of the discourse. The claim of the superiority of God's eschatological speech through the Son begins by listing the attributes and ministry of Christ, perhaps borrowing from an early Christian hymn for some of this "high" christological confession. The designations for Christ in 1:1–3 match the catena (chain) of First Testament quotations in 1:5–14, while 1:4 serves as an announcement for 1:5–2:18. The time distinction between "long ago" and "in these last days," is an essential dimension of the theology of Hebrews, a theme that will be elaborated on as the sermon progresses.

1:5–2:18. Christ Superior to the Angels and Like Us

1:5–14. Son superior to the angels (exempla/conclusion)

The preacher first compares the Son with the angels. The rhetorical device called *synkrisis*, or comparison, is used at least thirty-two times in Hebrews. Again and again, the preacher examines the quality and effectiveness of Christ's ministry over against other proven models of faithfulness. The conclusion: Christ is better.

While some scholars have speculated that the addressees were guilty of placing the angels above Christ, the more likely explanation for the emphasis of the Son's superiority to the angels is rhetorical. In Hebrews 2:6ff., the preacher has chosen Psalm 8:5 as his proof-text introduction to Jesus' essential incarnation, identification with humanity, and willingness to suffer. Before identifying Jesus as the One who "for a little while was made lower than the angels" (2:9), the skilled rhetorician establishes the superiority of the Son to those angels.

The writer does not simply quote from scripture to confirm his argument; these quotations–the speech of God–*are* his argument. The quote from Psalm 45:6–7 in Hebrews 1:8 is especially worth noting as one of the few New Testament texts in which Jesus is called God!

2:1–5. THEREFORE, PAY ATTENTION (EXHORTATION)

An *a fortiori* argument (a type of analogical reasoning intending to make a case "from the lesser to the stronger") exhorts the congregation to "pay greater attention to what we have heard" (2:1). If the message through the angels was valid and disobedience worthy of penalty, how can we escape if we neglect the word spoken by the Son?

2:6–18. JESUS MADE LOWER THAN THE ANGELS, LIKE US FOR US

Hebrews 2:6–3:6 also follows the "word of exhortation" form, offering a mini-sermon on the relationship between the hearers and Jesus. The preacher begins the scriptural exempla with a quote from Psalm 8:4–6 and concludes by quoting Psalm 22:22 and Isaiah 8:17–18 (see also 2 Sam. 22:3 LXX; Isa. 12:2). In the center of this exempla is one of the most dynamic proclamations of the incarnation to be found in the New Testament: the evidence of Jesus' humanity and the efficacy of Jesus' ministry lie in his suffering (2:9–10).

The conclusion (2:14–18) following these exempla summarizes the significance of this christology and introduces the theme of Jesus' ministry on behalf of those who are being tested (i.e., the hearers!). Hebrews 2:17–18 summarizes 2:6–18 and announces 3:1–5:10.

Hebrews 2:17–18 is an example of parallelism, in which the second verse repeats or elaborates on the thought of the first, followed by the use of the chiasm, in which the author reverses the order of elements in successive clauses or sections. Thus:

A 2:17 "So that he might become a *merciful*
B and *faithful* high priest in the service of God, to make expiation for the sins of the people.
A 2:18 For because he himself has *suffered*
B and been *tempted*, he is able to help those who are tempted." (RSV)
B' 3:1–6 Encomium on Christ as *faithful* using Moses as model with reflection on response to *temptation* (3:7–4:13).
A' 4:14–5:10 Encomium on Christ as *merciful* high priest with reflection on the function of Christ's *suffering* (5:7–10).

Hebrews 2:17–18 thus highlights Jesus as (a) *merciful* because he has *suffered* (illustrated in 4:15–5:10), and as (b) *faithful* even though he has been *tempted* (illustrated in 3:1–4:14). These adjectives define the christological foundation for the remainder of the sermon.

3:1–7:28. Christ, faithful and merciful, for us

3:1–6. CHRIST AS FAITHFUL, WORTHY OF MORE GLORY THAN MOSES (EXHORTATION WITH ENCOMIUM)

Hebrews 3:1 begins as an exhortation to the hearers: "Therefore, brothers and sisters, holy partners in a heavenly calling, consider that Jesus, the apostle and high priest of our confession..." The preacher moves, without pause, into an encomium on Christ as faithful, using Moses as a model. Here the author presents Christ and Christ's faithfulness as the foundation for instruction to the believers. This is the second portrait created by means of *synkrisis,* designed to build the argument of the superiority of Christ.

The comparison of Moses and Christ is common in early Christianity (cf. Jn. 1:17; 3:14; 6:32; 9:28–29; Acts 13:38–39; 1 Cor. 10:1–4; 2 Cor. 3:7–16). Hebrews uses the comparison here, focusing on Moses' scripturally attested attribute of faithfulness (see Num. 12:7). Faithfulness is the second of the qualities attributed to the Son as high priest in Hebrews 2:17 where Jesus is described as "a merciful and faithful high priest in the service of God." These christological verses provide the thesis statement from which the writer moves to warn the hearers of the dangers of not living by faith.

After Hebrews 3:1–6 establishes the faithfulness of Jesus over God's house, Hebrews 3:6 functions as a transitional statement that moves the argument from Jesus' worthiness toward a warning against the dangers of "un-faith." What does faith look like? How do members of the community maintain confidence and hope? For an illustration to clarify this exhortation to faithfulness, the preacher turns to the Psalms, considered to be God's words.

3:7–11. FATE OF THE UNFAITHFUL (SCRIPTURAL EXEMPLA)

In 3:7–11, the preacher appropriates the psalmist's account of those who rebelled in the desert, to whom God swore they would never enter the rest, as a "proof" of faithfulness "from the opposite," a common kind of didactic reasoning in which some form of the opposite case or circumstances would cinch the positive point. In the rhetoric of the day, choice of appropriate examples or illustrations for proof of one's argument was understood to be of utmost importance for the speaker to convince the audience of his or her position. Hebrews has carefully chosen the textual example of Psalm 95:7–11.

The verses are closely copied from Psalm 95:7–11 (LXX version); verses 7, 8, and 11 are copied exactly. The writer uses the vocabulary of Psalm 95:7–11 throughout the exhortation in Hebrews 3:12–4:13. By "today" (3:7; cf. 3:15; 4:7) the writer understands a distinction between the present age (today) and the promised age, typified by God's rest (Hebrews 4:1–10).

This reference to "rest" in Hebrews 3:11 (Ps. 95:11) alludes to the narrative in Numbers 14:23, 28–30, where God swears that the people will never see the land that had been promised. (References and allusions to this event in Numbers 14 occur again and again in ancient Jewish and Christian literature. See Deut. 1:19ff; 9:23; Ps. 106:24–26; Pseudo Philo, *Liber Antiquitatum Biblicarum* 15; *Siphre Num* 82 to 10.33; 1 Cor. 10:5, 10.) The psalmist has made the leap to equate the land with God's rest, a leap inconsistent with the text in Numbers, but not inconsistent with other texts in the Hebrew scriptures (see Deut. 12:9 and Josh. 21:43–45).

3:12–19. FATE OF UNFAITHFULNESS ANALYZED (EXEMPLA/ARGUMENT/EXPOSITION)

"From the living God" in Hebrews 3:12 and "the word of God is living" in Hebrews 4:12 constitute the outside pair of a carefully constructed chiasm marking the main body (3:12–4:13) of the writer's argument that the faithful enter into the rest. The title, "the living God," used later in Hebrews (9:14; 10:20, 31; 12:22), provides a vivid contrast to the death of disobedience.

Hebrews 3:12–19 contains two carefully structured sets of instructions, tied together by the key word/inclusio *apistis*, "unfaithful," found only in these two verses (3:12, 19) in Hebrews. The first instruction warns the community to beware of the dangers of unfaithfulness. The second instruction is a quotation from the Psalm, expanded by a series of questions highlighting the disobedience of those "in the rebellion" referred to in Exodus 34 and the account of the psalmist.

The fate of those who went away from the living God is illustrated in Hebrews 3:17 as those "whose carcasses dropped into the desert" (author's translation). The caution is given in Hebrews 4:11 "that no one may drop (dead) by the same pattern of disobedience" (author's translation). The need to be faithful is presented as a life-and-death matter.

Sin Greek: (*hamartia*) is a major issue for the author of Hebrews, who refers to it a total of twenty-five times. In the context of this word of encouragement, the writer defines sin as deceitfulness, which hardens the heart, and as disobedience (cf. Heb. 3:18; 4:11; Heb. 10:26–29). Problems have arisen because some have begun to fall away, unable to maintain their confidence in Christ through difficult times. The illustration from Psalm 95 and Ex. 34) provides an example by which sin and disobedience and unfaithfulness are defined as synonymous. This sin will prevent one from entering the rest.

The writer emphasizes the immediacy of the concern and the remedy, urging action "today" (Heb. 3:13). The goal is a community ethic for the present. The call to "encourage one another" comes again later in Hebrews 10:25. The preacher allows no illusion that anyone can stand alone and remain faithful (see also Heb. 10:24–25; 11:39–12:1; 13:1).

With a series of staccato questions and answers (Heb. 3:16–18), the preacher provides more depth to the brief psalm account of the peoples' rebellion and God's anger, jogs the hearers' memory of the story, and begins to clarify the warning about unfaithfulness. Finally, the preacher clearly states the theological conclusion intended for the hearers: Unfaithfulness causes persons to be unable to enter the rest.

4:1–10. ON ENTERING THE REST TODAY (CONCLUSION AND DISCOURSE)

The warning, more strongly worded this second time, contends that the consequence of "an evil, unfaithful heart, leading away from the living God" (3:12, author's translation) is failure to reach the rest (4:1). Hebrews 4:2 is so central to the theology of Hebrews that brief commentary is in order. In the Greek text, the case of the participle, *sugkekerasmenous* ("they were not united"), and, therefore, its subject, is unclear. My own translation reads:

> For indeed, the good news came to us just as it did to them;
> but the word they heard did them no good
> because they were not united in faith with those who have heard.

The claim that "the word they heard did them no good because they were not united in faith with those who have heard" is a bold one. Discomfort with the author's claim is no doubt the source of the great variation of textual emendations at this point. The preacher's claim is that the word heard in the wilderness did not and *could not have* done them any good because they were not united with the present generation who have now heard the word of faith in Christ.

Hebrews returns to this theological claim again in Hebrews 11:39–40, at the conclusion of the hero list. After listing both those whose faith led to victory and those whose faith was followed by terrible consequences, Hebrews continues:

> Yet all these, though they were commended for their faith, did not receive what was promised, since God had provided something better so that they would not, apart from us, be made perfect.

Even those giants of faith history, though commended for their faith, did not and could not receive the promise, because all of salvation history was waiting for us! The writer of Hebrews believes that salvation history finds its fulfillment only with Christ and in community with those who hear and respond to the good news in Christ.

The power of Hebrews 4:8–9 unfolds in light of translation possibilities and of the rhetorical dynamics at work. In the NRSV these verses read: "For if Joshua had given them rest, God would not speak later about another day. So then, a sabbath rest still remains for the people of God." The Greek word for Joshua is the same as the Greek word for Jesus: *Iēsous*. Mental gymnastics are required of the hearers when, suddenly, the preacher refers to *Iesous* (Jesus/Joshua) as having failed to give them rest. In English translation, the shift to Joshua remains unrecognized as momentarily shocking to the hearers. The context sets the record straight, but those who listened in Greek were required to change their vocabulary from *Iēsous*, Jesus, to *Iesous*, Joshua. This unexpected cognitive shift was a common Christian homiletical device. (For more discussion of this rhetorical technique in early Christian preaching, see Wray, 144–45.)

The word *sabbath* is not found in the Greek text of Hebrews. The preacher uses an obscure term, *sabbatismos*, a word found only here in the New Testament. By *sabbatismos* Hebrews means, not the practice of sabbath-keeping, but the very rest of God, which remains available for the people of God. The writer very deliberatively avoids calling Christians to any practice of the Jewish cult, consistent with the supercessionist theme of the entire document.

4:11–13. Make Every Effort to Enter the Rest (Exhortation)

The word of God, here identified in Hebrews 4:12 as "living," functions to judge and discern and provides "the cutting edge" to the exhortation to "strive to enter the rest...in order that no one may drop...by disobedience." (The word of God as sword, not Christian in origin [cf. Isa. 49:2], appears as a common metaphor in other late first-century Christian documents [cf. Eph. 6:17; Rev. 19:15], where it also appears as an instrument of judgment.) Nowhere does the preacher make the explicit claim made by the writer of the gospel of John 1:1–4, identifying Jesus the Christ as *ho logos* ("the Word"). While the major doctrinal element of Hebrews is an elaborate and distinctive christology, Hebrews 3:12–4:13 makes no christological claims.

Hebrews 3:7–4:13 has served as an effective sermon illustration on the necessity of faithfulness. "Rest," however, never becomes a part of the christology of Hebrews and is never mentioned again. Hebrews retains the key word, "entering," speaking in 6:19–20 of Jesus' entering the inner shrine; in 9:12, 24–25 of Jesus' entering the Holy Place, into heaven itself; and in 10:19–20 of our having confidence to enter the sanctuary. The warning against unfaithfulness has been well-served rhetorically by the example of those who failed to enter the rest; to seek a theological doctrine about rest based on Hebrews 3 and 4, however, would demand more than the preacher was providing. Later Christian theologians and preachers will allude to and develop a theology of rest far beyond this text; "rest" becomes a major soteriological theme in some second- and third-century Christian texts (cf. *Gospel of Truth; Barnabas XV; 2 Clement*).

4:14–16. Jesus, Our Sinless High Priest, Prepares Our Way (Exhortation Continued, with Introduction to 5:1–7:28)

Hebrews 4:14 summarizes the christological discourse of Hebrews 3:1–6 on Christ as faithful and introduces the christological discourse of Hebrews 4:15–5:10 on Christ as merciful high priest, with reflection on the function of Christ's suffering (announced in Heb. 2:17–18). Hebrews 4:14 also provides a conclusion for the christological exhortation in Hebrews 3:1–6. Thus the discourse that begins, "Therefore, holy sisters and brothers, sharing a heavenly calling, consider the apostle and high priest of whom our confession speaks, Jesus," (Heb. 3:1) is concluded by, "Since then we have a great high priest who has passed through the heavens, Jesus, the Son of God, let us hold fast the confession." (Heb. 4:14, translations mine).

Hebrews 4:14–16 establishes the main themes for the lengthy presentation of 5:1–7:28 on Christ as merciful and faithful high priest for us. Jesus, our high priest, has been tested as we are, yet without sin; therefore, we can approach the throne of grace boldly.

5:1–7:28. Word of Exhortation Based on Psalm 110

5:1–10. Background Information about Priests; Christ as Priest Like Melchizedek (Exempla, with Argument)

The word of exhortation based on Psalm 110, about Christ as merciful high priest (Heb. 5:1–7:28), begins in 5:1–4 by presenting some background information about the Aaronic priesthood. The narrative alludes to Leviticus 9:7 and 16:6, which instruct that the high priest shall first offer sacrifices for himself and his family before offering sacrifices for the rest of the people. A scriptural exemplum in 5:5–6, quoting from Psalm 2:7 (cf. Heb. 1:5) and Psalm 110:4 (cf. Heb. 6:20) establishes Christ as a high priest, "according to the order of Melchizedek" rather than according to the order of Aaron (see also Gen. 14:18–20 and the discussion of 7:1–10 below). Hebrews 5:7–10 proclaims that Christ's reverent response to his human experiences of suffering guarantees his qualifications as an effective high priest and source of salvation.

The theological premise of Hebrews 5:1–10 is restated in conclusion at Hebrews 7:28:

> For the law appoints as high priests those who are subject to weakness, but the word of the oath, which came later than the law, appoints a Son who has been made perfect forever.

The consequent exhortation and discourse (5:11–6:27) are solidly christological and serve as the foundation for later presentation of the ministry of Christ and the necessary response of the faithful (8:1–10:38).

5:11–6:12. Exhortation to Diligence and Growth

Hebrews 5:11–14 presents an introductory caveat to the exhortation in 6:1–12 by accusing the hearers of becoming "dull" in understanding; the phrase forms an inclusio with the closing encouragement (6:12) that they not become "dull" ("sluggish" in the NRSV). The orator uses a common Hellenistic rhetorical apology for the difficulty of the material being presented. The apology shifts quickly to a critique of the hearers, commenting that while they should now be teachers, they need someone to teach them the basics.

The preacher aims to get the hearers' attention and to cajole them, or even to shame them, into listening carefully to the message. While explaining his metaphors about infants needing milk and the mature needing solid food, he accuses them of still needing milk. Of course, the implication is that the message that the preacher brings belongs to the "solid food" category; the rhetorical challenge, by implication, urges the hearers to move beyond whatever "infantile" reservations they may have to his message, in order to appropriate "the word of righteousness" he brings and to progress toward a mature faith.

Hebrews 6:1–3 lists certain foundational principles, apparently standard in the church at that time. The six elements are grouped into three pairs: (1) the foundation of repentance from dead works (cf. 9:14) and the foundation of faith toward God, (2) teachings about baptisms (a general term that probably includes more than basic instruction about Christian baptism) and laying on of hands (probably referring to the conferring of the gift of the Holy Spirit after baptism), and (3) teachings about the eschatological doctrines of resurrection and eternal judgment. The caveat, "if God permits," while probably sincere, was conventional rhetoric.

The opening theological warning in Hebrews 6:4–8 about the impossibility of restoring fallen Christians to repentance, while certainly representing a doctrine held by the orator (cf. 10:26–31; 12:15–17), functions rhetorically to encourage the church to faithfulness, rather than to condemn them. The goal is made clear in 6:9–12 as the preacher praises the hearers for their love and service for the saints and urges them to continuing diligence "to the very end."

6:13–20. The Power of God's Oath

Hebrews 6:13 picks up where Hebrews 5:1–10 left off to develop a doctrine of Jesus as a merciful high priest. (Note: Nowhere else in the New Testament is Jesus referred to in these terms.) By using God's promise to Abraham (Gen. 22:17) as exemplum, the orator first establishes the nature and power of an oath, which "puts an end to all dispute"(6:16). He then, by means of another *a fortiori* argument, concludes that because of God's clear oath to the heirs of the promise, the hearers can be strongly encouraged to seize the hope set before us. God's unchangeable purpose and promise belong to *us*.

Even though in Hebrews 6:4–6 the preacher stated that "it is impossible (*adulation*) to restore again to repentance those who…have fallen away…," he proclaims what he hopes is the encouragement to prevent such falling away: "it is impossible (*adulation*) that God would prove false" (6:18). Reminding the hearers of the hope they have, the preacher brings them back to Jesus, a forerunner on our behalf, who has become a priest forever according to the order of Melchizedek (cf. 5:6, 10; Ps. 110:4).

7:1–10. On Abraham and Melchizedek

The author revisits and reinterprets the Genesis 14:18–20 narrative, playing on the meanings of the name "Melchizedek" and of "Salem." A Jewish exegetical move allows him, in the absence of a recorded genealogy for Melchizedek, to claim that Melchizedek was "without father, without mother, without genealogy, having neither beginning of days nor end of life, but resembling the Son of God" (7:3). (Note that the reference in Genesis 14:18 to Melchizedek's bringing of bread and wine may also bring to Christian minds the accounts of Jesus at the Last Supper. For an example of the mysticism that surrounded Melchizedek as a heavenly figure, see the Dead Sea Scrolls, *11Q Melchizedek*.) The Genesis narrative says that Abraham shared the spoils of war with Melchizedek, who was also "priest of God Most High." The preacher reinterprets the narrative to say that Abraham, thereby, gave a tithe to Melchizedek, as the people are to give tithes to the priest (cf. Num. 18:21). That Melchizedek blessed Abraham becomes to our preacher the sign that Melchizedek was greater than Abraham. Understanding that Levi himself, then in the loins of Abraham, gave tithes to Melchizedek, establishes, for the author of Hebrews, that the Levitic/Aaronic priesthood is inferior to a priest according to the order of Melchizedek.

7:11–19. The Priority of the Priestly Order of Melchizedek over that of Aaron/Levi

Lack of "perfection" and the inability to make "perfect" by means of the law associated with the Levitical priesthood, form an inclusio (in 7:11 and 7:19) that marks this small section. The preacher reasons that, since another priest according to the order of Melchizedek is spoken of (in Ps. 110:4), then perfection could not have been attainable under the Levitical priesthood. He then discusses Jesus' qualifications, not as one physically descended from the tribe of Levi, but as one who "arose" (NRSV–"descended" [7:14]) from Judah. (The verb "arose" [*anatetalken*] was not usually associated with physical descent, but was normally associated with the messiah [cf. Gen. 49:9–10].)

7:20–28. God's Oath Appoints Jesus a Priest after the Order of Melchizedek

Hebrews 7:20–28 returns to the themes of 6:13–20, especially to the theme of God's oath, by which Jesus is appointed a priest after the order of Melchizedek. Hebrews 7:27–28 summarizes the introductory presentation of the high-priest christology in Hebrews 4:14–5:10. The orator has stated his thesis, gathered scripture and argument to support his position, and finally returns to his thesis that God's oath has appointed a Son as a perfect high priest. Note that the discussion of the perfection of the Son in 5:9 and in 7:28 surrounds the discussion of the Levitical law's inability to confer perfection.

8:1–10:39. Christ's Ministry as Superior: Word of Exhortation Based on Jeremiah 31:31–34

8:1–6. JESUS, OUR HIGH PRIEST: A MORE EXCELLENT MINISTRY, MEDIATOR OF A BETTER COVENANT, THROUGH BETTER PROMISES

Hebrews 8:1–6 functions both as a conclusion of 6:13–8:6 and as an introduction to 8:1–10:38. This discussion in Hebrews 8:1–6 of Jesus' heavenly ministry in the sanctuary over against the earthly ministry of the Levites assumes the heavenly tabernacle set up by God is true, while the earthly tabernacle is a copy or shadow. The concept that all earthly things were created after a heavenly prototype was quite common in the Near East, and the version, here and elsewhere in Hebrews, which incorporates both temporal and spatial dimensions of the archetype/type theme, more nearly reflects Near Eastern than Neo-Platonic influences (cf. Ex. 25:40; 1 Chr. 28:19; Wis. 9:8; Isa. 60:11–14; Ezek. 40–48; 4 Ezra 7:26; 8:52; *2 Bar.* 4:2–7; *Tobit* 13:16).

8:7–13. SCRIPTURAL ATTESTATION THAT MAKES THE FIRST COVENANT OBSOLETE

In Hebrews 8:8–12 the preacher calls on God's words in Jeremiah 31:31–34 as scriptural exempla to prove that the first covenant must be obsolete, since God speaks of "a new covenant." The section, marked by the inclusion word, "first" (in 8:7, 13), adds only a brief introduction and conclusion to the Jeremiah text. In Hebrews 8:13, "first" also serves as a catchword to introduce the next unit, which speaks of the first covenant and the first tent (9:1–2).

9:1–10. THE FIRST TENT AND ITS SYMBOLISM

An extended exemplum with argument and exposition (9:1–28) begins with a focus on the first covenant, with its regulations for worship, and an earthly sanctuary. The descriptions of details are presented in inverse order. First, Hebrews describes the sanctuary–the tabernacle of the exodus generation–with its arrangements and its equipment (9:2–5). The order and placement of the furnishings varies from the descriptions found in Exodus 25:1–31:11; 36:2–39:43; 40:1–38. The second half describes "regulations for worship," contrasting the multiple daily sacrifices of the priests in the outer tent (9:6; cf. Num. 18:2–6) with the once-a-year ritual of the Day of Atonement performed by the high priest within the inner portion (9:7; cf. Ex. 30:10; Lev. 16:2, 14–15). The preacher interprets this to mean that the limited access to the inner sanctuary signifies a lack of effect on the conscience of the worshipers (9:8–9), since the rituals only concern earthly and temporal externals (9:10).

9:11–28. CHRIST'S ENTRY INTO THE HOLY PLACE ONCE FOR ALL

The first and last of the three units (9:11–15a / 9:15b–23 / 9:24–28) in this part of the discourse are clear christological statements about the effectiveness of Christ's ministry as the high priest who entered into heaven with his own blood, once for all! The first unit (9:11–15a) uses an *a fortiori* argument ("from lesser to stronger") that compares Jesus' sacrifice and cleansing with the sacrifices offered by the Aaronic priests. The following chart summarizes how the efficacy of Christ's ministry as high priest in Hebrews 9:11–14 addresses the inadequacies of the first covenant as they are listed in Hebrews 9:1–10:

Aaronic priesthood (9:1–10)	Christ's priesthood (9:11–15a)
"A tent was constructed, the first one"	"The greater and perfect tent (not made with hands)"
"the priests go continually into the first"	"[Christ] entered once for all into"
"not without taking the blood that he"	"the blood of Christ"
"gifts and sacrifices are offered"	"through the eternal Spirit offered"
"cannot perfect the conscience"	"will…purify our conscience"
"the first covenant"	"mediator of a new covenant"

The middle unit (9:15b–23), in order to justify the necessity for Christ's death, begins by giving the rules and customs by which ordinary wills are executed, then reviews how cleansing is ordinarily obtained under the instructions given to Moses. Since "without the shedding of blood there is no forgiveness of sins" (9:22), the need for a heavenly sacrifice is established.

The third unit (9:24–28) repeats most of the proclamation of the first unit (9:11–15a). The third unit shifts the emphasis to the "once for all" theme that is increasing in intensity as this word of exhortation progresses (in 7:27; 9:12, 26b; 10:2, 10).

Hebrews 9:26–28 offers a succinct statement of the author's eschatology and understanding of salvation: The end has come. Christ has dealt with sin, once and for all by the sacrifice of himself. Christ will appear a second time–to *save* those who are eagerly waiting for him. The responsibility of Christians is to be eagerly waiting for Christ.

10:1–18. WE HAVE BEEN SANCTIFIED THROUGH CHRIST ONCE FOR ALL (EXEMPLA SUMMARIZED)

Claiming the authority of God's speech by returning to scriptural "proofs" from Psalms 40 and 110, Hebrews 10:1–18 reiterates the earlier presentation of Hebrews 8:1–9:38:

Heb. 10:1 summarizes Heb. 8:1–6: earthly worship a shadow of the heavenly
Heb. 10:2–4 summarizes Heb. 9:1–10: the first tent and its symbolism
Heb. 10:5–7 summarizes Heb. 9:11–14: Christ's entry into the Holy Place once for all
Heb. 10:8–9 summarizes Heb. 9:15–23: the better sacrifice

Heb. 10:11–14 summarizes Heb. 9:24–28: Christ's once for all sacrifice
Heb. 10:15–18 summarizes Heb. 8:7–13: Holy Spirit's testimony about a
new covenant

At the same time, these eighteen verses are arranged in the form of a chiasm, the center of which proclaims, "And it is by God's will that we have been sanctified through the offering of the body of Jesus Christ once for all" (10:10). This verse provides a concise statement of the theological point of this word of exhortation section (8:1–10:38).

10:19–39. CONCLUSION AND EXHORTATION TO FAITHFULNESS

Hebrews 10:19–39 is one integral unit, arranged in a fascinating chiastic structure:

A   19–23: "we have confidence to enter the sanctuary" (conclusion)
B   24: "provoke one another to love and good deeds"
C   25: "encouraging one another"
D   26–27: "a fearful prospect of judgment"
E   28: death as consequence of violating the law of Moses
E' 29: "How much worse punishment…?"
D' 30–31: "a fearful thing to fall into the hands of the living God"
C' 32–33: past experiences of solidarity
B' 34: past demonstrations of love and good deeds
A' 35–39: do not abandon your confidence (conclusion reiterated with affirmation)

At the center of this chiasm is an *a fortiori* argument about the serious consequences of spurning the Son of God, profaning the blood of the covenant, and outraging the Spirit of grace, a theme visited three times in this sermon (cf. 6:3–6; 12:15–17). The preacher sees this word of exhortation as a life-or-death matter for his hearers. They are in danger of becoming complacent, of losing their confidence and, therefore, of letting go of their confession of hope in Christ. This is, indeed, the *raison d'être* for the sermon.

The conclusion (10:19–23 and reiterated in 35–39) is clear and concise: Christ has opened a new and living way through the curtain. Now we have a great high priest over the house of God, so that we can have confidence to enter the sanctuary by the blood of Jesus. Confident that the hearers now understand his proclamation, the preacher exhorts them to action.

Hebrews 10:23, "Let us hold fast to the confession of our hope without wavering, for he who has promised is faithful," serves to announce the next section of the sermon (11:1–12:3), with "hope" as the catchword that will begin the final word of exhortation about the results of faithfulness. Before the preacher makes that move, he continues the exhortation, encouraging them to love and good deeds and to regular attendance at community gatherings. Hebrews 10:26–31 returns to the warnings about the consequences of willfully sinning after having received the knowledge of the truth (cf. 6:4–6; 12:15–17), but ends with encouragement that reminds them of their past faithfulness.

11:1–12:29. Final Exhortation to Faithfulness

11:1–38. HEROES OF THE FAITH (EXEMPLA)

Hero lists were common in antiquity (cf. Sir. 44–50; 1 Macc. 2:51–60; Wis. 10; 4 Macc. 16:16–23; 4 Ezra 7:105–111; Acts 7). They always reflect the interests of their author, displaying an ideology consistent with their literary context. Several facets of this particular list make it unique. Women are included! There are no known hero lists in antiquity that included women (a fact that has led some commentators to posit a woman author, such as Priscilla or Phoebe, for Hebrews). And while Hebrews obviously draws on accounts from the First Testament, the preacher chooses selectively which faith acts to highlight and sometimes radically alters the information to suit his purpose. For example, while Exodus 2:14–15 speaks of Moses' fear, Hebrews 11:27 proclaims that Moses was unafraid of the king's anger.

This is not a retelling of biblical history. Beginning with creation, our orator creates an independent Christian faith history. Eisenbaum *(The Jewish Heroes of Christian History,* 11) observes that "most of the heroes' faith involves some ability to perceive the future, and this ability forms an historical link between one character and the next." The most important link is between these heroes of faith and those who hear the preacher: "Yet all these, though they were commended for their faith, did not receive what was promised, since God had provided something better so that they would not, apart from us, be made perfect" (11:39–40). The goal is not that the hearers would emulate these "heroes." The goal is that the hearers will recognize their responsibility to insure that these ancestors of faith actually receive what was promised. Without faithfulness on the part of the hearers, the ancestors continue to miss out on the fulfillment of God's plan.

This list begins by declaring that faith is "the conviction of things not seen" (11:1). Each person mentioned is recognized for some action based on an anticipation of God's future, even though that future was yet unseen.

The list is arranged symmetrically:

3–primeval figures: Abel, Enoch, Noah	Heb. 11:4–7
1–Abraham (and Sarah) with commentary	Heb. 11:8–19
3–patriarchs: Isaac, Jacob, Joseph	Heb. 11:20–22
1–Moses	Heb. 11:23–28
3–post-Moses: Red Sea wanderers, Jericho victors, Rahab	Heb. 11:29–31

After presenting his version of the acts performed "by faith" by Abel, Enoch, Noah, Abraham, and Sarah, the preacher pauses to interpret their status as "strangers and exiles on the earth" (11:13) who desired a heavenly country. This sets the hearers up to recognize their own superior status. God has prepared a city for these heroes of the faith, but the hearers have already come "to the city of the living God, the heavenly Jerusalem" (12:22).

The narrative about named heroes is followed by a quick-paced presentation of later figures that the orator claims among ancestors of the faith (11:32–38). He lists both "successful" acts by faith (conquered kingdoms, administered justice, obtained promises, etc.) and suffering experienced by the faithful (mocking, flogging, chains, imprisonment, death, etc.). Again, women are included among the faithful listed.

11:39–12:3. ANCESTORS OF FAITH, THE HEARERS, AND JESUS (CONCLUSION AND EXHORTATION)

The orator has built this heroes of faith list to a climax that proclaims the hearers are now in the continuum of this list. Indeed, they are the ones toward whom this list moves (11:39–40). The promises our ancestors received can now be fulfilled, that is, the ancestors can now be perfected along with us.

Therefore Hebrews 12:1–3 should not be read without 11:39–40. "Since we are surrounded by so great a cloud of witnesses," we have the responsibility to do whatever is necessary to remain faithful. These "witnesses" are not those who have made it, who are watching us and hoping we will join them. These "witnesses" are "martyrs" who have endured hardship and death and who await our completion of this race so that they may join us in the victors' circle, so to speak.

As we notice the ancestors who wait around us, we are to look forward to Jesus who defines the goal of the race we run. (Metaphors about athletic competition were common rhetorical devices in antiquity.) The challenge to run the race with endurance (cf. 6:1; 10:36) and to lay aside the sin that clings so closely leads directly into another christological proclamation, speaking of Jesus as pioneer and perfecter of our faith and highlighting, again, Jesus' suffering and exaltation. The Greek terms translated as "pioneer" and "perfecter" include an allusion to Christ's being "the first and last" (cf. Rev. 1:17; 2:8; 22:13). Earlier in the sermon, the preacher spoke of Christ's perfection (2:10; 5:9; 7:28) and of the believers' (6:1; 7:11, 19; 10:1; 11:40; 12:23). Faith, now, is the recipient of this perfection; the perfection of our faith has been accomplished by Jesus. Our task is to look to Jesus, so that we may not grow weary or lose heart.

In these verses and the verses to follow, the preacher "brings it home" to the hearers, concluding the word of exhortation with very personal applications of Jesus' faithful and merciful priesthood on behalf of the hearers. The allusions in chapter 12 to the themes presented in the earlier chapters are carefully chosen to bring this word of exhortation to a close.

12:4–17. Discourse on Discipline

Hebrews 12:4–17 explains the trials the hearers are enduring as God's discipline. This discourse on discipline is followed by a series of exhortations to urge community support of one another so that all may remain faithful (cf. 10:24–27).

12:18–24. Previous Terror and Present Celebration

The theme of approaching God has been woven throughout the sermon (cf. 4:16; 7:25; 10:22; 11:6). Hebrews 12:18–24 contrasts the approaching of God by Moses and the wilderness generation with the approaching of God by the hearers. A list of previous, terrifying experiences parallels a list of the present celebration of the faithful because of the ministry of Christ. The preacher proclaims that that which they approach is superior to all that went before.

12:25–29. The Unshakable Kingdom

Hebrews 12:25–29 concludes the sermon in the form of a final mini-word of exhortation. Beginning with an *a fortiori* argument that echoes Hebrews 2:1–3 and 10:28–29, the preacher warns of the danger of refusing "the one who is speaking." In context, the one who is speaking is God and "the sprinkled blood that speaks a better word than the blood of Abel" (12:24; cf. Heb. 11:4). The one who is speaking obviously includes the preacher, as well, who sees himself as speaking on behalf of God.

He appeals to a text from Haggai 2:6 that speaks of God's shaking earth and heaven in order to claim for the hearers an unshakable kingdom, and then exhorts them to acceptable worship (cf. 9:14; 13:15). Since Hebrews is a sermon to be preached within a worship setting, the invitation to worship is probably just that–an invitation to the congregation to move from listening to this word of exhortation into corporate "acceptable worship with reverence and awe" (12:28). The final verse, "for indeed our God is a consuming fire" (12:29; cf. 10:26–27) creates a warning inclusio, with Hebrews 12:25, around the proclamation of the unshakable kingdom.

13:1–25. Epistolary Postscript

The final chapter of "To the Hebrews" is also carefully constructed and includes some of the rhetorical dynamics of the sermon to which it is attached. There are enough similarities in themes and rhetorical techniques to justify assuming the preacher wrote the epistolary ending. It is presented in three major sections.

The central section, marked by an inclusio about honoring leaders (13:7; 13:17), begins with what was probably a traditional acclamation or confession of faith: "Jesus Christ is the same yesterday and today and forever" (13:8). The verse is unconnected with either the preceding or following verses, but effectively moves the presentation to a christological focus. Even in this epistolary section the author is still wanting to encourage faithful confession and responsible community life. The discussion about regulations about food and about the altar and sacrifice by the high priest recalls the earlier sermon (Heb. 9 and 10) and leads to the conclusion about Jesus' suffering and sacrifice. The exhortations, "Let us..." recall similar admonitions in Heb 10:22–24. In the sermon, the preacher spoke of the hearers' being able to go into the sanctuary (10:19–20) because of Jesus' sacrifice. Now the author switches the metaphor, and, noting that Jesus suffered outside the city gate, encourages the listeners to go "outside the camp" (13:13–14). The recipients, who experience themselves as outsiders, are urged to look beyond their present circumstance to the city that is to come.

The closing invitation to "pray for us" parallels other early Christian epistles and is probably formulaic (cf. 1 Thess. 5:25; 2 Thess. 3:1; Rom. 15:30; Col. 4:3; cf. also Ignatius *Trall.* 12.3; *Eph.* 10.1; 21.1–2; *Magn.* 14.1). The indication of personal travel plans is also a standard feature of epistolary conclusions.

The "benediction" or prayerful wish for the addressees (13:20–21) resonates with three major themes from the sermon: peace (7:2; 11:31; 12:11, 14; cf. also 1 Pet. 5:10); blood/covenant (mentioned 23 and 19 times, respectively); and God's will (2:4; 9:7–10; 10:36). The "word of exhortation" probably refers to the main document, to which the author has added a few words (almost as a cover letter). The final "grace be with all of you" is identical to Titus 3:15 and similar endings can be found in almost every New Testament epistle.

Theology of Hebrews

While "To the Hebrews" has much in common with other presentations of the gospel in the New Testament, Hebrews offers a unique articulation of the Christian gospel. The christology is a "high" christology, with a unique proclamation of an exalted Jesus as our high priest. This high christology is balanced by a unique presentation of the incarnation. Yes, Jesus was definitely like us (2:14), experiencing suffering and death. There are no details, however, such as can be found in "gospel" accounts, of Jesus' teachings or stories from his earthly life. Indeed, the designation "high priest" as applied to Jesus is so far removed from Jesus's earthly life as to suggest that this author had little regard for the details of Jesus' life and teachings. The writer's four favorite designations for Christ are: Jesus (13 times); Christ (12 times); high priest (11 times); the Son (15 times).

The soteriology of Hebrews is also unique. Unlike any other New Testament document, Hebrews proclaims that those who came before Christ depend on the faithfulness of those who come after Christ. Much like Paul, Hebrews proclaims salvation, freedom from sin, as completed in the eschatological moment of Christ's death and exaltation. For Hebrews, ongoing faith in the hope that Christ has provided is the essential nature of a Christian life, exemplified by regular participation in the worship and ministry of the Christian community. The faithfulness of Christ's present-day followers will allow the faithful ancestors to participate in the promises that they were unable to experience apart from the eschatological "today" available only in Christ.

Hebrews' goal is not a systematic doctrine of salvation. The preacher's motive is to encourage the church to faithfulness, so that they can avoid the terrible consequences of unfaithfulness.

Importance for the Church of the Twenty-first Century
Faith for Today

While our cultural situation may be very different than that of Christians of the first century, the danger of complacency is just as real. We do well to revisit the importance of faith "today." Surely, the admonition to love and good deeds and the warning not to neglect meeting together (10:24–25) are just as appropriate today as they were long ago. And while many faithful persons encourage diligence and faithfulness for the sake of our children, an emphasis on courageous acts of faith on behalf of our ancestors in the faith may bring new life and hope to congregations. Not that we are invited to repeat the past. God forbid! We are challenged in Hebrews to do better than our ancestors, to be more faithful, to see farther into the future and to take the risks that our hope in Christ allows, risks that our ancestors were either unable or unwilling to take (11:29–12:3).

A careful hearing of Hebrews does not allow an individualistic understanding of spiritual practice. While each person may face judgment alone, the staying power to remain faithful to the end requires the support of the community of faith. Hebrews affirms the essential nature of a faith community. None of us will make it without the rest of us!

Jewish and Christian Relations—Then and Now

While relying on the First Testament—the Jewish scriptures—to provide a narrative history for Christians who were both Jew and Gentile, the author of Hebrews felt a need to provide a Christian identity apart from Judaism. The result is a supercessionary presentation of the gospel, that the new covenant in Christ is both superior to, and replaces, the first covenant that God made with the people of Israel. This theology arose in a time of conflict between the early church and the Judaism out of which it came. It represented overstatement in the context of polemic; it does not wear well as a theology for the church in later generations.

What a tragedy, however, when a maturing Christian church continues to perpetuate the anti-Judaism and anti-Semitism that results from such a position. Christianity no longer needs to justify its existence apart from

Judaism. There is no longer a Christian identity crisis in which we must establish the validity of our proclamation apart from the structures of Judaism.

Jesus was Jewish. The first Christians understood themselves as faithful Jews who had experienced the advent of the Messiah, the Christ. The New Testament itself reflects various positions on the relationship between Judaism and Christianity. Our Jewish brother, Jesus, the pioneer and perfecter of our faith (Heb 12:2), surely expects us to be able to separate the passionate anti-Jewish rhetoric of the first-century sermon we know as "To the Hebrews" from a responsible doctrine of the relationship between Christians and our Jewish sisters and brothers today.

A Call to Excellence in Preaching

For the author of Hebrews, nothing less than the most exquisite, creative, passionate, persuasive rhetoric would suffice for the proclamation of the gospel. Maintaining faithfulness was a life-and-death matter, so this sermon was carefully constructed, using the finest rhetorical skills available at the time.

Our education system does not teach rhetoric with the same intensity as a classical education in the first century provided. Nevertheless, we who preach and communicate the gospel through various media would do well to take our clues from this preacher of "To the Hebrews." Christian exegetical practices have been honed through centuries of proclamation. In many of our seminaries, preachers have access to the various critical methods that can open a text and allow twenty-first–century exegetes to listen responsibly to texts. Women and other liberation theologians have taught us that the most faithful hermeneutic includes listening to the whole community, not just to those who look and think as we do.

The responsible preacher of the twenty-first century will, like the author of Hebrews, search the scriptures for new ways to hear God's word and will be open to the new thing that God may want to do among and through us "today." The message with which we have been entrusted today is no less a life-or-death matter than it was in the first century. The preacher who understands that will take the time that is necessary to study and pray and skillfully craft for oral presentation the word of exhortation needed by twenty-first–century Christians.

Suggested Resources for the Pastor's Library

Attridge, Harold W. *The Epistle to the Hebrews*. Philadelphia: Fortress Press, 1989.

Eisenbaum, Pamela Michelle. *The Jewish Heroes of Christian History*. SBLDS 156. Atlanta: Scholars Press, 1997.

Käsemann, Ernst. *The Wandering People of God: An Investigation of the Letter to the Hebrews*. Minneapolis: Augsburg, 1984.

Long, Thomas G. *Hebrews*. Interpretation. Louisville: Westminster John Knox Press, 1997.

Vanhoye, Albert. *Structure and Message of the Epistle to the Hebrews*. Roma: Editrice Pontificio Istituto Biblico, 1989.

Wills, Lawrence. "The Form of the Sermon in Hellenistic Judaism and Early Christianity," *Harvard Theological Review* 77 (1984) 277–99.

Wray, Judith Hoch. *Rest as a Theological Metaphor in the Epistle to the Hebrews and the Gospel of Truth: Early Christian Homiletics of Rest*. SBLDS 166. Atlanta: Scholars Press, 1998.

15

Consummation and Celebration
The Revelation of John

JUDITH HOCH WRAY

We are like two children in a dark room who are given a candle.
The one sits in fear of the dark and cries.
The other exclaims, "Look at the pretty light!"

"The revelation of Jesus Christ" are the first words of the epistle commonly known as "The Revelation" (*not* Revelation*s*). "Revelation" (or *apokalypsis* in Greek) means an uncovering or revealing. The opening words can be understood in two ways: as that which Jesus Christ reveals or as the revealing of Jesus Christ. While both of these perspectives can be found in the book, the latter is supported by the liturgical nature of the text. The Revelation is a witness to the victorious Jesus Christ, a testimony of faith in the triumph of good over evil, a celebration of the presence of God with the church in the midst of difficult times.

The Revelation (or its equivalent title, the Apocalypse) is *a Christian prophetic epistle using the genre of apocalyptic in the context of liturgy.* The significance of each of these designations will be explored in the following pages.

Often the Revelation has been read as if it were a handbook or calendar of events related to the end of the world, and much speculation has attended contemporary identifications of persons, places, and events described in the narrative. Such reading misunderstands the nature of the apocalyptic genre, to which the Revelation belongs, and removes the message from the context of the early Christian churches to whom the Revelation was written.

Reading from the perspective of the question, "How is Jesus Christ being revealed?" allows the church of today to appropriate the Revelation in ways that can be encouraging and transformative, as was intended for the churches to whom it was addressed. Jesus Christ is to the Revelation what a burning candle is to the dark of the night. Our speaking need not be, "What is the dark all about?" We can proclaim, "Behold, the light!"

Literary Genre

The Revelation appropriates the characteristic language-system utilized to convey the hope of Israel–"apocalyptic." Because of the nature of the Revelation, an understanding of the genre of apocalyptic necessarily precedes any other discussion, including presentation of basic data such as authorship and date. Lack of a foundational perspective on apocalyptic has led many an interpreter to faulty conclusions about the form and goal of this book.

While scholars continue to explore the fascinating and perplexing dynamics of apocalyptic texts, one of the standard works on the subject remains *The Apocalyptic Imagination: An Introduction to the Jewish Matrix of Christianity* by John Collins. I turn to Collins who explains the basics in this way:

> An apocalypse is defined as: a genre of revelatory literature with a narrative framework, in which a revelation is mediated by an otherworldly being to a human recipient, disclosing a transcendent reality which is both temporal, insofar as it envisages eschatological salvation, and spatial, insofar as it involves another, supernatural world.
>
> The [form] of the apocalypses involves a narrative framework that describes the manner of revelation. The main means of revelation are visions and otherworldly journeys, supplemented by discourse or dialogue and occasionally by a heavenly book. The constant element is the presence of an angel who interprets the vision or serves as a guide on the otherworldly journey. This figure indicates that the revelation is not intelligible without supernatural aid...In all the Jewish apocalypses the human recipient is a venerable figure from the distant past, whose name is used pseudonymously. This device adds to the remoteness and mystery of the revelation.
>
> The revelation of a supernatural world and the activity of supernatural beings are essential to all the apocalypses. In all there are also a final judgment and a destruction of the wicked. The eschatology of the apocalypses differs from that of the earlier prophetic books by clearly envisaging retribution beyond death.
>
> The generic framework...involves a conceptual structure or view of the world. It indicates some basic presuppositions about the way the world works, which are shared by all apocalypses.

Specifically, the world is mysterious and revelation must be transmitted from a supernatural source, through the mediation of angels; there is a hidden world of angels and demons that is directly relevant to human destiny; and this destiny is finally determined by a definitive eschatological judgment. (4–6, 8)

Apocalyptic as a genre does not easily translate into a modern or post-modern cultural outlook. Perhaps the most comparable literary genre is science fiction. Quality science fiction, while attempting to project some level of possibility or probability about future life, ultimately aims to critique the present, to provide social and political commentary on contemporary situations. Likewise, apocalyptic (along with other prophetic forms), while using the framework of prophecy about the future, has as its agenda a critique of the present world order and the transformation and/or equipping of the people of God for faithful life in the present.

The literary form of the Revelation is a construct, creatively and skillfully designed for greatest impact on the churches to which it is addressed. Does that negate the visionary nature of the message? Visions are documented throughout the history of Christian spirituality (cf. Mt. 17:9; Lk. 1:22; 24:23; Acts 9:10; 10:3; 16:9). Modern interpreters need not discard an ecstatic impetus for this epistle while exploring its rhetorical intricacies.

Reading the Revelation as information about the future usually leads to missing the goal of the text, which was (and is) to empower Christians to live faithfully in difficult times. Envisioning and celebrating the victory of God's agenda in the world provides encouragement in situations in which all that is easily discernable is defeat. The Revelation, like the great bulk of apocalyptic writing, does not suggest that the space-time universe is evil, and does not look for it to come to an end. It does, however, envision an end to the present world order and the transformation of the space-time world.

Basic Data

The Revelation is addressed as a circular letter to seven churches in Asia Minor, Christians who gathered in the cities of Ephesus, Smyrna, Pergamum, Thyatira, Sardis, Philadelphia, and Laodicea. Specific allusions in each letter clearly demonstrate that the author knew these cities and these churches. For example, there is at least some evidence that Laodicea was known for its banking, textiles, and eye balm (3:17–18). "Satan's throne" in Pergamon (2:13) may be a reference to the monumental altar of Zeus, known at the time as one of the seven wonders of the ancient world. While these seven churches are addressed explicitly, implicit in the number seven is the expectation that the message is for all Christian churches, since seven usually represents fulness or completion.

The nature of apocalyptic precludes using references to specific political and ecclesiastical forms as literal information for the purpose of dating. Elaborate charts have been devised to determine to which of the Roman emperors the texts refer. While such research is fascinating, no scholarly consensus on these identifications has been reached. At the same time, obsession with breaking the "code" for the various manifestations of Roman domination usually succeeds in distracting the interpreter from the theological proclamation of the Revelation.

For a long time, a scholarly majority has dated the text during the reign of Domitian (81–96 C.E.). Domitian ruled after the destruction of the Jerusalem temple and signed himself as "Lord and God" (Suetonius, *Domitian* 8.13; Martial, *Epigrams* 10.72). He could be understood as Nero, referred to in 13:18 as 666 (the numerical equivalent of the spelling of Nero's name), who was mortally wounded, come back again (Rev. 13:3). The historian Suetonius (*Domitian* 8.10) describes his last years as a reign of terror. Although some scholars believe that the characterization is an exaggeration, history does confirm that Domitian targeted political enemies and those with different philosophies, as part of his campaign for the purity of the official religion. Those refusing to worship the emperor were charged with atheism and treason.

While the most recent research does not support a persecution of Christians by Domitian that approached the ferocity of the earlier persecution by Nero (54–68 C.E.), some persecution of Jews and Christians under Domitian is documented. Christian reaction exaggerating the facts may account for historical reports of a major persecution. The end of Domitian's reign (90–96 C.E.) remains the best dating for the book.

The seer of the Revelation four times calls himself John (1:1, 4, 9; 22:8). John does not appear to be a pseudonym, as is common for other apocalypses. The author belongs to the same historical time and social situation as the recipients (1:9). Recognizing that "John" was a common name among first-century Christians, we have no reason to think that this John was any other than who he says he was: a Christian prophet or seer who had been exiled for his testimony of faith that Jesus Christ is Lord. He was almost certainly *not* the John associated with the gospel of John and the Johannine epistles.

The Greek of the Revelation is the poorest in the New Testament, to the point of being ungrammatical, so we can assume that the writer's native tongue was not Greek; it was probably Aramaic or Hebrew. This seer was fully conversant in the apocalyptic genre and, more than any other New Testament writer, alludes to texts from the Old Testament, although he never quotes from them directly. He knows the churches in Asia Minor to whom he addresses the letters and speaks, like the prophets of old, with passion and authority, understanding himself to be the voice of God's Spirit (Rev. 1:10–11).

This John demonstrates familiarity with both Jewish and Christian tradition. Some scholars have emphasized the interesting parallels between themes in the Revelation and in the gospel and the epistles that belong to the Johannine school, parallels such as an emphasis on witness, on Christ as light, on Christ as the Word of God, etc. Careful examination of the Greek text, however, brings into question the significance of the Johannine parallels. For example, both the gospel of John and the Revelation refer to Jesus as the Lamb. That analysis only works if one ignores the Greek, because the Revelation uses *arnion* and the gospel of John uses *amnos* for the word that is translated "lamb." The common references to Christ as "lamb" probably say more about early Christian tradition than about specific dependence on or relationship between John of the gospels and the epistles and John of the Revelation.

Elisabeth Schüssler Fiorenza (*The Book of Revelation*, 85–113) makes a very good case for the language, tradition, and form of the Revelation having more affinity with the Pauline texts than with the Johannine. For example, the letter form that frames the Revelation closely follows that which is common to Pauline epistles. Note the greeting formula, "grace to you and peace…" (Rev. 1:4, cf. Rom. 1:7; 1 Cor. 1:3; 2 Cor. 1:2; Gal. 1:3; Eph. 1:2; Phil. 1:2; Col 1:2; 1 Thess. 1:1; 2 Thess. 1:2; Philem. 3), and the benediction formula, "The grace of the Lord Jesus be with [you]" (Rev. 22:21; cf. 1 Cor. 16:23; 2 Cor. 13:13; Phil. 4:23; Philem. 25).

The non-apostolic authorship, the apocalyptic genre, an apparent focus on judgment more than on grace, the misuse of its message–these and other reasons have been used to explain why the Revelation's status as canonical has not always been secure. Though generally accepted by the Western church, the Greek-speaking church rejected the book for several centuries, and it continues to be rejected in Syria and by the Syriac-speaking church. Martin Luther assigned a secondary status to the Revelation; Zwingli denied it was scripture; and it was the only New Testament book on which Calvin did not write a commentary. Today, its canonical status is quite firm, even though it is omitted from many "canons within the canon." For example, very few verses of the Revelation are included in The Revised Common Lectionary, and some churches and preachers avoid the book altogether.

Methods of Interpretation

The first step in interpreting a text is reading it. I offer the following guidelines for reading the book:

- Read it aloud. The expectation of the writer was that people would hear the words, not just see them on a page (Rev. 1:3).
- Read it in its entirety, preferably at one sitting. Everything in these visions moves toward and anticipates the victory of the Lamb and

the glory of God envisioned in the last chapters. Reading any section apart from the full context increases the probability of misinterpretation.

- Read it (that is, *hear* it) in the context of a worshiping congregation. By entering into the experience of listening to and worshiping the revealed Jesus Christ, the interpreter ceases to control the text and grants to the revealed Christ the opportunity to transform the interpreter.
- Allow the metaphorical language to become a catalyst for the sensual imagination. The symbols, granted a life of their own, permeate the consciousness as angels, thrones, horses, beasts, and dragons. Allow the rhetorical dynamics of the text to have their way with the senses: the heat of the lake of fire, the trumpet blasts and the singing, the curses and the sounds of battle, the smells of sweet incense and acrid sulfur.

Such a reading of the text prepares the interpreter for a thorough examination of the liturgy, the christology, the ecclesiology and the eschatology of the Revelation.

Among the most helpful methods of interpretation for approaching a study of the Revelation are (1) canonical and tradition criticism—research into the relationship of the Revelation to the rest of the Bible and a knowledge of the history of the images, metaphors, and themes found in the Revelation; (2) liturgical appropriation—examination and experience of the Revelation as liturgy, a text written to be received and appropriated within worshiping congregations of Christians who were facing difficult times; and (3) rhetorical and form criticism—a study of the motifs, structural dynamics, and standard literary techniques that inform the meaning of the text. Each of these methodological foci deserves attention.

The Traditions behind the Revelation

The Revelation appears as the last book in the canon of Christian scripture. Since there was no Christian canon when the Revelation was written, the writer could not have planned it to be the last book of our Bible. Clearly, however, John understood the final vision of this letter to represent the consummation of God's intention as revealed in the story of the garden of Eden. Coupled with the picture of the garden of Eden in Genesis 2, the Revelation's vision of a new heaven and earth (Rev. 21:1ff.), with the tree of life on either side of the river of the water of life (22:1–2), provides a "frame" for the entire canon. With that in mind, the alert reader will understand the allusions in the Revelation to nakedness and clothing, to the fruit trees and rivers of water. The Bible begins in a garden and ends in a mighty, God-centered city, each filled with similar symbols of God's grace and provision.

The Revelation is full of allusions to other scripture texts, and awareness of those references will provide a foundation for faithful interpretation of the Revelation. Descriptions of the throne, of the heavenly city, of the four living creatures (4:6–11), of the sealed book (5:1–6:17; 8:1), the two witnesses/olive trees/lampstands (11:1–6), and a multitude of other seemingly esoteric images, all have their roots in Torah, the prophets, and other Jewish apocalyptic literature. The metaphors were familiar to Jewish Christians, intended to elicit recognition and assent.

General biblical literacy is essential for interpreting the Revelation. The interpreter will be aided especially by knowledge of other apocalyptic texts (parts of Daniel, Ezekiel, Zechariah, *4 Ezra, 1 Enoch, 2 Baruch, Apocalypse of Abraham, 3 Baruch, 2 Enoch, Testament of Levi 2–5*) as well as motifs basic to the Judeo-Christian proclamation of salvation history (creation stories, Moses and the exodus, exilic and post-exilic prophets, etc.).

The modern response of fear, or puzzlement, or the need to "decipher" the historical future would not have occurred to late first-century Christian readers. They knew that the beast and the harlot and all the other personifications of evil referred to Rome and the satanic power that supported the economic and social injustices of the Roman Empire. We need not consider the text as a "code" that remains mysterious. Those who read the Revelation as if it were written for our time alone risk being disrespectful of the text. When readers allow the text its own integrity, then the message, written *to* politically threatened late first-century churches, becomes life-giving *for* us as well. The challenge for the modern interpreter is to hear the gospel/prophetic message in the midst of the strangeness of apocalyptic language.

The Revelation as Liturgy

"Blessed is the one who reads aloud the words of the prophecy, and blessed are those who hear and who keep what is written in it; for the time is near" (Rev. 1:3). The expectation of the writer was that the manuscript would be read aloud to congregations gathered for worship.

On occasion, a gathered Christian community would receive a letter from one of the apostles or other leaders of the church with new teaching and exhortation to faithfulness. By the end of the first century these "memoirs" of the apostles were becoming standard fare. The community time together would include a common meal, the breaking of bread, receiving and remembering their Lord in this act.

About 138 C.E., Justin Martyr writes:

> On the day named after the sun, we hold a meeting in one place for all who live in the cities or the country nearby. The memoirs of the Apostles or the writings of the Prophets are read as long as time permits. (*First Apology*, 65–67)

Important letters would be carefully copied by someone so that they could be passed on to another group of assembled Christians. There the process would happen all over again. Each letter would be read and reread aloud to the assembled body so that everyone would be able to share in the teaching and encouragement.

The Revelation anticipates these patterns of worship. It comes alive as a book of worship. Hymns and testimonies and prayers and incense and silence—a whole half hour of silence! The closing words may surely be understood as an invitation to the communion table—not Paul's traditional words, of course, but an invitation to Christ's table:

The Spirit and the bride say, "Come."
And let everyone who hears say, "Come."
And let everyone who is thirsty come.
Let anyone who wishes take the water of life as a gift. (Rev. 22:17)

John was drawing on known liturgical traditions of the churches. The rich christology appears as more than theological speculation. In worship the many and varied names for Jesus the Christ stand out from the pages. The experience is of a Christ revealed to be more than common language can bear: Lamb and Lion; First and Last; Alpha and Omega; Beginning and End; Root and Offspring; human and divine; slain and victorious. This christology depends on rich symbolism of the godhead most effectively expressed in the apocalyptic genre!

Verses and sections devoted to praise of God and encouragement for the saints out-number details of negative, fearful experiences by a ratio of five to three. All significant action issues "from heaven" or "from the throne," which is the writer's way of reminding the hearers that God is in control! Perseverance results in blessings. The focus is praise. And when praise of God gets the church's attention, fear can be replaced with action.

The liturgical matrix in which the Revelation is disclosed presents an invitation, not to pietistic praise, but to worship that empowers people to overcome the evil that would destroy the world and all of God's people with it. As Raymond E. Brown (*Introduction to the New Testament* [New York: Doubleday, 1997], 810) puts it, "The Lamb standing as though slain is the ultimate guarantee of God's victorious care and deliverance, especially for the downtrodden and oppressed."

The vision that John reports is an invitation to worship and prayer that includes the act of one's testimony (*martyria*). The Greek word for "witness" or "testimony" is the source of our word for one who gives her or his life for a cause, *martyr*. This testimony sustains the faithful during times of crisis, persecution, and suffering. The power of *the testimony of Jesus* weaves its way through the vision (1:2, 9; 6:9; 11:7; 12:11, 17; 19:10; 20:4; 22:6). One's testimony of Jesus constitutes participation in the overcoming of evil, even though it may lead to personal death.

> But they have conquered him by the blood of the Lamb
> and by the word of their testimony,
> for they did not cling to life even in the face of death. (Rev. 12:11)

In the midst of worship, the churches are given a vision of God's justice for the whole creation. The saints are empowered to be witnesses *against* the principalities and powers of this world and witnesses *for* the victorious Christ, who stands as the Lamb who was slain.

Hymns of praise, probably known and used in the churches to whom this letter was sent, anchor other liturgical elements of prayer and encouragement to faithful testimony. The church throughout the ages has turned to the Revelation for worship material. Many magnificent Christian hymns and prayers are based on texts from the Revelation.

A worship celebration can be designed, following the complete text of the Revelation, with opportunities for the congregation to enter into the liturgical experience as prompted by the text. As John reports hymns, the people sing. Reference to prayer becomes an invitation to corporate petition. Silence, incense, trumpets, and testimonies: Each of these are incorporated into the worship, as the congregation shares in the hearing and the response to this revealing of Jesus Christ.

Organization

In the opening of this chapter, I said that *the Revelation is a Christian prophetic epistle using the genre of apocalyptic in the context of liturgy.* Now is the time to unpack that designation. A few basics about the organization of the Revelation set the stage for an examination of some of the details of the structure.

- The author derives some of his authority (rhetorical *ethos*) from patterning his work after the authoritative Pauline letter form. This is especially obvious in the formulaic introduction and conclusion.
- The movement of the visions is not linear. Spiral is probably a better description of the shape of the text.
- The narrative follows a basic prophetic pattern, flowing from promise to fulfillment. Everything moves toward the final consummation at the end of the vision.
- All time is *kairos* (eschatological), not *chronos* (historical). Therefore, references to time are not to be interpreted in a linear framework.
- The narrative movement is continuously interrupted by interludes. These visionary interludes are scenes of worship, hymns of eschatological protection, and general encouragement for the saints. These interludes function much as a Greek chorus would, to provide

commentary and explanation for the actions of the principles in the drama.

• Repetition of motifs and key words provide unity in the midst of complicated (or non-identifiable) patterns.

• At the center of the book is encouragement for the community in the context of prophetic interpretation of their present political and spiritual situation. The content of the Revelation can be summarized in the following form:

A Prophetic words of promise (Rev. 1–3)
B Heavenly visions (4–9)
C Encouragement for the church (10–12)
B' Eschatological warfare on earth (13–18)
A' Fulfillment of the prophetic words (19–22)

This overall chiastic arrangement points to the center (C) as the goal of the prophetic epistle, which is structurally framed by and spiritually encouraged by the revealing of the victorious Christ (A and A').
The setting, from the perspective of John and the churches, is worship, both on earth and in heaven.

Every attempt to clarify organization and structure of the Revelation will fall short, because apocalyptic, by its very nature, defies linear logic and control. Literature intent on speaking about the inexplicable will eschew logical categories. The following outline respects, as much as possible, the various rhetorical dynamics of the Revelation, that is, epistolary, prophetic, apocalyptic, and liturgical, but makes no attempt to identify all of the intricate structural patterns.

Outline of The Revelation

I. Prophetic words of promise (Rev. 1–3)
   A. Epistolary introduction of the author and purpose (1:1–11)
   B. Visionary introduction to the "one like the Son of Man" (1:12–20)
   C. Letters to the angels of the seven churches (2:1–3:22)
II. Heavenly visions (4:1–9:21)
   A. Worship of the Lord God Almighty (4:1–11)
   B: The Lamb and the scroll; worship of the Lamb (5:1–11)
   C. The opening of six seals; ecological disasters (6:1–16)
   D. Protection for God's people (7:1–8)
   E. The multitude from every nation at worship (7:9–17)
   F. The seventh seal (8:1–9:21)
      a. Silence, incense, and prayers (8:1–5)
      b. Six trumpet blasts and more ecological disasters (8:6–9:21)

III. Encouragement for the churches (10:1–12:17)
   A. The little scroll (10:1–11)
   B. The two witnesses (11:1–14)
   C. The seventh trumpet and worship (11:15–19)
   D. The woman and the dragon (12:1–17)
      a. The woman and the dragon in heaven (12:1–6)
      b. The dragon thrown down to earth; heavenly celebration (12:7–12)
      c. The woman and the dragon on earth (12:13–17)
IV. Eschatological warfare on earth (13:1–18:24)
   A. The two beasts (13:1–18)
   B. Protection and encouragement for the church (14:1–13)
   C. The reaping of earth's harvest (14:14–20)
   D. Glimpses of what is to come from heaven's perspective (15:1–8)
   E. The bowls of God's wrath poured out on the earth (16:1–21)
   F. God's judgment on Babylon (17:1–18:24)
V. Fulfillment of the prophetic words: Eschatological Consummations (19:1–22:21)
   A. Heavenly celebration and invitation to the marriage of the Lamb (19:1–10)
   B. The victorious rider on the white horse (19:11–21)
   C. Final battles and final judgment (20:1–15)
   D. The new heaven and the new earth (21:1–8)
   E. The new Jerusalem (21:9–22:5)
   F. Epilogue and commentary on the visions (22:6–20)
   G. Epistolary benediction (22:21)

A brief examination of each of these sections will not "explain" the contents of the Revelation. The letter is meant to be experienced in worship and appropriated as encouragement to remain faithful in difficult times. The wondrous vision of God's final triumph over evil unfolds, folds over on itself, and unfolds again until the assurance of the victory won by the Lamb that was slain becomes integral to the believers' lives and testimonies. The following section summaries refer the interpreter to some of the tradition history behind this dynamic and creative letter John writes to the churches.

Prophetic Words of Promise (Rev. 1–3)

After the epistolary greeting and introduction of the prophet John, we are told of the circumstances of his vision of Christ (1:1–11). The inaugural vision of Christ (1:12–3:22) should be read as a unit, with the letters to the angels of the churches as a continuation of the introduction of this One who is being revealed. The introductory description of Christ in each letter comes from the opening appearance in Rev. 1:12–20. Many of these identifying characteristics of Christ Jesus appear again in the concluding section of the book (Rev. 19–22).

In spite of the structural elusiveness of the Revelation as a whole, the organization of the letters to the angels of the churches in chapters 2 and 3 is easily identified, and, by their very form, these letters display an understanding of the grace of God that rivals any in the New Testament. Even in these letters, the revealing of Jesus Christ is a priority.

In these letters, God's grace and God's judgment work together as one and, thereby, set the stage for the rest of the vision. Each letter follows a general form: (a) address to the angel of the church; (b) description of Christ; (c) evaluation (positive and/or negative) of present condition of the church; (d) changes needed; (e) penalty for failure to repent; (f) a call to hear; (g) blessings. A quick look at each part of the letter form reveals the rhetorical dynamics that convey John's understanding of God's grace in Christ Jesus:

(a) Address to the angel of the church. Note that each letter is addressed to "the angel of the church," not just to "the church." While the word for "angel" (*angelos*) can also be translated "messenger," these need not be distinguished from other "angels" that do God's bidding throughout the Revelation. The idea of an angel being given responsibility for a certain group of people is not new (see Dan. 10:13–14, *1 Enoch* 89:59, Heb. 1:14). While each church must face judgment, none is left without help.

(b) Description of Christ. Like the plumb line that Amos saw (Amos 7:7–8), a specific attribute of the Christ becomes that against which each church is measured.

(c) Evaluation of present condition of the church. Spiritual evaluation of each local church follows the description of the Christ. Evaluation may contain praise for faithful living and/or a warning notice concerning things that need to be changed.

(d) Changes needed. Only two alternatives to the present condition are presented: repent or hold fast. The church can no longer plead ignorance of God's judgment.

(e) Penalty for failure to repent. Being judged by that standard of perfection which is Jesus Christ [see (b) above], the penalty for failure to repent is directly related to the description of Christ presented in the introduction to each letter. Note that one church (Laodicea), which has absolutely no righteousness to commend it, is given no penalty for failure to repent. Only to this church is Christ's coming associated with blessing. How unlike the judgment we would mete out! How typical of the Jesus who came to seek and to save that which was lost!

(f) A call to hear. What is the Spirit saying to the churches? She is saying, "Behold, Christ Jesus!" Behold this One who is for you! Behold Christ's perfection, Christ's judgment of you, Christ's love for you, Christ's blessings prepared for you!

(g) Blessings. Near the end of each letter is recorded a blessing or blessings; in each case the blessing is a result of the perfection of Christ being applied to a deficiency or hardship experience by the church. The Christ, whose strength is made perfect in our weakness (2 Cor. 12:9–10), blesses us at our weakest points.

Some scholars and preachers throughout the centuries have assigned a historical time period to each of these churches, or by some other means tried to determine which of the letters to the churches accurately critiques various churches today. Such efforts ignore the fact that these were real churches in late-first-century Asia Minor. Many details pertinent to each church reflect actual historical realities within the cities and churches to whom they are addressed.

An exegetical process more conscious of the rhetorical, theological, and historical dynamics in these chapters goes beyond the question, "Which of these letters speaks to my church?" After a careful study of the vision/ letters in Rev. 1:10–3:22, the challenge is to write a letter, consistent with the form addressed to these first-century churches in Asia Minor, that the Christ might write to the angel of *your* church in the twenty-first century. How is Christ being revealed to *your* church and what specific message does the Spirit give to *your* church?

Heavenly Visions (Rev. 4:1–9:21)

The vision moves to a heavenly scene. John is invited to "come up here…" (4:1) and finds himself in the midst of heavenly worship of the Lord God the Almighty. The scene draws on material from Ezekiel 1 and 10 and Isaiah 6.

The sealed scroll, introduced in chapter 5, is an image common to apocalyptic literature (cf. Isa. 29:11, 18–22). Most apocalyptic visions end, however, with the scroll being sealed until the end times (cf. Dan. 8:26; 12:4, 9). This apocalypse is understood by John as the final revelation in which the scroll is unsealed and the vision is available for all (Rev. 22:10). Only one is found who is worthy to open the scroll; this one who has conquered is identified as "a Lamb standing as if it had been slaughtered" (5:6). The victory has been guaranteed, not by military might but by the sacrificial death on the cross! The rest of the vision continues the revealing of the Christ, who is the Lamb who was slain. After spectacular scenes of worship of the Lamb, the Lamb begins to open the seals of the scroll.

In chapter 6, the opening of the first six seals unleashes war, famine, and plagues on earth. The voices of living creatures (cf. 4:6–8) call attention to the action. The four horses with riders draw on imagery from Zechariah 1:8–10 and 6:1ff. Those who have been killed for the faith ask, "How long will it be before you judge and avenge our blood?" (6:10) and are given white robes and told to rest a little longer. The rich and powerful, along with slave and free, hide in caves (cf. Isa. 10:3; 22:5). These images of the day of wrath resonate with well-known apocalyptic images of "the Day of the Lord" (Isa. 5; Amos 5; Joel 2; Mt. 24, et al.).

The vision includes a promise of protection for "the servants of God" (7:1–8), God's seal for 144,000. While many speculate about the identity of these 144,000, they are defined in the text as Jewish and later (in 14:1–5) as virgins and blameless. We must not forget that this is apocalyptic, metaphorical language. The 144,000 is the sacred number twelve (twelve tribes of Israel, twelve apostles) squared and multiplied by 1000. These 144,000 probably represent the totality of those who have been faithful (spiritually virgins) to Christ. (Compare Paul's reference in Gal. 6:16 to "the Israel of God.")

The scene that follows (7:9–17) includes multitudes from every nation at worship. They are martyrs now in heaven. The description of these worshipers includes metaphors commonly associated with eschatological bliss in the prophetic tradition (Isa. 25:8; 49:10).

The seventh seal is opened and heaven is silent for half an hour. (For other instances of silence associated with the day of the Lord, see Amos 5:13; 8:3; Zeph. 1:7; Zech. 2:13). After a description of the action at the altar of incense (cf. Ex. 30:1–10), fire from the altar is thrown on the earth, with attending thunder, rumblings, flashes of lightning, and an earthquake (cf. Ex. 19:16; Rev. 4:5; 11:19; 14:2; 16:18). Such phenomena are commonly associated with eschatological events.

This opening of the seventh seal now becomes the signal for seven angels to blow seven trumpets. The first six of these trumpets are blown in chapters 8 and 9, each trumpet signaling the unleashing of another plague or ecological disaster upon the earth. These are reminiscent of the plagues in Egypt (Ex. 7–12). Before the seventh trumpet blows, the vision is interrupted by an angel who comes down from heaven to interact with the prophet John.

Encouragement for the Churches (Rev. 10:1–12:17)

The rhetorical center of the Revelation offers encouragement to the saints in three movements: the presentation to John of a little scroll that he is to eat, the account of the "two witnesses," and the dramatic vision of the woman and the dragon. John's being given the little scroll to eat confirms his prophetic call (cf. Ezek. 3:1–3). Then John is given a measuring rod and told to measure the temple, the altar, and those who worship there (cf. Ezek. 39–48; Zech. 1:16; 2:1–5).

The scene continues with the identification of two witnesses, the two olive trees and the two lampstands, all of which are found in Zechariah 4:1–14. John's vision, of course, has its own version of this apocalyptic motif. The two witnesses have great authority, testify, and are finally killed by the beast. After three and a half days they come back to life and are called up into heaven. The attending earthquake kills many, but the rest of the people of the city are terrified and give glory to God. In the long run, the witnesses are vindicated and their testimony results in God being glorified. This segment, using well-known apocalyptic imagery, serves to encourage and justify all those who maintain a faithful testimony, assuring them of resurrection after martyrdom.

The seventh trumpet blows and we hear worship in heaven, the announcement of God's victory, the beginning of God's reign. The temple opens and the ark of the covenant is glimpsed, along with flashes of lightning, rumblings, peals of thunder, earthquake, and heavy hail (11:19).

Then begins the cosmic drama between the woman and the dragon. The woman is "clothed with the sun, with the moon under her feet, and on her head a crown of twelve stars,...pregnant and...crying out in birth pangs, in the agony of giving birth." (12:1–2) Scholars have variously identified this woman as Israel, as Mary, and as the church. The multivalent nature of apocalyptic allows for any or all of these interpretations. The drama begins in heaven; the woman's child is rescued from the dragon at birth and snatched away and taken to God while the woman flees into the wilderness. War breaks out in heaven and the dragon is defeated by Michael and his angels and is thrown down to earth. A chorus in heaven comments on these events and then the dragon pursues the woman, who is provided with natural and supernatural protection. The conclusion provides a dynamic mythological rationale for the experience of the church fearing or facing persecution:

> Then the dragon was angry with the woman, and went off to make war on the rest of her children, those who keep the commandments of God and hold the testimony of Jesus. (12:17)

Eschatological Warfare on Earth (Rev. 13:1–18:24)

The cosmic encounter between the woman and the dragon, both now on earth, provides a transition to various accounts of eschatological warfare on earth. The first-century recipients of John's letter would quickly understand the apocalyptic imagery to refer to Rome and its various officials. The head of the dragon who had received a mortal death-blow was Nero, whose persecution of Christians in the 60s C.E. is well-documented; Nero's symbol on coins was 666 and these coins were required for certain transactions. Domitian (81–96) is feared to be Nero come back to life. The call for endurance and the faith of the saints includes resistance to the powers of economic, social, and spiritual domination. This long section describing the eschatological conflict is continually interrupted by reports of worship in heaven and encouragement for the saints (14:1–7, 11–13; 15:1–8; 16:5–7, 15, 17; 17:14).

Chapter 17 and 18 are one unit, focusing on the fall of "Babylon." In chapter 17, John is carried away in the spirit into the wilderness (cf. Ezek. 3:12–14; 11:1, 24; 37:1; 43:5). The angel who guides him is identified as one of the angels who had the seven bowls (Rev. 15:7–16:21). By identifying the angel thusly, the writer provides continuity between earlier plagues and the fall of "Babylon."

The dialogue between John and the angel who guides him is a typical motif in apocalyptic literature (cf. Zech. 1–6). Picturing a city as a woman is common in the prophetic Jewish tradition with which John identifies, and prostitution is a traditional metaphor for idolatry (Ezek. 16; 23; Hos. 1:2; Rev. 14:4). Chapter 18 includes poetic angelic proclamations about the downfall of the great city and mourning by those who have profited from her wickedness. The language points to the city of Rome; the "Babylon" metaphor would have been transparent to any who hear this letter, including Roman officials. Rather than being engaged in "secret" communication, the writer uses evocative symbolic language to engage the hearer in multiple levels of meaning.

Evil is portrayed in the context of the relationship of the representative of evil to the saints. Thus, for example, "the great whore…was drunk with the blood of the saints and the blood of the witnesses to Jesus" (17:1b, 6); and a voice from heaven calls to the saints in "Babylon": "Come out of her, my people, / so that you do not take part in her sins, / and so that you do not share in her plagues" (18:4). The goal of this section, also, is the revealing of Christ Jesus, assuring the saints that their persistent nonviolent resistance will eventually be honored by the destruction of all that is evil.

Fulfillment of the Prophetic Words (Rev. 19:1–22:21)

The eschatological conflict on earth being concluded, John's vision moves to a heavenly celebration and an invitation to the marriage of the Lamb. The participants in this celebration include the twenty-four elders (4:4, 10; 5:6; 11:16), the four living creatures (4:6–8; 5:6, 8, 14; 6:1, 6; 7:11; 14:3; 15:7), and the voice of a great multitude (7:9). The magnificent hymns in chapter 19 continue to find their way into the liturgy of the church today.

One final bloody battle is fought; the beast and its armies are defeated. Rev. 19:11–21 is the sole description of Christ in warrior-like mode (cf. Wis. 18:14–25). These names, however, are not new. This chapter provides the consummate revealing of the Person and the consummation of the promises given in chapters 1–3. Many of the descriptions of Jesus Christ found in earlier chapters find their fulfillment in the description of the victorious Christ presented in chapter 19.

The rider on the white horse is joined by an eschatological army; the beast and false prophet are captured and thrown into the lake of fire. Thus Satan's agents are disposed of. The dragon (12:1–17), that ancient serpent (Gen. 3:1–2), who is the Devil and Satan, is still at large. But not for long.

The rhetorical dynamics of the temporary binding of Satan in Rev. 20:1–3, (7–10) can be lost if the interpreter forgets the nature of apocalyptic. No historical event is intended. The eschatological "binding" or "imprisonment" of the powers of evil was developed in Jewish and Christian apocalyptic thought in a variety of ways (*1 Enoch* 10:4–10; 18:12–19:1; 21:1–6; *Testament of Levi* 18:12; cf. Mk. 3:26–27; 5:3; 2 Pet. 2:4; Jude 6). The picture presented by John offers both hope for the future and commentary on the present: The power of evil is temporary and operates by the permission of God. While this may invite major questions about our own theology of good and evil, John's portrayal is a continuation of his literary revealing of Jesus Christ, the Lamb that was slain, who was and is and will be victorious over evil.

John does not move on to the rest of the story until he assures the hearers that Satan will be defeated for all time and thrown into the lake of fire (20:7–10). The dead are judged; Death and Hades are thrown into the lake of fire. The final battles and final judgment are complete (20:11–15).

The stage has been set for a revealing of eschatological bliss prepared for the people of God (cf. 7:15–17). The scene draws upon the imagery of Isaiah 51:1–11 and Isaiah 65:17–25. John is enabled to see "a new heaven and a new earth, for the first heaven and the first earth had passed away, and the sea was no more" (Rev. 21:1). The sea symbolizes chaos (Gen. 1:1) and the home of the dragon (cf. Isa. 27:1; Ezek. 32:2). The opening scene proclaims the presence of God among mortals (Rev. 21:3) and notes that those who do evil and the consequences thereof are no longer present (21:4, 8).

John is carried away in the spirit once again by an angel (17:1ff., cf. Ezek. 3:12–14; 11:1, 24; 37:1; 43:5). Earlier, John was shown the downfall of the great city "Babylon" (17:1–18). Now John is shown "the holy city, the new Jerusalem, coming down out of heaven from God" (21:2). For the description of its magnificence, John draws on images from Ezekiel 42–28 and Isaiah 60. How does one describe the glory of God? To understand the picture literally is to reduce God's glory to the limits of human imagination. John pushes the hearers beyond their wildest imaginings to envision the glory that belongs to them in Christ Jesus.

The motifs in Rev. 22:1–2 proclaim the consummation of that which was begun in the garden of Eden. There the tree of life was in the midst of the garden (Gen. 2:9) and a river flowed out of Eden to water the garden (Gen. 2:10). Now God dwells among mortals and the river of life flows from the throne of God. The tree of life produces unlimited fruit to eat, and its leaves are for the healing of the nations.

John's prophetic mission is once again validated (22:6). The theme of Christ's coming is reiterated (cf. 1:7–8; 2:5, 16; 3:3, 11, 20) and a blessing promised to those who keep the words of this prophecy (22:7). The prophet John provides an epilogue (cf. 19:10) encounter with the angel that includes instructions *not* to seal the words of the prophecy of this book. This is in sharp contrast to other apocalyptic visions, which end with the scroll being sealed until the end times (Dan. 8:26; 12:4, 9).

Just about the time that the hearers believe that the message is finished (one more time, since the narrative appears to conclude at least four other times, in 6:12–17; 7:9–17; 14:1–5; 15:1–4), the writer adds one final message from Jesus himself, without an angelic intermediary and without narrative comment (22:12–20). Thus the writer summarizes the several messages of the letter in the voice of Jesus, in effect saying, "Just in case anyone missed the point, here it is." Echoing the frequent references to "come" throughout the vision, the letter ends with the early Christian liturgical refrain, "Come, Lord Jesus!" and epistolary benediction (cf. 1 Cor. 16:22–23).

Theological Themes

Most of the theological themes of the Revelation can be summarized under three categories: christology, eschatology, and ecclesiology. Noting that these are presented within a liturgical matrix can focus the interpreter's hermeneutic perspective on the means of spiritual empowerment, rather than on linear, rational theological explanation.

Christology

The prevailing theological theme is christological, the revealing of Jesus the Christ, the cosmic Christ, not the historical Jesus of the gospels. The presentation of the cosmic Christ comes in the context of cognitive dissonance in which the victorious Lion of Judah is revealed in the present only as the Lamb who was slain. This is a christology to empower the poor and oppressed, not by emphasizing the teaching of a historical Jesus, but by celebrating the crucifixion and exaltation of Jesus the Christ. Acquaintance with this Lamb who was slain, known by faith as the Lion of Judah, expands one's repertoire for prayer, for worship, for envisioning justice in the world.

Each image of the Christ (Jesus Christ, the faithful Witness, the ruler of the kings of the earth, the living One, one like the Son of Man, the first and the last, the Amen, the faithful and true witness, the origin of God's creation, the Holy One, the Lion of the tribe of Judah, the root of David, the Lamb, Jesus, Lord of lords, King of kings, Faithful and True, the Word of God, Christ, the Alpha and the Omega, the beginning and the end, the bright morning star, Lord Jesus) is presented in the context of worship, with the expectation that in the revealing of this One, the church will be strengthened and encouraged in the spiritual persistence necessary to see the justice of God prevail.

Eschatology

The term "eschatology" comes from the Greek word for "end," *eschaton.* *Eschaton* can be used for the last in a series, such as the last chapter in a book; it can refer to the last scene or the conclusion of a story. In theological terms, *the eschaton* can apply individually, nationally, historically, or cosmically. The Revelation offers an eschatological vision of God's providence bringing a final chapter to history. While the vision prophesies the destruction of evil, it also includes a joyous hope to be celebrated and entered into. As such, Revelation does not present a picture of "the end" so much as a "sneak peek" at the last chapter of the book of history so that the actors will have the courage to play their parts today. Readers do well to examine how this "last chapter" is presented, for the language used belongs to the tradition of apocalyptic, with metaphorical imagery that, if interpreted literally, may be misunderstood and abused in contemporary settings.

TRIBULATION AND HOLY WAR

Volumes have been written on "the tribulation." At this point, interpreters enter a theological minefield. Divisions have been caused among sincere Christians by disagreements about when and where and for whom. In the minds of most people the word "tribulation" stirs a fear of punishment, when the wrath of God shall descend. Twenty-first–century Christians can heed the message while avoiding panic by understanding the nature of John's apocalyptic eschatology and by placing the contents of this prophetic letter within the context and mindset of late first-century Christianity. John's account of his vision depicts God's use of destruction as having two facets: tribulation as a way of drawing people into the acknowledgment of and knowledge of God as God (Rev. 9:20–21; 16:9,11; cf. Dan 4.); and tribulation as holy war, with God's heavenly armies destroying everything of the enemy so that God's people may not be tainted or compromised by those who refuse to acknowledge the Lord God (Rev. 18:2–6; cf. Deut 7:1–26; 20:1–20).

The social and political reality of the late first century included real or potential persecution for those who dared to honor as Lord anyone other than Caesar. The agenda of this literature, therefore, is to strengthen the faith and resolve of those who testify to the Lordship of Jesus Christ by celebrating the ultimate victory of God's domination-free "kingdom." Tribulation, then, in the context of these apocalyptic visions, expects of the interpreter questions other than "when?" and "for whom?" In spite of apocalyptic penchant for numbers, including numbers of days, weeks, and years, the question being addressed is not "when?" but "why?"

Apocalyptic struggles with the nature of and limits to evil. And, if God is truly God, then where is God when evil is unleashed upon the world? In the Revelation the conflict is never a personal/spiritual struggle; the conflict is envisioned as political/spiritual warfare. The forces of domination and economic abuse are judged; resistance in the name of the Lamb who was slain is integral to the prophetic nature of the church (19:10).

The nature of apocalyptic blurs time distinctions; the references to time are not to be interpreted literally. John seems most interested in assuring Christians that, if they are martyred for their faithful witness to Jesus Christ, they can be assured of the rectification of all things after death (6:9–11; 14:13).

Let the interpreter never forget that confrontation with the forces of evil is presented in the context of the revealing of Jesus Christ. The challenge to the church of the twenty-first century is to find a hermeneutic that interprets or reinterprets tribulation in ways that promote, rather than mock, God's justice and grace in the world. History warns against those who pronounce judgment and declare war in the name of God. This letter to people facing potential persecution and death daily presents "holy war," not as an excuse to kill others or even to defend oneself, but as a promise of the judgment of God on their behalf.

The participation of the faithful in this "holy war" is repeatedly defined as "conquering." Eleven times conquering is an activity attributed to the saints; the blessings in the letters to the angels of the churches are for "everyone who conquers." A careful reading uncovers the nature of that "conquering" as nonviolent resistance to economic and political domination. The saints are expected to refuse to cooperate with corrupt institutions; they must witness to their faith at the risk of their own lives. The faithful neither initiate nor participate in violence against another (13:10; 14:12). The eschatological battle and victory belong to God and to the Lamb for the sake of the saints, not to the saints for the sake of God.

An expectation of judgment and justice are integral to this eschatological vision. The eschatological restoration envisioned is neither personal nor escapist. The ecological devastation of the earth (8:7–12) is mourned and, in the end, the earth is renewed. The final goal is not destruction, but the renewal of all things (21:5).

ESCHATOLOGICAL RESTORATION

Who then shall be saved, according to the Revelation? The answer is not a simple one. The writer never uses the verb "save" or the noun "savior." "Salvation" appears three times (7:10; 12:10; 19:1), each time as an acclamation of God, never as the destiny of humans. The eschatological restoration of communion with God envisioned in the Revelation is sometimes portrayed as limited (14:9–10; 20:11–15) and sometimes portrayed as all-inclusive (1:7; 4:3; 5:13; 15:4; 21:5; 21:22–22:3).

Shall twenty-first–century interpreters pick and choose among the possible end-time scenarios presented in John's epistle? The thoughtful reader, initiated into apocalyptic, will recognize that the writer never intended to answer our questions about who shall be saved. The writer sees both judgment against evil and all-inclusive restoration to communion with God as signs of God's faithfulness to God's people. The goal is never that we will judge others, but that we shall examine ourselves and remain steadfast in our witness for Christ and against evil in all its forms.

Ecclesiology

The locus of the eschaton is the "kingdom," yet the letter makes it clear that this "kingdom" is the faithful people of God rather than a historical location. Thus John presents a cosmic ecclesiology, referring to the church as "a kingdom and priests to our God, and they shall reign on earth (Rev. 5:10, RSV).

A note about language seems appropriate at this point. *Kingdom* is one of those words we almost take for granted in many Christian circles. In corporate and private worship we pray, "Thy kingdom come." The language is part of our tradition. Yet, some are quite wary of political structures defined as kingdoms in our contemporary world. And many who wish to take seriously the vision of God and community proclaimed by Jesus are beginning to seek nonhierarchical models to speak of God's "shared shalom." Texts such as Luke 14:2–14 and Rev. 21:1–5 invite metaphors other than "kingdom," metaphors that more accurately reflect the vision of shared peace, justice, and wholeness. Some Christians prefer "household" or "realm" or "commonwealth" or "*kin*dom" or other contemporary political terminology with fewer oppressive, hierarchical connotations. Our language still waits to catch up with our theology, to reflect accurately the nature of God and God's "shared shalom" as revealed in Jesus the Christ.

Nevertheless, entering the biblical world view of the late first century C.E. through the text of the Revelation, hearers are drawn into a vision of an almighty God, sovereign in all things, acting to protect, to encourage, and finally to bring all into the safety and security and healing of the Divine Presence. As John writes, the church catches glorious glimpses of that realm of God, shares in that *kin*dom, and exercises its priesthood through worship and praise of God and the Lamb. In these pages all significant action is "from heaven" or proceeding "from the throne." However chaotic things may seem, God is in control and always places limits on evil (cf. Job 1 & 2). Those who hear and enter into worship join with those who already experience God's shalom (Rev. 7:15–17).

This shared shalom, this *kin*dom, envisioned in the Revelation illuminates John's fundamental understanding of church, of Christian community. The narrative moves back and forth between this cosmic vision of the *kin*dom and the reality of conflict and persecution in the churches of Asia Minor. The letter begins by proclaiming the cosmic, triumphant nature of the community and its relationship with the Christ who is being revealed:

> To him who loves us and freed us from our sins by his blood, and made us to be a kingdom, priests serving his God and Father, to him be glory and dominion forever and ever. Amen. (Rev. 1:5b–6)

Yet in chapters 2 and 3, the letter addresses specific congregations facing internal and external conflicts. External persecution has not fostered internal unity. The prophet John is in conflict with certain factions and individuals, rival prophets or leaders within these churches. Behind the metaphorical/mythical polemics are theological and political power struggles, actual churches and leaders with conflicting concepts of church stability and faithfulness.

John's eschatological ecclesiology is much more inclusive, however, than these specific congregations. Those who praise the salvation of God include "a great multitude that no one could count, from every nation, from all tribes and peoples and languages, standing before the throne and before the Lamb, robed in white, with palm branches in their hands" (7:9).

Importance for the Church of the Twenty-first Century

We, too, live in troubled and troubling times. We know the ravages of life brought about by guns and drugs and corporate greed. We can name the danger and stress of living in a world frequently defined by terrorist attacks, a world that systematically perpetuates racism and tolerates "ethnic cleansing," a world that still believes in wars and rumors (or threats) of wars as a way of achieving "peace." And more specific to the message of the Revelation, claiming and living the way of Christ remains a hazardous profession. More people were persecuted and martyred for their Christian faith and actions in the twentieth century than in all of the previous centuries put together.

The Politics of Interpretation

Gender, class, race, and other power-determining characteristics of the interpreter influence every reading of a text. This is especially pertinent in a text such as the Revelation, which so clearly addresses the structures of domination and abusive power in the world. The Revelation was addressed to churches that were feeling threatened by the dominant and abusive power of Rome. The letter was not written *to us* in the twenty-first century. The message, nevertheless, is *for us.* How we read the text or, more accurately, how we allow the text to have its metaphorical and rhetorical way with us, will determine its importance for the church of the twenty-first century.

The Revelation speaks to the question, "How shall we maintain faith and courage to persevere in the face of daily troubles and a threatening future?" The answer offered by the prophet John is: Perseverance is enabled by a vivid vision of Christ's completed work, bringing the universe to its fulfillment. The task of the Christian is faithful witness and persistent nonviolent resistance to the powers of greed and domination.

Interpretive Pitfalls in the Twenty-first Century

In the Christian task of faithful witness, one danger comes if we fail to acknowledge our own participation in the structures of domination. Unless we hear the call to repentance and the vision of judgment as directed at ourselves, we shall miss the grace offered to all. The Revelation invites sobering reevaluation by the faithful with respect to our own participation in systems that perpetuate economic and political exploitation.

In the context of the Christian task of persistent nonviolent resistance, another danger comes as people today continue to embrace the concept of "holy war" as the will of God. Many governments and terrorist organizations, both domestic and foreign, demonize the enemy and justify violent actions based on principles of "holy war." Such actions are inconsistent with the revelation of Jesus the Christ that the church has embraced in the gospel accounts of Jesus' life and ministry. There is nothing holy about human warfare. Nevertheless, throughout history, many, by misunderstanding apocalyptic writing, have turned to "literal" readings of the Revelation to support violence against those named as evil. When people of faith take their scripture seriously enough to understand the nature of apocalyptic literature in general and the Revelation in particular, these chapters can become humility-inviting, life-giving, and justice-making.

Women in the Revelation

To put it bluntly, women do not come off well in these visions. The symbols for both oppressive and eschatological redemptive communities are female because cities are personified as women. Idolatry, in the prophetic and cultic language of Israel, is symbolized as "whoring" or as "defilement with women." Revelation engages the imagination of the contemporary reader to perceive women in terms of good or evil, pure or impure, heavenly or destructive, helpless or powerful, bride or temptress, wife or whore. Rather than instill "hunger and thirst for justice," the symbolic action can perpetuate prejudice and injustice. An understanding of the dynamics of apocalyptic and ancient polemics can begin to ameliorate the negative images of women. A pro-active, pro-women hermeneutic, conscious of the need to end the abuses of sexism in church and society, will approach these metaphoric references with caution.

For example, the condemnation of "that woman Jezebel, who calls herself a prophet and is teaching and beguiling my servants to practice fornication and to eat food sacrificed to idols" (Rev. 2:20), if read without comment, may add credibility to those who distrust and/or deny the leadership of women in the church. Accusing the opposition of idolatry and adultery were standard political ploys in the ancient world, just as in today's. The name, "Jezebel," (1 Kings 18, 19, 21; 2 Kings 9) carried the implication of a sinful woman, then as now. Polemics aside, the historical data we can recover most clearly from this reference suggests that in the church at Thyatira was a strong woman leader/preacher/prophet who was distrusted and despised by this rival prophet, John.

For good or ill (and usually for ill), women and women's bodies have borne the weight of archetypal evil and good. Thus in the Revelation, the evil of Rome is personified as a woman, the great whore, who becomes the focus of God's wrath. On the other hand, a woman becomes the symbol of the persecuted righteous and the recipient of divine and natural protection (Rev. 12). In Revelation 19, a great multitude celebrates God's vengeance on "the great whore" and then celebrates the marriage of the Lamb, whose "bride has made herself ready."

No real women can be found in the Revelation. Let the interpreter be wary, lest the archetypal symbolism be allowed to perpetuate the oppression and abuse of women, women who are surely included in the justice and shalom of God envisioned by John.

At the Dawn of a New Millennium

The third millennium in the Common Era (C.E.) actually began on January 1, 2001, since the Gregorian calendar moves from 1 B.C.E. to 1 C.E. without intervention of the year 0. Even that date is arbitrary since the calculations of Jesus' birth by a sixth-century monk, Dennis the Little, commissioned to draw up a standard liturgical calendar, were off by several years. Current historians usually locate the birth of Christ between 4 and 6 B.C.E.

History teaches us that millennium speculation about the end of the world will not cease. Dedicated apocalyptists are not easily discouraged by failed prophecy. When the millennial year 1000 passed without incident, new deadlines were established, at 1010, then at 1033.

In the early twenty-first century, some persons will seek to know or claim to know more than the witness of scripture permits of humanity (Acts 1:6–7; Mt. 24:42; Mk. 13:33). Thoughtful reclamation of the purpose and the proclamation of the Revelation can be an antidote to arrogant speculation and doomsday predictions. The Revelation calls for persistent, faithful witness to the Lordship of Jesus Christ and persistent, nonviolent resistance to the powers of domination and greed. With John of Patmos, in anticipation of the consummation of God's inclusive shalom, we proclaim and celebrate Christ's victory.

The Ongoing Revelation of Jesus the Christ to the Church

The Revelation probably raises more theological questions than it answers for twenty-first–century Christians. For example, are we really expected to pray for the destruction of our enemies (Rev. 6:10)? Or are we to love our enemies and pray for those who persecute us (Mt. 5:44)?

The Revelation has been used and abused by Christian and non-Christian alike. For example, the conquering Christ riding on his steed with his "robe dipped in blood" (19:13) has been used to justify slaughter of enemies in the name of Christ. The text, however, elaborates on the image of the One who has been baptized in suffering through the cross. The victorious Christ does not conquer with human warfare but with heavenly armies. The use of such images in the Revelation to justify human violence of any kind denies the grace of the God who calls for nonviolent resistance to evil in all its forms.

However strange the apocalyptic genre may be, contemporary readers can hear the prophetic challenges to the way we live our lives today. As we nurture a synthesis of imagination, revelation, and reason, the Word spoken to John speaks again to us and furthers our journey toward wholeness. The test of essential, integral revelation is never the amount of information received but the quality of life-change that is brought about.

Suggested Resources for the Pastor's Library

Aune, David E. *Revelation.* Word Biblical Commentary. Three volumes. Dallas: Word Books, 1997–98.

Barr, David L. *Tales of the End: A Narrative Commentary on the Book of Revelation.* Santa Rosa, Calif.: Polebridge, 1998.

Boring, M. Eugene. *Revelation.* Interpretation. Louisville: John Knox Press, 1989.

Collins, John J. *The Apocalyptic Imagination.* New York: Crossroad, 1989.

Prévost, Jean-Pierre. *How to Read the Apocalypse.* New York: Crossroad, 1989.

Schüssler Fiorenza, Elisabeth. *The Book of Revelation: Justice and Judgment.* Second edition. Minneapolis: Fortress Press, 1998.

_____. *Revelation: Vision of a Just World.* Proclamation Series. Minneapolis: Fortress Press, 1991.

Wainwright, Arthur W. *Mysterious Apocalypse: Interpreting the Book of Revelation.* Nashville: Abingdon Press, 1993.

Wink, Walter. *Unmasking the Powers.* Philadelphia: Fortress Press, 1986.

Index

This index may also be used as a glossary–definitions and definitive discussions are indicated in bold.